SPAD XIII   1917

HAWKER FURY I   1931

MESSERSCHMITT Bf 109G-6   1942

MIKOYAN-GUREVICH MiG-15 FAGOT   1948

McDONNELL DOUGLAS F-4E PHANTOM   1967

scale   50 ft.

TUPOLEV Tu-22 BLINDER   1961

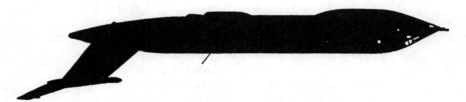

HANDLEY PAGE VICTOR B.Mk1   1958

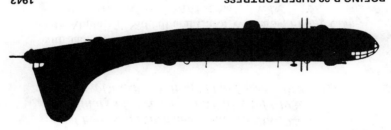

BOEING B-29 SUPERFORTRESS   1943

MITSUBISHI Ki.21-Ia SALLY   1938

GOTHA G.IV   1917

scale   100 ft.

Other books by Robin Higham:

Britain's Imperial Air Routes, 1918-1939
*The British Rigid Airship, 1908-1931: a study in weapons
    policy*
Armed Forces in Peacetime: Britain, 1918-1940
The Military Intellectuals in Britain, 1918-1939
Diary of a Disaster: British aid to Greece, 1940-1941

and as Editor,
with Jacob W. Kipp, *Soviet Aviation & Air Power*
with Abigail T. Siddall and Carol Williams, *Flying Com-
    bat Aircraft of the USAAF/USAF, 3 vols.*
Official Histories
A Guide to the Sources of British Military History
A Guide to the Sources of U.S. Military History
with Donald J. Mrozek, *ibid, Supplements One and Two*
Civil Wars in the Twentieth Century
with Mary Cisper and Guy Dresser, *A Brief Guide to
    Scholarly Editing*
*Intervention or Abstention: the dilemma of American For-
    eign Policy*
with Carol Brandt, *The United States Army in Peacetime*
with Jacob W. Kipp, *The Garland Library of Social
    Science Military History Bibliographies*, a multi-vol-
    ume series

Air Power:

A Concise History

Robin Higham

Sunflower University Press®

1531 Yuma (Box 1009), Manhattan, KS 66502 USA

To those who have made it possible to tell the history of aviation — those who have lived it and those who have preserved it.

Enlarged, second edition, 1984
Revised third edition, 1988

ISBN 0-89745-115-5 hardback
ISBN 0-89745-116-3 paperback

Contents

Preface   xi

Part One: Origins and Concepts   1
1 Early Attitudes towards Air Power   1
2 Some Patterns or Models of Development   2
3 The Principles of War and the Military
    Setting for Air Power   5
4 The General Background to 1914   9
5 Training and Manufacturing   10
6 Operations: Tripoli, 1911-1912   11

Part Two: The First World War:
    The Baptism of an Ancillary Service   13
1 Training, Command, and Equipment   13
2 Fighter Operations   16
3 Air Power in Action: The Ideal   20
4 Air Power at Sea   21
5 Strategic Bombing Campaigns   24

Part Three: The Inter-War Years   28
1 Progress towards New Roles
    and Relationships   28
  Evolution of the Flying-boat   36
  Aircraft Production, 1919-1939   39
2 Airline Development and Aircraft Production   38
3 Record-Breaking   42
  The International Scene, 1938   43

  Seen in the Mid-Thirties   44
  Origins of the World War II Fighter   45
  Bomber Development, 1920-1940   46
4 Operations   48
  The Saga of the Smaller Air Force
    — Sweden to 1939   50
  The Changing Aircraft-Carrier   54
  The Growth of the Airliner   56
5 Attitudes at the Outbreak of War   59

Part Four: The Second World War:
    Land-based Air Power   60
1 Preparation and Progress in Equipment,
    Training, and Command   60
2 Blitzkrieg and Airborne Campaigns   63
  Europe and North Africa   63
  The Evolution of Engines and Propellers   64
  Bombers of 1939-45   71
  Allied Personalities of the Second World War   72
  The Air War on the Eastern Front   75
  Asia   77
  Grand Strategic Bombing   82
  The Bomber Offensive against Germany   87
  Bombers in the Pacific   89
  ULTRA   100
  Noted Designers   100
3 Air Power and National Defence   79

The Lockheed C-130H Hercules is an advanced version of the turbo-prop transport which has been in production for a quarter of a century. This version is in use for Coast Guard patrols of 2,500 miles or more at a cruising speed of 350 miles per hour. **Lockheed-Georgia**

4 Strategic Air Offensives 91
5 Land-based Air Power at Sea 96
6 Analysis 98

Part Five: The Second World War:
　Seaborne Air Power 101
1 The General Nature of Air Action at Sea 101
2 The Atlantic-Mediterranean Area 101
3 The Pacific Theatre 109
4 Analysis 124
　The Swedish Air Force: another look 126

Part Six: Cold and Limited
Warfare since 1945 128
1 Background: Strategic and Technological
　Reactions to Nuclear Power 128
　The New Look in the Jet Age 130
　The New Shape in the Sky 131
2 Military Policy, Organization,
　and Equipment 132
　The Changing Airliner, 1945-75 136
　The Evolving Aircraft, 1945-84 138
　Naval Aircraft, 1960-80 139
3 Airlines and Aircraft Industries 140
　Changing Aircraft (cont.) 141
　Transport Aircraft Transition 1941-56 144

4 Operations 146
　Air Intelligence 146
　Berlin Airlift, 1948-1949 147
　Korean War, 1950-1953 147
　Vietnam, 1950 onwards 149
　India-Pakistan, 1965 153
　Arab-Israeli War, 1967 153
5 The Legacy 154
　Soviet Aviation — links & innovations 157
　1971-1983 160
6 War on the Airways, 1945-1988 163
　Lessons: Spares and Maintenance
　　and Safety 167

Part Seven: Patterns and Philosophies:
　Some Lessons 177
1 The Ideal 177
2 Realities 178
3 The Wave Pattern over Fifty Years 180

Bibliographical Essay 184
1984 Supplement to the Bibliography 192
Additional Bibliography for the 1988 Edition 195
Index 198

The **North American Rockwell** B-1B grand-strategic bomber.

List of Illustrations and Diagrams

Front End Paper   The Growth of Fighters
                              & Bombers
Contents   Lockheed C-130H Hercules
                       North American Rockwell
                         B-1B bomber
Preface   Boeing 707 and Short Empire
                         flying-boat
Introduction   Boeing Air Transport
                         Stewardesses, 1934

1   The Wright Modified Model B Flyer
     Fairchild Cornell
2   Early American flyers
3   *The Wave Cycle of Development*
     H. H. Arnold
4   The Wright 1909 Military Flyer
5   Glenn L. Martin
     International Air Racing
6   Early U.S.N. flying-boats at Pensacola
7   International linkages — Russia, 1914
8   Aircraft manufacturing, Los Angeles, 1914
9   Aircraft manufacturing, Los Angeles, 1914
10 The Martin Co., Los Angeles, 1914
11 Lockheed — Georgia, Atlanta, 1983
12 The first air war, Tripoli, 1911-1912
13 Repair & maintenance
14 A hated reconnaissance machine
15 Caudron bomber
     Fokker Triplane fighter
16 Vickers Vimy patrol bomber
17 Fighter pilots
18 Vickers Gun-Bus
19 Fokker D-VII
20 Pilotless aircraft
     Sopwith Pup
21 Capt. Guynemer
22 Zeppelin *L-33*
     R-34
23 The rigid airship *R-38/ZR-2*
     Brooks Field, Texas
24 Rumpler CIV
     Curtiss JN ''Jenny''
25 Bristol Fighter
26 SE-5A
27 Fokker Triplane
28 *The Spirit of St. Louis*
     Hawker Hart
29 The Douglas World Cruisers
30 Building a World Cruiser
31 Sherman Fairchild
     Igor Sikorski
32 DH-4's, 1928

33 Johns Multiplane
34 Army ideas of air power!
35 Grass airfield
     Early Sikorski passenger plane
36 Evolution of the Flying-Boat
     HS2L
     NC-4
     Martin PM-2
     Sikorsky S-42
     Cdr. Rodgers *et al.*
     Read's crew
     PAA Twin Boom
     Excalibur
37 C.L. ''Kelly'' Johnson
     Consolidated Vultee VII's
38 Pilot's delight — Boeing P-12B
39 Aircraft Production, 1919-1939
     Working on a wing
     Spirit of St. Louis airframe
     Sheet-metal inspection
     Beech's line, 1939
     Clyde Cessna & Co.
40 Gens. ''Billy'' Mitchell and Mason M. Patrick
     Foulois, Rickenbacker, and Fechet
41 USN Curtiss racer, 1926
42 Supermarine S6B
43 The International Scene — Switzerland, 1937
     Fairey Fox
     Czech (single-seater)
     Dornier Do-17
     Bristol Bombay
     Fiat CR-32
     Henschel HS-123
     Dewoitine D-510
     Hawker Hart
44 Seen in the mid-Thirties
     DeHavilland DH-51
     Bücker 133 Jungmeister
     Bücker Jungmann
     Junkers Ju-86
     Junkers Ju-52
     Consolidated PT-1
     DeHavilland DH-88
     Focke-Wulf Fw-200
45 Origins of the World War II Fighter
     Curtiss P-6E Hawk and Boeing P-26
     Boeing P-26A
     Curtiss 75A
     Bristol Bulldog
     Brewster Buffalo
     Grumman FM-4F
     Supermarine Spitfire

46 Bomber Development
    Curtiss NSB-1
    Handley Page Heyford
    Boeing B-17
    Fiat BR-20
    Martin B-10
    Vickers Wellesley
    Vickers Valentia
    Bristol Bombay
47 Soviet bomber-transport (Pe-4?)
    Douglas XB-19
48 Douglas SBD Dauntless
    Curtiss SBC Helldiver
49 Curtiss SBC front and rear cockpits
50 The Saga of the Smaller Air Force — Sweden
    Bleriot XI's   Thulin K
51 Albatros
    Baron Carl Sederström's flying school
    Testing the wing of a new fighter
52 Breguet ambulance plane in service
    Heinkel HD-36
    Fokker CV-E's
    SK 11A (DH 82) Tiger Moth
53 USS *Akron*
54 The Changing Aircraft-Carrier
    Taking off from *Langley*
    Vickers Vildebeeste
    USS *Ranger*
    USS *Yorktown*
55 USS *Akron* as an aircraft-carrier
    USS *Saratoga* off Panama in 1934
56 The Growth of the Airliner
    Canadian Airways Stearman
    Junkers W-13
    Bellanca Pacemaker
    Fokker F-7
    Boeing 226
    Northrop Gamma
    Boeing 247D
    Boeing 247D Cockpit
57 Boeing 247D cabin interior
    Douglas DC-2
    Douglas DC-3's
    Lockheed Lodestar
    Beech 18
    Beech 18 cockpit
    Dassault Type 220
    Boeing 307B Stratoliner
58 Junkers Ju-52
    DeHavilland DH-89
    Sikorsky S-42
    Short Empire *Caledonia*
59 Building Lockheed Hudsons
60 Edwin A. Link and Link trainers
61 Boeing Kaydet and Consolidated-Vultee BT-13
62 Beech AT-11's being bombed up.
63 The wartime airfield — the shape of the target.
    An expensive, but vital resource — aircrew
      cadets.
64 Pratt & Whitney Twin Wasp

65 Hamilton Propellers
66 DeHavilland Mosquito night-fighter
    North American P-51 Mustangs
    Confederate AF Spitfire and Me-109
67 Supermarine Spitfire
    Republic Thunderbolt
68 Heinkel HE-111's
69 Scenes from *The Battle of Britain*
70 Junkers Ju-52
    Hawker Hurricane
71 Bombers, 1939-1945
    Bristol Blenheim
    Bristol Beaufort
    Bristol Beaufighter
    Cant Z 2506B
    Lockheed Hudson
    North American Mitchell
    Martin B-26
    Petliakov Pe-2
72 Allied Personalities of the War
    The Leaders at Casablanca
    "Hap" Arnold
    Curtis LeMay
    Maj. Don Gentile
73 General Carl Spaatz
    General Ira Eaker
74 Messerschmitt Me-323
75 On the Eastern Front
    I-16 naval fighter
    Pe-2's attack bombers
    Ant-24 (front and rear view)
76 Pe-8 heavy bomber
    Il-2 Sturmoviks
    La-4 fighter
    Il-4 medium bombers
77 Dakota and Horsa
    Inside a Waco CG-4A glider
78 Mitsubishi Zero fighter in China
    C-47 dropping supplies
79 Airfield building in India
    Waco CG-4A glider
    Gen. Arnold in a light observation plane
80 Aircraft production in World War II
81 The breach in the Moehne Dam
82 Grand Strategic Bombing
    The mass-produced B-24 Liberator
    A B-24 crew
83 A bad landing in a B-24
    Nose-wheel problems
84 Target: Petfurdo oil refinery, Hungary
85 Before and after bombing: Berlin, 1943-44
86 Aircraft indentification: Me-109 and Fw-190
87 The Bomber Offensive against Germany
    Long-range P-38
    Boeing B-17
    V-1 Buzz Bomb
    Consolidated B-24
    Avro Lancaster
    Lancaster ground crew
    Bombing up Halifaxes

	Bombs for a B-17
88	Women ferry pilots of the US Army's WASPs
89	Bombers in the Pacific I
	B-24 gunners
	B-17 and B-29
	Baka bomb
	Atom bomb
90	Bombers in the Pacific II
	Aircrew in the Aleutians
	Cockpit of a B-29
	B-29's dropping bombs
	Overhead a B-29
	Low-level bombing run
	B-25 with 75mm gun
	B-25 attacking a ship
91	Mechanized mass-production of B-24's
92	Handley Page Halifax on a daylight raid
93	Consolidated B-32
94	Low-level attack on Ploesti
	Defoliation
95	B-29 navigating P-51's on raid against Japan
96	Consolidated Catalina on patrol
97	Catalina beached
98	Baby flattop as aircraft transport
99	Douglas A-20 in anti-shipping strike
100	Noted Designers
	Barnes Wallis
	Ed Heinemann
	Willy Messerschmitt
101	Savoia-Marchetti SM-79 torpedo bomber
102	Fairey Swordfish
103	Macchi 205 fighter
104	Lancasters against the *Tirpitz*
105	F4F Wildcat
106	Hawker Sea Fury
107	Vought 0S2U scout-observation-rescue seaplane
108	Grumman TBF Avengers
	Douglas TBD Devastators
109	Dauntlesses on the attack
110	Martin AM-1 Maulers
111	Curtiss SB2C Helldivers
112	Vickers on beaching gear
113	USS *Franklin D. Roosevelt* (CVA-42)
114	Chance Vought Corsair
	Grumman F6F Hellcat
115	Pearl Harbor
	Cdr. Minoru Genda
116	The Doolittle Raiders
	Martin Mars flying-boats
117	Generals Chow and Chennault
118	Japanese Zero in Chinese hands
119	Japanese Helen medium bomber
120	Noemfoor Island Airstrip
121	Japanese Sally heavy bomber
	Grumman Tigercat shipboard night-fighter
	Martin PBM Mariner
122	Ed Heinemann's SBD Dauntless
123	Consolidated PB4Y2
124	Japanese Kawanishi H8K flying-boat
	Sikorski H-3 and H-5 helicopters
125	The Shapes of Things to Come
	The German V-2 rocket
	Aircraft on exhibit at the USAF
	Museum, 1960's
126	The Swedish Air Force — another look
-127	SK-14/NA-16
	J-22's under construction
	DeHavilland Vampire
	Saab J-29
	Saab Draaken
	Cessna Birddog
	SK-60
128	The Cold War — Lightnings and Bison
129	Wright R-4360 Wasp Major multi-row radial engine
	Rolls-Royce RC-211 by-pass jet engine
130	The New Look in the Jet Age
	Dressed for flight in anti-G suits
	Bell XP-59 Airacomet
	Boeing B-47
131	The New Shape in the Sky
	Dassault Mystère
	Mig-15
	Convair F-106A
	Supermarine Attacker
	McDonnell Banshee
	North American F-86 Sabre
	Republic F-84
132	The new radar
	Sikorsky HUS-1 Marine helicopter
133	B-29 and B-36 Peacemaker
134	Avro Vulcan and Boeing B-52
	Republic F-105 "Thud"
135	Vickers Valiant
	Modern wind tunnel
136	The Changing Airliner I
	The Bristol Brabazon I
	The Bristol Britannia
	Douglas C-124
	Douglas DC-7
	Vickers Valetta
	Martin R4Y
	Boeing Stratocruiser
	Vickers Viscount
137	The Changing Airliner II
	DeHavilland Comet I
	Convair 990
	BAC 111-500
	Tupulov Tu-134
	Boeing 747 and 707
	Vickers VC-10
	Boeing 737
	Lockheed Tri-Star
138	The Evolving Aircraft
	Convair F-106 Delta Dart
	Lockheed C-5A unloading attack helicopter
	Fuselage plugs for a C-130
	A powerless cockpit computer
	Workers inside a C-5B wing
	Rolls-Royce RB 211-524 turbofan engine

139 Naval Aircraft, 1960-1980
   Lockheed P2V Harpoon
   Grumman S-2D Tracker
   North American RA-5C Vigilante
   Douglas A-4 Skyhawk
   Vought A-7A Corsair II's
   Lockheed WV-1 Super Constellation
   Grumman E-2A Hawkeyes
   McDonnell F-4J Phantom II's of the
     Blue Angels
140 Dassault Mystère IV
   General Dynamics B-58 Hustler
141 The Changing Aircraft (cont.)
   Republic F-84 cockpit
   General Dynamics F-111 Aardvark
   North American XB-70 Valkyrie
   F-80 engine change
   Dassault Mirage V
142 The Changing Aircraft (cont.)
   Lockheed F-104's and McDonnell F-4 Phantom
   Dassault Etendard
   DeHavilland Caribou
   Saab 37 Viggen
   Fairchild A-10 Warthog
   North American B-1
   General Dynamics F-16
   Boeing KC-135 refuelling Lockheed C-5A
143 USS *Forrestal*
144 Transport Aircraft Transition, 1941-1956
   Douglas DC-3
   Avro York
   Douglas C-54/DC-4 Skymaster
   C-54 interior
   Lockheed 049/C-69 transport
   Lockheed Model 749 Constellation
   Constellation cockpit
   Convair XC-99
   Lockheed XR60-1 Constitution with P-51's
145 Stretching a Lockheed Hercules
   A Soviet aircraft factory
146 Douglas DC-8
   Douglas DC-10 and F-4 fighter
   Douglas DC-9 (now the MD 100)
   Airbus Industries A-300
147 Lockheed SR-71
   Douglas DC-9 production line
148 North American F-86 in action
   North American F-100 Super Sabre
149 Fairchild C-82 Packets
   Mig-15 pilot bailing out over Korea
150 Grumman F9F Panther
   Vought A-7D coming in to refuel from a KC-135
151 HMS *Bulwark* with Westland Wessex helicopters
   HMS *Eagle* with Blackburn Buccaneers
152 Air/Sea Rescue by helicopter in Vietnam
   Heavy-lift helicopters
153 Folland Gnat light fighter
   Passing Lockheed F-104's
154 Polish Sukhoi Su-7 fighters scramble

155 McDonnell Phantom I
   Phantom I cockpit
   Lockheed P2V Harpoon with jet pods
   Lockheed P-3B Orion
   Aircraft Accident Comparison
156 McDonnell F-3H Demon on the elevator, USS
   Ticonderoga
   Douglas AD-1 Skyraider leaving the angled deck,
   1965
   Aircraft Accident Comparison (verso)
157 Soviet Aviation: Links & Innovations
   Lend-Lease C-47/Li-2
   Navy Fresco jet fighters
   Polish Air Force Mig-19
   Mig-15 flown out of North Korea
   Yugoslav Mig-21
158 Tupulov Tu-114 Moss
   Tupulov Tu-20 Bear
   Tupulov Tu-28B Backfin
159 A 201M Bison
   MA-25 Hormone helicopter and a USN Sea
     King
   The helicopter carrier *Kiev*
160 Soviet helicopter carrier *Moskva*
161 Command and Control — SAC's underground
   headquarters
   Space Shuttle *Enterprise*
162 Backfire heavy bomber. *RSAF*
   F-16 Fighting Falcon. *USAF*
165 DC-4 and Concorde
166 Douglas DC-6B
167 Wichita, KS, Municipal Airport
168 Boeing 707
169 Douglas DC-10
   Boeing 737-100
170 Fokker F-50
   North American Rockwell B-1B
171 Pratt & Whitney engine
172 United Parcel Service Boeing 757PF
173 Fokker F-100
   Cessna Citation II
   British Aerospace BAe 146
174 Saab SF 340
   Embraer Brasilia
175 British Aerospace Hawk
176 Boeing 747-400
177 Junkers Ju-88 at Wright Field
178 RADM William A. Moffett, USN
179 Boeing 727
180 Kawanishi Shiden (George)
181 Boeing Model 299
182 North American B-25
   Sikorsky S-44a *Excalibur*
183 Focke-Wulf Fw-190
   BMW-801D engine for the Fw-190
   BAC/Sud Concorde
194 USAF Thunderbirds
Back End Paper   The Growth of
                        Aircraft-Carriers

Preface

THE aim of this book is to demonstrate how some of the principles of air power have developed: the story of the rise of aviation is used for this purpose, rather than presented simply as a detailed historical coverage. The variety of events and elements in the history of airpower is stressed, but only those which seem to hold lessons for us are emphasized. Thus the Second World War is treated more fully than is the period before it, and even the former is given detailed treatment only when tactical lessons seem to merit it. Occasionally the focus is on minor details, where these provide significant examples of the practical impact of war upon theory, or of the conflict between absolute obedience to rules and achievement of larger ends.

The arrangement of the book is only partially chronological, in order to present in one place material, such as that on tactical air forces, where the lessons are interconnected, and so not weary the reader by repetitions. For instance, there is no lengthy section specifically on the tactical air forces over Russia in 1941–45. In this way, the book aims to present an overall picture of the rise of air power within which both beginners and professionals can set their own knowledge. It is thus a synthesis and explanation of a particular twentieth-century phenomenon.

If the book appears to be overbalanced in the use of material relating to the British and American air forces, there are several reasons for this. The author's own interests and training have been primarily in the field of British aviation. There is a dearth of materials on others air forces available in English and a severe lack of useful monographs and single-volume works on the history of aviation comparable to Potter and Nimitz's *Sea Power*. Lastly, much of the important development work was done by the victorious air forces, British and American, which eventually domin-ated the skies during and after the two world wars. Nevertheless, prejudices of all sorts notwithstanding, some basic lessons can be drawn and comments made which it is hoped will serve as guides for others, whether or not they agree with them.

One last point must be taken up. There is an assumption that those of us who write on military history are enamoured of war, and some will insist that we do not mean it when we say that we are much more concerned with maintaining peace than we are with war. The study of military matters is beset with difficulties of this sort as well as with paradoxes. War has been one of the most common and also one of the most expensive of human activities. States-men can be accused of starting wars just as easily as can generals, and of starting them at the one extreme by pursuing aggressive policies or at the other by failing to provide sufficient armaments to deter a potential aggressor. In peacetime the military have the job of preventing conflicts and in war of winning them. For military leaders as well as for commercial and political leaders, the problem is to find the balance point between what is sufficient simply to maintain peace and low taxes and what is necessary to win a war quickly and thus inexpensively. The examination of a military organization is the reverse of the study of a corporation or a state, though it may mirror it in that reverse. For corporations and states peace means the constant engagement in the activities proper to them, but for the armed forces peacetime is a period without chal-lenge, in which they may well fall into inefficient or out-dated habits. The study of any organization must include its successes as well as its failures and point to the reasons for both; and it will be necessary within this context to point out occasionally that for air forces wars are a good thing, using the term "good" not in a moralistic way but in terms of efficiency.

*The Short S.23 **Champion**, a 1936 Empire flying-boat taking off under a superimposed Boeing 707-436 of 1960. The photographic images are to the same scale courtesy of BOAC, now **British Airways**. The Empires cost £61,000 each in 1936, the 707's £2,200,000 each twenty-six years later giving some measure of growth, but speed and carrying capacity had also gone up six-fold.*

AIR POWER

Introduction to the Third Edition

The major change in this 1988 edition is the addition of a section dealing with War on the Airways. This aims to make plain that the world's major airlines are now as big as many air forces — Aeroflot has 2,000 aeroplanes, the larger U.S. carriers over 300 each — and that they run a war daily. The largest U.S. carriers despatch more than 1,500 sorties (departures) daily seven days a week. Air cargo operators shuttle tons of cargo in and out of a central terminal, in one night moving parcels between any two points in the United States as much as 3,000 miles apart within 18 hours door-to-door. Moreover, for the aircraft and ancillary industries, the airline market now exceeds the military in value, consistency, and likely future growth. In years to come, defence contracts may only pay because they provide access to new technology, but at political hazard.

Aviation is not yet a century old, yet its story perfectly reflects that of the societies from which it has sprung. Speaking generally, from the Wright Brothers to Sikorsky it was founded by the sons of well-to-do parents on the aircraft side and by auto and cycle mechanics on the engine. Some of these people were practitioners and others were merely managers. (Indicative of the short span thus far of aviation is that Sir T.O.M. Sopwith, one of the founders, is still alive today.) These aircraft industry pioneers controlled company destinies until after 1945, and the airline founders until after 1960. They started in the wood and cloth days and left when all-metal jets were operational. They started with engines that weighed eight pounds per horsepower, got down to less than one pound, and departed when power was measured in pounds of thrust.

That such changes were feasible was due to the advances in the chemistry of fuels and of metallurgy, and these were made possible both by public and private setting of standards and testing, and by the dedicated work of a few men who spurred parts of the industry ahead. That this was possible at all was due to the two World Wars and the Cold War, which loosened the purse strings, and to the actual suc-

cesses and salesmanship of aviation, which attracted investment capital as well as government spending. Thus by 1941 not only was aluminum available and critical, but also high octane gasoline could be had. Equally important, airlines were buying significant quantities of passenger-carrying machines in international transactions and governments were following suit.

In the acceptance of aviation, the role of displays, journalism, books, and films, not to overlook later media, must not be underrated. Aircraft and air power were natural romantic symbols from the beginning, especially for urban populations. In the USSR they were the symbol of the Revolution.

If World War I made people conscious of the aeroplane, World War II as a global war took advantage of its new reach, a fact airmen were quick to grasp. By the end of the war and especially by the end of the decolonialization of the 1950's, an airline had become a sign of independence, no matter if the flight crews were still imperial.

Aircraft as the visible symbol of aviation became the master of progress and success, and also of modernization. But at the same time all powers were forced to recognize the costs involved whether of owning an airliner or an air force. The economics of words, deeds, national aspirations, and power politics have also been reflected in equipment. Thus super powers seem to have a mindset towards big bombers and air superiority fighters. Whereas lesser powers have to be more concerned with role, numbers, and price.

Early flyers used to argue that aviation history did not exist because the subject was too new. Hopefully readers of this volume will discern that the patterns of air history are the same as those found in all history because those who make this story are humans, too.

R.H.
Manhattan, Kansas
20 June 1988

Boeing Air Transport stewardesses about 1934; it was forty years before women got seats in the cockpit.

PART ONE

Origins and Concepts

This modified "Model B" Wright Flyer was still used for flight instruction in 1916 and was last flown in 1924. It was presented to the **USAF Museum** at Wright-Patterson AFB in 1962.

1. Early Attitudes towards Air Power

The history of air power has been much confused, both by the glamour surrounding flight and by a lack of historical perspective on the part of its exponents. To pierce this confusion we must examine the context in which the aeroplane first flew.

Its arrival coincided with the beginning of widespread industrialization and with the closure of frontiers in the United States, Australia, and South Africa. Man was now confined to known bounds and his frustration was accentuated by the stalemate in the mud of the First World War when airmen appeared to be as free as the birds, the romantic frontiersmen of the day.

Man began to fly just after the tabloid newspapers of the sensational yellow press were started; this, and the fact that flying grew up with the cinema and shared its young heroes in the twenties with radio, made glamourization inevitable. Flying somehow fitted into the idealized characteristics of each nation. The Wright brothers were practical mechanics in the American mould; elsewhere the pioneer flyers were more often gentry, manufacturers, or engineers in Britain and France, or even nobility in Germany and Japan. That at least was the popular impression, if not always the fact. Above all else there emerged the picture of the daring pilot (other members of the crew were largely ignored even in wartime), his white scarf streaming in the wind as man once again battled against nature.

There was another form of sensationalism. Those publications which raved about the magic of flight also delighted in portraying its accidents. In the early days these were often spectacular, though

Throughout the history of air power, training has played a vital role. This is the author in a Fairchild Cornell over Alberta, Canada, in 1944 — halfway between the Wrights and the present (1984).

not always fatal. But because of the apparently dreamlike, fantastic quality of early aviation, the public, enchanted by the misfortunes of those who dared, liked to read about air disasters, though far fewer people were killed in these than in vehicles on the ground.

Somehow, too, the impression was created that the air was a new element with unknown dangers and unknown rules. Past history did not apply. Everything seemed new. But actually, in order to fly, man had converted the automobile engine and the ship's propeller and adopted for his vehicle the shape of the bird. His organization of the developing air forces followed that of ground-bound military services, armies and navies. In fact, the utilization of most new weapons is perforce based on old organizations, because adaptable manuals exist; and service aviation was originally manned by men who saw it only as another branch of their own service, like cavalry or submarines.

The history of air power has also been confused by the bragging of its prophets and the derision of its enemies. Too often vision has outrun reality and resulted in disappointment and reaction. As newcomers, forced to plead from a position of weakness, airmen carried arguments to their logical extremes and talked about what air power was going to be able to do; and their listeners tended to forget that these were prognostications, accepting them instead as imminent realities. For instance, not until the post–1945 perfection of air-to-air refueling and the creating of the atomic bomb was it technically possible for the aircraft of any one power to devastate a city anywhere in the world. Before that the psychological impact of air power on civilians was greater than the physical impact, in terms of numbers involved. And in spite of the actual destruction that did take place in war, it is notable that the impact of air power was discussed more widely by its partisans than by its victims, not all of whom died. The real effect of air power thus in many ways fell far short of the claims of its early supporters.

The history of air power must be considered within the general intellectual and emotional background sketched above, but it must also be approached in other terms and from other angles. In the first place it must be seen within the general patterns not only of military history but of all history. The means and the medium were novel, but human elements have remained unchanged. One of the failures of earlier students of air power was to claim for it immunity from the laws of history, but we can now see that the usual patterns of administrative and logistical history apply, with their changing political and economic pressures, feasts and famines, bureaucratic rigidity, and human foibles.

2. Some Patterns or Models of Development

The development of British aviation provides patterns which are known to be applicable to American development, but which have not as yet been tested for other aeronautical countries, in particular France, Russia, Germany, and Japan. The cycle of peace and war is a wave pattern: a peacetime equilibrium, disturbed by rearmament, then settling into the controlled activity of full wartime production; and, when the war is over, renewed instability due to disarmament, phasing into new equilibrium.*

A second pattern can be discerned in the overall history of aviation since its beginning. The aeroplane, the airship, and aero-

---

*This pattern was first developed from a study of the British aircraft industry, in which the process could be measured in terms of either the numbers of aircraft produced or the money appropriated for the air force. In either case the pattern emphasized that, at least in a technological service, the beginnings and ends of wars do not coincide with the formal dates assigned to these phenomena. Thus accelerated purchasing began in 1913 and 1934, many months before war was declared. (The Korean War caught the government in Britain flat-footed, and the instability of rearmament thus began *after* the crisis started and continued after it ended.) The level of steady wartime production was not reached until 1916 or later in the First World War and carried on till shortly after it ended. In the Second it was not reached until about 1942 (about the same three years after the war began as before) but the running-down process began in 1944, nearly a year before the conflict terminated. After 1918 the political situation at home dictated using war-surplus aircraft for years in order to save money in a day of orthodox finance; the continuing unsettled state of Europe created the demand for the Home Defence Air Force of 1923 which resulted in some aircraft purchases, but that programme was stretched out over ten years, during which technology changed rapidly.

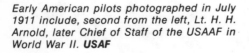

Early American pilots photographed in July 1911 include, second from the left, Lt. H. H. Arnold, later Chief of Staff of the USAAF in World War II. **USAF**

PART ONE

Origins and Concepts

*This modified "Model B" Wright Flyer was still used for flight instruction in 1916 and was last flown in 1924. It was presented to the **USAF Museum** at Wright-Patterson AFB in 1962.*

1. Early Attitudes towards Air Power

The history of air power has been much confused, both by the glamour surrounding flight and by a lack of historical perspective on the part of its exponents. To pierce this confusion we must examine the context in which the aeroplane first flew.

Its arrival coincided with the beginning of widespread industrialization and with the closure of frontiers in the United States, Australia, and South Africa. Man was now confined to known bounds and his frustration was accentuated by the stalemate in the mud of the First World War when airmen appeared to be as free as the birds, the romantic frontiersmen of the day.

Man began to fly just after the tabloid newspapers of the sensational yellow press were started; this, and the fact that flying grew up with the cinema and shared its young heroes in the twenties with radio, made glamourization inevitable. Flying somehow fitted into the idealized characteristics of each nation. The Wright brothers were practical mechanics in the American mould; elsewhere the pioneer flyers were more often gentry, manufacturers, or engineers in Britain and France, or even nobility in Germany and Japan. That at least was the popular impression, if not always the fact. Above all else there emerged the picture of the daring pilot (other members of the crew were largely ignored even in wartime), his white scarf streaming in the wind as man once again battled against nature.

There was another form of sensationalism. Those publications which raved about the magic of flight also delighted in portraying its accidents. In the early days these were often spectacular, though

Throughout the history of air power, training has played a vital role. This is the author in a Fairchild Cornell over Alberta, Canada, in 1944 — halfway between the Wrights and the present (1984).

not always fatal. But because of the apparently dreamlike, fantastic quality of early aviation, the public, enchanted by the misfortunes of those who dared, liked to read about air disasters, though far fewer people were killed in these than in vehicles on the ground.

Somehow, too, the impression was created that the air was a new element with unknown dangers and unknown rules. Past history did not apply. Everything seemed new. But actually, in order to fly, man had converted the automobile engine and the ship's propeller and adopted for his vehicle the shape of the bird. His organization of the developing air forces followed that of ground-bound military services, armies and navies. In fact, the utilization of most new weapons is perforce based on old organizations, because adaptable manuals exist; and service aviation was originally manned by men who saw it only as another branch of their own service, like cavalry or submarines.

The history of air power has also been confused by the bragging of its prophets and the derision of its enemies. Too often vision has outrun reality and resulted in disappointment and reaction. As newcomers, forced to plead from a position of weakness, airmen carried arguments to their logical extremes and talked about what air power was going to be able to do; and their listeners tended to forget that these were prognostications, accepting them instead as imminent realities. For instance, not until the post–1945 perfection of air-to-air refueling and the creating of the atomic bomb was it technically possible for the aircraft of any one power to devastate a city anywhere in the world. Before that the psychological impact of air power on civilians was greater than the physical impact, in terms of numbers involved. And in spite of the actual destruction that did take place in war, it is notable that the impact of air power was discussed more widely by its partisans than by its victims, not all of whom died. The real effect of air power thus in many ways fell far short of the claims of its early supporters.

The history of air power must be considered within the general intellectual and emotional background sketched above, but it must also be approached in other terms and from other angles. In the first place it must be seen within the general patterns not only of military history but of all history. The means and the medium were novel, but human elements have remained unchanged. One of the failures of earlier students of air power was to claim for it immunity from the laws of history, but we can now see that the usual patterns of administrative and logistical history apply, with their changing political and economic pressures, feasts and famines, bureaucratic rigidity, and human foibles.

2. Some Patterns or Models of Development

The development of British aviation provides patterns which are known to be applicable to American development, but which have not as yet been tested for other aeronautical countries, in particular France, Russia, Germany, and Japan. The cycle of peace and war is a wave pattern: a peacetime equilibrium, disturbed by rearmament, then settling into the controlled activity of full wartime production; and, when the war is over, renewed instability due to disarmament, phasing into new equilibrium.*

A second pattern can be discerned in the overall history of aviation since its beginning. The aeroplane, the airship, and aero-

---

*This pattern was first developed from a study of the British aircraft industry, in which the process could be measured in terms of either the numbers of aircraft produced or the money appropriated for the air force. In either case the pattern emphasized that, at least in a technological service, the beginnings and ends of wars do not coincide with the formal dates assigned to these phenomena. Thus accelerated purchasing began in 1913 and 1934, many months before war was declared. (The Korean War caught the government in Britain flat-footed, and the instability of rearmament thus began *after* the crisis started and continued after it ended.) The level of steady wartime production was not reached until 1916 or later in the First World War and carried on till shortly after it ended. In the Second it was not reached until about 1942 (about the same three years after the war began as before) but the running-down process began in 1944, nearly a year before the conflict terminated. After 1918 the political situation at home dictated using war-surplus aircraft for years in order to save money in a day of orthodox finance; the continuing unsettled state of Europe created the demand for the Home Defence Air Force of 1923 which resulted in some aircraft purchases, but that programme was stretched out over ten years, during which technology changed rapidly.

Early American pilots photographed in July 1911 include, second from the left, Lt. H. H. Arnold, later Chief of Staff of the USAAF in World War II. **USAF**

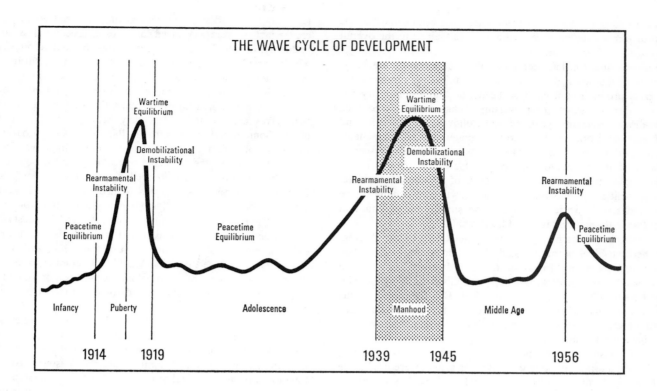

THE WAVE CYCLE OF DEVELOPMENT

Wartime Equilibrium

Demobilizational Instability

Rearmamental Instability

Peacetime Equilibrium

Wartime Equilibrium

Demobilizational Instability

Rearmamental Instability

Rearmamental Instability

Peacetime Equilibrium

Peacetime Equilibrium

Infancy | Puberty | Adolescence | Manhood | Middle Age

1914 | 1919 | 1939 | 1945 | 1956

nautics in general were in their infancy before 1914. Only about 1917 did military aviation begin to mature. Its period as an ancillary weapon in war was very short and came to an effective end with the Armistice of November 1918. Like the boy born about 1900 who enlisted in 1917, it had scarcely been properly blooded when fighting stopped. Untrained for other jobs but with airy dreams, aviators sought for a significant place in a world where until then they had been nothing more than a Sunday afternoon entertainment. It was a long and painful struggle for military and civil aviation, for manufacturer and airlines alike, and it lasted for nearly two decades. Air power did not reach maturity until well into the Second World War, and only after 1945 did it enter a full hardworking middle age. At least this was true for the United States and the Soviet Union; in other countries, notably Britain, the manned air forces after a brief resurgence as a result of the Korean War began a gentle decline toward retirement.

Corresponding to the growth of aviation from infancy to middle age and retirement are the careers of many of the men who have taken part in this development. Sociologically airmen form a group, drawn largely from the middle and lower middle classes, which has certain recognisable characteristics (though this caste awaits a study such as Janowitz's *The Professional Soldier*); the young airmen of 1914 were only retiring as chiefs of staff in the 1950s. In the aircraft industry, many of the people who pioneered the aeronautical business were actually leaving it only in the 1960s. Thus the management of the industry, at least in Britain, has tended to reflect the age of the founder of the firm. A powerful leader rarely produces an equally dynamic heir, for who with ambition wants to play second fiddle to a strong man unwilling to give up the reins of power in the foreseeable future? This is true for any nation or industry, though in the US, where competition has been more ruthless than elsewhere, the aviation companies were by the end of the Second World War becoming far more corporate and far less one-man shows. Yet in the American airline business, the founders Juan Trippe, Six, C. R. Smith, Patterson, Eddie Rickenbacker, were still, in the sixties, running systems which were none the less highly competitive and dynamic. The aircraft industry and the airline provide

the basis for the exercise of air power outside its purely military aspects, and thus the aircraft industry—more than the airline indus-

Lt. H. H. Arnold at College Park, MD, on a "Model B" Wright illustrating what the well-dressed flyer wore. **USAF**

try, which was born at least a decade later—has been subject to the pattern of war and peace described above, as well as to the overall growth pattern of air power.

The aircraft industry has been more often the target of attacks on profit-making than most others. Aircraft manufacturers have indeed made great profits. But it has also been true that the industry has enjoyed enormous short sharp wartime peaks and suffered long hand-to-mouth peacetime years as well, followed, after the Second World War, by a drastic rise in costs of materials and components and a compelling need to undertake increasingly expensive research. One facet of the history of air power which is at present inadequately studied is the combined influence of economic considerations and political developments on the growth and decline of the aircraft industry in various nations. The simple assumption that competition is the solution is not of itself tenable.

It is ironical that the first graduate of the RAF College at Cranwell to become Chief of the Air Staff did not do so until 1956, when the British air force was already starting to fade away. It remains to be seen whether or not Parkinson's Law of Great Buildings applies to the USAF Academy, founded in 1954. But these two events occurred at a time when it appeared that missiles would replace manned aircraft; the arrival of the practical ballistic missile inspired talk of its being the ultimate weapon which would make all others obsolete. Yet historical analogy suggests that this may not happen. The field gun did not outmode the pistol. As armies were used more and more merely to guard frontiers, pistols became less important to them, but there was a long period in which the pistol remained useful in minor contests. And so it appears to be with air power. The nuclear ballistic missiles may well have created their own stalemate, so making the manned tactical aeroplane, or the transport aeroplane, far more valuable.

In the early days, in their state of peacetime equilibrium, the air services simply strove to be recognized and survive. Officers were attached on a temporary basis so as not to ruin their careers, and equipment was flimsy and scarce. Then came the mushroom wartime expansion when regulars were promoted rapidly to high command or high heaven, and massive recruitment and constantly changing material disrupted the services. Wartime equilibrium in the First World War was reached about 1917. At last the machinery

ran smoothly, and with the arrival of properly trained pilots and crews tactics were stabilized and losses became less alarming. Suddenly, in late 1918, came demobilization and its uncertainties, which started before the end of the conflict with the cutting back of orders, then, once the fighting had stopped, continued with the wholesale movement of men and the disposal or storage of equipment. Those who had hoped to make the air force a career found themselves demobilized unless they belonged to the correct 'in' clique. Some found employment in the airlines, a few barnstormed, but most could only dream of the good old flying days. Those who did stay in found themselves dropped two ranks, bound into an often boring routine, and compelled to wait years for promotion. Equipment remained war surplus. With little room at the top, many younger officers found the flying career limited and wound up elsewhere. The result was that in the Second World War most of the top posts went to those who had served in 1914–1918 and who often thought in terms of that war; much of the theory and doctrine of 1919–1939 was based on First World War combat experience and its apparent lessons—or upon colonial conditions of limited validity in conflicts between modern armed forces—and not on the history of war.

But after the Second World War the civilian airlines were expanding at a rate of 14 per cent per annum. Their need for manpower and equipment created an increasing demand for pilots and kept the surviving aircraft manufacturers in business. At the same time the private or general aircraft market at last blossomed, twenty years after predictions, providing more jobs in aeronautics. In countries where defence or the airlines became big business, retirement from the services often meant only a sidestep into a new career in defence industry or the airlines. But in the air forces of powers with no belligerent future, notably in Latin America, careers became sour enough for pilots to turn to politics. In these countries the future of the air forces remains a question mark.

The airmen's struggle for identity during the growth cycle of airpower was not an abnormal phenomenon, but one to be observed in many human groupings. Thus airmen sought a separate service and uniform, in order to fight as equals and brothers with the older services and even ultimately, in some cases such as in Canada, to wear the same uniform again in one single triphibious service.

*The "1909" Wright Military Flyer was a little more complex than the earlier models as this **USAF Museum** replica shows, but it could carry two men for an hour and could average 42 mph. For successfully passing these requirements and exceeding the 40 mph demanded, the Wrights were paid $30,000, a large sum for those days.*

The pattern revealed in the choice of Permanent Under-Secretaries (the highest rank civil servant) for the British Air Ministry and ministries associated with it is of some interest. In the early days the post of Permanent Under-Secretary (as opposed to that of Secretary of State, who is always a politician) was usually filled from civil servants already working inside the Air Ministry; but in the Second World War, when the position became more powerful and important, it was taken over by a small coterie of high civil servants associated with the Board of Trade, with the result that the permanent 'managing director' was a man who knew the civil service rather than aeronautical technology. After the Suez debacle and the 1957 White Paper, the Permanent Secretary at the Air Ministry was again chosen from inside that organization, for the post enjoyed declining prestige.

3. The Principles of War and the Military Setting for Air Power

Air power is an integral part of warfare, and any historical or theoretical study of its use must take into account the general principles of war. In Britain at least, even in 1920, the principles of war, though often referred to, had not been spelled out. Nowadays they are usually given as Concentration of Effort, Control, Simplicity, Cooperation of All Arms, Surprise, Speed of Action, Seizing the Initiative. To these may be added Liddell Hart's Adjusting your ends to your means, Keeping your object (once selected) always in mind, Choosing a line or course of action of least expectation (Surprising), Exploiting a line of least resistance, Taking a line of operations that offers alternative objectives, Ensuring that both plan and disposition are flexible and adaptable to the circumstances. And two negative ones: Don't throw your weight into a stroke when your enemy is on guard; never renew an attack along the same line or in the same form after it has once failed. And to these we may add the principle that the line of communications must always be protected.

The principles of war can be applied on the grand-strategic, the

One of the Intrepid early flyers was the Californian Glenn L. Martin, seen here in the cockpit with Gladstone bag, dead wolf or coyote, and ship's style wheel. **Martin Co.**

strategic, and the tactical levels. And here more distinctions must be made: Grand strategy is that combination of political, diplomatic, military, economic, ideological, and social factors which is made into a national plan; it is continuous in peace and war; Strategy is the concern of the high military command; Tactics are the methods employed when engaged with the enemy. These three elements are combined in war, which is the continuation of national policy by other than outwardly pacific means.

The theory of war, in spite of the writings of a number of authors from Machiavelli to Jomini and Clausewitz, was not well studied in the nineteenth century. Too often writing was limited either to compiling manuals or to reporting on campaigns. This has been less true in the twentieth century, but airmen have written relatively little on theory. The only air-power theorists worth mentioning are Douhet, Mitchell, de Seversky, Slessor, Kingston-McCloughry, Trenchard and Asher Lee. None of them has attempted a balanced history of air power, and only a very few books about development within single countries have yet been published.

Clausewitz, in the early years of the nineteenth century, placed the theory of war in its context as the extension of diplomacy, recognizing that in the modern state system it was unlikely that most disputes would lead to more than limited wars for limited objectives. In other words, the objective of war would usually be an early peace, normally to be achieved by seizing and holding small territories with or without the decisive defeat of the enemy's forces in the field. The British application of this theory, if there was any awareness of it at all, was naval and consisted generally in picking up colonies overseas while preventing the opponent from coming to their rescue.

Towards the end of the nineteenth century and into the twentieth Clausewitz's common sense was lost sight of, if indeed military men had ever read Clausewitz. Instead they fastened upon the Napoleonic *ésprit* or the will to win battles. A logical extension of this was to couple it to the democratic idea that a nation responds to the will of its people, and, therefore, the will of the people must be broken. To airmen this meant quite logically skipping over the battlefields to strike directly at the people. And this in its turn became linked with the old fascination which capital cities had long

Air racing and international meets were an important way in which aircraft and engines were proved and ideas exchanged — a scene somewhere in France. **Dassault**

The **US Navy** early adopted Pensacola, Florida, as its major flying training base. This 1914 view shows Curtiss flying-boats on their ramps in front of the canvas hangars.

held for generals. Thus the temptation with the aerial weapon was to turn wars for limited objectives into unlimited ones on the grounds that a paralysing stroke at the enemy's capital would destroy his will to fight and thereby quickly assure victory. The fallacies in this argument were that it presupposed accurate destructive capacity, denied any patriotic feelings or natural human resentment on the part of the population, and failed to realize that occupation of the ground, or at least defeat of the enemy's surface forces, was a prerequisite to success. Moreover, airmen tend to be unwilling to credit the enemy with totally effective stopping power, assuming that some of the bombers will always get through. In fact, until the massed raids of 1944 and the advent in 1945 of the atomic bomb, the amount of damage that could be done was strictly limited both by the power of the bombs available and by the inaccuracy of the bombing.

Thus a paradox developed in the application of the aerial weapon within the total military effort. Powers whose policy was normally defensive tended towards the counter-strike deterrent theory, while those with aggressive intentions developed tactical air forces to enable their surface forces to take and hold ground. Defensive powers assumed that aggressors would think as they did, and thus prepared themselves against the wrong kind of attack. *Blitzkrieg,* for instance, was specifically designed to avoid a war of attrition on the ground or in the air. Thus aggressive powers intended to wage a limited war whereas the reaction of the defenders created the conditions for an unlimited one.

In the past, independent use of air power has at times led to the neglect of the whole war effort, notably in the Second World War. Air strategy must be effectively related to both grand strategy and any particular surface campaigns either current or contemplated. Whether or not a nation can afford to use air power depends, as Mahan pointed out for sea power, on its territorial position and resources as well as upon its human might and technical skill. Psychological factors also affect the use of air power, and they vary considerably. For instance, both British and German civilians proved unexpectedly stoical under bombing in the Second World War, to the surprise of most British politicians and even such a military expert as Major General J. F. C. Fuller. Leaders had perhaps been unduly impressed by the airmen—who could point to the

impact of the German raids on London between 1915 and 1918—with the devastating effect of bombing; and they forgot that veterans of the First World War trenches, who had gone through worse experiences in Flanders, were by the Second World War among the citizens undergoing attack at home, and were providing stiffening for their will to resist. In fact, recent evidence seems to show that a naturally stoical people such as the North Vietnamese have responded to bombing much as did others in the Second World War in Europe. Such attacks close to home have increased their resolution and support for their leaders because the conflict has had immediate meaning to them.

Air power has also been used inappropriately or inadequately in maritime warfare. Nations whose lifeblood depended upon the sea should have thought in terms of protecting their shipping by both air and sea arms. But in the Second World War both the Germans and the Americans scored heavily on the convoys of their opponents, for air power had not been applied to safe-guarding lines of communication, one of the most elementary of all principles of war.

It is clear that many aspects of the utilization of aerial warfare within the context of overall military theory are yet to be adequately understood. Even in limited wars, air power must be used with swift tactical restraint, and its effectiveness will be restricted by the many factors determining grand strategy. Particularly in such wars, for example, numbers and readiness may be more important than the most modern equipment or most sophisticated methods. These considerations hold good for all warfare, and they can only be applied by a commander who understands his object. This may well mean, in terms of air power, a single air force commanded by an airman—a force perhaps including contingents from several different air arms, with a commander who is the immediate deputy of the supreme commander of all the armed forces involved. By the end of the Second World War the Allied Higher Direction understood this. Even so, efficient command depended upon personalities, planning, production, and communications, no matter which service was involved.

War is intended to obtain the political objective as quickly as possible with the least cost to either side. It calls for the most efficient use of all the forces available to bring victory so that peace may be restored and trade resumed. Marshal Saxe in the eighteenth century, and Field Marshal Wavell in the twentieth, said that a pyramid of skulls or other evidence of butchery are not the signs of good generalship; to this may be added the claim that politicians who go to war without a policy, a plan, or the power to wage the war dynamically are not good statesmen. The efficient conduct of war depends upon the development of doctrines which are flexible enough to be applicable to the situations which emerge. German success with *blitzkrieg* in the Second World War was due to the development of a doctrine and the appropriate equipment in the inter-war years and to their correct application until mid-1941 in limited campaigns. Similarly, the most effective use of carriers was made by the Japanese and the Americans because they had developed the doctrines necessary for intelligent command (including the rudiments of re-supply) and because they saw carriers as weapons in themselves and not just as vessels subordinate to the main fleet.

In assessing the place of air power in war it is useful to go back to the thoughts of a surface pundit. In 1890 Captain Alfred Thayer Mahan of the United States, after a lengthy study of the British experience in controlling the seas, argued two things: first, that sea power was the ability to go where desired when required and to prevent the enemy from doing like-wise; second, that there were six things which made one nation, Britain, a successful sea power: geographical position, physical conformation, extent of territory, numbers of population, national character, and character of the government. To combat such sea power, grand strategy in air warfare, or what might be called grand-strategic bombing, has to take all of these factors into account. Success presupposes that the enemy's geographical position can be reached; that the enemy has concentrated vital industries and transportation or military facilities; that the loss of any of these would leave no alternative for warlike action; that his population cannot stand losses and has not the will to war; and that the national government is weak and ill-prepared mentally and physically. A nation with adequate room in which to disperse its vital organizations, with a government prepared to wage war, and with a people experienced in war or strongly policed, will not easily crack. A lack of understanding of this point from misreading the evidence of the First World War left some leaders believing that the Second World War could be won by an

air blow. But in that sort of blow the campaign has to be as much psychological as physical to have immediate effect; in 1940 the Germans underestimated Mahan's intangibles in the case of Britain. True, fighter airfields were vital, but even more so were the ports and the railways and roads leading out of them. The Japanese in China and the Germans again in the Soviet Union made the same mistakes. The United States in the pre-intercontinental days enjoyed all the assets Mahan required for success. Whether the atomic and hydrogen weapons have nullified some of these remains to be seen.

War in the twentieth century has been a legacy of the industrial and technological revolutions. In the Russo-Japanese conflict and the First World War most soldiers and seamen saw the solution to their troubles simply as bigger and better guns, more shells, and a greater wastage of manpower. But in the Second World War the younger officers who had faced the actual bloodbath caused by the machine-gun in 1914–1918 knew they could not afford to repeat those tactics; instead they made greater use of improved mobile and armoured warfare. Navies, too, moved beyond the point at which the Royal Navy, the only major fleet with an air component, and the German navy, which had advanced ideas about using air power, left off. This meant at least a beginning of three-dimensional warfare.

But the air forces were split. The British, the Italian in theory, the American, and possibly the Japanese Army forces favoured 'strategic bombing' but had not the wherewithal to carry it out; when their bluffs were called, they were not in a position to do more than engage in a war of attrition on the 1918 scale. The real successes of 1939–42 were won by tactical air forces in cooperation with surface forces. And that includes the Battle of Britain. The ultimate absurdity of the called bluff was reached in Vietnam in 1968 where strategic bombers were used to drop anti-personnel bombs in tactical raids, and tactical aircraft were used in strategic raids on grand-strategic targets. Insult to air power was added to injury by a slow escalation which vitiated the grand-strategic air force's most important weapon—a devastating surprise blow. The blame for this kind of mismanagement has to be placed on those political leaders whose knowledge of military affairs is too limited to enable them to understand their professional advisers, let alone overrule them when their proposals or doctrine run counter to the

One of the fascinating things about aviation has always been its international linkages. Here French-built Farman pushers stand ready for review at Russian army maneuvers just before the First World War in 1914. **US War Department General Staff (National Archives)**

*Aircraft manufacturers, as the following series of pictures show, tended like any other establishment to reflect the society in which they operated. This is the **Martin Co.** front office in Los Angeles, perhaps 1914.*

possible, credible, or acceptable in both political and military terms.

The air weapon is essentially a technical weapon. Such an instrument in trained professional hands can be a superbly efficient tool for a *coup de main*—a knockout blow at the beginning of a conflict, whether declared or not; but it must have the power to be used quickly, ruthlessly, and absolutely effectively. The trouble with complex new weapons is that their effectiveness decreases rapidly when the professional force has to be diluted with 'hostilities only' civilians, though ultimately they may well make it a better weapon than it was in regular hands. The irony is that in the interim period they may do enough damage to stimulate the opponent's fighting spirit. In addition to the American bombing of North Vietnam, the German use of U-boats and the German air attacks on London in the 1914 war, and British attacks on Germany in the 1939–1945 war, are examples of this. In recent years the Israelis seem to have understood this best, and their 1967 pre-emptive strike against Arab aggression was a perfect example of the proper use of air power: simple, direct, and limited to military objectives. Civilians without martyrs cannot long be venomous; to attack them is to arouse the uncommitted.

Success or failure in war is of course directly related to the weapons available and how they are employed. A notable feature of air power has been the rapid and significant increase in the kinds of weapons which aircraft have been able to bring to bear on an opponent. Armament has been directly related to technological developments in manufacture, logistics, and maintenance; to operational suitability and command imagination; and last, but by no means least, to the lifting capacity of the aircraft itself. The power of aircraft has increased immensely. In 1914 aircraft could carry a bombload of less than 1,000 pounds of gunpowder about 100 miles, while fighters could with difficulty lug one machine gun and a few hundred rounds into the air. By the end of the war bombers were capable of delivering a 2,000-pound bomb several hundred miles, while fighters carried two or more machine guns. The next jump came in the late thirties and during the Second World War with the introduction of cannon in fighters and the development of a better range of high explosives and the mass production of incendiary bombs. (The latter particularly emphasized another factor in war: the bigger and better weapon may not

be the most effective; the cheap 4½-pound incendiary proved to be perhaps the most destructive non-battlefield weapon of the 1939 war.) Both at sea and on land the airborne rocket gave aircraft new hitting power. Another new armament was napalm, a jellied gasoline fire-bomb for battlefield use, which has become an emotional and political target. A further ramification of wartime research, in this case into means to protect friendly soldiers from natural hazards, was the development of herbicides. Thus even the transport, fitted with tanks and spraying apparatus, has become a combat aircraft capable of defoliating the countryside. The atom bomb, developed under a crash Anglo-American programme, at last enabled one airman to hold a whole city to ransom, and the mating of the nuclear weapon with the ballistic missile has now raised the question of the future role of manned aircraft.

It can be argued that it takes technology about fifty years to reach an acceptable peak of development, after which for some time the public is unwilling to support further progress. Reaction to the use of some of the new weapons, including rapid-fire guns used specially for strafing, has concentrated on the air forces because they have been the most spectacular users. Airmen have become, in countries like the United States by 1970, the victims of their own successes and of their own well-developed public-relations systems. Yet such activity on the part of air-power supporters has stimulated, especially since 1935, scientific and technological advances of all sorts. Nor would it have been possible if the governments had not been willing to support these developments, albeit often without comprehending their significance for the future of mankind, and at the same time driven by their fears that 'the enemy' would go ahead and develop them anyway. And in a vague tacit way, their peoples supported them, although radar and the atomic bomb demonstrate that often significant weapon development has been undertaken in secret, so that knowledge of a weapon's existence may not become public until after it has been used. But now the massive cost of new systems, sub-systems, and their antidotes are effectively limiting the number of new developments, even of airframes and engines.

Airmen, especially in the United States, like to talk about air superiority, especially with reference to certain fighter types. Like so many phrases, this has often been misinterpreted. Air space, unlike the seas, has almost no boundaries, though in the past distance and ceiling have imposed limitations upon air activity, and today radar forms a kind of barrier. In the First World War, however, when bombers followed spotter planes, some air commanders saw their responsibility as keeping the skies clear over whole battlefields, a policy wasteful both in wear on patrolling aircraft and crews and in casualties. With forces spread over greater areas in the Second World War, commanders learned, using radar, to attempt to achieve air superiority only over decisive points, either for attack or for defence. In some local wars, of course, air superiority may go to one side by default. But as in Vietnam the grounded opponent can develop effective anti-aircraft defences and adapt his tactics to his lack of air cover.

4. The General Background to 1914

Before 1914, even really before 1917, air forces hardly existed. In 1914 the major European powers each fielded about fifty aircraft. Each squadron was composed of assorted types, monoplanes or biplanes. None had reliable engines nor were they equipped to fight. In fact, exactly what they were there for was not very clear. The German general staff took the tactical view that aircraft might provide battlefield information after a movement had started, though the French were more anxious to use them to locate enemy armies and observe their movements in order to prepare for battle. The Germans had the means in the Zeppelins to cruise well behind the front lines while the French did not, and, because the Zeppelin was the symbol of German power, the French favoured aeroplanes. Thus national pride, among many other factors, entered into the creation of air forces.

By the 1880s, before the Wright brothers, both the British and the Germans had developed military balloon units run by engineers. But, just as the engineers did not always control automobile transport when it appeared, the artillery officers could claim that powered aeroplanes came under their jurisdiction. They argued that aero-

planes had to be transportable by road, just as the navy was apt to lay down that since an *airship* was a *ship* it had to carry an anchor, capstan, and towing hawser. On land the transport staff emphasized that aircraft must be stowable, and easy to erect or disassemble; this requirement made for a lack of airworthiness, but not until a number of accidents had occurred because of structural weakness was it changed. Thus, early designers and aviators, and they were sometimes the same people, had to fight vested interests which laid down rules that had no relevance to the problems of flight.

At the same time reaction to the arrival of the aeroplane and the airship varied. Some of those who feared or disdained these craft criticized them unreasonably, discounting, for instance, the Zeppelin because it could not turn as tightly as the non-rigid airship; and they saw to it that aircraft were not given scope on manoeuvres to demonstrate their real abilities. Those who supported aeronautics sometimes claimed too much for their fragile, temperamental, and unweatherly birds. But the enthusiasts also went ahead with their own experiments in bomb-dropping, mounting machine guns, and aerial photography. None of these developments had reached a useful stage or had been adopted officially when the First World War broke out, except in the veteran Italian air forces. Nor had artillery spotting been accepted, except, again, by the Italians, because until the advent of workable wireless sets communication between spotter and gunner was better maintained via a telephone line from the new sausage-shaped observation balloons.

Those who were worried about aircraft also sought the development of anti-aircraft guns. Here again the conflict between established groups was evident. The artillery advocated the adaptation of field-guns, but these could not be traversed fast enough or elevated sufficiently to be effective even against the very slow aircraft of the day. A much better device appeared to be special guns mounted upon automobile chassis and firing shrapnel. But no resolution of this conflict had appeared before the war broke out.

Another unanswered question concerned the actual size of the air arms. In the 1960s there was talk of a 'missile gap'. In the early 1900s, and indeed again in the thirties, there was talk of an aeroplanes or machines gap. Politicians faced with vociferous and well-intentioned, though not always well-informed, questioners, made their usual vague statements. There was, of course, a vast difference

*The sheet-metal department at the **Martin Company** in Los Angeles where cockpit coamings, seats and other items were hand-made to order.*

The Martin Los Angeles plant's wing department — the picture tells a good deal about both the premises and the work. It was an age of wood with a second story not designed to carry heavy loads. Nor were the wings, by modern standards. Wing-loadings were in the order of five to ten pounds per square foot and speeds still below 150 mph. Nevertheless, it resulted in elegant carpentry as these wing panels awaiting their fabric outer coverings make clear. **Martin Co.**

between the number of aircraft officially on charge and those actually able to fly; and a vast difference, too, between the latter and machines ready for war. This problem and the related matter of the money for aircraft caused the fall of a French government in 1912, while in Britain it reached a ridiculous point when members of Parliament actually went around counting aircraft on the various fields. Rumours flew, secret missions were sent abroad, and journalists were encouraged. The new aviation magazines took up the cry, for it was good business to demand more orders for their advertisers. National pride was appealed to. Subscriptions were raised to help pay for new aircraft for the French Army, or 'condolences' for a dead Japanese flyer. International competitions were sponsored and prizes and orders given to the winners. Sometimes this backfired, for on occasion the judges made their award to a product which turned out to be useless. Yet they can hardly be blamed, for nobody had a very clear idea about what was really wanted.

The Germans and the British were in some ways more concerned with quality than with quantity, while in the US almost no aeroplanes were on hand till 1916. The military desire to standardize came early to the fore, and by 1912 the British were seeking the ideal aeroplane. It was early recognized that at least three of each type should be built. One would be used as the basis for production, another for the development of modifications and for training, and the third as the basis for the next generation. The rapidity of progress was largely limited by the development of engines and the survival rate of pilots.

5. Training and Manufacturing

Pilots were a commodity both in great potential supply and in acute actual shortage. When volunteers were called for, bored young officers happily stepped forward. But few could be taken, since training facilities were limited by the lack of instructors and aircraft, and the need for perfectly still or windless flying days. The whole training process was hampered by lack of flying knowledge

and by the non-existence of a training philosophy. It was not until the development of such simple things as the intercom tube and dual controls that an instructor could both run through his patter and demonstrate in the air. Moreover, accidents were not investigated with any understanding either of what airmen were trying to do or of likely causes and the complex factors involved. Even such commonplace phenomena as stalls and spins were not understood until well into the war, though some skilful pilots had worked out how to get out of them before the war started. The result was that many pilots were injured or killed in accidents close to the ground when quick recovery was essential. The monoplane was banned in Britain as inherently unstable. Structural testing was also somewhat primitive, while dynamic testing did not exist. Moreover, parachutes, though available by 1913 as static models attached to the machine, were not used until late in the war, and then only by the Germans. Here another tradition came into play, that of the white feather. It was argued that if airmen could bail out they would abandon costly equipment in the face of the enemy. Already before the war the attitude was abroad that airmen were not to be trusted (largely owing to the boisterous behaviour of this younger generation), and this was coupled with the failure to consider what high casualty rates could mean to an élite branch which was to be relentlessly ground down in continuous combat. The attitude to fear was that it could be prevented by yet more flying.

Training up to and during the First World War remained primitive. At the worst, pilots might be sent into action with as few as seventeen hours of flying time; they were easy victims. In the better organizations and as training became a better recognized and standardized operation, pilots were given some fifty hours, which included both elementary flying instruction and advanced work on the kind of craft they would use in combat, together with gunnery and navigational work. By 1939 this had risen to some 150 hours before combat, and by 1945 was likely to have reached 300 or more as aircrew became a surplus commodity on the Allied side. But in countries such as Germany in 1918 and 1945, and Japan by 1945, fuel shortages sharply restricted training in days before useful simulators existed.

In contrast with sizes and methods of 1914, seventy years later **Lockheed-Georgia** workers were preparing this router with which to make frames for 50 C-5B giant transports on order. Note diameter of the fuselage as compared to the size of the men.

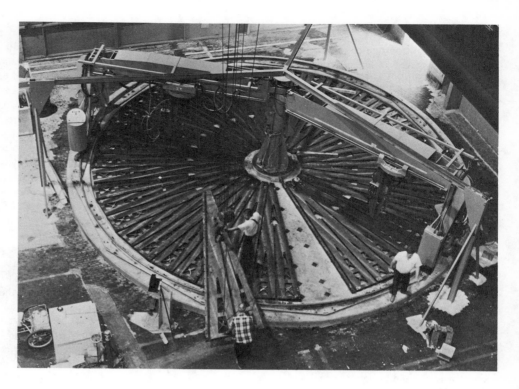

One of the enduring problems of training organizations was their detachment from operational realities. Before 1914 the small élite stations, mostly catering to officers, did not know what they were really training their pilots for, since the role of aviation in war was largely undecided. Thus the emphasis was upon learning to fly; employment on manoeuvres was largely limited to primitive tactical reconnaissance. Training staff tended to be non-operational personnel; they stuck to peacetime concepts and rules, and were loth to change unless forced into it by an influx of men experienced in fighting. Even then jealousy could make it more important to vanquish the expert than to train the fighting force. This hostility was less notable at operational training units, which were closer to battle both in terms of men and machines, and which were more heavily staffed with veterans and so lacked the often petty outlook of training commands. No doubt there were exceptions, but in general this account applies to training in both World Wars.

It was also at this period that special pay was granted to those who obtained a pilot's brevet or wings and that flying pay was introduced. These steps reinforced the idea that the airman was something special. And perhaps he was—few others in the services were likely to have such a short life.

If training was primitive, so was manufacturing. Up to the start of steady orders in 1914, design and manufacture was strictly a small-team, limited, manual operation. Small rival establishments scrambled for orders, gloated over others' failures, and loudly touted their own wares. Firms got off the ground with one wealthy silent partner, who might also take a hand at sales, a designer (who might or might not be an engineer or a pilot or both), a pilot, and a half-dozen workmen. Each model was hand-built and, after each accident, rebuilt. Most aircraft were a combination of wooden frames, fabric covering, and wire bracing, powered by an unreliable reciprocating petrol engine. Airships used heavier fabric, metal framework, and sometimes diesel engines, as well as highly inflammable hydrogen for lifting power. On the other hand, planes were not too expensive for some officers to possess their own, just as they owned cars and horses.

6. Operations: Tripoli, 1911–1912

Despite their primitiveness, the Italians took aircraft to the war in Libya in 1911. Aircraft had been assigned to the army in 1910, and on manoeuvres in August 1911 each of the contending armies had been allotted four. It was soon obvious that far more aircraft were needed; in a matter of three days half of one 'air force' was out of action owing to forced landings. Other lessons were learned: observers were needed to make notes of ground activity; more pilots as well as more aircraft had to be available; these in turn required a better servicing organization. In these early manoeuvres airborne observers, who had been given a crash twenty-day course, undertook strategic reconnaissance of some sixty-five miles each way twice a day, then scouted for the attacker, and finally located the units engaged and plotted the extent of the front. It was the results of these operations which convinced the Italian armed forces of the value of small airships and led to their dispatch to the Libyan front.

Because of transportation problems and bad weather, active operations in Tripoli with airships, balloons, and aeroplanes were not begun until 23 October 1911. In November the magazine *La Stampa Sportiva* of Turin sent out two flights of its own to Derna and Tobruk under the command of the President of the Italian Aero Club. Naval aviators were established at Benghazi.

These actions in Libya again made plain some of the things which needed to be done as well as uses to which aircraft could be put. The first requirement was for better maps, and this led to aerial photography; observation of bombardments was less fruitful, since airmen could not communicate with the gunners to correct their aim or choice of target. The first bombs dropped from the aircraft were 4.4-pounders which the pilot flung over the side after pulling the pin with his teeth. The effect on the press was probably greater than that on the Turks. Immediately the moral-humanitarian issue was raised. The Turks claimed a hospital had been hit, though the bombs used were basically hand grenades lobbed a somewhat abnormal distance. The early bombs were soon followed by a special box which held ten; a safety-catch was released automatically when a bomb fell from the box, and the pilot or observer in an airship could choose to drop one or all ten bombs at a time. Occasionally airmen also engaged in leaflet dropping and night-flying, for which they soon devised instruments, lighting, and runway illumination.

At the same time consideration was given to the possible challenge posed if the Turks got aeroplanes, and to the more immediate challenge of the increasing accuracy of their rifle and anti-aircraft gunfire. Despite all these side developments, the main task of the pilots was observation, and this they performed so well that headquarters came to rely to a great extent upon their confirmation of intelligence gathered from other sources that were not always reliable.

It is interesting that not until 25 August 1912 was the first pilot killed, and that was when he lost conrol after take-off and plunged into the sea. On 10 September the first pilot was captured by the enemy when his engine failed and he landed behind the lines. There were other incidents, but on the whole very few considering the nature of the country, the fact that the aircraft could not reach over 3,000 feet even with only one man aboard, and the remarkable accuracy of the enemy gunners.

As the Italians demonstrated in Libya in 1911–1912, there is nothing like a war, especially a minor one, for pointing up weaknesses and showing the lines along which developments may be profitable. Participation in such a campaign counts far more than manoeuvres, for the targets are real and there are no umpires, except the press. Success or failure depends upon training, equipment, tactics, leadership, and empirical response. Yet the lessons learned can be as misleading as those from manoeuvres, for the enemy may not be typical or the results may be over-interpreted.

Just as the Russo-Japanese War provided many lessons for the coming holocaust, so did the Libyan War, as far as air power was concerned. Too few Europeans troubled to learn them, or even to observe them, but the Italians gained invaluable experience and in a quiet way their air force undertook a number of unusual operations in the First World War. The Libyan campaign had taught the Italians, at least, the usefulness and the rapidity, as well as the reliability, of air reconnaissance of the other side of the hill; the need for accuracy in bombing; the dangers of ground fire; and the limitations of equipment.

In conclusion it can be asserted that up to 1914 air power was hampered by many problems, but it was also learning roles to develop for the future. In peacetime, aviation attracted the bored, the adventurous, and the ambitious. But it also required that they be either wealthy enough to pay for flying lessons or technically bright enough to be useful. The military air arm was both an extension of and a potential rival to artillery and engineers; as international rivalry became more dangerous, and as aircraft began to receive the support of such notables as Prince Henry of Prussia, funds started to flow and growth became assured. In both peace and war airmen were quick to seize opportunities for publicity and to combine their efforts with those of popular journalists to impress the general public as well as politicians and senior officers. And they were doing this at a time when the major aeronautical powers were well aware of the growing political power of the man in the street.

Yet at this time air power was still frail; young officers were discouraged from associating with it on a permanent basis for fear they might ruin their careers. Senior officers perhaps also recognized that, if an élite were created, other units of the services might well be weakened by a syphoning off of the best officers. Certainly before 1914 the air services were regarded largely as another arm of the surface forces and not as separate services. Moreover, their equipment made them capable of no more than tactical action and strategic reconnaissance. The war in Tripoli showed that the air service had much scope, but it also demonstrated that its role was essentially ancillary and not independent. It would be a long time before airmen would have the power and the range to operate independently in an effective manner. But visionaries talked and wrote as though their dreams were already about to become reality.

The first war in which aircraft played a part was the Turco-Italian one in Libya in 1911-12. Here the Italian air base on the shores of Tripoli with the airship hangar in the center shows what was historically the first forward airfield for operations against an enemy.
USAF

PART TWO

The First World War:
The Baptism of an Ancillary Service

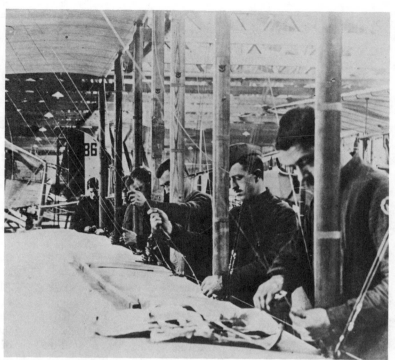

Repair and maintenance, the rebuilding and remanufacturing of aircraft and engines was a major factor in keeping air forces airborne in both World Wars. Here riggers are under instruction in an Allied repair depot learning to swage and tension the cross-bracing wires. **USAF**

1. Training, Command, and Equipment

During the First World War airmen continued their struggle for recognition and independent power, against a background of romantic journalism and an often hostile military establishment. Neither in 1914 nor at the end of the war were they in a position to deliver decisive military blows independently, although under certain conditions air power could exert considerable psychological pressure. The complaint of soldiers in the trenches, however, was centred on the fact that flights by enemy observation planes brought down *artillery* fire upon those on the ground. Aircraft of themselves made little direct impact, except perhaps in strafing runs along the length of a trench, and that only late in the war. Aircraft were more effective generally in bombing raids over civilian and resource areas, as was demonstrated in German raids on London; the argument for a strategic air force independent of an army commander was based on this function.

Bombers could have been more effective than they were if army commanders had had more imagination in their employment, and if airmen had been more rational in their assessment of the damage they were doing. The Royal Naval Air Service, for instance, found that at night its heavy bombers could range more widely, unmolested by enemy fighters, than in daytime; they could fly lower and bomb more accurately. But while naval commanders were less afraid of night operations than their landlubber brothers, the latter generally regarded night fighting as ungentlemanly, liable to confusion, and downright dangerous to their reputations. The real reason for this prejudice may well have been that in fact it was almost never tried in training exercises, so that none of the hazards were thoroughly examined and means of overcoming them devised. Apart from a few attempts at night flight made in early 1916 by the RFC, bombing was limited until the German breakthrough in March 1918.

It is difficult to glamourize a bomber crew unless they undertake some spectacular daylight operation and a cameraman is along. But the lone fighter pilots appeared to the public as valiant gentlemen of the clouds, like the knights of old, fighting gallant duels in the air. The newspapers were clamouring for popular heroes, and the massive bloodbaths in the Flanders mud produced few. But the realities of aerial fighting were little understood or analysed. Fighting between aircraft started largely to prevent enemy observers from gaining information, and not until the last year or so of the war were the forces engaged sizeable. This is a point often overlooked.

It should also be noted that although a great deal of glamour was attached to the fighter pilots, many died. A single day's loss of aircraft could be as high as 23 per cent in squadrons engaged in low-level work; on 8 August 1918 the RAF lost forty-five aircraft over the front lines and fifty-two wrecked or damaged on landing. Wastage in aircraft in Britain ran 66 per cent per month. The French replacement rate for the last two years of the war was 50 per cent. The reasons for these figures are not hard to find. Many of the casualties were officers who scarcely knew how to fly—but the breakfast table was never allowed to have empty places. So insistent was Trenchard on the offensive, for instance, that in 1917 pilots were being sent into action who had flown less than twenty hours. They could hardly have been masters of their machines, let alone of aerial combat. British casualties in the air were high also because, unlike the Germans, British airmen often took the offensive regardless of the odds; it was considered cowardly not to. This hangover from a knightly code and colonial warfare was costly.

The offensive *à l'outrance* in the air eventually killed almost all the aces.* Those who survived, and after a few combat victories

---

* An 'ace', for the French and the Americans, was anyone who had shot down five enemy aircraft. In the German Air Force, twenty victories were required. The RFC did not recognize the concept for some time, while the Russians, Austrians, and Italians never did, thus, perhaps, putting more emphasis on doing the task assigned than on scoring.

their experience placed them way ahead of the fledgling, were generally those who, like the Canadian Billy Bishop or the American Eddie Rickenbacker, entered the game late. Aces were sometimes killed because their judgment was warped by combat fatigue and a sense of honour, or fear of accusations of loss of nerve, which kept them airborne when they should have been on leave. Fatalities were unnecessarily high because, although parachutes were available before 1914, they were not actually used until towards the end of the conflict. In all, 55,000 airmen were lost in World War I.

Although the British air force acquired some 50,000 machines during the war, the increase in strength was slow. In January 1915 there were six squadrons in France, a year later about twenty-four; in early 1917 there were fifty-eight, and at the beginning of the last year of the war around 100. In March 1918 the Germans had about 200, while the French ended the war with 260 squadrons on the Western Front alone. British aircraft elsewhere overseas were spread far thinner, though here the French often took up the slack. Allenby at Megiddo in September 1918 had only four RAF, one Australian, and one French squadron, compared to some 100 under Haig. In the great German March 1918 offensive the British in two months lost 1,032 of their 1,232 machines on hand when the battle started, and of these 528 were fighters. On the last day of March, when only three combats were fought in the air, the RFC lost ten aircraft in action and thirty-eight wrecked. The fact that most of the latter were in landing accidents emphasizes the costliness of inadequate training.

The command of the air forces was still evolving. The history of organizational change shows that a new administrative unit is developed according to a pattern which the founder already knows. Army practice was to model the new force upon the cavalry, as a reconnaissance arm; in the navy the organization followed that of cruiser squadrons. But while it was easy to organize an ancillary air service on paper, it was a much greater problem in fact. In the army there was less awareness than in the navy of the heavy demands that complex, and as yet unreliable, machinery makes upon man-power resources. The British air services grew from some 2,000 officers and men to about 300,000 but the destruction of the élite youth in the flying services was very high, and it can be roughly

calculated that one in every four officers who joined the British air services died.

To be fair to those who commanded the air forces, it must be noted that their position was not an enviable one in some respects. Owing to the very youth of air services, those in command were generally low in rank, sometimes no higher than major. They had, then, more tactical skills than experience in commanding large forces. Some of them—and later in the war, many of them—had never been to staff college. Furthermore, some of the air commanders were misfits or gadflies from other units. In general, officer aircrew lived fast and developed rakish traditions of conduct and dress which tended to appal stuffy senior officers. Thus commanding an air unit required a combination of political finesse and fatherly oversight that was often foreign to those in charge. Moreover, anxious to build their own empires while at the same time not letting the side down, airmen made promises they could not carry out, and, when they failed, they blamed lack of equipment rather than poor generalship.

In the higher headquarters their position was also difficult. Although there were a few admirals, such as Jellicoe and Beatty on the British side and Scheer among the Germans, who had some knowledge of aeronautics and who had helped in its development, the bulk of generals were not so trained. Thus as the importance of aviation was thrust upon them, they sought out a congenial air adviser. So Trenchard found himself suddenly raised from major in charge of a training base to major general and chief air adviser to the Commander-in-Chief of the British Expeditionary Force in France. And no doubt there were those who were jealous. Until more thorough studies are available, it is only possible to suggest that one of the problems in the First World War was that airmen had not been trained for command, while after the war, because they had exercised it, they had a tendency to feel they knew all about it.

But the conduct of war in the air is not simply a matter of man-power and commanders; it is also a technical battle. The aircraft available in 1914 were underpowered and could often barely climb with two men aboard. Moreover, their speed was so slow (50 mph) that with any headwind they had trouble returning to base. Gradually new craft appeared with higher horsepower, able to climb first

Snapped over the lines a German two-seater reconnaissance plane was the target of Allied fighters. Hated and feared by the infantry, reconnaissance planes were far more deadly than bombers or attack aviation in the 1914-18 war because they called down artillery fire. **Source unknown.**

to 10,000 and later to 20,000 feet, although slowly. At the start of the war most units were outfitted with a ragged assortment of aircraft which could neither fly together effectively in the air nor be easily maintained on the ground. But by 1915 the need for co-ordinated firepower in the air and for ease of maintenance began to dictate changes. Formation flying in pairs, flights, squadrons, and finally in wings or groups or circuses demanded aircraft of a standard type, and the development of these automatically eased the spares and maintenance problem.

A further technical problem was the location and operation of guns. The pusher aircraft gave a pursuit a free field of fire forward, but it was generally slower, and it had to rely for protection to the rear on alertness and manoeuvrability. And the pusher was not thought of as a weapon itself but as a platform for a movable gun. Thus it had to carry more weight in a gunner. The single-seater tractor machine carried less weight, but for some time an insuperable problem was that the pilot had to stand up and fly while trying to fire a machine-gun mounted on the top of the upper wing, or aim one aligned nearly 45 degrees out of the flight path. Moreover, early airborne machine-guns were drum fed, and in the case of the British Lewis the drum originally only held forty-seven rounds and had to be changed while manoeuvring. On top of all that, the guns frequently jammed because of wind pressure and had to be cleared with a wooden mallet. The French first invented a system of protecting the propeller blades with metal wedges, allowing a fixed machine-gun to be fired through the propeller arc, but this system made the blades of the airscrew less efficient. Technologically it was fortunate that the only French machine so equipped was forced to land behind the German lines and was captured intact before the pilot could destroy it. The Germans promptly turned it over to Fokker, the Dutch designer's company, which in four days produced a proper interrupter gear that enabled the pilot to fire fixed guns at random through the propeller arc, aiming his whole machine at his opponent. The Allies, owing in part to the prevailing wind and in part to German defensive tactics which forced them to do most of their fighting on the German side of the line, did not have the German luck; it was nearly mid-1916 before they had aircraft equipped with an effective interrupter gear.

One of the truisms of aeronautical development has been that airframes have generally been available before engines. At the beginning of the war the Germans were ahead with 200 hp motors

The German Fokker Triplane was a very popular fighter late in the war due to its rate of climb and tight turning circle. It had the lift of a monoplane with a fifty-foot span but a very inadequate fin and rudder. This is a recent US-built replica. **Source unknown.**

while the Allies lagged with most of theirs closer to 80 hp, and production difficulties delayed the output of aircraft. Again, it was not until after 1916 that many of these problems began to be solved. Designing was simpler than production, since most aircraft manufacturers were amateurs with little or no idea of mass production. Moreover, the military were not well equipped to write specifications for new equipment, and often, in the absence of an overall ministry of munitions to allocate industrial resources, the services competed against one another for supplies. This was most true in Britain, where the Royal Naval Air Service was a very clear rival to the Royal Flying Corps. Rivalry was less acute in Germany, France, Russia, and Italy, where the navy was no more than an auxiliary. The position in the United States was similar to that in Britain, but far more chaotic because of confusing counsel and industrial haste, as America entered late into the war.

Some indication of the amount of effort that went into the production of aeronautical material for the war can be gauged from the few figures available. Germany turned out 48,000 airframes and 41,000 engines; France, 51,000 airframes (of which 9,500 were for her allies) and 92,000 engines (of which 28,000 were for allies, especially the British); Britain, 52,440 airframes and engines. The Italian figures give some indication of the growth of manufacturing, for in 1915 only 382 aircraft and 606 engines were produced, while for 1918 the figures were 6,488 and 14,840, respectively.

A great deal of the success of aircraft production depended upon flexibility and the availability of topnotch designers. What happened without these is best illustrated by the American case. In April 1917 there were 350 aircraft on order, but of such obsolete designs that the manufacturers asked to be released from their contracts. An ambitious programme was then developed of producing 22,000 aircraft by July 1918, which with spares meant about 40,000 machines. Production lagged badly, sometimes because of such simple errors as the use in drawings of dimensions unfamiliar to American craftsmen. In the end the United States produced only 11,950 planes for the army, which bought 5,198 abroad. Engine development in the United States was another story, because the automobile industry was at that time still closely related techno-

When the US Air Service began operations in France in 1918, it had to use foreign machines as no US-built designs made it to the battlefields before the war ended. Here Americans start up a French-built Caudron bomber. Note both the bird-like airfoil and the many drag-inducing bracing struts. **USAF**

logically to the aircraft engine business. Thus the Liberty engine was a success, and 15,572 were delivered by the end of November 1918.

2. Fighter Operations

As soon as the war opened all the participants sent airships, aeroplanes, and balloons to the front. The four squadrons of the Royal Flying Corps together with their mixed collection of aircraft were shipped over to France. The French mobilized the aircraft and talents of the free-lance flyers who had been entertaining civilians in the years before the war. The Germans sent their little Taube monoplanes. The Russians trundled out some early Sikorskis, and a varied collection of French Farmans and Voisins in various states of repair. At first most of these machines, with the exception of the Russian ones, bore no national markings, and in many cases they were hard to identify, because nobody had been trained in aircraft recognition.

On 22 August 1914 the first engagement in the air took place, and it at once became obvious that markings would be needed. The RFC first adopted the idea of painting a Union Jack on the aeroplane, but left it up to each pilot to decide on size and arrangement. Identification from the air was not the only problem. Troops who had hardly ever seen an aeroplane fired at anything that came within range, though fortunately for the early fliers very few units had anything approaching anti-aircraft guns. To counter this, British Field Headquarters ordered full-chord Union Jacks to be painted on the underside of the wings. But even this was unsatisfactory because it could be confused with the cross *patée* used by the Germans and Austrians on both wing and rudder surfaces; and it was the French who, by October 1914, found a satisfactory solution – the roundel. The British simply reversed the French colour scheme so that red was the central concentric circle. Almost the only change in this scheme made from late 1914 to the present has been that the tailstripe order was reversed for the Second World

War. Roundels soon appeared on fuselage sides and on the top of the wing, and with the introduction in 1916 of camouflage a thin circle of white was used to outline them.

Early aircraft were easily visible. British aeroplane finishes came out in shades varying from buff to primrose pink, depending upon the varnish used on doped fabric, though most metal was finished in grey or black. German machines were pale cream, but this usually became a dirty white on operations. Then in 1916 came black-dot grey followed shortly afterwards by a blotchy effect of green-purple and brown. In 1917 the Germans went further and introduced an octagonal lozenge printed fabric, while the Allies went to khaki-green, though the shade varied tremendously. As in the 1939 war, however, not everyone attempted to merge with his background. The Fokker triplanes of the Richthofen Circus were painted bright red, while RNAS flying-boats adopted the same dazzle-paint applied to ships from 1917 onwards.

Most of the time relatively little damage was done by pilots and observers firing rifles or pistols at enemy planes, largely because the very few aircraft in the air at any one time had a great deal of trouble even getting near each other. British pilots found that their BEs with a speed of 60 mph and a ceiling of 3,000 feet simply could not catch other aircraft. A German was shot down by two Britishers on 26 August, but though the British pilots landed at once and pursued the enemy with pistols drawn, the German aircrew escaped into a forest and disappeared! It still was not quite an aerial war. But it soon was to be.

Even before the war individual pilots had tried out machine-guns on their aircraft, but to the German ace Oswald Boelcke must go the credit for developing the first disciplined attack techniques. Aged 23, he had by the end of 1914 made forty-two operational flights without being involved in a fight. Early in 1915 he asked to be transferred to a squadron which was equipped with the new C two-seater, which had been fitted with a machine-gun in the after cockpit. On 6 July 1915, after a thirty-minute stalk and twenty minutes of combat at speeds from 35 to 80 mph, he shot down an enemy aircraft. As luck would have it Fokker delivered the first of his new E-1s to Boelcke's airfield, and Boelcke was given the job of testing the new machine in combat. He soon found that the best scheme was to loiter at his 5,000-foot ceiling and to pounce

By the end of the war a number of heavy bombers were in service capable of bombing well behind the front lines. This Vickers Vimy with Roll-Royce Eagle engines is similar to that flown across the Atlantic in 1919 by Alcock and Brown except that it mounts a 37-mm cannon for anti-submarine patrols. **Vickers**

from cloud or sun on any Allied plane which strayed below him. He then dived down, closed as quickly as possible, aimed his plane, fired, and climbed away. About this time Max Immelmann, another pilot in the same squadron, developed the technique of diving below his opponent, pulling up so as to fire into him from the vulnerable position under the tail, then at the top of his climb kicking on hard rudder and dropping back down for a new strike from the opposite direction. This method worked as long as the Fokker was faster than its opponent, but as soon as the Allied planes developed the power to climb after him the German pilot was vulnerable as he made his stall turn.

The British RFC continued to fly offensive missions and long reconnaissance flights, and Boelcke's tactics, now with Immelmann as his wingman or extra pair of eyes, were paying handsome dividends since the enemy constantly came into his territory. Their successes were not unnoticed in the German command, and more pairs of scouts were ordered upon the initiative of Major Stempel, the 6th Army's Aviation Staff Officer. But in the spring of 1916 the Allies began to dominate the little Fokkers with new types, the DH-2, the FE-2b, and the Nieuport 17, and by midsummer 1916 the Allies were using early formation tactics. At first formation had simply consisted of providing three escorts for each reconnaissance machine, but as the escorts were often nothing more than other two-seaters, the system resulted in a formation, rather than in a proper escort arrangement. To counter escorts Boelcke had already begun to consider formation flying and was by 1916 organizing his fighters into squadron formations. Hand signals were required, since aircraft were not until many years later fitted with voice radios or R/T. To identify the squadron leader, streamers were tied to his wingtips; these were supplemented by the use of coloured paint, reaching its culmination in Richthofen's bright red Fokker triplane.

Tactical formations not unnaturally developed from infantry and cavalry manoeuvres practised at first in pairs and then in fours, and finally in squadron formations of twelve or more aircraft. Each squadron was subdivided into diamonds of four led by a flight commander. The slow evolution of these tactics must be stressed. The aircraft themselves were not easy to fly, the pilots were often not very experienced, and the leaders were anxious to avoid non-battle

casualties; while formation flying itself demanded that 75 per cent of a pilot's attention be devoted to watching his leader. As in the case of escort work, the development of formation flying was considerably retarded by the long lag in equipping squadrons with a single kind of machine so that all pilots would have aircraft of more or less identical performance. The Germans had largely achieved uniformity in late 1915 with the Fokker *Eindeckers*, but the RFC, the French, and the Italians did not reach this stage until the summer of 1916. By July the Fokker scourge, as it was called, had been mastered, but as the Germans brought out new aircraft and developed new tactics, aerial supremacy continued to move from one side to the other.

It was during the summer of 1916 that one aeronautical debate was settled. The RFC, like some French units, had been equipped with pusher aircraft which countered the synchronized guns of the Fokkers by a freely mounted gun. The French, however, continued to work on the tractor aircraft and in the Nieuport 17 produced one which could reach 10,000 feet in nine minutes and fly at 107 mph, in contrast to the single-seat British DH-2, which took twenty-four minutes to gain the same altitude and could only do ninety. Thereafter pushers became oddities, until the advent of the jet engine in the 1940s.

In August 1916 the Germans started forming their new élite *Jagdstaffeln* or *Jasta*. These were equipped with the Halberstadt D-11, with two synchronized machine-guns, and the Albatros D-1. Though the former did not last long, the latter remained in service with the German air force till almost the end of the war. Boelcke's *Jasta* 2 was extremely effective, and by the time of his death on 28 October, in a combat collision, he had shot down thirty-five Allied aircraft.

The winter of 1916–1917 saw many changes. The German air force units were redistributed into fighter, reconnaissance and bombing units. Even larger formations were developed to counter the arrival in the field of new Allied aircraft such as the Sopwith Pup, the first British aircraft fitted with a synchronized machine-gun. On the British side, the RFC was licking its wounds from the Battle of the Somme, in which airmen had been thrown into action just as ruthlessly and with about as little point as had troops on the ground. Albert Ball, one of the British aces, was in twenty-three

*A rather unusual photograph of a group of British pilots in front of an FE-2 pusher aeroplane showing both the varied uniforms worn flying by officers temporarily seconded in many cases from their regular regiments as well as in this case the early handcranked movie camera mounted tripod and all in the observer's cockpit. Casualties in these units were as in the infantry often 50 percent. **USAF***

The Vickers FB-9 Gun Bus was one of several early WWI types built to take advantage of the pusher aircrew with the resulting smooth flow of air over the fuselage and the wings. The gunner-observer normally stood up in action — and after a few were flipped out, safety chains were introduced. **Vickers**

battles in fourteen days before finally being allowed to go home for a rest. Though at the beginning of 1917 the RFC had thirty-five squadrons at the front, most of these were ill-trained and no match for the élite German *Jastas*. The French also had suffered from the mauling they had taken at Verdun and had sensibly largely withdrawn their squadrons for refitting.

The Anglo-German contest still favoured the Germans in the spring of 1917 because their fighters were superior to the FE-2b and the BE-2c which the British were using. And, although the RFC now could deploy some 550 aircraft or more, in April 1917 it lost 140. Manfred von Richthofen was in his prime and shot down five aeroplanes in one day, while at the same time seriously damaging the faith of the RFC in the Bristol F-2B, a new two-seater with a powerful armament of a forward-firing synchronized gun and twin Lewis guns for the observer. In the vital action on 28 April Richthofen attacked a group of six Bristol F-2Bs led by Leefe Robinson, the man who had won a VC for shooting down a Zeppelin. Robinson's crews were not yet used to their powerful machines and their tactics had not been properly worked out. The result was that four aircraft were lost and Robinson captured. Training improved, however, and by the end of the war the Bristol was the dominant British two-seater.

At the same time, the Germans also began to face the SE-5, which in the hands of British squadrons proved to be a highly efficient counter to the thirty-five German *Jastas*. In addition the RFC was beginning to get the DH-4, a two-seater day bomber that was at least as fast as many enemy fighters. Ludendorff had decided the air arm needed its own separate organization, and had placed General Ernst von Hoeppner in command of the air forces in October 1916. To counter what appeared to be dangerous developments on the Allied side, including the American declaration of war, Hoeppner now organized four *Jastas* into a *Jagdgeschwader*, or wing. Richthofen was placed in command of the new circus, as the Allies called it, and his duty was to lead his outfit to battle over any part of the front upon which the Germans found themselves threatened. Thus reorganizing their forces, Richthofen and his experienced fighters followed, successfully, the principles of concentration and economy of force. The circus flaunted brightly coloured Albatros aircraft as

a psychological threat to all who saw them. But even when equipped with the new Pfalz D-III scouts, the circus increasingly came up against tougher opposition as the SE-5s and the new Sopwith Camels came into action, not to mention the newer French fighters such as the SPAD and the Nieuport 28. Even when the circus got its Fokker Dr-I triplanes, which were extremely manoeuvrable but slower both in level and climbing flight, it never regained the supremacy that it had enjoyed in the early summer of 1917. While Germans like Werner Voss still occasionally made lone sorties across the lines on stalking expeditions, the British had finally learned to operate in groups, such as the one which jumped Voss on his last flight. Moreover, the Fokker triplane turned out to have a weakness – its canvas-covered upper wing disintegrated in steep dives. By the end of the war the Fokker D-VII was the mainstay of the German fighter force, and indeed its surrender was required as part of the peace settlement in order to make sure that the Allies maintained their aerial-fighting superiority. Not as fast as some Allied fighters, its biggest asset was its manoeuvrability at the then high altitude of 10,000 or more feet.

Hoeppner's plan of June 1917, sometimes called the *Amerika Program*, was designed to help win the war before trans-Atlantic power could be applied on the Western Front. Helped by the collapse of Russia, the German Air Force was built up to 155 squadrons and seven heavy bomber groups by the time the great March 1918 offensive was opened. But the leaders were beginning to suffer from chronic battle fatigue brought on by daily dicing with death. Richthofen had become in many respects an old man. He was obsessed with thoughts of fire in the air. On 21 April, just as the German offensive petered out, he entered one more dogfight, unerringly picking on a fledgling pilot. The conflict was fought at a low altitude, and whether he was shot down from the air or from the ground has remained a matter of argument. Certain it is, however, that he went the way of most aces who stayed too long in combat. His immediate successor was killed testing a new craft designed to replace the well-worn Albatroses still in use, and command of his circus for the rest of the war devolved upon a lesser ace, Hermann Goering, later to be the leader of the German Air Force in the Second World War. But so much had the Richthofen myth been built up in the German Air Force, that his death caused a steady

Regarded as the scourge of the Western Front in 1917-18, the Fokker D-VII was a highly maneuverable German fighter. This replica at Old Rhinebeck, NY, is authentic in its mottled camouflage. **Living Museum of Old Aeroplanes**

deterioration of morale amongst men pushed hard against increasingly great odds.

Production was by now seriously hampered by the Allied blockade, which was at last having a material effect, and the airmen were hard-pressed, increasingly facing the same losses due to inexperience that had earlier weakened the Royal Flying Corps. Yet in many ways the Germans failed to learn the lessons of the First World War and in the Second made the same fatal mistakes of standardizing too early and of not estimating the wave pattern of war so as to be able to take advantage of the flow and stem the ebb.

By the end of the war the RAF on the Western Front had been built up to 97 squadrons with 36 more overseas, 55 at home, and 199 in the training system. The French Air Force contained 260 squadrons on the Western Front, of which 135 were reconnaissance, 10 were for strategic observation for army headquarters, 83 were fighter squadrons, and 32 were bomber units. In addition there were 72 squadrons on home defence or overseas, including 3 in Russia and 1 in Palestine. In March 1918 the German Air Force had about 200 squadrons spread between the Western and Italian fronts with 6 squadrons in Turkey.

The Italians did not enter the war until late May 1915, and their opponents, the Austrians, were not of the same fighting calibre as the Germans. Moreover, because the Italians suffered the great reverse at Caporetto in 1917, because they became Hitler's ally in the Second World War, and because little has been written in English of their actions, it has long been assumed that the Italian air effort was not worth recording. The truth is the opposite. Italian exercise of air power was conditioned by geographical location and physical features. Ground fighting quickly became stalemated along the Isonzo. But the Austrians had to be supplied through the Ljubljana gap, and the mountainous nature of the terrain meant that they were forced to concentrate in other areas as well. At the same time, their navy operated from the few bases available at the head of the Adriatic, notably Fiume and Pola. Because of the limited number of enemy supply routes, the Italians were able to develop a number of features of air power which received less attention elsewhere. Rather than merely fighting for air superiority, Italian airmen undertook long-range photo-reconnaissance (PRU) flights which

took them as much as 300 miles through enemy territory, along the enemy communication lines. Control of PRU work was at Army headquarters, and the information gathered was used for strategic raids to disrupt the Austrian rear. Though the Caporetto disaster lost the Italians many forward airfields and compelled a reorganization of the air service on a more independent basis, it did not stop the Italian air offensive, as most raids flew directly across the Adriatic. In view of the claims of the American propagandist General William Mitchell it should be pointed out that the Italians used massed air power as early as 1916 during ground operations, while at the battle of Vittorio Veneto (October–November 1918) the Italians employed 600 aircraft, 36 balloons, and 7 airships.

On the Russian front the situation is much less clear, owing to the general absence of historical reports, at least in English, and to the historiographical impact of the Revolution. It appears that the Russian Air Force never amounted to more than some 300 effective machines, many of which were cast-offs from the Allied air forces in the west. Some craft of foreign design were manufactured under licence in Russia itself, together with a few advanced designs of Russian origin such as the Grigorovich seaplanes, and the Sikorski Ilya Mouromets four-engined bombers, sometimes used for PRU. But Russian maintenance was pitiful, and much of the equipment was in disrepair even before the Revolution. The fact that on the whole they did not face great opposition on the Eastern Front, except for occasional raids by the large Russian bombers, allowed the Germans to concentrate upon the West. Very little is known even of the desultory naval strikes in the Baltic which produced Alexandre de Seversky, later an apostle of victory through air power.

The United States' contribution to the air war was at first limited to volunteer pilots in oufits such as the Lafayette Escadrille, but gradually an army air force using Allied equipment was built up. Its most notable operation was the 1,500-aircraft cover provided during the reduction of the Saint Mihiel salient in September 1918, and in October Mitchell followed Italian practice in using large bomber forces against concentrated targets.

On the whole both sides overlooked the significance of massing additional air power in the lesser theatres where victories even if of no great strategic import could be used for propaganda leverage elsewhere. Aircraft in these overseas theatres were particularly valuable for reconnaissance, although they were in short supply. The British also used aircraft occasionally for resupplying forces, and the destruction of the German raider *Königsberg* in the Rufiji River was accomplished by monitors guided by two naval aeroplanes. One notable attempt by the Germans to make use of air transport was the abortive flight of the Zeppelin *L-59* to take ammunition and medical supplies to the elusive German commander in East Africa, von Lettow-Vorbeck; the Zeppelin turned back to its Balkan base after reaching the vicinity of Khartoum.

The Dardanelles campaign might have been more successful if a more advanced and less heterogeneous collection of aircraft had been sent out to Gallipoli. As it was, the aircraft operating from the island base of Tenedos (for only one temporary landing ground was made available on the Gallipoli peninsula) made a number of significant contributions to the development of aerial warfare, including the first successful destruction of a ship with an air-launched torpedo. In particular, more squadrons with better equipment might have panicked Constantinople by psychological bombing as well as providing competent photographic reconnaissance before the Gallipoli landings themselves.

The Sopwith Pup was a rotary-engined fighter with a performance matching its light wing-loading. In naval use in a 30-knot wind it had a take-off run of less than 15 feet. **Air Portraits**

3. Air Power in Action: The Ideal

The Palestine campaign under Allenby during the last months of the war was for its day as perfect an example of the proper application of air power as the German blitzkriegs in 1940 or the Israeli campaign of 1967. While it was true that the Turkish army was weakened by malnutrition and lack of supplies, and was therefore a less formidable opponent than some other units, Allenby's operation was the almost romantic breakthrough and envelopment that leaders on other fronts had dreamed about all through the war. He achieved it by a combination of tactical deceptions and feints, cavalry, armoured cars, and air power. He made use of five air squadrons, all but one with modern aircraft, to achieve complete

Pilotless aircraft appeared in the First World War, the Kettering Aerial Torpedo, being the world's first guided missile, was in development when the war ended. **USAF Museum**

domination over the opposing air force, so that by September 1918 the Turks were virtually without either reconnaissance or air cover. Immediately prior to the attack, aircraft bombed the central Turkish telephone exchange and Turkish army headquarters, upsetting the enemy's balance in a way the cavalry could not get through to do. A patrol of two SE-5As flew constantly over the main Turkish airfield, dropping bombs from time to time as an additional harassment. As the British advanced on the ground, RAF aircraft provided them with smokescreens and intelligence. Late on the nineteenth two Turkish divisions were in retreat, and they were caught in a narrow defile by RAF fighters and bombers and badly mangled. Good photo-intelligence had enabled Allenby to predict all routes of Turkish retreat and to intersect them with cavalry and armoured cars. The psychological effect of the sudden appearance of these units caused a precipitate retreat which the RAF was able to turn into a rout. Further out in the desert along Allenby's right flank, the forces of the mysterious T. E. Lawrence suffered from the attacks of German aircraft, which the three British fighters assigned to him could not beat off until Lawrence managed to arrange a reinforcement of three more fighters.

Much of the success of Allenby's subsequent campaign, which moved some 300 miles in six weeks, was due to the way in which supplies were rushed forward, often by air, so that the fighters and bombers of the RAF could continue to supply both a physical and a psychological spearhead, while the Turks found themselves without air cover. Strangely the ability to move squadrons forward with great rapidity had to be learned all over again in the Western Desert in the Second World War.

This use of the RAF in Palestine was much more imaginative, while at the same time of a sounder tactical nature, than were its assignments in Europe. The explanation for this lies both in the mentality of the high command and in geography. On the Western Front, Allenby had been under the command of leaders of generally conservative vision. But when he, and the same could be said of Maude in Iraq, became a Commander-in-Chief himself, he was free to operate as he saw fit. The maps of the area, in comparison to those of Europe, lacked detail, and aircraft were sent out to undertake long reconnaissance flights, in the Italian manner. It was necessary to consider great distances in moving supplies, over ground not potholed by incessant shellfire but rather so arid that water supply was one of the chief limitations. It can be claimed that lack of supplies and the difficulty of transporting them, together with the small number of aeroplanes available, meant that resources were used with more skill than in France, where abundance stultified generalship.

Another theatre in which air power was used efficiently was Macedonia. The British diversionary attack in September 1918 was supported by only three squadrons, but by the end of the month the Bulgarians had started to retreat and had been caught in a mountain pass and demoralized. Here, as in the Palestinian campaign, part of the secret of the air force's success lay in the nature of the country, which was sparse, mountainous, and with very few roads along which any army could move. Thus the side with command of the air was likely to be the victor, from the application of both psychological and physical pressure.

4. Air Power at Sea

Naval air power in the First World War was heavily dominated, as might be expected, by the Royal Navy, which was then the largest fleet in the world. Moreover, though the British navy was moribund in many respects from a century of peace, it did have the advantage of officers with technical competence, and in the formative years first Jacky Fisher followed by Churchill and then the combination of the two to command it. Fisher launched naval aviation and Churchill became an enthusiastic supporter. Naval airmen, despite the precedent of the Royal Dockyards, were not tied to an official factory and energetically sought material from other sources. Thus for much of the war the RNAS enjoyed superior material to the RFC. In addition, its officers apparently understood the need for training better than did those in the other services, and this, coupled with a less recklessly offensive policy, meant that on the whole it developed more highly qualified squadrons. While the bulk of naval air activity was connected with the Fleet and the protection of trade, as an offshoot of these responsibilities it operated a bomber and fighter base on the northern French coast. Almost all its flights had a tactical purpose; a few were strategic strikes.

Other naval air forces were less prominent. Apart from Zeppelins, most of the German naval air effort was either connected with the few sorties made by the Fleet or defensive against the incursions of British ships or aircraft. French and Italian efforts were concentrated mainly in the area of anti-submarine warfare. The embryo United States naval air service followed in the wake of the RNAS. Under these circumstances, then, any description of the war at sea must inevitably deal primarily with the British experience.

The RNAS established bases at Dover and Dunkirk when the Germans seized the Belgian coast. Seaplanes were used to raid the new U-boat bases, but with little effect. When intelligence showed that the Germans were assembling coastal U-boats in the shipyards at Antwerp, a strike against these was laid on, but the three aircraft which succeeded in dropping a total of twelve twenty-pound bombs did little damage. The Admiralty decided upon a much wider programme, to include better protection of shipping, and their plan led to two important developments: the SS or submarine-searching (or scout) airships, and the heavy bombers. The former were very rapidly improvised from non-rigid airship bags and the fuselages of BE-2c aircraft, an arrangement that produced a ship capable of an eight-hour flight with a crew of two, 160 pounds of bombs, and most importantly a wireless set. But since throughout the war the anti-submarine craft were not fitted with electronic detection aids, their effectiveness was limited to visual distances.

While the attacks made by non-rigid airships were not many, their presence was disliked by U-boats since they could call up destroyers. Thus shipping escorted by a blimp was generally immune to U-boat attack. The truth of this was shown in the Mediterranean, where the blimps were slow to arrive and losses to U-boats were high until they appeared. By the end of the war blimps had been developed until they were able to stay on patrol for nearly two days and could achieve speeds close to 60 mph. But they were always limited by the weather, and attempts to use them with the Fleet were unsuccessful when the wind rose to 30 mph, for this reduced their surface speed into the wind to that of the cruisers. British attempts to imitate Zeppelins and provide long-range fast airships

*One of the famous aces of the war was the French Captain Guynemer, who flew a SPAD with an "Eclair" propeller, made by one of the ancestors of the present **Dassault** company.*

for Fleet scouting and long anti-submarine patrols over the Western Approaches were nullified by the fact that designs were copied from the Germans and were thus usually four years behind.

The other solution, then, to both the U-boat problem and Fleet requirements was the development of aeroplanes. For the ASW role both seaplanes and flying boats were produced. The former had the advantage that they could be carried at sea by ships and launched from smooth water alongside, while the latter were generally operated from harbours, though some attempts were made to tow them closer to their patrol areas on lighters from which they could be slipped for take-off. The seaplane was more manoeuvrable, but the flying-boat had much greater range and could carry a heavier armament including a 37-mm recoilless gun. (The latter, however, was not always successful, for it did not use a rocket but provided a bag of buckshot to absorb recoil which was exhausted to the rear, sometimes to the detriment of the upper wing or the engines!)

The Germans were unable, owing to American pressure, to start on a full-scale U-boat offensive until February 1917, and by then the Allies had been able to develop much of the equipment, though not yet the convoys, needed to protect commerce. It might, however, be argued that if the Germans had attacked earlier at a time when they had fewer submarines, the advantages would have been placed more firmly in Allied hands, for they would have been forced to undertake convoying and other measures much sooner than they did. As it was, convoys, started in June 1917 to and from the United Kingdom, were soon given air cover, and the same practice was adopted in the Mediterranean.

Besides protecting trade, the British navy took rapid steps to make use of air power in its strictly military operations. When on the outbreak of war the Admiralty appointed the quiet Sir John Jellicoe to command the Grand Fleet it sent to sea a man who was familiar with submarines, and who was the one flag officer to have flown in a Zeppelin. Jellicoe was alarmed by these two weapons, since the British navy had no counters, and he set to work with the help of Fisher, who had been recalled to the Admiralty to join Churchill, to remedy the deficiency. Thus throughout the war the RNAS engaged in a strong programme to take air power to sea. Seaplane tenders were developed to enable aeroplanes to be used either from secluded harbours or with the ships at sea. Platforms were

mounted on the turrets of battleships from which aircraft could be flown off, and platforms were erected over the sterns so they could be landed on. And eventually it was recognized that a ship was needed that had its funnels set over to one side, so that planes could land and take off on an unobstructed surface immune to the deflecting fumes from the ship's funnels. All of this took a great deal of time and had not been realized in practice when the war ended. Nevertheless, when the Grand Fleet went to sea in 1918 it carried with it some 150 fighters ready to fly off and do battle with any enemy, and was shortly to include torpedo-bombers for attack on the opposing German High Seas Fleet. At the same time, the submarine menace had been partially countered by towing kite balloons, which, while they tended to give away the Fleet's position, warned U-boats that they were likely to have destroyers directed onto them if they approached.

To carry the war home to the Germans in their own waters, S. C. Porte, who commanded the naval air station at Felixstowe, began building some large flying-boats on the American Curtiss lines. These machines dwarfed the standard aeroplanes of the day with their two 345-hp engines, crew of four, up to seven machine-guns and two 230-lb bombs, and overall weight of 11,000 lbs (compared to the 1,200-lb Sopwith Pup fighter). Able to patrol for eight hours, they were assigned to the so-called spider-webs in which they searched that part of some 4,000 square miles of sea in which the Admiralty suspected a U-boat was lurking. On 20 May 1917 *UC-36* became the first submarine sunk from the air when hit by a bomb from a Porte flying-boat. The flying-boats also managed to pick off two Zeppelins (*L-22* and *L-43*) while the latter were flying over their home waters. This sort of insult compelled the Germans to strengthen their naval air service, with the result that offensive seaplane patrols began to become a nuisance to British airmen, and a see-saw battle continued to the end of the war.

The development of a naval strategic strike force came from the desire of the Fleet to be rid of Zeppelins. On 22 September 1914 the RNAS had staged a pair of raids with two aeroplanes each against the Zeppelin sheds at Düsseldorf and Cologne. Only one pilot reached the target and only one of his bombs, the one that missed, exploded. But on 6 October two planes set out. One jettisoned its bombs on the Cologne railway station, but the other hit the sheds

*The German naval airship **L-33** had but a short life before being shot down over England in Spetember 1916. As she was not totally destroyed, the British took off her lines and the British R-33 class emerged in 1919 as viturally absolute copies. And yet another link in the chain was forged when **R-34** of that class became the first aircraft to make a round-trip crossing of the North Atlantic — England-Long Island-Scotland. **Douglas H. Robinson: Beardmore's***

Aviation 1914-1918 was responsible for large construction in the form of air bases such as Brooks Field, Texas, above **(USAF)** *and airship works, such as Cardington, England. At the former many hangars were needed for maintenance, while at the latter the complex structure of the large rigid airship exceeding 750 feet in length and 100 feet in diameter was developed out of duraluminum. The airship shown here under construction is the ill-fated* **R-38***, a British copy of a German height-climbing Zeppelin being built for the US Navy.* **Captain Garland Fulton,** *USN (CO)*

at Düsseldorf and destroyed the brand-new Army Zeppelin *Z-IX*. On 21 November a strike of three Avros hit the Zeppelin plant at Friedrichshafen, but just failed to do any damage. A penetration of 150 miles into enemy territory was a notable achievement in itself in those days. A further attempt to damage the Zeppelins was made on Christmas Day 1914 by seaplanes ferried to their take-off point in converted cross-Channel steamers. Though none of the seven planes found the Cuxhaven sheds, a thorough reconnaissance of the Wilhelmshafen naval base was accomplished. No new attacks were made until 19 July 1918, when the new aircraft-carrier *Furious* was used to launch a strike against the airship sheds at Tondern. This was successful with two aircraft destroying Zeppelins *L-54* and *60* by dropping 50-lb bombs from a height of only 100 feet as they passed over the sheds. Not only was the German Naval Airship Division left in a state of nerves that lasted to the end of the war, but at Tondern, used as an advanced emergency landing ground, both a strategic and tactical surprise had been achieved and a psychologically strategic effect created.

Meanwhile in an attempt to deal with the Germans on the Belgian coast, the British Admiralty had asked in 1915 for a true heavy strategic bomber. The response was the Handley Page 0/100, but the first was not delivered to the Dunkirk base until November 1916 and the third was, due to a navigational error, landed intact behind the German lines two months later. At first they were employed as intended in patrols off the coast, but during the summer they switched over to night bombing, striking at strategic points behind the German lines but refraining from attacks on purely civilian targets. Though one squadron of the four available was lent to the RFC for strategic bombing, on the whole the Navy was successful in keeping these bombers for its own purposes.

5. Strategic Bombing Campaigns

The Italian, British, and German strategic (a better term for some of them is *psychological*) bombing campaigns started as much from

The major training aircraft in North America was the Curtiss JN-4 Jenny of 1915, which after the war became the barnstormers' hack. **The Flying Circus**

the demands of the navy as from those of army commanders. Many claims were made before the war that air power would strike at the heart of an opposing power, but this was largely long-term guessing. The Italian Giulio Douhet's claims must be taken with a pinch of Caproni salt. Strategic bombing divides into two categories: attacks against targets which were legitimate military objectives, such as ammunition dumps, supply routes, and factories out of tactical reach of surface forces; and attacks against enemy cities undertaken for psychological reasons. Into the first class clearly fall many of the early French and British raids against German rear areas in France and against airship sheds and constructional facilities in Germany, together with Italian raids on Ljubljana, Pola, Trieste, and Fiume. Into the second must be placed the raids starting with the French reaction to the German attacks on Paris in September 1914. Apart from a lone raid in August against a Zeppelin shed near Metz, the French waited until the end of the year, when they began to organize first five- and then twenty-bomber squadrons. Under Captain Happe they began to penetrate as far as Karlsruhe (13 June 1915), and one aircraft struck Munich (17 November). It is not at all clear that a deliberate doctrine of retaliation upon civilian centres had yet evolved, but by 1916 the French consciously began such retaliation with an attack on Karlsruhe in reprisal for German attacks on French towns which had been declared 'open'. It was probably a combination of the early German Zeppelin attacks and naval bombardment of Britain with the friction between the politicians in London, Paris, and Rome and their generals in the field in 1917 which brought on in frustration the development of an independent bombing force, and the decision on the part of some leaders that this should be a destructive retaliatory force.

Another element in the decisions to bomb civilian centres stemmed from the still-primitive nature of air warfare. As defences developed, as inevitably they always do, the planes were forced to drop their bomb loads from higher altitudes or to fly at night. Both courses led to greater inaccuracy. In part, therefore, to justify inaccurate bombing politically, airmen developed the defensive thesis that war workers in their homes were directly connected to the will to make war and could properly be attacked.

A peculiarity of the British system under Churchill was that the navy had been put in charge of home defence in general, in addition

*This Rumpler C IV of the **Shuttleworth Collection** in England is said to be the only World War I German aeroplane still flying. Eventually these machines could reach 24,000 feet with the crews sucking oxygen and wearing electrically-heated clothing while taking pictures.*

One of the ultimate developments of the WWI fighter was the two-seater Bristol Fighter, known as the "Brisfit, which served in the RAF until the 1930's. Note the varnished, lenticular interplane struts and the gleaming doped fabric of this factory-fresh example. **British Aircraft Corporation** (Bristol/Filton)

to its particular responsibility for that of Fleet bases. In the early German raids the Zeppelins had several advantages. Not only were they simply frightening, but they could hover while dropping their bombs, and the defences were so sparse that neither anti-aircraft fire nor aeroplanes were for some time very effective against them. In fact it was not until June 1915 that the first Zeppelin was brought down by an aeroplane, and not until September 1916 that one was brought down over England. On the whole, these early Zeppelin raids on Britain were not very effective in physical terms. *LZ-13* dropped the first high-explosive bombs on London on the night of 8 September 1915, killing thirteen and wounding eighty-seven persons, but at that time casualties in Flanders were already running to several thousand a day. As far as the defences were

concerned, the Zeppelins had greater effect; they raised a political storm which ultimately resulted in air defence being handed back to the War Office, and they stimulated the defences to prepare for the next challenge, which came in the form of daylight German aeroplane raids starting on 28 November 1916. Night attacks followed, however, and in pre-radio and pre-radar days, finding an attacking enemy aircraft was difficult; though by 1917 many aircraft were scrambled to intercept enemy raiders, few were even attacked, let alone shot down. The Germans were able to obtain a great deal of information about the effectiveness of their raids, and they were encouraged to believe that they could quickly bring Britain to her knees.

The cycle of German raids against Britain was the same for Zeppelins and Gothas: first came daylight attacks, then night raids, then the raids were finally abandoned because the defences became too accurate and the losses too great. Even the Gothas flying in daylight could not be escorted by long-range fighters, for not until the 1930s would the Japanese Navy develop long-range tanks for operational use. The Gothas usually escaped destruction at the hands of fighters because their defensive armament and formation were sufficient to counter the few defending fighters which reached them. (The lessons learned from this were rudely shattered in 1939 when the RAF relied on formation flying and First World War machine-guns against cannon-armed fighters, and in 1942 when the USAAF repeated the mistake.)

Although it was not ultimately directly successful, the German bombing of Britain did accomplish several things. The threat of air raids and the sounding of the air raid alarms caused suspension of production, and the fear of air raids caused the withdrawal of some fighter squadrons from France. This in itself was not really serious, despite the insistence of Haig's headquarters that every aircraft possible should be diverted to his cause; it could well be argued that the rest period in England was, in fact, beneficial to men who were being flown too much. More importantly, German raids meant that Allied squadrons were not sent to the Middle East, where even one extra unit made the difference between air superiority and inferiority. Also the raids meant some diversion of resources into attempts to develop long-range raiders to conduct retaliatory operations against German targets and eventually against

Total bombs dropped on Great Britain During the First World War   Key

1918

1917

1916

1915

500   1000   1500   2000   2500   3000   3500   4000

Bombs from airships

Bombs from aeroplanes

9,000 German bombs totalling some 280 tons were dropped in 51 airship and 52 aeroplane raids. 1,413 people were killed and 3,408 wounded.

Berlin, though no machines were ready for this great adventure until the war was over. But lastly, and most important of all, the raids brought to a peak the complaints about air defences and production problems which led to the formation in Britain of the independent Royal Air Force.

It is true that the newly arrived Field Marshal Jan Christian Smuts of South Africa was the man who wrote the final report to the Cabinet which called for this turn of events, but it was by no means simply the few daylight raids which he witnessed that convinced Smuts. The German attacks acted as a catalyst in a political-industrial quarrel which had been raging from the start of the war. The Royal Naval Air Service had steadily worked to acquire a large chunk of British aircraft-manufacturing facilities. Naval officers had also applied their knowledge of technological developments to produce increasingly effective aircraft, while at the same time they had not had to waste their aircrew in constant battle over the Western Front. In contrast, the Army had attempted to standardize too early, and it was concurrently undertaking constant offensive action. To this basic dichotomy of outlook has to be added the fact that private manufacturers had a direct interest in putting the Royal Aircraft Factory out of business. And on top of all this, not only was a former private manufacturer calling the government murderers in Parliamentary debates, but his targets were themselves not at all sure that the army's conduct of the war on the Western Front was right.

Asquith's Liberal government had attempted to get around the problem by the usual British compromise, the establishment of a joint Air Board, which under Lord Curzon, himself a strong character but with no training in technological matters, was supposed to arbitrate without any executive powers. This unsatisfactory position continued until well after Lloyd George became Prime Minister in December 1916. After the German raids in July 1917, Smuts was asked, as someone fresh to the English scene and therefore untainted with political or military prejudices, to adjudicate. He was supplied with a lengthy memorandum by General Sir David Henderson, a man high in the direction of the RFC. Henderson urged that air defence and retaliatory bombing would have to be undertaken by the air service. Smuts was willing to go along with this, while at the same time turning down the rebuttals supplied from British

Headquarters in France. The assumptions upon which he made his decisions, however, predicated that there would be a surplus of aircraft over the army's needs by mid-1918. In fact his assumptions were optimistic and were largely vitiated by problems with engine production and by the failure of the American aircraft programme.

Still, the Smuts report of September 1917 did not go all the way. It was only in October that a War Production Committee was finally established when Churchill pressed for the total rather than piecemeal allocation of resources so that the whole of the war effort was logically planned. This in effect meant that when the new Air Ministry came into being in January 1918 it was really an Air Board with executive powers. The creation of the Royal Air Force was a logical, if debatable, afterthought. Certainly it would cause endless trouble in the years to come.

One other side effect of the German raids should be mentioned. Damage was actually very light (£3,000,000 in four years; it has been calculated that rats destroyed material worth £70,000,000 per year.) But the freak casualties of a raid of 28 January 1918, in which one bomb hit Odhams printing plant and caused thirty-eight killed and eighty-five wounded were used in the following years by statistically unsophisticated air force planners to create a horrible spectre of the power of the bomb; although the vision was largely out of touch with reality, it may be said to have played a part in the coming of the Second World War. A little knowledge is a dangerous thing.

British response to German psychological bombing was the development of a retaliatory strategy for the new air force, calling for raids against targets in German cities. The British had been persuaded in the summer of 1916, before the Asquith government fell, to add a force to the French strategic bomber squadrons; the Admiralty had supported this while Haig protested against dilution of effort. But before all the difficulties could be resolved, and they centred about problems of aircraft procurement, the German daylight raids caused urgent government acceptance of an expansion of the air forces to include forty long-range bomber squadrons. Haig opposed the idea again, but by mid-October 1917 a wing had begun to operate. By May 1918 it had four squadrons, and on 6 June these became officially the Independent Bombing Force. The name change was prompted by three motives: to remove the force

*The **Shuttleworth Trust's** SE-5A is the quintessence of the 1918 fighter and of the progress made by aircraft design and production in the four years cauldron of war. Small, fast, well armed and high-powered, and very much a fighting machine. It, too, also represents the international linkages, being powered by a Swiss-designed engine manufactured by a Spanish company in France (hence the Hispano-Suiza name) and licensed for further production in Britain.*

A lone Fokker Triplane sounds a fitting end to the chapter by providing a linking image to the present not only in what it conveys but also in the other image of Snoopy and the Red Baron, the heroic mythology of the first great aerial war.

from the Commander-in-Chief in France and from the control of the new Allied Generalissimo; to provide a high-sounding post for Trenchard, recently relieved as Chief of the Air Staff of the new RAF; and to provide the government at home with a retaliatory air force. Owing to its small size it accomplished little during the war, but by misinterpretation of the word 'independent' a great deal afterwards.

Strategic bombing on the Italian front, where tri-motored Caproni bombers were available to the Italians by August 1915, began with a raid on Ljubljana on 18 February 1916. This was followed by occasional sorties against targets behind the Austrian lines, including Army headquarters, and by a succession of attacks in August and September 1917 against the naval base at Pola; the last of the series, on 2 October, involved 148 Caproni bombers and 11 flying-boats. A year later the last major raid of the war was again against Pola when on 22 October 1918 142 flying-boats and 56 Capronis took part. These strikes are correctly called strategic, in that they were aimed at essentially military targets.

After the retreat from Caporetto had been halted at the Piave, the suggestion was made that a token psychological 'raid' be made against Vienna. Work started at once with a trial long-distance flight within the Italian lines on 4 September 1917. The poet Gabriel d'Annunzio, later famous for his post-war capture of Fiume in 1919, took up the cause, and on 9 August 1918 he led five aircraft on a long leaflet-dropping journey, using evasive routeing both going and returning. The Italians appreciated the raid at its face value—a psychological effort rather than strategic bombing—and at least semi-official Italian sources do not give Douhet credit for this conception.

On the whole the psychological lessons learned from bombing in the First World War were that the shock effect was at first great upon civilians long undisturbed by war, especially when the defences appeared to be unable to stop the attackers; but that both physical and psychological defences were fairly quickly built up. Churchill was undoubtedly right in the long run when, in a lengthy memorandum to the British Cabinet of October 1917, he pointed out that attacking civilians only in the end stiffened the opponents' will to make war. What the effect upon the German nation would

have been of one psychological raid against Berlin before the end of the war remains an interesting speculation.

In the last two years of the war material was more plentiful than in 1914 and 1915, but the problem of standardization still plagued all air forces. In feverish attempts to gain air superiority a plethora of designs were rushed into production, of which only a very small number actually proved useful on operations. Maintenance problems were often accentuated by trying to keep too many kinds of aircraft in the field. Those in power did not always recognize that it was necessary to standardize yet at the same time to deal with the constant challenges of the rapidly developing aerial warfare. Flexible measures were required in defence against aerial attack and in the training of crews, as well as in production. As warfare in the air became more complex it was necessary to undertake more thorough training; and, as fighting became more regular, it was necessary to organize bigger formations and plan mass tactics. At the other end of the spectrum it was equally vital to recall that the war in the air was still a conflict in which the principles of war applied. Concentration, surprise, protection, mobility, and a clear objective were still important. And to these could now be added the knowledge that a comparatively small diversion of force to a theatre in which existing forces were weak could make a significant contribution psychologically as well as physically.

In the First World War were sown the seeds of future progress and of future disaster. Many heroic traditions were created and many illusions generated. The fighter pilot was glorified and the ace immortalized. Too much credit was given to bombs which often in the early years were no bigger than portable typewriters. And just as myths emerged so did mythical personalities. Trenchard for one and Mitchell for another came out of the war with reputations that history does not substantiate. Trenchard was originally an advocate of a tactical air force, and in the long run he may well have been right in opposing strategic bombing, but he made the mistake later of adopting it. Mitchell was at his best as a tactical man and a propagandist of air power. His postwar fame overshadowed the real work he did during the conflict in forming the American air services. Douhet also achieved a reputation in later years that is today much more open to question than it was in 1933.

The German Air Force ended the First World War as it concluded the Second, gallantly fighting despite increasing supply difficulties and rapidly dwindling reserves of men and machines. Its commander, von Hoeppner, remains a shadowy figure, at least in the English-speaking world, yet he should rank as one of the geniuses of early aviation organization.

Too much of the writing of aviation history has taken place in the Anglo-Saxon world with the result that erroneous impressions have persisted. The RAF managed to put about the claim that it was at the end of the war the world's biggest air force; in fact, history shows that it was not—the French force was bigger. An impressive British claim, however, is that of the 55,000 airmen lost, about 30 per cent were British. It was a magnificent show, but it was not war the way a war should be fought.

PART THREE

The Inter-War Years

The Fortieth Anniversary replica of Lindbergh's "Spirit of St. Louis" flying over the St. Louis Arch is a reminder of the tremendous impact which "the Lone Eagle's" solo flight to Paris had in 1927 and of the confidence which it created for aviation. **McDonnell Douglas**

1. Progress towards New Roles and Relationships

The end of the First World War left the victorious powers with a large surplus of material and a mixed bag of officers and men, some eager to be demobilized as fast as possible and others still dreaming of glory and anxious to make flying a career. Many were too young to have known any other.

The vanquished were left with shattered forces which were soon eliminated, either under armistice or peace-treaty terms or at the hands of their own men. In the case of Germany, at least, technological advantage lay ultimately in being defeated, for all her material was destroyed and she was forbidden to undertake military construction. Thus she was compelled to concentrate upon the development of new, technically reliable, and efficient machines while at the same time training her personnel outside her borders, operating them in such climatic extremes as Russia and Latin America.

In all countries, demobilization brought a severe constriction in terms of men, material, and monies. And since air services had in most nations to compete against older services and better-established arms, the members of the newest and youngest branch of war had again to attempt to justify their existence. Doctrine and conceptions once more sometimes outran reality; at other moments airmen's claims annoyed their fraternal opponents into taking more active parts in the over-all military reorganization. This was particularly true in America, for example, where opposition to the messianic views of Billy Mitchell drove the United States Navy along the

The **Hawker** Hart was the epitome of the standard two-seater developed for RAF general-purpose use, largely in colonial areas.

path to the creation of the carrier task force. Perhaps even more than in wartime, it is essential for a military force in peacetime to have an 'enemy', even if it is only a rival service or arm—with victory in terms of money, not territory—for a challenge may lead to coherent planning. Of course if political power is too oppressive on one side or the other, or if verbal combat is mostly acrimonious, then the effects may be undesirable.

Even more than words, deeds were essential to make industrialists, politicians, and the public—and thus the legislatures—aware of the importance of air power. Here airmen were gifted with an ideal vehicle for publicity, in an era of individualism and demonstration. Throughout the interwar years, at least until the Great Depression, airmen sought to stir the public mind with record-breaking headlines and aerobatic displays. And not unnaturally while some of these activities, such as the development of racing and long-distance machines, had practical applications in the creation of material and techniques, inevitably other facets tended to become ends in themselves. Thus a squadron might spend nine months of the year practising a set of manoeuvres for the annual public display. The other three months left little time for military training once leave had been taken.

Peacetime brought other problems. Since the air services had hardly existed before the war, they had no permanent bases, schools, or positions in the defence spectrum. Nor did they have traditions, which may have been a good thing. In each case it was necessary to establish an organization to create a permanent force, which would in itself form the cadre of another wartime air force, if one should be needed. Yet how was this to be done with the money available?

The solutions varied according to the situation each nation faced. The Germans created a disguised air force in their airlines, and through advisers sent to foreign air forces. The French, then possessing the world's largest air force, stayed tensely on guard against another German attack, remaining especially fearful when the Anglo-American Guarantee Treaty failed to be ratified after Versailles, and even regarding Britain as a likely enemy in the critical days over the Ruhr in 1923 when British airliners flew currency into that area soon occupied by the French. The Italians followed the British lead and established an Air Ministry, as a rehabilitated

Douhet, in favour with the newly risen Mussolini, found acceptable his ideas of a counterstrike deterrent against the enemy while the infantry held the Alpine passes. The British, unable to re-divide the RAF as originally planned, took the view that as there would be no major war for ten years the best thing to do was cut the service back to a cadre force while building anew from the ground up. Trenchard was, perhaps fortunately, inarticulate—unlike Billy Mitchell—while British Parliamentary procedure did not allow the public brawling between services that was possible in American Congressional committees. In the United States, however, there were the unique opportunities of a vast amount of internal space and reasonably good weather.

While both British and American doctrine developed the concept of an air defence against a seaborne invasion, the controversies resulted in different conclusions. In Britain the naval air arm was subordinated to and manned by the RAF. In America the Navy retained and developed under Moffett its own air force, to counter Mitchell's claims. Ironically, the ex-Royal Naval Air Service professionals followed naval tradition and went out to train the Japanese naval air arm, thus laying the trap for the humiliation of the Royal Navy in 1941–1942. The Royal Navy was allowed to start Fleet Air Arm training in 1924, but it was not until 1937 that the FAA was brought fully under Admiralty control. It is interesting to speculate about the outcome of the war at sea if the RNAS had remained a naval air arm after 1918 and had not trained the Japanese. British airmen have claimed the Admiralty did not want them until the RAF took them, but the challenges created by both the Americans and Japanese, whose first carrier entered service in 1923, coupled with the evidence of air-mindedness in Jellicoe's 1919 proposals for a Far Eastern Fleet suggest that a naval air arm of some kind would have been maintained. And Japanese-American rivalries would, no doubt, have created an oriental carrier fleet anyway.

If the Royal Navy was uncertain about the future of naval aviation and was entangled in fights with the Air Ministry, the United States Navy moved rapidly ahead. It owed its progress to several things, not the least of which was that the country's leading practical airman-politician was a naval officer. Rear Admiral William A. Moffett was the Hyman Rickover of his day and also the

The US Army's Round-the-World Cruisers, one of which remains on exhibit today in the National Air and Space Museum, are seen here at the start of the Air Service's historic flight in which the machines operated some of the time on wheels and sometimes on floats. **McDonnell Douglas**

Building the World Cruisers was a task which employed most of the staff of the Douglas Company, including Donald Douglas himself, seen leaning out of the cockpit. The design was a modification of the company's Navy torpedo-bomber, a simple, rugged wooden structure powered with a single in-line engine. **McDonnell Douglas**

Trenchard. Like the RAF leader, he enjoyed an exceptionally long tenure of office (1921 till his death in 1933) as head of the Bureau of Aeronautics. It was Moffett who guided the Navy past Mitchellian rocks and along the lines of the carrier task force. Moffett was careful; he never openly antagonized either his superiors or Congress, but he took full advantage of the power of a Bureau chief and of the publicity value of aviation. As a result the USN found itself escaping the odium heaped upon the Army's Mitchell, whose antics and attacks made Navy brass all the more ready to fight fire with fire.

To prevent the usurpation of the Navy's traditional coast-defence role by the Army Air Force, the Navy developed patrol bombers and carriers. At the same time Moffett was helped by the fact that by 1922 the great battleship advocate, Admiral William S. Sims, had become converted by games played under his own command at the Naval War College, and Sim's endorsement of carriers influenced other officers. Aviation was included in annual fleet manoeuvres starting in 1921, but not until Fleet Problem V in 1925 was a carrier, _Langley,_ present, and not until 1929 were two modern carriers, _Lexington_ and _Saratoga_ available. From then on progress was steady. The USN was able to order its own aircraft and train its own crews, and a permanent cadre of naval aviators came into being with equipment which they specified, tried, and modified.* The Navy's grasp of politics was one of the basic reasons for its ultimate success.

While the French helped the Japanese army, it was a British Air Mission, sent out in April 1921 and staying until the end of 1923, which helped with naval developments. Though not regarded as particularly apt pupils by their instructors, the Japanese were aware of what needed to be done. Thus _Hosho_ was laid down in 1919 as a carrier and commissioned by early 1923, when active flying trials aboard her began. Though an economy drive in 1923 created some problems, the Japanese were vigorous in their desire

* It was American naval airmen who worked up the dive-bomber, and it was their Curtiss Helldiver which Udet saw in 1935, bought with state funds, and took back to Germany, and 'sold' to Goering and the _Luftwaffe_. Thus the USN was indirectly responsible for the Stuka design, which started operational life in the Spanish Civil War, then spearheaded the 1939–40 _Blitzkrieg_ before being used in the war at sea.

to learn about flying and soon acquired British aircraft and equipment, which they often proceeded to copy as the first step towards creating their own home-built aircraft. The Mission suffered from the British Air Ministry's reluctance to release the latest information, as it wished to keep its developments at least a year ahead of rivals; but the Japanese in any case soon progressed more rapidly than the Fleet Air Arm, even as early as 1923 engaging in night-flying operations. As an island kingdom, Japan had good reason to develop a naval air arm and was in a political position to do so.

Yet in both the Japanese and the American navies airmen had trouble developing their tactics, because the navies were dominated by battleship admirals who predicted that the next war would be won at sea in one great big free-for-all battle of the Tsushima type. Thus carriers were tied to the battle fleet, not always with happy results, as when in the 1929 games _Lexington_ was caught by the 'enemy' surface forces while steaming away from her own battle line to launch her planes. Though in the 1930 American manoeuvres a separate striking group was built around _Saratoga,_ the idea seems not to have occurred to the Japanese, who began fleet air manoeuvres in 1931. Their vision was blinded by the apparent necessity, similar to that facing the Germans up to 1918, to cut down the USN's battle line. The ratio established at the 1922 Washington Naval Conference was that the American and British fleets would be equal and the Japanese only 60 per cent of the size of either; and the Japanese placed too great an emphasis upon the possibility of the presence of all the American fleet in the Pacific at one time. In preparing to reduce the American battle line, their carriers were heavily outfitted with dive- and torpedo-bombers, while American carriers had a higher proportion of fighters. Only gradually did the Japanese realize that the US carriers were their main problem, and not until about 1940 were these made the principal objective.

What influenced the Japanese were the ideas brought back by their naval air attaché from Britain in 1940. He concluded that air superiority was essential, that strikes must be by at least 100 bombers, and that carriers had to have armoured decks. Partly as a result of these observations and of a newsreel of the four US carriers steaming together, the Japanese had by 1941 developed the doctrine that for attacks on land targets their carriers should steam

Early designers and manufacturers were sometimes very much 19th-century style engineers in their wide interests. Sherman Fairchild, right, was one of these, seen here discussing the first flight of the new Fairchild-Caminez engine with Harold Caminez and Dick Pepew, the test pilot, about 1928. **Fairchild**

One of the great designers, Igor Sikorsky, whose career began in Russia and ended in the United States. **United Aircraft**

together, but in order to avoid 'mutual kill' as they termed it, in air actions at sea the carriers should be separated. The object of the characteristic Japanese separation of forces was the entrapment of the enemy fleet in a box which would allow them to strike from four directions at once, the tactic they had in mind at Midway.

What gave strength to both the Japanese and American naval airmen was the fact that their services were separate from other air forces; their struggles were fought within the navies, which controlled their own material and expected to fight battles basically in their own environment.

In their search for a post-war role, airmen could justify themselves in part by their wartime actions. But here, on the whole, they found themselves really doing no more than making a case for an arm of one of the surface services. Naval airmen could not, for instance, show that they had played a significant independent role against enemy navies; even in anti-submarine warfare their role had been ancillary. They sought to claim that they could sink ships with torpedoes and that they could take over the coast-defence role, and they did demonstrate that bombs could harm battleships, although in this they were out-shone by Mitchell and the Army.

In Germany naval airmen for a while were given a role in coast defence, but this was more an arbitrary administrative division of covert activities than a real function. What naval airmen basically could claim, a fact which the RNAS had demonstrated and which the US and Imperial Japanese Navies would prove, was that unless the fleet controlled its own air arm it suffered from three fatal defects. First, its aircraft were not designed for its own needs, but were usually variations of land-based machines whose operational weaknesses became more apparent as size increased. (It must be noted here that the poor design of British naval aircraft came from a variety of factors connected both with the history of the Fleet Air Arm and with the nature of the aircraft industry.) Second, its personnel were not dedicated naval officers, but belonged to an alien service. And third, most clearly demonstrated in the German case in the Second World War, its entire air arm could be siphoned off to other tasks more rewarding in the eyes of the air force high command or of other career officers. Even in Britain, the great example of an independent third service was compromised, as Trenchard had envisaged that it would be when money was avail-

able, by the creation first between 1924 and 1937 of the Fleet Air Arm, and then in the midst of the Second World War of an Army air arm, manned partly by army officers and partly by 'hostilities only' RAF aircrew who had no overriding loyalty to either service. Two other factors must be noted as affecting the issue. Most of the difficulties and rivalries were amongst the prima donnas in the top echelons; individuals at the lower levels got along when they had a common concern. But in the days of strapped budgets anything that could be passed over to someone else's account scored a point in budgetary gamesmanship. There was also the adverse publicity that could easily be associated with air crashes and with excessive profits of aircraft firms, singled out in particular by the disarmers whose attacks on private manufacture of arms reached their climax in the American Nye Committee hearings in 1935.

If naval airmen had their problems, in some countries they were able to make progress by quiet work at sea and successful efforts on manoeuvres. On the other hand, German and Soviet naval aviators got almost nowhere, and in the British navy airmen were hampered by their affiliation with the RAF and by the fact that umpires on manoeuvres were often conservative officers who might overlook the contribution of aviation. Thus tactics tended to become sterile, and only real warfare would sharpen them to viability in combat.

Land-based airmen had an equally difficult time arguing that they had a separate role and were not an arm of the Army. Even in Britain it was only intended that the unified air service should exist until wartime production problems were solved; after the Armistice it was assumed that the RNAS and the RFC would be recreated, if not under the same names. In Italy, the United States, and Britain airmen sought a separate identity because of their frustration at operating under control of older groundbound officers, who they felt did not understand air power. Progress towards complete separation between air and surface commands, however, was slow and uneven.

Acceptance of new technologies appears to go through a cycle, starting with battles in which the lines are sharply drawn in public between unabashed admirers and fervently reactionary opponents. If the item is eventually accepted, it is assumed at first to be a cure-all. Once that adulatory phase passes in some disillusionment, it is possible to come to a rational understanding of the real capabilities and limitations of the new technological creation. In the meantime, in the twenty years or so which this process takes, technology itself may have advanced far enough to give some realism to the claims made for the machine in its early days. With air power the twenty year period was up in 1939.

While it was true that airmen discovered that in colonial operations against tribesmen lacking even anti-aircraft guns they could act swiftly, economically, and therefore effectively as policemen, colonial activities between the wars produced little more than tactical air forces used in a limited strategic sense. Moreover, the very conditions under which these forces operated created a frame of mind that was a liability in a modern mechanized continental war. British airmen suffered, too, from their isolation, in such activities, from the very people with whom they would have to co-operate in wartime. That the RAF, for instance, did not do worse in the Second World War was probably in part due to a dominant aspect of the British character—the willingness to team together, in spite of diversity, to get a job done. In the United States, where Army airmen had few if any tasks, they were never able to obtain more than Corps status until 1942, when the corps was promoted to the US Army Air Force. In other countries such as Japan and the Soviet Union, to whom no grand-strategic targets were open, the air arms remained essentially tactical. And in Germany, where former fighter pilot Goering made much of his air force as opposed to the needs of the navy, he nevertheless saw it in basically a First World War style tactical role, in support of the army.

In their attempt to achieve a self-confident independent identity —necessary before they could willingly join their strength to that of a larger community—airmen found an area in which they could make a special claim, though even that could be disputed by anti-aircraft proponents. The apparent lessons of the German air attacks on Britain in the First World War were that the next war would open with a devastating air attack and that only an independent air force could protect the nation from this third-dimensional blow. A corollary developed was that the best defence was a good offensive threat. But the intellectual simplicity of these approaches was made difficult by internal political and economic clouds as well as by diplomatic and geographic obstacles. Thus if the air-power

nations of the inter-war years are surveyed, it will be noted that each reacted in a different way and suffered a different fate. And at least a part of the result was due to semantic difficulties over the word 'strategic', which we have suggested should be redefined as either 'strategic' in the older army sense—designating military contacts beyond the immediate battlefield—or 'grand-strategic' in the sense of independent operations not directly connected with a surface campaign. That this confusion arose and still persists was due to the lack of defence education on the part of politicians and their unwillingness even to listen in an era in which the emphasis was upon disarmament, and to a natural human tendency to assume that both parties in a dialogue are using the same terms in the same way.

The attitude taken by the Soviets and the Japanese was largely governed by the lack of an apparent grand-strategic threat and by a dearth of external targets. But it was also governed by the absence of a champion within the state. In the Russian case, Igor Sikorsky and Alexandre de Seversky left the country for the United States, where Sikorsky turned to building passenger aircraft and helicopters, as the idea of grand-strategic bombing was given little support in an isolationist era. Despite the fact that the Germans had been the instigators of grand-strategic bombing, the German officers who trained the Soviet Air Force were essentially tactically oriented. The 1936–38 Soviet purge of general officers ended any chance that those who had read Douhet, whose doctrines the Germans did not accept, would have power. By 1939 Soviet heavy bombers were obsolete and converted to transport roles, while the rest of the air force was recuperating from the Spanish Civil War.

By the time the Sino-Japanese incident broke out in July 1937 the Japanese air forces had developed long-range bombers which were used first for strategic attacks against Chinese airfields and then, when these first strikes caught and nearly destroyed the CAF on the ground, for larger strategic raids against the principal bases outside Chinese cities. In the 1939 Nomonhan war against the Soviets, however, the Japanese never were in a position to undertake strategic bombing owing to the overwhelming numbers of Soviet fighters. Each side, of course, claimed the other suffered severe losses, but neither established air superiority.

In Germany, where the air force was suppressed until after the

One of the major curses of peacetime was the availability of war-surplus materiel. Here during a 1928 US Air Service inspection crews stand in front of American-built, British-designed DeHavilland DH-4's. **USAF**

rise of Hitler, the concentration was on air transport and after 1933 on tactical aircraft, in part because Goering, the head of the *Luftwaffe*, had been a fighter pilot and in part because the only advocate of grand-strategic bombing, General Walther Wever, was killed in an air crash in 1936. Moreover, it is questionable whether grand-strategic attacks would have suited Hitler's policy, which was to avoid arousing other powers while quickly snapping up victims. As for the French, even in the First World War they had been most careful not to arouse the Germans because of the fragile state of their own morale, because they had already lost many of their industrial towns to the German army, and because they did not want retaliation. Thus they had resisted the British establishment of an Independent Air Force outside the control of the Allied Generalissimo for these very reasons. If the British wanted to retaliate against the Germans, they reasoned, let it be clearly a British action with the consequences quite clearly upon the heads of their stubborn allies.

But in the case of three, possibly intellectually interlinked, air forces, the doctrine of 'strategic bombing' or of 'the counter-strike deterrent' held sway. In Italy and in Britain the air-power enthusiasts were led to advocate a doctrine of offensive bombardment by the willingness of politicians to consider some other way to win the war than through appalling casualties for local ground actions that brought no apparent result in a war of attrition. After the 1914 war military men themselves began to appreciate that no nation could fight another war with manpower losses of anything near a similar level. Instinctively people sought a weapon which would prevent another war from starting or win a war in a very short order without terrible casualties to either side. In Italy the chief advocate of this cause was General Giulio Douhet, though the impetus may have come from Count Caproni, a bomber manufacturer. The Italian situation reflected the frustrating battles of the Izonso and the Caporetto disaster, which Douhet had predicted. Douhet and Caproni could argue from a geographical environment that provided a natural defensive position from which there was little prospect of sallying. To Italy, air blows which would paralyze her adversaries made good sense as a defensive grand strategy. But, ironically, the whole Italian approach lacked vitality for two reasons. The first was that war when it came was fought not against

a Continental power with vulnerable industrial centres, but against primitive Ethiopians and then against colonial British forces in the desolation of the Western Desert. (The battle against France in 1940 was over a corpse.) The second was that not only was Italian equipment going out of phase in 1940 and 1941, but the Italian character was not that of Julius Caesar and the Roman legionary. Individually daring and superb flyers, collectively the Italian Air Force of the Second World War, with the possible exception of its anti-shipping strikes, was ineffective.

American officers had had some contact with Caproni, who tactfully had his doctrine printed in English. Strategic bombing and the concept of an independent air force for them went hand in hand. But they had no enemy, and equally significantly they had in the first crucial years Mitchell as their mouthpiece. Mitchell was intellectually, in the best military habit, a plagiarizer and temperamentally a propagandist. Mitchell's and Douhet's careers have a number of parallels, but the timing was significantly different. Douhet was court-martialed and imprisoned in 1916, but a turn of the tide of war (Caporetto in 1917) exonerated him, and the rise of Mussolini in 1922 catapulted him into a place of influence in a government determined to glorify Italy. Mitchell was just about three years too late. Isolationism lasted a full decade and a half after his 1925 court-martial. Even more ironically, although Douhet's name appeared in English as early as 1922, and some of his writings became available within the US Army in 1933, his renaissance and fame in the English-speaking world did not come until the publication of the Dino Ferrari translation of his *Command of the Air* in 1942. And then he was glorified because he was an outside expert who posthumously backed up the ideas of American air-power strategists.

In the meantime, what America really needed was an Air Corps Hyman Rickover, a quiet, knowledgeable, and able advocate of air power who could win the genuine support of Congress; or even a man like General Amos Fries, who saved the Chemical Warfare Service in 1919. As it was, after the court-martial Mitchell's friends took up his legacy in the remote safety of Randolph Field, Texas, and evolved an offensive doctrine of [grand] strategic bombing. They believed that the advent of the Boeing B-17A in 1935 gave them their victory weapon. The Second World War was to prove

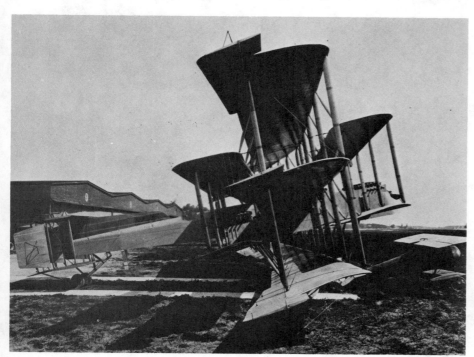

Early attempts to design a super-bomber resulted in interesting structures, some of which never even got off the ground. Others struggled into the air, but could not get over the surrounding terrain. The Johns Multiplane was one example. An idea of its size may be had by comparing it with the fighter on the right. **Source unknown.**

Perhaps nothing better illustrates the frustrations of dealing with the military mind of the mid-twenties than these pictures of Army airmen forced to conform to paradeground inspection rules. The picture above shows artillery being loaded in transports in the Philippines in 1933, while that below illustrates a Departmental Review in Puerto Rico in the same year — note the aircraft neatly drawn up in the top lefthand corner. **Anonymous gift.**

One of the advantages of grass airfields was that many planes could operate at the same time, an especially valuable feature for military formations wishing to take-off at the same time. On the other hand, in dry weather, the dust was not appreciated. These Air Corps machines of the late twenties would have had a take-off speed of about 60 mph on their way back to Kelly Field, TX, in June 1930.

An early Sikorsky design for a twin-engined passenger aeroplane carried on his Russian approach of a forward view for the passengers, while the pilot sat above and well aft still in an open cockpit. **United Aircraft**

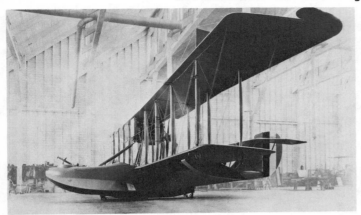

HS 2L

Rodgers et al

NC-4, 3 May 1919

Read's crew.

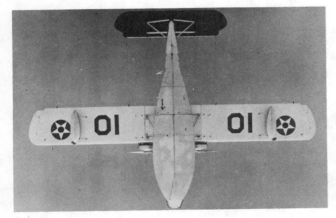

Martin PM-2

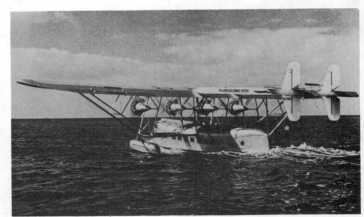

PAA Twin Boom. S-62534-M

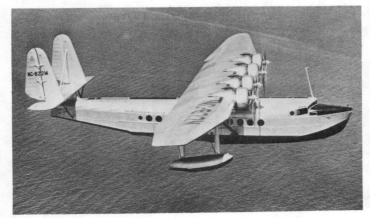

Sikorsky S-42

Excalibur

Young C. L. "Kelly" Johnson, the Lockheed design wizard, monitoring a 1930's test-flight by radio. **Lockheed-California**

how over-optimistic they were and to what extent they, like most airmen, over-estimated the power of the 500-lb. bomb and under-estimated the toughness of populations either inured to hardship as in Spain and China, endowed with a stoic outlook as in Japan, or stiffened with veterans of trench warfare as in Britain and Nazi-dominated Germany. Moreover, by the Second World War the novelty of air power, and the horror leading to panic with which it had been viewed in 1914–18, had worn off; women evacuated from London in September 1939 returned that same night, preferring to face bombs in a familiar environment rather than the unknowns of a blacked-out countryside. The US Army Air Corps in 1941 had bomber advocates firmly entrenched in its leadership, when in fact it needed armour-oriented tactical airmen. This is not to say that it did not develop tactical doctrine and planes; but in terms of the war that had to be fought, the emphasis turned out to be un-balanced and had to be reshaped in the cauldron of war to include fighters and fighter-bombers.

Yet, for all this, it must be recognized that it was perhaps inevit-able that in the search for an independent and respectable identity the brass of the Army Air Corps should seek out the one role that appeared to free airmen from domination by the older service chiefs. Such action was a form of escapism, often politically neces-sary within the establishment, but marred by the vitriolic nature of the Mitchell crusade which made it difficult to reconcile roles and budgets.

What happened in the United States was in many respects parallel to what happened in Britain, but as the British national character was more privacy-, privilege-, and Parliament-conscious than the American, the battle was fought out largely behind closed doors, proving almost equally dangerous. One thing that can be said for the British pattern was that it probably owed absolutely nothing to Douhet, since Britain had produced its own air-power theorists at least as early as the Italian general in F. W. Lanchester, P. R. C. Groves, and Sir Frederick Sykes. It is questionable if Trenchard would have adopted these views if he had not heard in 1921 that Generalissimo Joffre accepted them, if the Royal Navy had not pushed the RAF over coastal defence, and if Trenchard himself as head of the RAF had not had to become concerned about its separate survival. Trenchard was a tactical and strategic

man only in the limited army sense of those terms. He was closer, that is, to a Haig than to a Sykes.

In Britain the RAF discovered that it could have three roles: colonial policing, air defence, and anti-invasion. In the inter-war years it managed to keep its active squadrons largely abroad engaged in policing, while it argued at home for roles in air and coastal defence. It was awarded the former in 1922 and 1923 Cabinet decisions, and a Home Defence counter-strike deterrent force—composed two-thirds of bombers—was initiated. The logic of this decision was marred because anti-aircraft equipment and troops were never placed under RAF command. Trenchard, in fact, did not want them; not only would they have hurt his budgets, but he did not believe that there really *was* a defence against bombers —the civilian population would just have to grin and bear it until the morale of the enemy population broke in an aerial war of attri-tion. The argument that the bomber would always get through was in large measure true only because little work was done in defensive measures by offensively-minded air marshals who refused to take into account the lessons of the 1915–1918 battle of London. In fact, one of the problems of the post-war RAF was that Trenchard vir-tually hand-picked the officer corps from RFC veterans of the Western Front. Others, too, overlooked the study of all-round defence until their cities were attacked and political pressures upset rational defensive planning and diluted resources.

Yet it must also be remembered that what was said and what was done were two quite different things, as a study of RAF procure-ment shows. At the very time when the counter-strike deterrent force concept was accepted, when the Cabinet adopted as policy the idea that a weaker democracy could protect itself by threatening to devastate the cities of any potential aggressor, the RAF ceased to issue specifications for long-range heavy bombers. Instead, the cadre force maintained was equipped with medium bombers with a striking range inadequate for any target beyond Paris. The majority of the aircraft in the RAF were general-purpose machines designed to be used as fighter-bombers in colonial operations. More-over, if the RAF was to play an anti-invasion role and if the torpedo was *the* weapon at sea, then surely it should have developed efficient ones for this work. But it did not, a point which the 1942

For most aircraft industries exports became vital. Some-times these consisted of types never sold at home, but at others the sale of machines which could have sold well was stopped by national security. Here Consolidated Vultee VII's over Rio de Janeiro. **Convair**

fall of Singapore, the one place in which it was specifically charged with this duty, showed.

In fairness to the RAF and to Trenchard, it should be noted that he concentrated much of the limited resources on creating a sound force of mechanics through the Halton programme and a proper officer cadre through the RAF College at Cranwell. And the RAF emerged victorious from the Second World War because its officer corps, old and new, was able to work in harmony on the operational level with its navy and army counterparts.

In France, Douhet's ideas had been accepted in the early twenties and a good deal was done then to prepare a bomber striking force for use against any opponent; but in the thirties, despite the use of French equipment in Spain, the whole conception sagged. Knowledge of exactly what happened will have to await the production of official French air histories.

The important change in the United States came not in the Army Air Corps Act of 1926 but in the MacArthur-Pratt Agreement of 1931 and in the Baker Board recommendations of 1934. The former provided that army bombers would assume responsibility for coast defence, thus freeing the navy for offensive roles, which the new carriers made attractive; while the Baker Board, though rejecting the idea of an independent air force, did agree to the establishment of the General Headquarters Air Force which would have central control so as to be able to strike in any direction. These two decisions coincided with the technological revolution whose first fruit was the Martin B-10 twin-engine bomber, which had barely entered service before the prototype four-engine B-17 appeared. The 1934 Air Corps 'Project A' request for an aircraft which could carry a one-ton bomb 5,000 miles was not met, owing to cost. In fact the Army Air Corps was so strapped for funds that the first orders for B-17's were very small, cheaper aircraft being purchased instead. In 1938 the B-17 squadron intercepted a liner 725 miles at sea to demonstrate the army's ability to frustrate attacks on the US coast, and the Army and Navy Joint Board supported the army general staff in saying that nothing bigger or longer-ranged than the B-17 would be needed, a vote of confidence which nearly killed the B-29 of later long-ranging Pacific fame. Thus when war came the US had no aircraft capable of being a grand-strategic—let alone an intercontinental—bomber.

Thus doctrinal and technological developments were enmeshed in political problems. For air forces to grow in peacetime they had to convince either military or political superiors or both that they could play a more economical role than some other arm in national defence, or that they were the only shield against certain hazards. Unfortunately these two roles might produce incompatible equipment, and, with only limited funds available, compromise or calculated risk were unavoidable. They led either to general-purpose aircraft most suited to colonial operations, or to an investment in a very limited number of squadrons flying up-to-date craft, supposedly prototypes for an expanded procurement which rarely came. Too often these hand-crafted prototypes proved unsuitable for mass-production.

2. Airline Development and Aircraft Production

Coupled to the serious dichotomy between theory and practice were two linked problems: airlines and the aircraft industry. Of all the nations in the world, only the United States probably had the climate, the wealthy population, and the distances to make the development of airlines a feasible internal matter. While the Russians lacked a wealthy population, they saw air travel both as a national status symbol and as the solution to their roadless and railless vastness. Only the Germans had no such other outlet for their aerial energies. Owing to technological problems, costs, distances, weather, and public reluctance—combined in some cases with subsidy problems and mail payments—airline development was slow. Though it was true that by the end of the thirties both the Atlantic and the Pacific had been spanned, so that it was theoretically possible to fly around the world commercially, the lines were still very small.

The arrival of all-metal monoplanes with useful economic characteristics took place in the mid-thirties, starting with the German Ju-52 and the American Boeing 247 and Douglas DC-3; and the

Working on a wing.

Spirit of St. Louis frame.

Sheet metal inspection.

Beech's line, 1939.

Clyde Cessna and Co.

American Sikorsky and Boeing, the British Short, and the German Dornier, flying-boats. Strangely, when war came, air-power leaders, though controlling a highly mobile weapon, failed to understand the role of air transport. Except for the Germans, they still thought of 1914-style trench warfare. Just as in the First World War an immediate mobilization of skilled workers seriously hampered munitions production, so in the Second—at least in Britain, where the airlines were just being nationalized—both men and equipment were siphoned off to the RAF for other purposes, to make good the lack of foresight in peacetime. The German and Soviet air forces, being tactical in outlook, had integrated transports into their systems for paratroop operations by the late thirties. In the United States, not only did there exist an aircraft industry attuned to air transport, but the relative plethora of available airline managers in 1941 enabled the airlines to capture control of the military air transport system, seeing it as a heaven-sent means of acquiring knowledge of international air routes.

In a number of respects the confusions which had plagued disarmament discussions until 1934 over the ability to convert transports into bombers continued in the minds of some air force officers, who in an unsophisticated way continued the peacetime habit of specifying bomber-transports, which were generally neither one thing nor the other. It is true, of course, that the differences between bombers and transports were not great in the 1920s. But as airline management came out of the war-surplus era it began to demand real reliability and ease of maintenance coupled with economy of operation. This led to certification problems, since the testing standards were those of the military, who controlled aviation, and not of the civil operators. Even before the technological revolution, the bomber and the airliner were moving apart, for the needs of airline men were in direct conflict with stated military demands. Airlines had no use for the many things like bombs and guns which the military tended to hang on the outside, so that a machine which might start out with an aerodynamically clean configuration lost this during modification to service specifications. Thus airliners led the way into the technological revolution which included all-metal construction, retractable undercarriages, flaps, streamlined cowlings, constant-speed propellors with variable pitch, and higher octane fuel followed in the late thirties by radios and other gadgetry.

Leading lights of US aviation — BG Benjamin D. Foulois, Capt. Eddie Rickenbacker, and MG James E. Fechet. **USAF**

Operationally airlines tended to lead the way in navigation, though naval airmen were quite sophisticated here, and night-flying. Some of the conflicts that developed within air forces during the Second World War came from the interaction of traditional officers with airline personnel. In part, the latter's standards were higher because they had accumulated far more experience in the same period of time. Airlines aimed for an annual utilisation per aircraft of some 2,000 hours a year, while the military might get 200. Airline men were frequently ex-officers whose ambitions could not be satisfied under peacetime military conditions, and they regarded themselves as professional airmen and the military as amateurs.

Airlines developed carefully because their survival depended upon fare-paying passengers and freight, and because they were the most heavily supervised of all transportation systems. Moreover, they had stockholders who demanded profits. They tended to choose those routes on which there was the least competition from ground transport. All over the world, the story was about the same. Some companies folded as their war-surplus equipment was destroyed and they could no longer raise capital for new machines. Others merged, voluntarily or otherwise, in order to obtain subsidies or mail payments. By 1930 the basic structure of the modern airline system was visible. Then a second generation of small operators moved in to feed the bigger systems and were themselves eventually merged into bigger companies. In the meantime the main air routes were being pioneered by the Dutch KLM to the East Indies, Air France to Indochina and Africa, Lufthansa within Europe and into the Soviet Union, Imperial Airways to South Africa, Australia, Hong Kong, and to New York in conjunction with Pan-American, who also operated to South America and across the Pacific. In running all of these lines, whether they were state companies such as Lufthansa and Air France, or semi-private such as KLM, or subsidised like Pan-American and Imperial Airways, political contacts at home and abroad counted for as much as technology. The directors of these companies fought a constant war against international competition and waste. Thus, when they had to buy aircraft or run a military air transport service, they tackled the job with 'combat' experience behind them.

Airline equipment orders were limited, though in terms of airframe weight a large passenger flying-boat of 1935 was the equiva-

Leaders of the US Air Service in 1922: BG William Mitchell and General Mason Patrick, US Army.

lent of a squadron of fighters. For a handful of companies airline orders were more rewarding than military orders, and after 1935 there was a chance of making a reasonable profit on them while at the same time developing the latest technology with a design team attuned to performance and maintenance economics, points which were not without value in military competitions. But, at the same time, the technological revolution began to bring American dominance with the emergence of the fast Boeing, Douglas, and Lockheed airliners. War gave American manufacturers an additional advantage, but that it was so great was in part Europe's own fault for failing to understand the need for transport aircraft in war.

A close and interesting link between the military, the airlines, and the aircraft manufacturers, was the rigid airship. While Japanese and Italian efforts were limited to blimps or semi-rigids, the Germans, Americans, and British experimented with full-blown dirigibles. These great streamlined beasts were both civil and military, political and commercial, successes and failures. They might have served as very-long-range scouts and transports, as indeed the *Graf Zeppelin* did, but on the whole they suffered the fate of peripheral weapons in peacetime. Their development was stopped by the loss of their leading proponents in well-publicized crashes, two of which (*R-101* and *Hindenburg*) might not have been fatal had the US seen fit to export helium. But their basic problem was that they were too expensive, too slow in gestation and development to compete with the technological progress of the aeroplane, and too unwieldy on the ground. The cost of docking and housing them as much as anything else was their downfall, for it limited their use to specific routes in spite of the apparent lessons of the *Graf Zeppelin's* South American service. Yet for all this, the rigid airship contributed significantly to technological developments in terms of structures and stress measurement, streamlining, and diesel engines.

One other aspect of aircraft production deserves mention. When rearmament began, a number of problems arose. In the first place the beginning of rearmamental instability coincided with the technological revolution. This meant that both designers and production engineers had to learn new techniques with new materials. Moreover as the switchover from wood took place, capital costs rose sharply because metal-working machine tools had to replace those

of carpenters. These in their turn demanded a labour force with new skills at a time when every other defence industry, not to mention new consumer ones, was competing for talent in an evaporating market.

For some the American dominance began to be felt at this time because it was the Yankees who had taken the lead in developing machine tools. The Germans, it is true, had them. But the Germans in 1934 were engaged in their own revolution. They were quietly tooling-up secret aircraft factories which were putting into production the types which would suddenly, with a public announcement from Hitler in March 1935, boost the *Luftwaffe* from last to near first place amongst the world's air forces, not so much because of numbers as because of the appearance overnight of what seemed to be a fully-trained, cohesive, and coherent modern air force with the latest equipment. The whole emergence of the *Luftwaffe* was a consummate piece of showmanship, and it was effective. The British and the French began a hasty rearmament which saw the continued production of obsolete types to provide training experience. It was another five years before American industry received orders from its own government, though it managed to get through much of the first part of its own rearmamental instability on British and French demand and financing. Meanwhile the Soviet Air Force had initiated its own five-year plans and was busy turning out tactical aircraft, some of which were still copies of western designs, but others of which were ahead of them. Much the same thing happened in Japan, except that there Japanese designers took over from the imported Europeans and began to produce their own long-range, high-performance aircraft for the incidents in China and other possible actions. In all these developments, skilled management became as critical a commodity as raw materials and machine tools.

In studying the history of air power, the low level of peacetime usage must not be overlooked, particularly when coupled with the artificial nature of manoeuvres. These factors led for one thing to a failure to find flaws in equipment, in the absence of skilled professional maintenance and long-term pilots. Modern accident statistics can be used to show that the fewer hours flown per month before the war broke out made pilots much more accident-prone than in wartime, when intensive usage became the rule. The one advantage of crashes, in terms of technical progress, was that they did dispose

The way to test equipment and prove it, to gain publicity and appropriations, and to achieve progress in design was to undertake record breaking or win air races. How rapidly such work could make refinements can be seen by comparing this 1926 US Navy Curtiss racer with the earlier 1918 fighters. **U.S. Navy**

The ultimate in the racing seaplane was the Vickers Supermarine S-6B fitted with a specially built engine which became the progenitor of the famed Merlin of World War II, it carried its fuel in the floats and like others before it had its radiators buried in the wings and the tail fin. **Vickers**

of aircraft which would not otherwise be retired and replaced. Another defect of peacetime was the limited numbers of any one type ordered, often no more than enough for one squadron with a few spares. Squadrons tended to develop their own techniques with a consequent lack of uniformity throughout the service, and manufacturers, able to count on only a trickle of government orders, tended to hand build most aircraft. Thus peacetime aircraft factories were design establishments with workshops attached, and flaws were ironed out by the shop foreman. When in the late thirties rearmament began and demands for aircraft rose from one and one-half per month to 500, at a time when amateur management and unskilled workers had to be employed in the midst of a technological revolution, errors in mass-production multiplied. The many modifications and masses of paperwork now had to be passed on to production establishments no longer across the corridor from the designer's office. It was these things which the stilted peacetime manoeuvres did not bring out, but which had a significant effect on the next war.

3. Record-Breaking

The inter-war years saw a number of interesting specific developments in civilian aviation; record-breaking for one was an area in which the future of military aviation was anticipated by about a decade.

In 1919 the Schneider Trophy contests for high-speed seaplanes were revived. These soon became national events. In 1923 the US Navy entered a team with full official backing, and the French Navy followed suit, though less enthusiastically. The Americans used Curtiss racers incorporating the radical new Curtiss D-12 inline V engine and won with a speed of 177.38 mph. The contests then seesawed back and forth until the British using Supermarine aircraft flown by a special RAF high-speed Flight ended the contest by winning the Trophy for the third time in a row in 1931, at a speed of 340.6 mph. Just after that event one of the Supermarine S-6bs was

flown to a world speed record of 407 mph, using a specially souped-up engine which gave 2,530 hp. In 1939 the Germans, flying a Messerschmitt Bf "109R", raised the record to 469 mph.

There were, of course, other races. The reasons for entering them were twofold. They attracted great publicity and in a dull period provided considerable excitement, especially as a running commentary could be given on the new public radio systems and the races could be seen in newsreels at local cinemas. In theory, the winner brought in orders to the manufacturer and recruits to the service. But a more important reason for racing was the chance to prove engines and airframes under something like operational conditions. The Schneider Trophy aircraft led directly to fighter designs used in the Second World War. Experience was gained with monoplanes before the world's air forces were willing to accept them, and engines were boosted to horsepowers which would not become operational for another ten years or more. Contests for prestige provided a way in which both manufacturers and the services could put pressure on governments for funds to pay for experimental work.

Experimental work, of course, was the heart of peacetime air forces, because it enabled them to keep up-to-date so that when a war started their equipment would match that of the enemy. The real problem lay in balancing an operational plane with a much better one on the designer's drawing board. To do this, money was put into prototypes whose fate often rested in the hands of a test pilot or two and upon the impression the machine made in flying past the groundbound top brass. In some air forces, however, new machines had to pass airborne handling by senior officers with results that were sometimes fatal to both. In others each mediocre aircraft arrived with a case of champagne, and the judgment was based more on its alcoholic than its octane rating.

Equal to speed in importance was altitude, for the fighter with the greater altitude always had an advantage. In 1920 the Americans captured the record at 33,000 feet; by 1930 it had been pushed up to 43,000; and in 1938 it went to the Italians with 56,000. By 1942 photo reconnaissance aircraft were operating at 50,000 feet. The benefits from pursuing these records accrued mostly in the areas of cold-weather technology, pressure suits, oxygen systems, and meteorology. All of these were important both to aviation medicine generally and to fighter, PRU, and bomber technology specifically,

Fairey Fox

Fiat CR-42

Czech (single-seater)

Hs-123

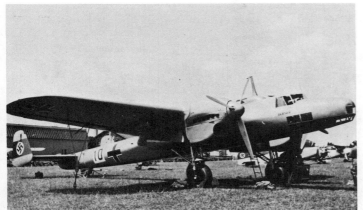

Do-17

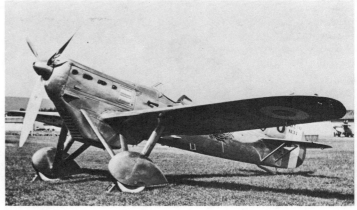

Dewoitine D-510

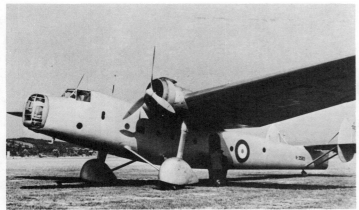

Bristol Bombay

Hawker Hart

Seen in the Mid-Thirties

DH 51

Ju 52

Bucker 133

Consolidated PT-1

Bucker Jungman

DH 88

Ju 86

FW-200

Curtiss P-6E Hawk & P-26.

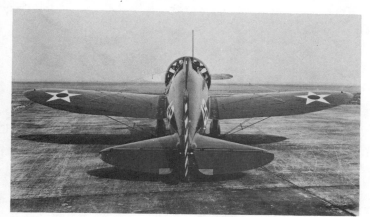

P-26A

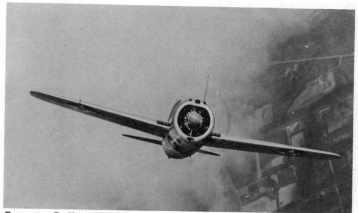

Brewster Buffalo XP2A-1

Curtiss 75a

Grumman FM-4F

Bristol Bulldog

Supermarine Spitfire

Bomber Development, 1920-1940

Curtiss NSB-1

Martin B-10

HP Heyford

Vickers Wellesley

Boeing B-17

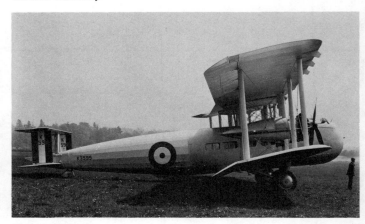

Vickers Valentia

Fiat BR-20

Bristol Bombay

By the mid-thirties the Soviets were operating large four-engined aircraft not so much as strategic bombers, since they had little use for them in spite of the original Sikorskis, but as parachute-troop transports. **USAF** In contrast in the United States where the nucleus of the USAAC bomber leaders were working out their theories at the Air University at Maxwell, AL, the trend was towards strategic bombing aircraft of great range, a program that led on one leg to the experimental Douglas XB-19 of 1940. **McDonnell Douglas**

though for a long time not nearly enough attention was paid to crew comfort and flying fatigue.

But in view of the avowed strategies of the British, American, and Italian air forces and of their need to protect shipping, the records they should have been most interested in were for range. For in attempting to span the greatest distance non-stop, men and machines faced many of the problems which bomber and ocean reconnaissance crews would have to combat. Long-range flight called for absolute reliability in engines, economy of operation, comfortable crew positions, and excellence at both day and night navigation. The machine used also had to be capable of lifting very large quantities of fuel. The first post-war attempts were to cross the Atlantic and to reach the outer colonies of the European colonial empires, and these experiments, mostly with war-surplus aircraft, focused on the long-distance record. In 1925 the French held it with a flight of 1,967 miles; by 1929 they had raised it to 4,911, but in 1938 the RAF captured it with 7,158 miles, an achievement made the more remarkable by the fact that the two aircraft which accomplished this non-stop feat were single-engined machines, as was the Soviet aircraft which flew over the North Pole to California.

The Italians with their genius for showmanship undertook long-range mass formation journeys, following the lead the United States Army had set in its 1924 round-the-world flight. General Italo Balbo led a massed formation of twelve Savoia S-55 flying-boats across the Atlantic and back. The Italians also participated in polar flying and in giving aerobatic demonstrations, at which they excelled.

But again, peacetime and display formation tactics did not always prove as valuable as they were thought to be. What looked wonderful at an air display became downright vulnerable in combat, and it took real warfare to bring about more effective deployment. In fighter squadrons, the symmetrical *vic* of three was replaced with the functional pair, and bombers tended to group into defensive 'hedgehogs' or flying boxes. In any case, apart from formation, the validity of a defensive system depended upon its firepower vis-à-vis opposing fighters and upon the provision of adequate close and distant fighter escorts.

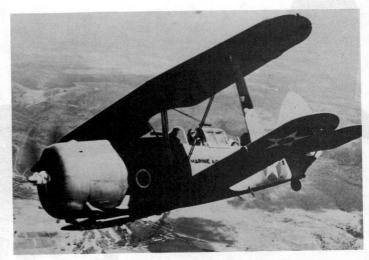

The US Navy went in for compact shipboard dive-bombers such as the biplane Curtiss SBC Helldiver of the Marines. **US Navy**

4. Operations

Fortunately for their technical progress, some air forces were allowed to participate in occasional wars. In the conflicts of the twenties only one side, generally, had aircraft, but in the thirties there were several real tests.

The wars of the twenties were mostly colonial skirmishes in which a European power equipped with a war-surplus squadron or two engaged in reconnaissance and punitive sorties with general-purpose aircraft against rebellious or over-exuberant tribesmen along the frontiers of valuable imperial holdings. The effects of these actions may well have been overrated, but so far little study has been devoted to them, even though the British use of air policing was one of the major innovations in aviation, and even though operations from Aden went on for some forty-five years (a fact which raises some question as to their effectiveness). In addition to the general-purpose two-seater fighter-bomber and single-seaters, these actions also saw the use of twin-engine heavy bomber-transports, whose most spectacular action was the evacuation of the British colony from Kabul, Afghanistan, in 1928.

In many ways the Italian campaign in Ethiopia in 1935–36 was also simply a colonial operation, since it pitted a modern army and air force against a feudal, medieval country. Yet in spite of the fact that the Italians enjoyed overwhelming air superiority and employed gas, and in spite of the internal dissensions of the Ethopians and their faulty ground tactics, it took the Italians eight months to conquer the country and another year to finish pacifying it. And all this occurred at a time when the *Regia Aeronautica* was at its peak with new equipment and a fine professional force in its ranks. The use of gas aroused considerable ire, but it was not particularly effective in the field, and modern operational research analysts would probably argue that it was an inefficient weapon. Certainly, airborne gas was not favoured by other air forces since it was easily protected against in addition to being heavy to carry and awkward to dispense accurately.

Much more significant for the use of air power were two other conflicts, the wars in China and Spain, of which only the latter was

Just before the US involvement in World War II, Ed Heinemann of Douglas designed the rugged SBD Dauntless, which served the USN as a dive-bomber throughout the 1941-45 war. **McDonnell Douglas**

The relatively simple front (above) and rear (below) cockpits of the Curtiss SBC Helldiver are shown in these two pictures. The Pilot's was taken in a hangar resulting in extra clutter in the windshield. The rear cockpit contained the radio-man/gunner. Both show the state of the art in 1938. **US Navy**

really known to western advocates of air power. The Manchurian Incident of 1931 coincided with the emergence of aircraft designed and built in Japan by the Japanese themselves. In the events that followed, Japanese air power was of first-class significance. In subsequent actions against China, the Japanese had things much their own way, for the sky held few Chinese fighters and virtually no bombers. The reasons for this were the old Chinese warlordism which constantly eroded the central control of their forces, coupled with graft and inefficiency. In addition, many Chinese pilots were mercenaries who arrived in the Far East claiming to be aces, but who, as Chennault later found, could wreck a whole air force in a day all by themselves. In general the lessons must be drawn from the Japanese side. With superior aircraft and airmen they quickly dispatched the opposing air force by a combination of swift bombing attacks upon airfields and brisk fighter battles. Once freed from opposition, Japanese bombers engaged in grand-strategic raids against Chinese cities. At the same time, however, the Japanese tended to become over-confident, with the result that occasionally the remnants of the Chinese Air Force could strike a blow; on one occasion they caught Imperial Naval fighter and bomber squadrons drawn up in neat rows on a Chinese airfield and ruined nearly all 200 aircraft. And when in 1939 the Japanese found themselves compelled again to fight the Soviets along the northern Manchurian border, as they had off and on since 1929, they made little progress and were forced to fight a defensive air war to maintain the status quo on the ground.

Nevertheless, in the meantime, the Japanese had been getting valuable experience. Starting in the summer of 1937 they had undertaken long-range raids of some 1,250 miles in which naval Mitsubishi Nells bombed the Chinese positions around Shanghai to support a beleaguered Japanese marine garrison there. Based on Kyushu and Formosa, the Nells made long over-water raids in many kinds of weather, and the Japanese learned that neither Nells nor carrier-based bombers were immune to enemy fighters and that they must have cover. In one raid, when the carrier *Kaga* launched a strike of twelve Val bombers, they missed their escort and eleven were shot

down. *Kaga* was at once ordered home to take on a full complement of Claude fighters, and thereafter her escorted bomber formations were not molested.

After a series of air battles in late 1937, the Chinese moved their bases out of range of marauding Japanese fighters; but the Japanese countered by setting up advanced refuelling fields so that their fighters could make very-long-range sorties, thus achieving the advantage of surprise and again catching the Chinese on the ground. Naval aircraft also acted in a tactical role for the army, and naval airmen came out of the war with two convictions: that naval aircraft could operate over land and that the key to success was command of the air. Moreover, naval airmen argued that the special demands for range which they had made were justified, as it gave them a greater radius of action than had so far been considered by others, a factor especially important in the Pacific and in China where targets were scattered over vast distances. But the younger officers who had done the fighting still faced in both the navy and the army frustrating conservatism in the High Commands, which continued to insist that the air weapon was auxiliary and not of itself a prime instrument for victory.

Japanese bombers striking the withdrawn Chinese airfields were suffering high casualties, but in late 1938 the Mitsubishi Zero became available. The Zero, a sleek monoplane fighter with long-range fuel tanks, gave the bombers continuous escort, and even raids against Chunking, started in May 1940, were escorted for the entire thousand-mile round trip. It would be another eighteen months before a former American fighter pilot, observing these actions from the ground, would begin to have his revenge.

All his life Claire Chennault was a late comer. Dispatched to China after being retired from the USAAC, the author of *The Role of Pursuit Aviation,* he had had a stunted career in the bomber-minded Army Air Corps. In 1934 an American air mission had been forced out of China by Japanese pressure on Washington. Four years later Chennault arrived in the theatre, inherited a Keystone Cops air force which managed to write itself off in training accidents, and settled down to observe the Japanese and establish an early-warning network, while waiting for diplomatic, economic, martial, and physical impediments to a new Chinese air force to be removed. In 1940 it was decided to build the Burma Road, and in 1941 Franklin Roosevelt declared for all-out aid to China. But it was not until the end of 1941 that the idea of defending the Burma Road was accepted and 100 Curtiss P-40 fighters, declared by the British

THE SAGA OF A SMALLER AIR FORCE —
the Royal Swedish Air Force to 1939
All photos courtesy of the RSAF

One of the first requirements with which armies burdened air services was that aircraft had to be able to march with the troops. A French-built Bleriot is seen being prepared to go on the 1915 maneuvers and on the road.

The first aeroplane in the Swedish national defence forces was built at Landskrona and presented to the Navy by the director of a Stockholm brewery. This Bleriot was flown by Swedish aviator No. 3 who was trained in London. By 1917 Sweden was building the Thulin K, a 1917 copy of the early WWI French Moraine-Saulnier fighter, but with skis for the local weather.

When at the end of July 1914 the first German Albatros biplane landed and overturned in a field near Stockholm, the Army took it over and it became the model for a great number of the type built in Swedish factories and equipped with locally-made Mercedes engines of German design. Early flying instruction in Sweden as elsewhere was given in private schools. Here Baron Carl Söderström, who had trained with Bleriot in France in 1910, stands in front of a Bleriot with his Army pupils and mechanics.

By 1923 structural design was becoming better understood and in the land of wood craftsmanship, the wooden monoplane was making progress. Here the designer, test pilot, and staff test the wing of a new Malmen J-23 fighter.

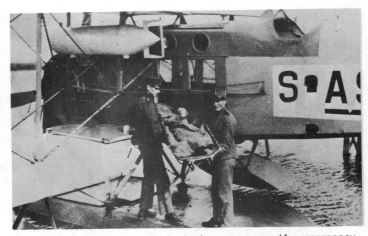

In a flat country such as Sweden which was full of lakes, in much of the year seaplanes made good sense for both passenger and for emergency service. Here a Breguet ambulance, another French design, of the Swedish Red Cross is seen operating in Laplandia flown by an Army crew.

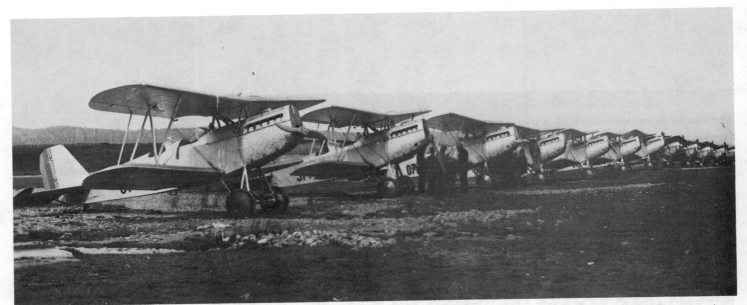

Popular trainers in 1929 were these Heinkel HD 36's of German design, where they compared with the Swedish built Fokker C V-E's across the field at F5 Flying Training School.

Starting in 1928 the very popular British De Havilland Moth series of trainers were introduced, with the DH-82 Tiger Moth coming into service in 1933. However, by 1936 the Swedes considered it was altogether too easy to fly and began replacing it with the German Focke-Wulf Fw-44.

The 1920's saw the development and refinement of the big rigid airship and the 1930's its demise. Here the US Navy's **Akron** flies near the entrance to the Panama Canal. **Source unknown.**

to be too obsolete for use in Europe, were made available. In the meantime, Chennault had been allowed clandestinely to recruit experienced flyers in the United States. Both flyers and crated aircraft were in Rangoon when Pearl Harbor was struck. What Chennault then proceeded to prove was that a professional force, even with outdated equipment, when properly led with an understanding of the enemy's tactics and weaknesses, could first fight a defensive battle and win it and then go over to the offensive. Forced to operate on the cheap, Chennault made his outfit economic, efficient, and effective, because he could not afford to have it be otherwise. He put into practice the ideas he had written about, which showed—a lesson the Japanese had already learned from the Chinese—that the bomber was unlikely to get through if opposed in the air unless properly escorted. He made plain that early warning prevents surprise and that a defence against attack is always possible if properly undertaken. While Chennault's study of the Japanese saved many American lives in the Pacific theatre, his work could also have been usefully studied in Europe, where bomber losses were unnecessarily high until the arrival of proper escort fighters in 1944.

But it was the war in Spain from 1936 to 1939 which was seen in the West as the most significant combat experience prior to the Second World War. Here on both sides there were professional airmen and modern equipment, some sent officially and others voluntarily. In Spain air power was not, however, decisive, even if the neutral press, just as in China, played up horror stories of bombings of civilians and the glories of aerial combat.

In addition to the Spanish air force, three regular air forces fought over Spain: the Soviet, the Italian, and the German. From elsewhere came volunteers, though the British, French and American governments held strictly aloof. The French, however, supplied aircraft, so at least to that extent their equipment was tested in war.

The Soviet air contribution to the Spanish Civil War was a politically involved one. Since there was a mistrust of those sent abroad and a general suspicion of air force personnel, those sent to Spain from mid-1936 onwards were captains and above. They flew I-15 and I-16 fighters and fast SB-2 twin-engine bombers. Their commander, General Smushkevich, succeeded Alksins, the Commander-in-Chief of the Soviet Air Force when the latter was executed in 1938. All told, the Soviets had about 1,500 aircraft in Spain for

some two years, of which at any one time perhaps a third were serviceable. Soviet personnel obtained lots of experience, but the air force's showing was not high, in part owing to Nationalist possession of the German Me-109 fighter, which was easily the best combat machine in Spain. Its appearance in quantity in the summer of 1938 caused Stalin to withdraw his air contingents. At home the Soviet aircraft industry found it hard to explain its failure to develop a comparable fighter, except that it was not so much design as production know-how which was the trouble. The other Soviet lesson was the inaccuracy of their bomber forces, a problem which was not theirs alone. Even the much-vaunted German Condor Legion had the same troubles.

The *Luftwaffe* became involved shortly after it came into the open as the revived German Air Force, and Goering was determined to use Spain as a real testing ground. Germans who had been running training establishments in the Soviet Union and who had themselves done a post-graduate course with the Italian *Regia Aeronautica* in 1935 were sent to gain experience. And for the Germans it was just as well that they were, for the *Luftwaffe*, whose historical section had had to work quietly and had been unable to publish, had forgotten a great deal. In Spain it fought primarily against Soviet machines. At first its He-51 biplane fighters found themselves outclassed by the newer Soviet I-16s with retractable undercarriage, and its Ju-52/3m transport-bombers were too slow. But by 1938 the Me-109 was on hand as a fighter and the He-111 and the Do-17 as bombers, either of which could out-run most opposing fighters.

What nearly defeated the Germans at first were their own tactical formations, which made no use of the lessons of the First World War. In tight formations, so beloved for showing-off in peacetime, there was no room to manoeuvre and too little time to look around for opponents while holding an exacting position. So the German fighters quickly went back to pairs, with two pairs to a finger-of-four, and twelve aircraft all told to a squadron. A loose formation, this was far more flexible and much less easy to surprise. Using the force tactically, the Germans quickly developed a forward air controller system so that aircraft could be vectored in visually to targets in front of the troops. If anything, the Germans in Spain gained a reputation for ruthlessness and efficiency, and perhaps never more so than in the bombing of the market town of Guernica, in which

The Changing Aircraft-Carrier

Taking off from **Langley**.

Vickers Vildebeeste

USS **Ranger**

USS **Yorktown**

*Off the Panama Canal the **Akron** releases one of her scouting aircraft (in circle), giving an idea of the size of these giant airships.* **Source unknown, but original defective.**

*One of the US Navy's two Washington Treaty battlecruiser-hull conversions to aircraft-carriers, the U.S. **Saratoga** off the Panama Canal in the early 1930's. With their 33 knots these ships were about ten knots faster than the battle fleet of the day.*

The Growth of the Airliner

In the 1920's and early 1930's, thanks to the technological revolution, the transport aeroplane grew from the single-engined biplane flown by a pilot esconced in the open to a reliable craft with both passengers and crew in a comfortable enclosed fuselage. The Northrop Alpha line of which the Ellsworth expedition plane was one represented the beginning of the great transition epitomized by the Douglas DC-3.

Canadian Royal Mail

Junkers W-13

Bellanca

Fokker F-7

Boeing 226

"Ellsworth"

Boeing 247D

247D cockpit

247D interior of cabin.

DC-2

DC-3's

Lodestar

Beech 18

Beech 18 cockpit

Dassault, type 220

Boeing 304

The German Ju-52 was a very popular pre-war transport and the backbone of the German Air Force's transport and paratroop fleet in World War II. These two aircraft belong to the **South African Airways.**

In spite of the revolution, some companies, such as **De Havilland,** continued to use steel tubing and fabric coverings to produce light, practical, efficient transports such as the DH-89.

The two big users of flying-boats down to the 1939 War were Pan American World Airways and Imperial Airways. The former had most of its boats designed and built by Martin or **Sikorsky**, whose S-42 shown here helped pioneer the North Atlantic routes. Imperial Airways stuck with Shorts, which produced the admirable, if rather small Empire class in the mid-1930's, designed basically for the imperial routes rather than the long transoceanic hops. **BOAC**

the object was to try out the bombing of cities rather than to break a strategic bridge. The attacks started with fighters strafing the crowded market-place; then followed methodical high-explosive bombing; and last came a deluge of incendiaries. Out of some 10,000 people, 1,600, mostly civilians, died. International charges of immorality did not improve the image of the Condor Legion.

The Italian contribution, like the German, started with helping Franco consolidate the Nationalist position on the mainland by ferrying troops over from Morocco. Like the Germans, too, the Italians were able to use their bomber-transports to good effect to keep supplies flowing and aircraft airborne. At the same time their bombing raids acted as a blockade of the southern Spanish ports. Ironically the Germans failed to understand the real significance of this aerial blockade and thus lost the economic battle of Britain in the spring of 1941.

5. Attitudes at the Outbreak of War

The first period of peace in the air-power history to cover a whole cycle from demobilization to rearmamental instability, the inter-war years provided many lessons for the future. Retaining the memory of an unnatural stalemated war, air forces tended to forget that the most effective wars are those of mobility in which basic equipment must be constantly adapted to new uses in both a technological and tactical chess game. Those air forces which were best prepared for the Second World War were those which had had their showmanship attitudes destroyed by the realities of combat. And the most effective air forces were the tactical ones which had the power to effect decisions on the surface by striking at the immediate military threats. Yet, it was not easy in peacetime in a highly political, economy-minded situation to gain support for even obvious short-term goals. To be successful, air forces had to play peacetime politics as a mixture of economics, public relations, and fear. Airmen tended to be blunt and to overlook the fact that indirect action can be as effective as and much cheaper than direct. It can be argued, of course, that this was the game being played by the democracies whose grand strategy was essentially reactive. But those whose move is based upon the enemy's taking the initiative must be provided with up-to-date equipment and ideas in the hands of professionals. Whether or not this requires numerical superiority is a moot question. So is the problem of determining what is enough defensive power and how nearly ready it is. The answers have to be found in planning which takes into account both grand-strategic desires and political and diplomatic as well as military realities. Readiness may well be conditioned not only by the supply of money but by whether or not the logistics plan is in step with grand strategy, if indeed the two have been linked at all. Even when there is centralized control, policies may not be executed centrally or soundly.

All of these things are closely tied to intelligence of enemy plans and abilities. These in their turn must be analyzed without wishful thinking as must the preparation of one's allies. In the period before the Second World War, Allied eyes were fixed on Germany and Japan, but neglected to look at France, Poland, Czechoslovakia, or Italy. Moreover, air forces were generally so offensively-minded that they failed to consider defensive measures adequately.

By the time peace ended in 1939 the air weapon was very much more sophisticated than it had been in 1918, owing largely to scientific and technological developments. But mentally there was a large disparity between those air forces that saw their role as strategic and those which regarded themselves as the hand-maiden of a surface service. As events were to show, the latter could often destroy the forces in the field before strategic bombers could have a paralyzing effect. By 1939 air power was no longer ancillary; it was a force in itself but not by itself.

By World War II when the Lockheed 18 was converted into the Hudson patrol bomber, aircraft construction had become largely an all-metal affair with rivets replacing nails as the principal fasteners.

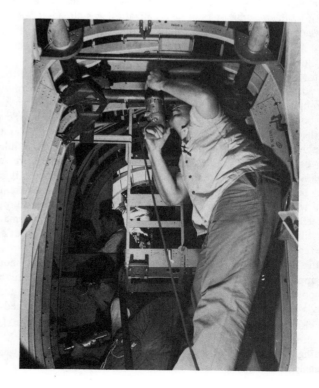

PART FOUR

The Second World War: Land-Based Air Power

By the Second World War flying was no longer a fair-weather sport, but a serious business. Ed Link invented the first widely-used simulators in which pilots learnt blind-flying. **Singer**

1. Preparation and Progress in Equipment, Training, and Command

In many respects the story of air power in the Second World War is one of continuity, both from pre-war peacetime and with the peace that followed. The war started in the middle of rearmamental instability, and wartime equilibrium was not reached until 1942-1943; by the autumn of 1944 demobilization was already beginning. It was a time of almost continuous change, of growth, and of constant technological progress, and it was also a period of history that gave rise to myths which die hard.

In analyses of the conflict, too much importance has often been placed on the glamorous events and too little on the sinews of war. Too often the tale has been of battle and too seldom of the realities, the boredom, and the long quiet applications of power. Moreover, in the historical study of air power in the Second World War the emphasis has been at best strategic and not grand-strategic. While it can be argued that the Pacific and the war at sea in general are separate subjects which can be treated in a parallel chapter, it can also be shown that the use of air power over land must be treated as a whole. In particular, the use of Allied air power over Europe, especially the so-called strategic air offensive against Germany, must be assessed in terms of the overall objectives of the Allies and the resources at their disposal.

In all of these assessments the principles of war can be and should be applied. That they have not been has been due both to the tunnel-vision of many writers and to the insistence of airmen that theirs was a new world. The use of air power was of course governed by the vision of its leadership and the willingness or failure of air staffs to accept the judgments of those who had seen combat firsthand. During the latter part of rearmamental instability there was a struggle to convince the leadership that air power could not do

what it said it could do and '*homo lagiens*', the human lag factor, came into play once again. At the same time, what had been learned in peacetime carried over into the war years. Those air forces which had had the benefit of combat experience moved ahead more rapidly and successfully. But those which started late and suffered early defeats, such as the Chinese, American, Soviet, and British, by learning the hard way ultimately, perhaps, learned better. They also operated, of course, from protected arsenals out of reach of an Axis which lacked long-range grand-strategic bombers with fighter escorts.

Just as the First World War saw tremendous strides in technology, so did the Second. Two air forces, the German and the British, started the war still with some biplane fighters, but ended it with a few jets. They started with visual early-warning and ended with airborne radar. The British started with 500-lb bombs and ended with 22,000-pounders. Speeds rose from 300 to 600 mph, while fighting heights rose to 30,000 feet and in exceptional cases reached 50,000.

The whole problem of locating the enemy began to be solved. While relative speeds in combat remained much the same, overall speeds were rising, and it became vital, especially at night, to be able to identify friend and foe. Visual signals were developed, first pyrotechnics, then lights, and finally a radar pulse called IFF Identification Friend or Foe). And where in 1939 an intercepting fighter pilot might be given a rough course, height, and location of the enemy, based upon ground observers' sightings, by 1945 he was vectored onto his airborne target by a ground controller or by his radar observer, whose information was fine enough to place him in shooting position. As the RAF learned in 1944 to provide night-fighter escort in the bomber streams (a lesson that the Japanese in the Far East had learned earlier in daylight raids), identification became still more critical. The war saw the development of techniques for making targets at night and for controlling the bombers operating over them, using combinations of radar, pyrotechnics, and radio-telephone worked both from home bases and by pathfinders

Primary training in the United States was generally in the "yellow peril," no matter what the air force. **Boeing** Kaydets.

In the American system the next step was from the primary trainer (the PT) into the basic (BT), of which the most widely used was the Vultee BT-13. **Convair/General Dynamics**

on the spot. Such achievements were major elements in the ultimate effectiveness of the bomber offensive against Germany.

Much more than the 1914 air war, this one was fought on the ground. It was not merely a war of flying equipment, it was a struggle between competing industrial systems. Design and production were important, but equally vital were materials, machine tools, and manpower. Forced once again to consider the total production picture, all air forces went back to the salvage and repair operations so cheerfully abandoned in peacetime, with the result that up to 35 per cent of some air forces were composed of rebuilt machines and equipment. This was a war, too, of technicians in radar laboratories, on direction-finding and listening posts, and on airfields. The latter in themselves became immensely important as the new heavier planes brought into being by the technological revolution of the thirties could no longer be operated off grass, but required concrete runways. Constructing the standard three-runway airfield involved moving some 30,000 tons of materials, just for the runways, not to mention revetted dispersal areas, fuel dumps, hangars, shops, stores, and living quarters. While such fields were fine in static warfare, they could not be produced overnight in the fluctuating campaigns which took place other than along the English Channel line. Thus a whole new organization had to be created to manufacture portable airfield materials and manage the rapid movement of entire landing grounds so that air support was always close to the battlefront. In the Italian theatre and in the Pacific this was even taken so far as to use aircraft carriers as airfields for covering air forces until bases could be established within the newly-won beachheads.

In such a technological war, aircrew also became of prime importance. Recruitment was rarely if ever a problem. Many were willing to become airmen because of the glamourous and, in theory, romantic consequences. But even with lowered physical and educational standards, not all were taken. Training depended upon the availability of planes, fuel, facilities, airspace, and instructors. The British and the Americans were best off in that they had vast unneeded air spaces in suitable weather belts and close to fuel supplies; training could be carried out in Canada and the United States as well as in South Africa without molestation by enemy intruders and without the penalties of fuel shortages. Moreover, the Allies did not make the German mistake of using instructors on hazardous

operations. They did suffer from the need to make use of instructors without war experience. While systems varied, in 1940 British fighter pilots had 150 hours of experience before entering combat, and by late 1944 they were getting 275 hours before they received their wings. By December 1944 the RAF had a year's supply of aircrew on hand and the training programme was being slowed down. While the Americans used a three-stage system to the award of pilot's wings and then further schooling before assignment to an operational squadron, the RAF used a two-stage programme. After pre-flight school, American cadets were given instruction and soloed in primary trainers, then moved to basic, and finally to advanced aircraft with variable-pitch propellers, retractable undercarriages, and radio aids. Meanwhile, for bombers, other members of the crew went to specialist schools and then to a gunnery course before reporting to an operational training unit for crewing and training on the type of craft to be used in combat. By mid-war pilots were getting instrument-flying instruction in Link trainers. while others were given work in primitive simulators.

Once a crew had completed six operational sorties it was regarded as invaluable, and all air forces became increasingly anxious to recover downed aircrew as well as aircraft. Air/sea rescue teams were developed, using special amphibians or high-speed launches, and on the east coast of Britain two large airfields, Manston and Woodbridge, were established which were essentially enormous (3,000 x 250 yards) concrete areas where badly damaged aircraft could be crash-landed and assisted by special rescue crews. Much work was also done to develop means of homing lost and strayed aircraft by vectoring fighters in to guide them. For airmen fighting over their own territories recovery was a less serious problem; for them new aircraft could be more critical. But for those airmen who landed in enemy territory escape rarely succeeded, and the vast majority spent the rest of the war in prison camps.

The air war depended, much more than its proponents for some time realized, on the gathering of immense amounts of economic as well as military intelligence. For effective grand-strategic bombing, it was necessary to possess precise details of an opponent's economic and business resources, inventory, and habits, as well as simply to be aware of his military installations. The air weapon was a rapier and not a sledgehammer. It had to be aimed at small vital spots and thrust in quickly, sometimes repeatedly, to be effective. For that to be done, air commanders had to know economic anatomy, and their sword arms had to be highly trained, well armoured and accurate.

At the start of hostilities in 1939 the warring air forces could be ranked in terms of their re-equipment as follows: The Germans were reaching their peak and basically fought the war with what they had in production then. The Italians had peaked in 1937 and though some of their equipment, such as the Macchi and Fiat monoplane fighters, was excellent, by 1940 it was already becoming dated and little was done to modernize it. Both the French, in a very small way, and the British, were in the midst of re-equipment programmes, but these were not expected to be completed until 1942. The Soviet Air Force was just undertaking to re-arm itself after the Spanish experience; it had already moved factories east of the Urals, in part to supply its separate Far Eastern air force facing the Japanese, who like the Germans were about at their peak in 1939. The United States, though possessing advanced airliners, was between re-equipments. The naval air force was in fighting trim, but the equipment of the US Army Air Corps was nearly obsolete and Congress was still being stingy. Roosevelt's 50,000-aircraft programme was still a year away.

The world's leading land-based air force was the German, the leading naval one, the Japanese. In fighters this meant the Messerschmitt Me-109 and the Mitsubishi Zero. Both were low-wing single-engine aircraft with a top speed of about 350 mph, a ceiling of 30,000 ft, a radius of action of 300 to 1,000 miles (the Zero was designed especially for long-range missions), and an armament of cannon and machine-guns. Both air forces possessed dive-bombers and twin-engine bombers. In the former category were the Ju-87 and the Val, single-engine aircraft capable of carrying a 2,000-lb bombload, but vulnerable to fighters when not in a dive. The German Heinkel He-111 introduced during the war in Spain was a fast, streamlined twin-engine bomber, indifferently armed but carrying a 5,500-lb bombload at 225 mph for 670 miles at 25,000 ft. By the end of the war the United States air forces possessed probably the world's best equipment, although the Soviet Shturmovik ground-attack aircraft was in something of a class by itself. The North American P-51 Mustang fighter was outclassed only by the German

and British jets just becoming operational. The P-51, with its 1,450 hp engine, maximum speed of 437 mph, and a ceiling of 40,000 ft, could bring six .50 calibre machine-guns and ten 5-inch rockets or two 1,000-lb bombs into action over a range of nearly 1,200 miles from base. The US Navy Grumman Hellcat with a slightly higher horsepower and a considerably higher weight was somewhat slower. Except for the USN's Curtiss Helldivers, attack aircraft were largely rugged fighters turned fighter-bombers and armed with bombs or rockets as well as 20-mm cannon. Bombers which because of their bomb loads had been considered heavies in 1939 had by 1945 become medium bombers; the North American B-25 Mitchell and the versatile De Havilland Mosquito were the best representatives, with variations ranging from level bombers to anti-shipping aircraft fitted with up to 75-mm cannon. Moreover, the Mosquito had replaced the German He-111 and Do-17 of the Spanish Civil War as the unarmed bomber which could outrun fighters. In the heavy class were the British Avro Lancaster, which could carry up to a 22,000-lb bomb, and the American Boeing B-29 with its stripped performance of 367 mph at 30,000 ft with 16,000 lbs of bombs over a range of 2,600 miles.

Vastly complicating the logistics problems of the war in the air was the great increase in weight and complexity between 1939 and 1945. The He-111 had an all-up weight of 25,000 lbs, while the B-29 weighed 135,000. Even fighters more than doubled in size from the approximately 5,000 lbs of 1939 to the Mustang's 12,000 lbs. Weight was by no means the only measure of change. By the end of the war a Lancaster carried a Mark XIV gyro bombsight and radar for navigation and defence, not to mention a large number of machine-guns, though these were not very effective, and photoflash devices both for photographing the impact of the bombs and for defence against fighters. All of this meant a drastic increase in the number of man-hours needed to produce aircraft, and the creation and training of much larger ground crews. At the same time, as enemy defences became better, up to 25 per cent of the force sent out might be lost or so badly damaged as not to be available for operations the next day. The need for spare parts led to the development of techniques for handling the supply of parts on an estimated replacement basis, and ultimately to breakthroughs in mathematical techniques.

*Air war meant bombing, either tactical, strategic or grand strategic. Here ground crew load bombs into **Beech** AT-11 Kansans preparatory to target practice.*

Airfields were both essential and popular targets. This French field northwest of Paris testifies both to the accuracy and the inaccuracy of USAAF 8th AF bombers on 4 July 1943. **USAF**

The whole question of making better use of what was available led to the creation of a scientific organization concerned with operational research whose personnel studied all aspects of the war in the air. At first these 'boffins' were unpopular with commanding officers and others, but as the value of their work came to be recognized they were increasingly in demand. All this led to another dilemma: more and more, instead of attempting to solve their own problems, commanders called for a boffin to do it for them, with the result that there began to be a shortage of these scientists, who were diverted from finding longer-range solutions. Even worse, commanders began to rely upon them to make judgments which were not within the boffin's competence or responsibility. And not only boffins had influence. Even more than in the First World War, staffs included sharp civilian minds with no career at stake who disputed, sometimes dominated, and often guided the thinking of senior commanders with their wider experience of the world and forceful logic. All of these things varied, of course, within different air forces in accordance with national characteristics as influenced by traditions, and according to combat losses, accidents, and personalities.

Nor must it be forgotten that the use of air power built up very gradually. For instance, only 17 per cent of the bombs dropped on Germany by the Allies had been delivered before 1944; and in the Battle of Britain, when Air Marshal Dowding was protecting the whole nation from a German aerial onslaught, he had only about 600 fighters available. Constant aerial activity could be misleading to observers on the ground. Much less than in the First World War were aircrews thrown continuously into combat if flight surgeons could prevent it and if operations did not call for it. The whole concept of tours of duty helped limit the time during which aircrews were subjected to the tensions of combat. American heavy bomber and fighter crews were unwilling to continue in combat as they approached the 200-hour mark. Recognition of this factor had its advantages in an air force with a growing pool of trained personnel, for it meant that those with combat experience could be phased into the training command to provide the no-nonsense reality which such systems were apt to lack when staffed for too long by people wedded to established, even peacetime, procedures.

The success or failure of air power in the war was not merely a matter of equipment and command; it was also intimately linked to anti-aircraft defence, which was sometimes an air force but more often an army responsibility and which thus necessitated liaison at all levels. This was particularly important for rapidly advancing armies and at sea, where sailors tended to shoot first and ask afterwards.

Throughout the 1939 war air power remained both a constant presence and a special force, and its capabilities were often over-rated by its friends and under-rated by its enemies.

2. *Blitzkrieg* and Airborne Campaigns*

Europe and North Africa. Though the war in Spain was a testing ground for air power, it did not see the realization of *blitzkrieg* tactics. These were first made evident in the German Polish campaign at the end of the summer of 1939, but the dazzling speed of that performance led unbelievers to discredit evidence of such tactics in favour of other more acceptable and traditional explanations for the German successes. This was a mistake for which they paid dearly in the summer of 1940.

The secret of the German *blitzkrieg* lay in meticulous planning coupled with lightning strikes to unbalance the opponent and render

* The term *blitzkrieg,* while normally associated with German mechanized operations in the years 1939 through 1941, can be equally well applied to some Allied operations in the sense that it consisted of a combination of armour, infantry, and air power providing a fast striking force. It is so used here in connection with the wave pattern. The Germans were shifting from rearmamental instability to wartime equilibrium in their *blitzkreig* operations by the summer of 1940, whereas both the western Allies and the Soviets were still rearming until late 1941 or early 1942. In the development of tactical air forces cooperating with ground forces the most significant change after wartime equilibrium was reached was in terms of numbers and power of weapons systems. For this reason, then, little is said of either Allied operations in Italy or after D-Day, or of Soviet support of the Red armies after Stalingrad, because in terms of historical lessons or techniques these contribute little to what can be gleaned from earlier operations. The same comments apply to the development of air transport support operations. The Germans set the style; others simply improved on it.

Three British Commonwealth Air Training Plan students in Canada in summer and winter uniforms relax against a Harvard (AT-6). **RCAF.** *Cadets were an expensive, but vital resource.*

The Evolution of Engines and Propellers

Anxious not to become enslaved to one engine firm, the US Navy encouraged the old established Hartford, Connecticut, toolmaking firm of Pratt & Whitney to enter the business. The company soon successfully created the air-cooled Wasp radial, then joined two together to make the Twin Wasp, and continued to develop the power of their piston engines to about 3,000 hp before the jet took over. To absorb the increased output, metal propellers were needed, and as part of the technological revolution the company became involved in Hamilton propellers. These interests and other eventually became consolidated in the present company, **United Technologies.**

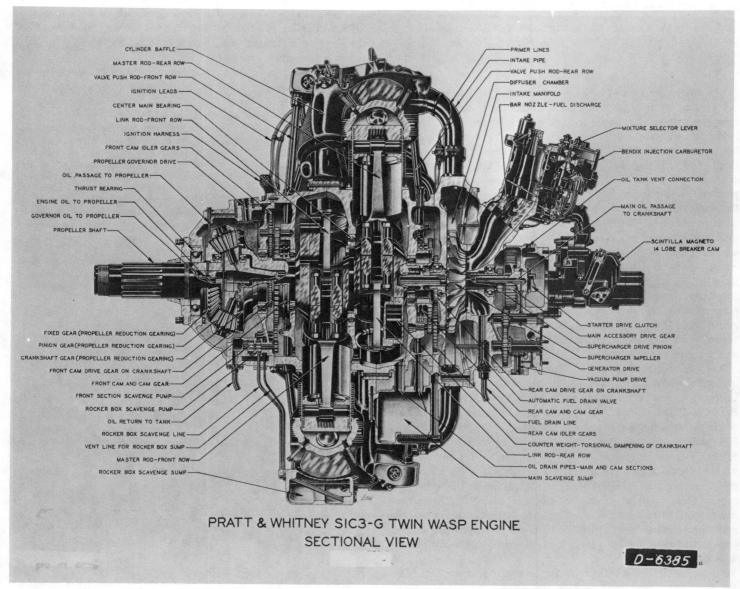

CYLINDER BAFFLE
MASTER ROD-REAR ROW
VALVE PUSH ROD-FRONT ROW
IGNITION LEADS
CENTER MAIN BEARING
LINK ROD-FRONT ROW
IGNITION HARNESS
FRONT CAM IDLER GEARS
PROPELLER GOVERNOR DRIVE
OIL PASSAGE TO PROPELLER
THRUST BEARING
ENGINE OIL TO PROPELLER
GOVERNOR OIL TO PROPELLER
PROPELLER SHAFT

PRIMER LINES
INTAKE PIPE
VALVE PUSH ROD-REAR ROW
DIFFUSER CHAMBER
INTAKE MANIFOLD
BAR NOZZLE-FUEL DISCHARGE
MIXTURE SELECTOR LEVER
BENDIX INJECTION CARBURETOR
OIL TANK VENT CONNECTION
MAIN OIL PASSAGE TO CRANKSHAFT
SCINTILLA MAGNETO 14 LOBE BREAKER CAM

FIXED GEAR (PROPELLER REDUCTION GEARING)
PINION GEAR (PROPELLER REDUCTION GEARING)
CRANKSHAFT GEAR (PROPELLER REDUCTION GEARING)
FRONT CAM DRIVE GEAR ON CRANKSHAFT
FRONT CAM AND CAM GEAR
FRONT SECTION SCAVENGE PUMP
ROCKER BOX SCAVENGE PUMP
OIL RETURN TO TANK
ROCKER BOX SCAVENGE LINE
VENT LINE FOR ROCKER BOX SUMP
MASTER ROD-FRONT ROW
ROCKER BOX SCAVENGE SUMP

STARTER DRIVE CLUTCH
MAIN ACCESSORY DRIVE GEAR
SUPERCHARGER DRIVE PINION
SUPERCHARGER IMPELLER
GENERATOR DRIVE
VACUUM PUMP DRIVE
REAR CAM DRIVE GEAR ON CRANKSHAFT
AUTOMATIC FUEL DRAIN VALVE
REAR CAM AND CAM GEAR
FUEL DRAIN LINE
REAR CAM IDLER GEARS
COUNTER WEIGHT-TORSIONAL DAMPENING OF CRANKSHAFT
LINK ROD-REAR ROW
OIL DRAIN PIPES-MAIN AND CAM SECTIONS
MAIN SCAVENGE SUMP

PRATT & WHITNEY S1C3-G TWIN WASP ENGINE
SECTIONAL VIEW

D-6385

(D-6385) This cutaway drawing gives some idea of the precision complexity of the piston aero engine, a piece of machinery delivering better than one horsepower per pound of weight by World War II, but requiring complete overhaul about every 300 to 1800 hours depending upon operational theater and type of aircraft.

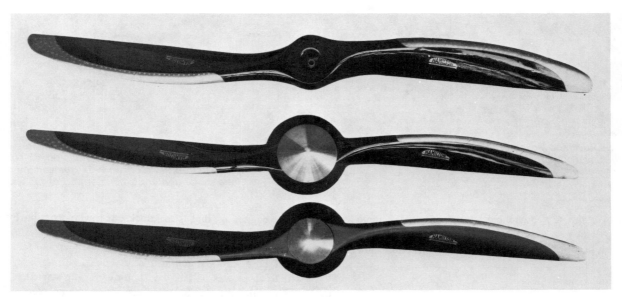

(1488) Early Hamilton wooden propellers of the 1920's for use on engines generally of less than 400 hp.

Early ground-adjustable metal propellers fitted to the Ford Trimotor **Kingbird** allowed adjustments to be made for more efficient angle of attack at different altitudes depending upon where the aircraft generally operated.

The 24E60 Hydromatic propeller fitted to the Republic P-47 Thunderbolt represented the perfection of the constant-speed idea. Pilots could adjust the pitch in the air to maintain any fixed number of engine revolutions for maximum climb or cruise or other performance requirements.

Left, by the end of World War II so much power was available that propeller designers went to contra-rotating propellers, two sets of blades moving in opposite directions, to absorb the output. Right, with the revival in the 1980's of interest in turboprops due to the high cost of fuel after 1973 and the availability of computer-aided design techniques, new blade shapes began to emerge. **All pictures United Technologies.**

*The wooden **De Havilland** Mosquito was both one of the most versatile and one of the faster aircraft of the entire six years, 1939-45. This is the night-fighter version.*

*The international marriage of British requirements, American design genius, and the Rolls-Royce Merlin engine made the **North American** P-51 Mustang the pre-eminent long-range fighter of the later part of the war.*

his control over the subsequent battle ineffective. The model was provided by Allenby at Megiddo in 1918, when he used aircraft to isolate Turkish headquarters while cavalry and armoured cars broke

THE EUROPEAN THEATRE
in the Second World War

through to the rear. The success of his tactics was capped with the aerial ambush of the retreating Turkish forces. German successes generally followed the same pattern until the tables began to turn in late 1942 when the Americans, British, and Soviets came on the field with escalated versions of the same system. But the Allies were never able at that stage of the war to do what the Germans had done

at the beginning, that is to knock out a whole nation by a surprise stroke which succeeded before any counter grand-strategic air bombardment could take effect. Moreover the German technique combined both military action and psychological warfare so that the will to resist was half broken before the war started.

The Japanese employed somewhat the same tactics, but in the jungles and undeveloped terrain over which they operated armour was omitted. Their judo *blitzkrieg*, therefore, used air power to strike at Allied air bases and naval power, so that surface, usually amphibious, forces could get ashore and pad swiftly to their objectives.

In both *blitzkriegs* the objective was a short quick victory to obtain economic resources and to destroy existing political and military organization.

German *blitzkriegs* can be divided into two phases. The first was a series of brilliant successes from Poland in September 1939 to Crete in May 1941; the second was the campaign in the Soviet Union. Having taken Austria, the Rhineland, and Czechoslovakia without a shot, Hitler selected as his next victim Poland, created in 1919 out of eastern Germany and western Russia. The usual propaganda campaign was mounted and the Poles were thus warned that they were the next on the list. This saved them for a few days, for although Hitler struck without warning they were already forearmed. All serviceable Polish air force units had been withdrawn to special landing strips, but unserviceable and obsolete machines were left visible on the old airfields. For the attack on Poland the *Luftwaffe* could deploy 648 bombers, 219 dive-bombers, 30 ground-attack planes, 210 fighters, and 474 other aircraft. Of these some 285 were lost to enemy action in the twenty-eight-day campaign, and an additional 279 were damaged. To oppose the Germans the Polish Air Force could muster 159 fighters, 36 medium bombers and 84 reconnaissance machines. Of these and aircraft in reserve the Poles lost 333 in the first two weeks and the remaining 116 were flown to internment in Rumania on 17 September.

The Polish campaign did not go as the Germans had intended. The plan was to destroy the Polish Air Force on the first day, next to help the army attain its objectives, and then, when time could

*Constant opponents throughout World War II were the British Spitfire and the German Messerschmitt Me-109. These examples belong to the **Confederate Air Force** in Harlingen, Texas; ironically this Me-109 was built in Spain and has a Merlin engine.*

be spared, to go after the Polish aircraft industry. The one major question was whether or not Goering could stage the massed attack on Warsaw which he intended to use as a devastating blow, not against the Polish people as such but against the military, aircraft industry, and communications targets with which the area abounded. After one day's delay due to fog over eastern Germany and Poland, on 2 September the *Luftwaffe* swarmed over Polish airfields, meeting little opposition in the air and cratering runways, blasting hangars, and destroying aircraft on the ground. Not until the third day did the Poles rise from their new lairs. But the Germans had already won the battle for air supremacy, though they did not know it. Their attacks had severed Polish communications so badly that orders did not reach squadrons in intelligible fashion. The Poles had achieved surprise by their concealment of usable aircraft, but the Germans negated it by disrupting the control system.

The Germans had done more than they needed to do, however, and less well than they imagined. A secret assessment made after the campaign showed that the damage done to the abandoned airfields was superficial and that runaways could quickly be filled in again. Even worse, the attacks on the aircraft plants had been too effective and these facilities were not available to the Germans.

Nor did the rest of the Polish campaign go smoothly. Polish anti-aircraft fire was accurate and heavy, and German aircraft had to be ordered not to fly low except when necessary. Moreover, Hitler was most anxious to take Warsaw before the Soviets reached it and thus put on the pressure for its destruction. But for this sort of attack against a city the *Luftwaffe* was now not prepared. While Stukas could be used effectively enough with high explosives, deprived by effective anti-aircraft fire of the expected low-level bombers, the air commander had to use Ju-52 transports to drop incendiaries, and these literally had to be shoveled out of the doors. After a longer struggle than anticipated, heavily-defended Warsaw was eventually forced to capitulate in one hot day.

It was not in the air battle over Poland that the *Luftwaffe* really contributed so much to victory, for the Polish Air Force, though gallant, was inferior and soon disrupted, but in its aid to troops on the ground. The German air force was the eyes of the army (25 per cent were reconnaissance aircraft) and its long-range artillery. Using the lessons learned in Spain, the *Luftwaffe's* field commander,

The Spitfire captured the imagination with its elegance and got more credit than it deserved for winning the Battle of Britian because of its looks and handling qualities. **Vickers**

The Republic P-47 Thunderbolt represented the rugged, 2000-hp approach to the elliptical-winged fighter.

von Richthofen, placed forward air controllers with the leading army elements so that Stukas could be directed onto defensive pockets and strong points. The German communications system worked because it was direct rather than, as planned, being routed through channels.

The Norwegian operation in the spring of 1940 was not part of the German strategic plan, but it became necessary from their point of view because of British interference with German iron-ore shipments from Narvik and merchant shipping sneaking along the coast, together with an Allied plan to seize Narvik. In this respect, then, the German action was a countering or foiling one. This in itself did not make it unusual; what did was the way in which air transport was used as the instrument. Moreover, the Germans were willing to take risks, whereas the Allies were, as often in the war, too cautious and too prone to assume that the Germans were as fuzzy in their thinking as the British were in theirs. The Germans minimized risks by better planning and by taking the psychological initiative.

Four Norwegian airfields were to be captured by paratroopers who would have twenty minutes in which to do the job before reinforcement transports began to land; and an air-transport commander was appointed who was to be responsible for seeing that the 500 transports operated smoothly in and out of the four airfields. But, as in the attack against Poland, this phase of the German plan did not go according to schedule. Though the Me-110s sent to suppress the anti-aircraft defences at Fornebu-Oslo airfield got through the thick fog on the Norwegian coast, the cruiser *Blücher* carrying the assault infantry was sunk by a Norwegian fort and the transports were thus held up. The first wave of paratroopers had been turned back by bad weather, but the second wave of transports were able to land with the Me-110s as soon as the local Gladiator fighters had been defeated. X Air Corps Headquarters in Hamburg at once ordered up reinforcements, who on the evening of 9 April seized the Norwegian capital. Stavanger airfield was successfully gained by paratroopers who were shortly reinforced by airborne troops. Small risks, in terms of numbers, were taken, but the prize was great. By the time the British reacted and put troops ashore on the fourteenth, the Germans were well enough established for the Allied landings to be untenable. Norway belonged to the Germans for the rest of the war and furnished them with valuable air bases for attacks on the British Home Fleet base at Scapa Flow and later for strikes against the Russian convoys.

Norway was just at the extreme range of British naval fighters based on northern Scotland, and at this stage of the war the British had neither the doctrine nor the escort carriers to make use of floating airfields. The Germans won in Norway because they took boldly calculated risks and had the air transport fleets with which to carry them out, and because the British were still using a reactive strategy which allowed the Germans the initiative. While it must be admitted that the Norwegians helped nobody with their intransigent neutrality, the British were unprepared to act in bold disregard of niceties to save the greater objective. In addition to being at that time involved in a Continental commitment in France, they were not yet geared mentally or physically to fight the war that was being forced upon them.

The next *blitzkrieg* was more conventional, and still shockingly effective. In a matter of weeks the Germans took Holland, Belgium and France. The techniques were much the same as before, but there were some interesting added touches. On 10 May Ju-52s left Cologne towing gliders which landed inside the key Belgian fortress of Eben Emael. The troops had practiced the operation for seven months and it went like clockwork; once again a complete surprise was achieved and the enemy taken from the rear. Other gliders disgorged their teams to seize key points and hold them until infantry could arrive, as they had done in Denmark in April.

Included in the attack on Holland and Belgium was another decisive blow at a principal city, in which speed was emphasized as it had been at Warsaw and Oslo. In Holland, a country easily flooded so that troops would be confined to single elevated roads or rail lines, speed was especially vital to prevent the sluices from being opened. Surprise and secrecy were partly lost when a staff officer carrying the secret plans made a forced landing in Belgium; and with the plans for the invasion partly compromised the Germans switched to a variant. Although hampered by the flatness of Holland, which made the target airfields difficult to find, as well as by stubborn Dutch resistance, the Germans managed to take the vital bridges across the New Maas river in Amsterdam by flying seaplanes right up to them and seizing the bridgeheads. Almost simultaneously

airfields on the outskirts were bombed, and paratroopers dropped outside their perimeters to make the defenders face outwards. Ju-52s landing on the fields were torn apart by obstacles placed on the runways, and other airborne attackers got lost or could not land on the fields already choked with wrecks, but eventually an infantry force hemmed the Dutch defenders into a triangle to the north of the vital pass through the centre of Rotterdam. There on 14 May occurred a tragedy that was due to a combination of communications and historical difficulties.

The Dutch colonel commanding refused to capitulate in the face of what he regarded as a ruse, and by the time he was undeceived the destruction of the city was under way. German communications, as so often at this stage of the war, were too elaborate, and no frequency had been established by which General Student, the airborne leader, could speak directly to *Luftwaffe* aircraft overhead. Thus try as he would he could not stop a 100-plane demonstration raid which had been laid on that morning for 1500 hours. It was only after fifty-seven aircraft had dropped their bombs from 2,300 feet that the leader of the formation saw the red Very lights fired by the general himself and halted the raid. Then history took over. The old timbered city was an oil and margarine trading centre. The Dutch, always thrifty, had no modern fire-engines, only handpumps of ancient design and a volunteer fire brigade. Thus the fires started grew quickly out of control and most of the old city burned down while the Dutch capitulation was taking place. Allied propaganda made a great deal of another Nazi outrage, but the Germans have truth on their side. Despite the tragedy of not being able to stop the raid in time, and in spite of what analysts—especially wartime propagandists—have said about it, the operation itself was no more immoral than the use of artillery by both sides at that time and place.

From the German point of view the major disaster of the attack on Holland was that it consumed 310 of the 430 transports employed; and as these were mostly flown by instructors from bomber training units the chain-reaction effect upon German operations was out of proportion to the value derived. In effect, the Germans suffered something of the same loss of experienced pilots which plagued the Japanese after the first seven months of the Pacific war in 1941-1942.

*From the movie, **The Battle of Britain**, repainted Spanish AF Heinkel He-111's are seen being inspected prior to take-off for an attack on Britain. **Confederate Air Force***

An Me-109 catches a Hurricane on the ground in a favorite German dawn attack. **Confederate Air Force**

The operations against France were yet another example of the *blitzkrieg* technique. Here once again *Luftwaffe* bombers flying at tree-top height struck at seventy Allied airfields. While they were not always successful in destroying the fields, the surprise was un-nerving. In fact the Allies were in poor condition to fight. The French Air Force had started to deteriorate in the early 'thirties, and its condition had steadily worsened, in spite of the developments of some promising new designs. Anglo-French relations were not always frank, and neither partner was really sure of what the other pos-sessed. The French had only 186 bombers, of which eleven were modern, 549 fighters of which 131 were obsolete, and 377 recon-naissance aircraft of which 316 were outdated. At their request RAF Hurricanes were stationed in their sector of the front to pro-vide fighter support. Even worse than the fact that this spread Bri-tish fighter strength very thinly behind the front, neither of the two British bomber-types available could survive in the face of German fighters unless escorted, and there were not enough Hurricanes to do that. The Fairey Battle was a three-seat single-engine light bomber weighing twice as much as a Hurricane but powered with the same engine. In the first three days of the campaign it averaged a 70 per cent loss rate, yet it was expected to make tactical daylight sorties. The Bristol Blenheim fared not much better. To supplement these machines Bomber Command in Britain had 200 heavy and medium bombers of the Whitley, Wellington, Blenheim and Hampden types, making a total of 544 bombers for all European operations. But even more than the technical inadequacy, theoretical considerations on the Allied side posed problems, for though there had been public debate in Parliament and about Mitchell, air power had never found its Fuller or Liddell Hart.

No one was sure that air power could stop a fast-rolling ground offensive, nor were they sure where to strike to attempt to do so. This was not only an Anglo-French bone of contention, but also one between the War Office and the Air Ministry in London. The French did not want bombers used except possibly right on the battlefield, because they were afraid of retaliation; some British air-men argued for their use tactically, others for grand-strategic attacks against the heavily concentrated German industrial targets in the Ruhr, and yet others for an attack on oil. The whole problem was that no one was really sure what results could be obtained and the

Commander-in-Chief of Bomber Command was not at all convinced that his Blenheims should be used at all. The only aircraft in France in which anyone on the British side had any confidence were the Hurricanes, and of these only ten squadrons were available to face some 1,200 German fighters.

The fact is that the Allies simply were not prepared to face the concentrated German fighter force, nor did they grasp the lightning nature of *blitzkrieg*. This kind of war required highly skilful, ruth-less, hard-hitting bombing of key passages or bottlenecks in repeated escorted raids; the Allies had neither adequate reconnaissance air-craft nor a gun which could equal the German 88-mm dual-purpose anti-aircraft gun or their 20-mm vehicle-mounted cannon. In addi-tion, air superiority had to be established to protect airfields and aircraft which could be concentrated on the enemy's armour, motor-ized columns, and supply lines. Attacking the industrial base of a *blitzkrieg* army was unlikely to be of much use, as the Germans planned carefully and the whole operation was designed to be car-ried out at lightning speed. Given their whole system, it is scarcely surprising that the Germans rolled over a France commanded by generals who thought in 1918 terms and were backed by a popula-tion with low morale.

The one mistake the Germans made was in halting their tanks outside the Dunkirk area. It was here for the first time that they had begun to run into British air superiority, as the *Luftwaffe* had not moved up fast enough. When von Richthofen did move his groups forward, many of them were at half their normal thirty-aircraft strength after two weeks of intensive operations. (In addition, the Germans normally considered that 10 per cent of any unit would not be available due to maintenance problems.) At this point Goer-ing, never backward, suggested to Hitler that the tanks be held back while the *Luftwaffe* finished off the surrounded Anglo-French forces. For two and a half days the tanks sat idle. On one of these Stukas and artillery combined to complete the fall of stubborn Calais. On 26 May the Germans launched an all-out attack on the Dunkirk bridgehead, but as it was within range of fighters based in Britain air cover could be provided and was. In addition there were several days of bad weather, and after only two and a half days of attacks during the nine days and nights of the evacuation the *Luftwaffe* was withdrawn and switched south, resuming its normal support

He-111 side view. **Confederate Air Force**

tactics until France fell. It had defeated the Allied air forces except over Dunkirk and helped defeat their armies. The operations, while expensive, were effective and well worth the price.

The next German *blitzkriegs* were into the Balkans. A German military mission protected the vital Rumanian oil fields about Ploesti against Soviet advances. Yugoslavia was attacked, Belgrade bombed, and the country over-run when a change of government refused German protection. And this was the beginning of a campaign designed to eradicate the sore in the Axis side created by Mussolini's ill-fated attempt to conquer Greece. Hitler, with his intuitive eye for grand strategy, saw as early as November 1940 that the island of Crete was the key to the whole area. No sooner had the Italians attacked Greece than the British occupied Crete. But just as the British under-rated German energy and thoroughness, so the Germans over-rated the British. Hitler feared that the British bombers based in Crete, or more likely in the Salonika plain of Greece, would be a threat to the Ploesti oil fields, and he had, therefore, proposed an airborne operation against Crete. Nothing was done about this over the winter while preparations for the invasion of the Soviet Union went ahead, but it was decided to clean up the Greek campaign even before the British landed there in March so as to secure the German flank for the invasion of the Soviet Union. Thus once again the Germans worked to an extremely tight timetable and relied on the momentum of surprise, experience, and organization to carry them through.

The campaign in Greece was short and decisive. It was an ideal area in which to use air power, since road and rail networks were almost non-existent and the defenders were constantly hampered by the terrain. The Germans were able to strike at key bridges, to disrupt traffic by bombing and strafing the closely packed columns on the few roads available, and to destroy aircraft on their landing grounds. In this they were aided by the British lack of an efficient early warning system. Thus the RAF, which by April 1941 was virtually the Greek air force, was wiped out very quickly at relatively small loss to the Germans. The whole campaign was a repetition of France the year before.

On 21 April, while the Greeks capitulated, Hitler assented to the completion of the campaign by an airborne assault on Crete. But he specified that this must be done by the airborne and paratroop divisions alone and that it must be completed by mid-May. Mussolini was persuaded to agree—although he was inclined to accept the German General Staff's appraisal that Malta was the more vital target, lying as it did across the supply routes to North Africa—and the formal order was given on 25 April. But it was not until 14 May that the assaulting forces were ready, and by then the airborne division, unable to move south by road from Rumania, had been replaced by an élite mountain division which had never participated in airborne operations. The irony of all these delays lay in the fact that if the British had put Crete into fighting order in the first place they would have had some three weeks in which to re-form and rearm the troops that had been evacuated from Greece. Moreover, if they had built airfields on Crete, and if they had had modern medium bombers rather than Blenheims available, they might seriously have disrupted the German preparations: the passes in the Macedonian mountains were clogged with panzers going north and troops trying to get south, and the airfields were jammed. Unfortunately on the British side almost everything was missing—including radar, which was vital to provide the necessary early warning against attacks on Crete. But this was merely an extension of the tragedy of involvement in Greece, the blame for which must be laid at Churchill's door. He failed to understand that the Middle East Command was a vast theatre (the distance from Salonika to Nairobi was five times the length of the British Isles) and that paper figures of numbers of squadrons were highly unreliable when vast distances and many campaigns were involved.

The campaign against Crete had to be delayed by the Germans for a number of reasons. In the first place the 500 Ju-52s used for the Greek campaign had to be returned to home bases for overhaul. It is a tribute to German efficiency that they were completely overhauled and 493 returned to Greece between 1 and 14 May. Unfortunately no fuel had arrived because the Corinth Canal bridge, though taken by German paratroopers, had fallen into the canal and the tankers could not get through. After the transfer into forty-five-gallon drums of the 560,000 gallons needed for the operation, these drums had to be taken over abominable roads to the airfields. Even worse, as the RAF had discovered earlier, Greek airfields were composed of either mud or dust. The *Luftwaffe* enjoyed the dry season. After one squadron took off, well over a quarter of an hour had to

The workhorse of Fighter Command, RAF, in the Battle of Britain was the Hurricane, a more rugged, slower aircraft than the Spitfire. **British Aerospace**

A Ju-52 in the movie **The Battle of Britian. Confederate Air Force**

Bombers of 1939-45 in Europe

British Bristol Blenheim I

U.S. Lockheed Hudson

British Bristol Beaufort

U.S. North American Mitchell

British Bristol Beaufighter

U.S. Martin Marauder

Italian Cant 2506B

Russian PE-2

Allied Personalities of the Second World War

The Higher Direction of the war at Casablanca in 1943. Seated from left to right are Arnold, King, Churchill, Roosevelt, Brooke, Pound and Marshall, while standing are (   ), Ismay, Mountbatten, (   ), Dill, Portal, and Hopkins. **USAF**

Below center, General H. H. "Hap" Arnold, Chief of Staff, USAAF.
Left, General Curtis E. LeMay, who was a colonel at the beginning of World War II, but rose to be Chief of Staff, USAF, in the 1960's. During the war he commanded both in Europe and the B-29 campaign against Japan.
On the right, Capt. Don Gentile's uniforms are now exhibited in the USAF Museum in Dayton, Ohio; they show what the well-dressed ace wore in 1944 when Gentile, who flew both in the RAF and the USAAF, was a Mustang pilot.

elapse before another could proceed. But on the morning of 20 May, hot, tired, sleepless, and dirty, the Germans took off for Crete. The RAF had missed its chance.

The first wave of fifty-three gliders and 5,000 paratroopers planned to seize the western airfield of Maleme, but the British had first-class intelligence and, despite a heavy pre-attack bombing, most of their concealed positions were intact. As a result during the first day the Germans were unable to seize the airfield, although enough anti-aircraft guns were silenced for a substantial German force to be scattered on the ground. Late in the afternoon, in much disorder due to the mess on their own airfields in Greece, where landing aircraft had collided and losses far exceeded the seven Ju-52s shot down over Crete, the second wave dropped near the other two British airfields. Student had intended that these be diverted to Maleme, but his staff were unable to get through on the telephone to the squadrons before they took off. Thus the second wave arrived in droplets and was unable to capture either Retimo or Herakleion airfields. By nightfall the British held a very narrow advantage. It might have been greater if the desperate German seizure of the vital hill overlooking the airfield at Maleme had met a counter-attack, for the paratroopers were out of ammunition and were only saved the next day by the arrival of a single Ju-52 which landed on the nearby beach with a supply. By the twenty-first, *Luftwaffe* aircraft controlled the air, as none of the British airfields was tenable and fighter cover could not be maintained from Egypt. Then at four in the afternoon Student's mountain division was successfully landed on Maleme airfield in a desperate stroke, at the cost of eighty transports. At last the Germans had a beachhead on the island. The Royal Navy beat back the seaborne reinforcements that night, but was forced the next day to withdraw, lacking air cover and nearly out of anti-aircraft ammunition. Though the battle went on until 1 June, it had been decided by the night of the twenty-second.

The irony of Crete is that it was the last great German airborne operation. It cost the Germans too many aircraft and too many élite troops to be repeated. Moreover, once again, as in the west in 1940, it was the cream of the bomber-instructor crop who were lost and the impact of this was felt all through the war. Even more than this, it was in part the decimation of the transports which hampered the speed of movement of the panzers in the Soviet Union; this was especially critical since the campaign there opened a month later than planned, not so much because of the Greek campaign as

General Carl Spaatz was the first Chief of Staff of the **USAF** when it achieved its independence after World War II. He was the astute leader of the USAAF in Europe in the 1942-45 period.

because of the slow spring thaw which made the ground too soft for tanks until June.

But it is also ironical that Crete convinced the Allies that airborne operations were a pre-requisite to success, and men and equipment were therefore diverted to the air forces. The argument against this policy is that it plucked the best men out of regular units and isolated them in special contingents which were rarely used and, when they were, suffered high casualties. The *coup de main* airborne tactic was valuable on occasion, perhaps, but it had to be used within clearly defined rules. Basically these were that the units had to be dropped precisely on time and on target and that they had to be relieved within no more than two or three days. Moreover, they had to have air cover and instant resupply even in those few days. And lastly, as the Allied Arnhem-Nijmegen operation showed in 1944 and as the history of war has all too often demonstrated, such a fragile force could only successfully be committed on the basis of accurate intelligence. In Crete, for instance, the Germans found that the hilly nature of the ground resulted in units landing out of sight of one another while being dominated by hidden defenders. At Arnhem the British landed on top of a panzer division.

As an extension of the *blitzkrieg* technique little need be said here of the German thrust into the Soviet Union. The mistake made was simply to attempt on a very broad front what had succeeded on narrow ones without allowing time to build up the necessary air striking and air support forces. In each of the previous campaigns the Germans had been able to strike decisively on the ground straight at the enemy's capital while receiving support from aircraft based at airfields established before the campaign started. In each case, moreover, the blitz had lasted no more than four weeks, yet even so *Luftwaffe* units were reduced to something like half their normal strength without allowing for the effects of battle fatigue. The *Luftwaffe* of 1939–41 was a tactical rapier, not a sabre, and it was not backed by an aircraft industry geared for a major war. The fact that it lacked a strategic bomber is a moot point which is discussed later. After 1941 it was placed on the defensive in a war which would last another three years and which would make great calls upon it both in many far-flung battlefronts abroad and in defence of the Third

General Ira Eaker commanded several air forces in the European theater and went on to become the beloved "father" of the **USAF**.

Reich at home. Though it survived to the end, it lacked the stamina to achieve victory.*

Just as in the Pacific the Battle of Midway in June 1942 marked the turning point of the Allied fortunes, so in Europe a subtle change took place. The Germans ceased to advance into Egypt or to break past Stalingrad, American forces joined the Battle of the Atlantic and arrived in Britain, where RAF Bomber Command had finally begun to receive its four-engine heavy bombers and to believe the unpalatable facts which its PRU people had been trying to point out for two years. Disappointing as it may be to some patriotic readers, it must be noted that the Allied tactical air forces owed their successes in the years to come to learning from the Germans, to intelligent leadership, and above all else to the arrival in the war zone of adequate material and men.

The change was visible first in the Middle East. There in 1942 Air Chief Marshal Sir Arthur Tedder, closely in touch with the Chief of the Air Staff in London by both official and unofficial means, was at last beginning to receive modern material. No longer did his pilots have to face the Me-109 in obsolescent Curtiss Kittyhawks and battle-weary Hurricanes; they now had Spitfires. The Westland Lysander was replaced as an observation plane by the Kittyhawk, and the Blenheims and Marylands gave way to Baltimores and Mitchells. And at last Tedder had not only radar to prevent surprises but an organization which could leap-frog squadrons up and down the battlefield so that troops could have continuous air cover. Even the faithful Wellingtons used for strategic attacks on Axis supply ports were supplemented with four-engine British and American bombers. Thus when Montgomery opened his offensive at El Alamein in November 1942 he was supported by a mobile tactical air force the likes of which the British had never before possessed. And the Allied invasion of North Africa was similarly

*One special advantage which German generals enjoyed until the middle of the war was a personal aircraft. In transport planes they had the means of getting to and from the front without loss of time, and in the Fieseler Storch they had the inestimable advantage of being able to move about the front rapidly. The Storch was the ideal plane because of its short take-off and landing characteristics, simplicity, and the excellent all-round visibility it afforded its passenger. More than this, German generals like Rommel were willing to use it.

blessed. In the wide open spaces of the Western Desert aircraft were hampered only by rain and dust. Montgomery's advance moved at such a pace that the tactical air forces could always keep the pressure up and at certain bottlenecks could get their revenge for similar German maulings in earlier campaigns.

As a result of the German successes with gliders, the Allies built large quantities of both light Wacos and heavy Horsas and some Hamilcars, the latter of which could carry a tank. Horsas were towed all the way from Britain to North Africa for the landings there, but the physical endurance required of the crews and their passengers was so excessive as to blunt their efficiency. In the later Sicilian campaign the airborne operation was also badly handled: the crews had to assemble their own gliders; the tug crews were unfamiliar with navigation in blacked-out, radioless, and maritime areas; recognition signals were lacking, and night landings were attempted. Army commanders overlooked a fact that the Germans had learned by 1940, namely that gliders were a special weapon with their own limitations. At Eben Emael the Germans had been guided to the dropping point by a line of lights within Germany, and the arrival of the gliders had been timed for first light so they could see the very precise landing zone and each other. At Sicily not only were the gliders dropped all over land and sea in the dark, but lack of liaison caused the assault force ships to open fire on the gliders as they passed low overhead, with the double result of casualties to the airborne and the alerting of the defenders. A year later at D-Day in Normandy the Allies had learned a great deal; they also had the advantage of staging from nearby main bases in Britain. They were successful owing to careful planning and intensive training, and to the development of radar landing beacons which could be planted as a guide for gliders and paratroop transports homing in the dark.

Allied tactical air forces owed most of their success to the development of material and techniques and to the masses of aircraft available. From April 1944 the Allied Expeditionary Air Force had 2,000 fighters and 700 medium bombers engaged in the transportation attack plan by which the Normandy area was isolated from the rest of German-held France. And despite the misgivings and protests of the Commander-in-Chief of Bomber Command, the 1,000 four-engine heavies he possessed were also on call. The Allies could not disguise the fact that they were going to assault northern France, but

The Me-323 was a six-engined version of the largest transport glider the Germans had, designed to carry tanks, it was used in the evacuation of Tunisia in 1943, when it became highly vulnerable to marauding Allied fighters and medium bombers. **USAF**

The Air War on the Eastern Front

I-16 naval fighter.

Pe-2 Medium attack bombers.

Long-range Pe-8's were the Soviet heavy bombers and also used as transports.

The vast, fast blitzkrieg into the USSR undertaken by the Germans in 1941 and 1942 was turned about by the Soviets starting as early as the winter of 1941. They used space, time, and winter weather to their advantage and by late 1942 had gone over effectively to an offensive which by mid-1944 gave them undisputed control of the air over their advancing tank armies. Because of distances and a lack of suitable targets within striking range, grand-strategic bombing accounted for only 0.02 percent of the sorties flown. By far the vast majority of the effort of the Soviet Army Air Forces (the VVS) was in air superiority, tactical support strikes and escort missions.

Just as in other theaters, so also on the Eastern Front, the evolution of air forces is to be seen. Hampered by its many theaters, the Luftwaffe gradually lost control, but it was never totally eliminated even though vulnerable at every turn. It was ground down, but it did not collapse. In contrast, the VVS which was dealt a "Pearl Harbor" blow at dawn on 22 June 1941 and lost some 1200 aircraft the first day, recovered, modernized, learned new management techniques, and became a highly effective, if massive fighting organization. Some of the changes were on the way in any case as a legacy of the Spanish Civil War, the dismal showing in Finland in the winter of 1939-40, the Stalinist purge of the high command, of the move of the aircraft industry east of the Urals, and of the normal cycle of design changes. War made their implementation imperative. Among the more interesting and productive ideas were that base maintenance and logistics organizations should be separate from that of squadrons or regiments so that the operational aircraft and their air and ground crews (170-

200 persons) could be switched quickly from one front to another. This was gradually developed during the war to such an extent that by the Spring of 1945, 209 regiments could be accommodated on 290 airfields within 65 miles of the front after an advance of over 1200 miles and still fly the maximum sorties desirable. At the same time command structures had been modified as the VVS had recovered from the devastation of 22 June, which largely saw material rather than personnel lost, so that as the reserves accumulated and trained personnel came forward to man the new fighters, bombers and attack aircraft, regiments could be increased from 10 to 20 and more aircraft and operate in larger and larger formations. At the higher levels this meant that whole air armies were created with such effectiveness that by the end of the war as many as three might be assigned to a single front under one overall air commander no longer simply the air adviser to the group commander but charged in full to gather reconnaissance intelligence, wage offensive action to gain air superiority, and to provide maximum support for the tank armies in both the preparation and the execution of ground operations. In 1942 these air armies had about 950 aircraft each, sometimes still in a composite force of fighter, attack and bomber regiments, while by 1945 they contained 3000 aircraft of one class, such as fighters.

Training and tactics went hand in hand. By October 1942 first the fighters and then the new Il-2 Sturmovik ground-attack regiments adopted the pair and the finger-four learned by the Germans in Spain. At the same time, the best personnel and machines were concentrated in the newly-designated elite

Twin-engined USSR torpedo bomber (a DB-3 or Il-4).

IL-2 Sturmoviks in typical low-level strike.

La-4 fighter.

Marshalling a Red Air Force Medium bomber for take-off.

Guards units and sent to do batte against the best of the Luftwaffe. In this they were helped by the arrival of the new fighters, the Yak-1 and 7 and the La-5, which were the equal of the Me-109's, especially at the low altitudes — usually below 3000 feet (1000 meters) — at which the Soviets operated over the flat steppes. Soviet bomber losses were high due to poor training, lack of maps except for the leaders, and the fact that almost all targets were in frontline areas heavily defended by flak.

Notable in the development of the VVS was the active role played by women, not merely in ground support roles as in all the Soviet forces, but also as combat pilots.

Though not noticeably operating on interior lines, the Russians did have the advantage of defending their own territories and of being closer to their sources of supply than the invaders were to theirs. One sign of maturity was that the management of the armed forces was run in something of the same manner as the well-known Five-Year Plans, which were themselves closely linked to defence. An offshoot of this was that the supreme headquarters, the Stavka, controlled the allocations of air resources, and by mid-1942 was holding about 40 percent of the VVS as a central reserve. This it switched to whichever front required offensive or defensive support, thus satisfying the principles of war called mass, mobility, and surprise. This became most apparent on 19 November 1942 when Stalin took the Great Patriotic War, as the Russians called the 1941-45 War, over to the offensive in the campaign against the ill-fated Germans lodged in Stalingrad. By the

battle of Kursk in July 1943 the VVS had grasped the initiative and could achieve local air superiority at will. By 1944 it could have it anywhere as the Germans could no longer parry air armies which had such a surplus that they could mount "hunter" fighter and, by Stalin's order, ground-attack operations whenever it suited them.

Even though the Soviets had carefully built their air armies one "steppe" at a time, from mid-1944 on they were faced by the fact that their ground organization could not keep up with the rapid pace of their tank armies. Thus occasional halts were necessary to allow the air arm to catch up and resite itself for the next great leap forward, as before the final battle of Berlin.

Readers and historians in the West have too often tended to overlook the fact that by 1945 the Soviets had 13 air armies in operation each with a formidable armada of aircraft, supported by flexible logistical and maintenance battalions, and ultimately by the aircraft industry which produced some 137,000 aircraft between 1941 and 1945, to which must be added some 14,000 supplied by Allied Lend-Lease. In addition, the VVS destroyed some 77,000 Luftwaffe aircraft, or about 57 percent of the GAF's losses, for the destruction of about the same number of its own machines. And all of this happened in a country where a large part of its prewar industrial and agricultural base area was overrun and occupied by the invading enemy. Luckily for the Allies in World War II space, time, the Russian winter, and Hitler's optimism and lack of long-range planning were on the Soviet side.

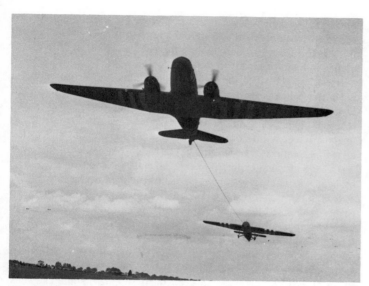

The Germans abandoned the glider and offensive use of paratroops after their Pyrrhic victory on Crete in May 1941. At that point the Allies took up the idea. Here a Dakota(C-47) has a Horsa heavy glider in tow. **USAF**

they achieved tactical surprise with the use of sophisticated electronic deception. Once ashore, they quickly laid down perforated-steel-plate (p.s.p.) airfields so that air cover could be based close behind the front lines. Already in earlier campaigns as Allied air power became plentiful and fuel no problem, British forward air controllers had developed the 'cab-rank' system: fighters and fighter-bombers orbited just behind the front line and were called in whenever a target appeared. Thus the reaction time from call to strike was cut to minutes.

On the Eastern Front the turning point in the war was the revival of the Soviet air force in the winter of 1941–42. The Soviet aircraft industry had been moved behind the Urals, to put it beyond German reach; and, as the Soviets began to put into practice the lessons of the Spanish and Finnish wars, modern material was on its way. The further the Germans advanced, the longer were their lines of communication and the tauter they became. The Crete campaign had seriously depleted their air transports, of which only 500 were produced in 1941, and the onset of winter found them without adequate clothing, oil, or other equipment, or even the experience with which to cope with severe winter flying. Eventually the Soviets built up equipment to levels technically comparable to the Germans but far superior in numbers, their transport system became adept, and they were aided by the western Allies both directly in the form of some 2,000 fighters and indirectly by the so-called strategic air offensive against Germany and by the pressure of Allied attacks in Italy and France. From 1942 onwards the Russian front had a low priority in German air force supply, with the result that the Germans were outnumberd as much as five to one in the Soviet Union and their less experienced personnel flying older equipment were operating there. After 1944, when the Soviets gained safe air superiority, the German armies were without eyes or much tactical support. Yet counter to the claims of air-power theorists, they fought on for nearly two years after they lost their air cover.

The Allies had learned well from the Germans. If there is one criticism of their technique, it is that generals became too prone to call upon air power rather than using artillery and risking tanks. The result was that in front of some generals villages were so destroyed by bombing that bulldozers had to be sent in before the troops could advance. There are, then, disadvantages to having too

much firepower available, as its profligate use is apt to slow rather than speed the advance, especially when controlled by a general who is unwilling to take risks. The Allies had also learned well from the Germans that air power and armies must co-operate. The successful model was worked out first in the Western Desert, where the RAF tactical commander had his headquarters alongside that of the army commander so that in both planning and execution at high and low levels there was proper liaison.

The Sicilian and Italian campaigns showed that air power was not necessarily able to dominate the battlefield under some circumstances. Allied air power did not prevent the German evacuation of Sicily nor did it prevent the Allies from coming close to disaster at Salerno and Anzio. Finally, it was not able to open the Cassino bottleneck. While it could make things difficult for the Germans in the limiting terrain of Italy, where supply lines ran within narrow grooves, it was not able to open the way for the infantry because the ground favoured the defence. Rather than an aerial 'Operation Strangle', the way to have won in Italy might have been to have mounted the 'Anvil' invasion against northern Italy rather than into southern France, but such a suggestion involves a very complex set of 'ifs' outside the scope of this work.

Asia. In terms of its future impact, the Allied campaign in Burma was both an innovation and the precursor of that in Vietnam. While it was true that in the victory in France in 1944 the US Ninth Air Force had been employed to shield Patton's right flank, in Burma the air forces were used both to shield and fully to supply the Allied ground campaign, air evacuation of casualties was developed to the full, and helicopters were employed. It was also the campaign to study for the future because it was a peripheral or forgotten war, last on the list for all the normal fighting perquisites, including mail for the men's morale, as well as being a theatre in which air power had to answer to many masters located anywhere from a thousand yards to thousands of miles away. Airfields were scattered over many miles of jungle; both supply and navigation were difficult in an area of few landmarks. Yet the lack of railways and roads, and the expense of building roads in a country notorious for its high rainfall, made air supply essential. Even without the jungles, the country was nearly impassable because of mountains and rivers, and the bridges

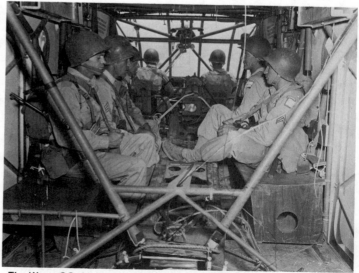

The Waco CG-4A was a medium glider which could deliver troops and a jeep. Construction was steel tube and canvas — they were expendable. **US Army**

Standing on a Chinese airfield in February 1943 a Japanese Zero in Chinese markings and a Flying Tigers' Curtiss P-40. Fast and highly maneuverable, the Zero suffered from failure to develop it. **USAF**

that did exist were major targets as the weakest links in the transportation chains.

When the campaign opened the British were being driven out of Burma into India and the Chinese back into their homeland. The year 1942 was not an auspicious time for the Allies to begin a build-up in the forgotten theatre. Apart from the competition of the European, Pacific, and North African areas, India was plagued with its own troubles. It was unusually hot and humid; malaria was prevalent, and mepacrine and atabrine pills were not yet freely available. The unusually heavy rains caused landslides on the road to the British advanced garrison-base at Imphal. The breakdown of the talks on Indian independence led to a slow-down of airfield construction work, which in pre-bulldozer days was bad enough anyway. The 30,000 tons of fill for runways was dug with shovels, stones were broken by hand, and all was moved in head-carried baskets by a patiently lethargic people. On top of this, at the end of the retreat from Burma there were but five squadrons in India, a subcontinent the size of Europe. Most of their equipment was obsolescent, to be polite, yet it had to be used until the end of 1943, when the last Curtiss Mohawks were withdrawn and the first PRU Spitfires were just beginning operations.

The first major operation in the theatre was the original Chindit expedition, which was supplied by Dakota (C-47) aircraft, rarely needing escort by the Hurricanes because of the scarcity of Japanese opponents. This expedition terminated as the monsoon broke in June 1943, but it had showed the value of an air transport force. At the end of 1941 it had been decided to develop such a service, and a plan was put into being in March 1942 to provide 215 airfields, internal air services in India, and a viable flying-control system. At the end of nine months five airfields were finished. By November 1943, however, a modified programme found 140 two-runway fields, sixty-four with one runway, and seventy-one fair-weather strips finished, with a further fifteen fields still building. Radar had been installed and ground-observer units established. In late 1943 Southeast Asia Command was organized and the British and USAAF forces merged. By this time there were more than forty-eight RAF and seventeen USAAF transport squadrons in the Command. Even so, this force was hard put to it to contain Japanese thrusts, which by coincidence began almost simultaneously with a British drive

down the Arakan coast. Success or failure hung on the ability of the Allies to supply their units by air and to shift troops rapidly from the Arakan front to Imphal when the need arose, even if it meant cutting into the Hump airlift to China to do so.

In early 1944, when the Japanese outflanked the British advance down the Arakan coast, the troops were ordered to stand and fight in a box, where they were supplied by air until the relief forces reached them. That this was possible can be credited both to imaginative gambling on the part of the high command and to the arrival in the theatre of Spitfire VIIIs, which were able to seize control of the air. Auster light aircraft, later in the campaign replaced by light American types, evacuated the wounded at the rate of 300 a week, immensely raising morale, and, at the same time, long-range bombers harassed the few Japanese airfields at night. The Japanese siege of Imphal was broken by a 758-sortie airlift of a whole division from the Arakan in an operation reminiscent of the German use of railways before Tannenberg in 1914. At neighbouring Kohima the garrison was wedged into a hilltop only 400 by 500 yards, yet planes flying at 200 feet managed to keep them supplied, some canisters even being so accurately dropped as to kill the recipients because the chutes had no time to open! Needless to say, some of the supplies benefited the enemy. At Imphal the situation was so critical that 30,000 support troops were flown out of the box together with the hospitals. The Allies were able to do for the British and Indians in Imphal what the Germans had not been able to do for themselves at Stalingrad. In part the success was a matter of scale, in part it was because the defenders kept six airfields in their hands, and in part it was due to the Japanese lack of the air power or the knowledge of how to interfere effectively. Throughout the siege the British were able to maintain fighters on the fields in daylight, flying them out for rest, maintenance, and safety at dusk. In the absence of radar, standing fighter patrols were used over the entrances to the valley to keep Japanese aircraft out. In the eighty-day battle the RAF lost two Dakotas and a Wellington while supplying 275 tons a day. One corollary of the airlift operations was the development by the Americans of a conveyor-belt conception of the handling of supplies, a system that saved time in many ways.

In between the Arakan and Imphal battles, in March 1944, the second Chindit operation was airlifted into Burma. This was a most

Supply-dropping was a major means of resupply, especially in the campaign in Burma, but called for tennis-court accuracy. **US Army**

Left: In order to build a World War II airfield, 30,000 tons of fill had to be moved in and concrete runways laid, often without machinery, as here in India. **USAF**

Below, left: The Waco could really glide. **USAF**

Below, right: Light aircraft replaced the old observation types for both spotting and communications duties. Here Hap Arnold visits a forward area in Italy in 1943. **USAF**

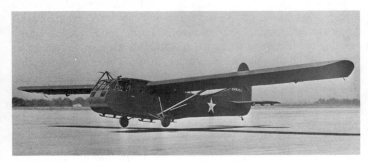

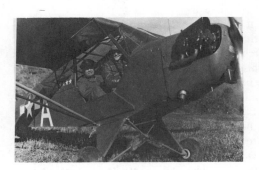

significant new development in that 10,000 riflemen were taken into a single strip in Burma that had been opened up by bulldozers landed in gliders only the night before. Conditions at Broadway were such that the original lift was cancelled for twelve hours, but that night the first two transports into the strip were piloted by the American and the British general officers; thereafter an aircraft landed or took off from the single two-way strip every three minutes all night. The Japanese detected and bombed an adjacent landing ground, but they did not discover Broadway for a week, even though it was 150 miles behind their lines. In the course of the campaign five fields were created and 100 strips for casualty evacuation established. Helicopters used any open patch as needed. All re-supply flights were made at night, as the columns were beyond escort-fighter range, but fighter-bombers and Mitchells provided air support, guided to targets by RAF officers with the troops and by smoke grenades fired onto the enemy positions at the crucial moments.

In the north the American General Stilwell used airborne troops to capture the Myitkina airfield for his Chinese troops. The siege of the town took seventy-nine days, but seventy-five Dakotas, the equivalent of 1,200 two-and-a-half-ton trucks, kept his force supplied; the aircrew used were less than half the equivalent force of truck drivers.

Another innovation, again presaging Vietnam, was that in the advance through the Valley of Death to Tamu the road was sprayed with DDT from the air to keep down malarial mosquitoes.

To disrupt Japanese river traffic, especially on the Irrawaddy, mines were sown by aircraft, while in daylight much of the river, road, and rail network was patrolled by Beaufighters, known to the enemy as 'Whispering Death' owing to the silence of their approach, especially in comparison with the Mitchells. The 'Beaus' also did well when compared to the wooden Mosquitoes because of their all-metal construction, which kept their flaps from being blown away in rough weather or on water-soaked runways, or their wings from coming unglued in the humidity.

The final triumph of air supply in Burma was the advance of the British XIVth Army to Rangoon in spite of both the threatened withdrawal of the American transport squadrons and the monsoon. Taking a calculated risk, the seventeen squadrons of the combined Anglo-American air supply force kept 300,000 men on the move

in the race down country. That they succeeded was due in no small measure to the effectiveness of the air cover supplied from new fighter strips and old Japanese airfields. So rapid, in fact, was the advance that the bombers were ordered not to destroy bridges for fear of holding up the attackers. Even so, some 8,000 bridges were attacked by aircraft, which ranged as far as 1,400 miles from their bases.

The whole reconquest of Burma was not accomplished without some headaches. The army came to regard air supply as the norm and began to demand greater and greater loads. The principal problems, apart from the overworking of aircrews (who often made three trips, totalling twelve flying hours, a day over the Arakan mountains to the front), were the failures to see that perishable cargoes cleared airfields before they rotted, to ensure that items were not flown in which were available locally behind the front, to land incoming transports ahead of the take-off of routine tactical patrols, and, lastly, to see that transport crews got food and rest while aircraft were being unloaded.

Success in South-east Asia Command was a matter of the right combination of ingredients in a tight schedule. As an adjunct to it the Hump route to China had always to be considered, but its problems were not peculiar, and once adequate aircraft and crews were available its operation was routine, even though the international personalities involved may have made it seem otherwise.

3. Air Power and National Defence

Periodically during the Second World War air power was called upon to defend the homeland of one of the belligerents. The ensuing battles were frequently a sobering experience for both sides.

Hitler needed to knock Britain out of the war so that he could get on with his other plans, and Goering claimed that this could be done by allowing the *Luftwaffe* to destroy the RAF before an invasion force crossed the Channel. The British had radar defences along the arc facing France and Germany, with fighter controllers who could vector defending fighters in by radio. But, although the

British had long considered the defence problem, they had never developed long-range fuel tanks to allow their fighters an extended patrol at fighting altitudes. Therefore a great deal depended upon the ability of radar and ground-observer warnings to give sufficient time for the squadrons to climb to height. The RAF had learned from the early French campaign: aircraft were dispersed on the forward airfields, and flexible communications and command centres as well as elaborate early-warning systems were created, more than this, the Commander-in-Chief of Fighter Command, Dowding, was one man who had in the First World War understood the need to rest aircrews. Thus when the forward airfields began to take a pounding, he withdrew squadrons out of range and rested them while new pilots were assimilated.

The first phase of the Battle opened with the Germans attacking coastal convoys to bring out RAF fighters. Dowding refused to rise to the bait, but Churchill forced him to assign six fighters to cover each convoy. While this was fine for morale—and perhaps necessary, since the 'coal-scuttle brigade' was being attacked within sight of the coast—it hardly helped the defence preparation because it put hours on machines and fatigued pilots. What probably saved Dowding here more than anything else were the poor, wet weather, which limited the Germans to sporadic raids, and the fact that the Germans themselves were not ready.

Hitler was an offensive gambler and neither he nor Goering was willing to get involved in long campaigns. They understood the nature of war too well, but not what to do when the opponent refused to give up. Only on 21 July did Goering order planning for the attack on Britain, which was to be carried out with a three-day knockout blow in early August.

On 12 August the *Luftwaffe* launched a series of attacks, first against the south coast radar stations and then against fighter airfields. But they ran into two difficulties apart from weather. First their timing was bad; the early fighter-bombers knocked out the radar stations, but the bombers did not show up until about two hours later, after the stations had been repaired and the defending fighters were once again ready for combat. Carrier commanders in the Pacific judged this better. Secondly, the Germans did not know England well enough, even though well briefed, and in some cases mistook one airfield for another, so that several training fields were plastered

while nearby fighter fields were unmolested. Airfields had been built to standard patterns, and such a mistake was not hard to make, especially in a countryside with too many landmarks. A number of fighter airfields were hard hit, however, especially by fighter-bombers, whose arrival had been ignored by radar controllers (they were not distinguishable on radar from fighters, which Fighter Command had been under orders not to engage). A third problem for the Germans was the inadequate range, due to insufficient fuel, of the Me-109 escorts.

Attacks continued during August, and major battles raged over southern Britain as the RAF adopted the tactic of first attacking the high escort and, once it was in a dogfight, sending in other fighters to hit the bombers. Both sides made claims which were about three times as high as the real losses; but in any case the Germans could not make good their losses as rapidly as the RAF, because their monthly production rate was about 200 fighters, compared with the British 475. Both sides were getting short of pilots, in spite of the fact that British pilots generally parachuted back to their own territory even if shot down. In an attempt to improve their poor showing in Goering's eyes, the *Luftwaffe* removed its older wing leaders and put the top squadron commanders in their places. This improved morale, and a shooting competition began; but the move did not settle the arguments between the bombers and fighters as to the best method of protecting the attackers, or, in fact, of acomplishing the destruction of the RAF.

The fighter-bombers might have held the key to the problem. Incredibly some of the key RAF fighter-controller rooms were not only above ground but on airfields. If the *Luftwaffe* had realized this, it might have paralyzed the whole system by systematically destroying these nuclei with rapier fighter-bomber thrusts. Indeed, the Germans did decide in the new phase which opened on 24 August to make an intense effort to destroy the RAF fighter fields with groups of fifteen to twenty bombers protected by sixty fighters; by thus striking at airfields they stood a chance of hitting the sector control rooms, which the Germans assumed were in underground quarters. In order to be more effective and save wear and tear on pilots already flying five missions a day, the scattered German fighter squadrons were grouped onto airfields close to Calais. At this point, if the British had been less concerned about invasion barges, they

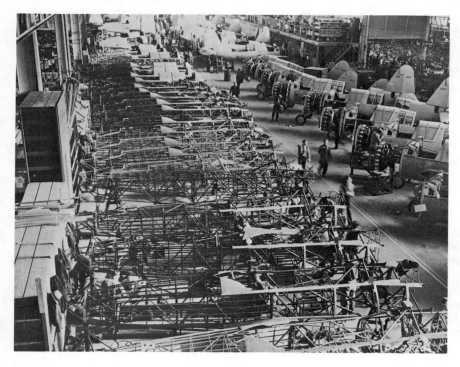

Vital throughout the war was aircraft production. Here Vought Sikorsky 0S2U Kingfishers are being built in Connecticut as part of the French order which helped stimulate the American aircraft industry before the United States geared up for war. **United Technologies**

MOEHNE DAM
(After attack)
K 1559
Neg. N° 24686

Though the 1939-45 War was notable for the development of complex technology and electronics, the equipment used in the classic 1943 night attack on the Moehne and Eder dams by low-flying four-engined heavy bombers is an acute reminder that the simplest system may still be the best. The aircraft approached from the bottom of the picture flying at 125 feet above the water, determined when the lights from two spots under the wings become one on the surface. The pilot aimed for the center of the dam and released the bombs when two dowels set on a stick on the cockpit coaming aligned with the towers visible on each side of the breach. The bombs then bounced and rolled over the anti-torpedo net and snuggled down the inside of the dam before exploding with maximum water-hammer effect causing the breach shown.

Grand Strategic Bombing

*The most mass-produced four-engined bomber of World War II was the **Convair** B-24 of which some 18,000 took the air, flying a total of 312,734 sorties and shooting down 4,189 enemy aircraft, according to company claims. They were used as heavy bombers, ocean patrol ships, and as long-range high-altitude transports operating on take-off at up to 72,000 lbs. With four 1200 hp engines, they cruised at up to 230 mph.*

*A typical crew of a B-24 is this one from the 827th Squadron, **484th Bomber Group**, USAAF, in Europe, with the navigator, bombardier, and two pilots standing, and four gunners, the engineer and radioman kneeling.*

Not all landings were successful, especially in muddy Italy in 1944 where this battle-damaged **484th** ship came to grief.

Nosewheels were an innovation and a source of grief and suspicion. Another **484th** aircraft, showing the vertical bombbay with the doors partly rolled up.

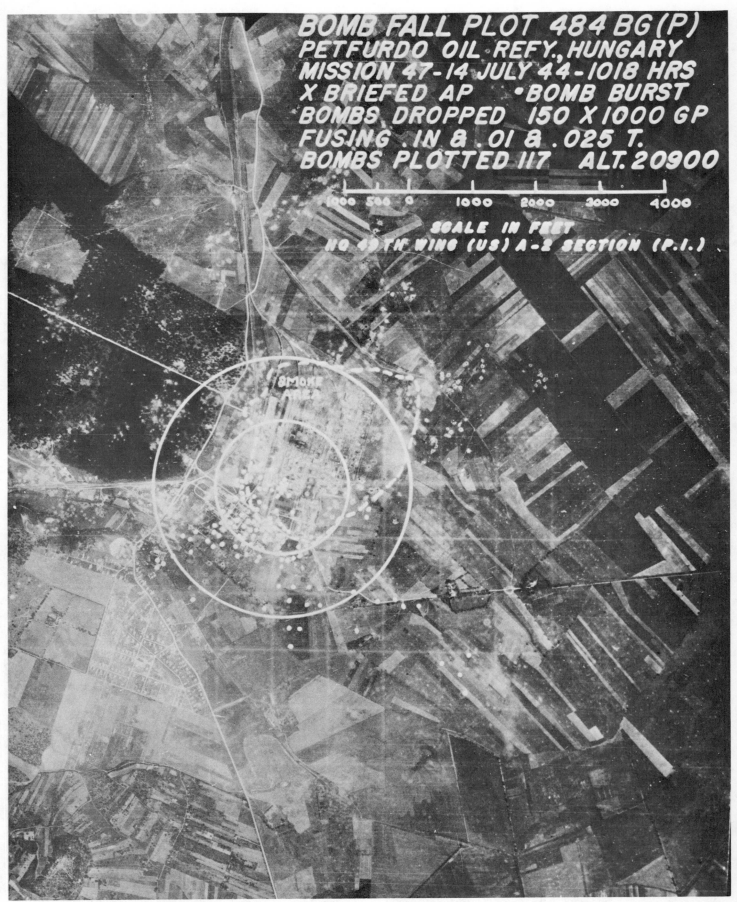

BOMB FALL PLOT 484 BG (P)
PETFURDO OIL REFY., HUNGARY
MISSION 47-14 JULY 44-1018 HRS
X BRIEFED AP   •BOMB BURST
BOMBS DROPPED 150 X 1000 GP
FUSING .IN & .01 & .025 T.
BOMBS PLOTTED 117   ALT. 20900

1000 500 0   1000   2000   3000   4000
SCALE IN FEET
HQ 49 TH WING (US) A-2 SECTION (P.I.)

SMOKE AREA

*Bombing analysis photo of the **484th** Bomb Group's attack on the Petfurdo Oil Refinery, Hungary, 14 July 1944. Legend shows 117-1000 pound general purpose bombs plotted within the target radius.*

might effectively have used their night bombers to attack these concentrations, on the principle that if bombs were dropping pilots would get little sleep and mechanics could do no maintenance, even if nothing was actually hit. Moreover, the *Luftwaffe* was so used to operating with air superiority that it was not attuned to defence.

On 31 August the British lost thirty-seven fighters, and the Germans, sixty, in melées over the bombers. The *Luftwaffe* believed, however, that it had passed the crisis. In the first week in September the RAF appeared to have slackened its effort, though 12 Group had switched over to two-squadron wings instead of individual squadron attacks. But then in retaliation for an attack on the outskirts of London, an area Hitler had forbidden, the RAF attacked Berlin; on 5 September Hitler ordered the attacks switched to London, and Goering took over personal command of the Battle of Britain. These events were critical, for the British were down to about a two-weeks' reserve of fighters. The Germans might have won the Battle of Britain if they had continued to attack RAF airfields. On the other hand, given its limited resources at the time and continued British withholding of fighters from the front lines, as the Germans were later to do in France, the *Luftwaffe* might still not have achieved victory. The answer is one of the tantalising 'ifs' of history. It would be interesting to 'game' it out. Some German generals have criticized Goering for starting the battle too early instead of saving the *Luftwaffe* for its usual *blitzkreig* support of invasion forces; they claim that Goering's plans were made without consultation, that they were unrealistic, and that they violated the principles of surprise and concentration.

The massive attacks on London by as many as 625 bombers were designed once and for all to get RAF Fighter Command committed and destroyed before bad weather set in. The climax of this operation came on 15 September, when Air Vice-Marshal Sir Keith Park, who commanded 11 Group, Fighter Command, made the decision—with Churchill sitting next to him—to commit all his reserves. The defence was successful because the exhausted German fighters could not escort a new wave before two hours had elapsed, by which time the RAF was ready once again. The *Luftwaffe* was discouraged. It had fought longer and harder and with greater losses than ever before, and yet the enemy could still field 300 fighters at a time. That Sunday afternoon battle resulted in a jubilant British claim of 185 Germans shot down (the actual number was fifty-six). It was a psychological victory and a propaganda coup. Hitler had already decided upon an attack on the Soviet Union; Britain would

The pictures on this page show damage to the German capital caused mainly by incendiaries during the battle of Berlin of late 1943 and early 1944. Note the later absence of roofs. **USAF**

be tormented by bombing, but was out of invasion danger once and for all. The battle petered out in November, partly due to aircrew fatigue, but Hitler left a fighting enemy in his rear to his later regret.

In the night-bombing attacks which followed, the Germans ingeniously fashioned radio beams along which their bombers could fly until they intercepted a second beam over the target, upon which they dropped their bombs. The British responded with ground anti-aircraft defences, beam-bending, and the development of night fighting. The last was at first crude, making use of Havoc light bombers equipped with searchlights to illuminate bombers for the accompanying Hurricanes. But the real solution was found in the Bristol Beaufighters, with airborne radar, vectored onto an invader by a ground controller, and carrying a powerful armament including 20-mm. cannon. When the Mosquito came into action, the RAF had a night fighter that was faster than anything flying at night against Britain for the rest of the war.

The Germans and the Japanese were hampered in air defence by their disbelief in its necessity and by old concepts in handling the problem. These restrictions were particularly acute in Germany. There in the late thirties defensive thinking was tied to the Siegfried Line with an Air Defence Zone West. It was a cordon system patterned on the First World War trench-type warfare. It provided for a defensive anti-aircraft belt through which bombers would have to fly, attacking and returning, if they were below 23,000 feet. But it was ineffective, for the British came in from the sea to the north in an end run. The line was backed by a very few squadrons attached to geographical zones, and it was not until 1943 that the Germans developed anything like an effective radio vectoring system to put fighters onto enemy aircraft. Even after that they suffered from difficulties with air defence to the end of the war. A major weakness came from the short endurance of their fighters; the Me-109, for instance, had only seventy-five minutes, half of which it needed for a climb to fighting altitude.

The Germans had radar, and the first British raid on Wilhelmshaven on the day war was declared was spotted on the experimental set and fighters were dispatched. But if the early sorties of 1939

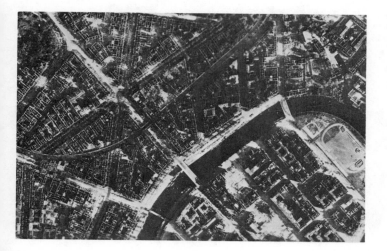

The problems of aircraft identification can be seen in these two pictures. Here a pilot bails out of an Me-109. **USAF**

taught the British that daylight attacks were fatal and that night operations were the solution, the Germans did not get the message from their own successes. When British night raids started in earnest in the autumn of 1940, the Germans could not counter them. The failure to develop a night-fighter system was due in part to overconfidence on Goering's part, in part to divided command structures and zone defence systems with rigid boundaries, and in part to poor technical direction. Again, it was 1943 before the Germans began seriously to try to deal with night raids, at a time when British attacks were having an adverse, though by no means critical, effect upon home morale. Night fighters of the Bf-110 (a radar-modified heavy day-fighter) and of the bomber-variant Ju-88 and Do-217 types equipped with radar were developed, but they suffered from lack of ground direction, altitude, range, speed, and trained crews. RAF tactics were confusing, at first because of the system of individual raiders flying to their own schedules, then—after the Cologne thousand-plane raid of May 1942—because a whole massive short stream of raiders would be routed evasively and would pass over the target in a very few minutes. And the RAF was by then being equipped with pathfinders and radar-bombing equipment so that it could operate in weather for which the German night fighters were unfit.

The light weight of the Allied grand-strategic bombing programme gave the Germans the chance to perfect their defences. But if the Germans were given a great deal of forewarning, they were not in fact forearmed, and a drastic escalation of German fighter and war production only took place from mid-1943 onwards, reaching its peak in September 1944. In this rush to make good neglected defences the Germans were forced—by their own stubbornness and by the usual run of failures incident to any attempt to develop new material hastily—to mass-produce the old tried and true designs, the Me-109 and the Fw-190. But these aircraft had already been out-developed by the Spitfire, let alone the newer American fighters, the P-47 Thunderbolt and the P-51 Mustang. The new spectacular German fighters, the rocket Me-163 and the jet Me-262, caused alarm but came too late. Moreover, even they were hampered by the German fighter-control system which was sometimes jammed by the Allies, or interdicted by German-speaking Allied interlopers giving

contrary instructions, or frustrated by the use of Window (the radar-reflective foil strips dropped by Allied aircraft).

On the ground the German defence system consisted of anti-aircraft boxes around vital targets. This scheme was acceptable as long as the British tackled only a limited number of precise militarily important targets. But once they abandoned these for the bigger urban complexes which were more easily hit, and which ironically did not always contain important factories, then the demands for protection far exceeded the means available, at a time when German operations in the Soviet Union and North Africa were calling also for increasing flak protection and U-boats were being armed. Flak belts were set up along the northern German coast and in the Netherlands, but the British often managed to achieve surprise even after crossing the belts, by evasive routeing and a choice of targets. From February 1942 to May 1945 flak accounted for 1,345 of the British bombers brought down and night fighters for 2,278. The rest (2,072) were lost for a variety of operational reasons from bad weather to engine failure to low flying, plus 112 in collisions. Of the 297,663 night and 66,851 day sorties dispatched, 13,778 were damaged; flak accounted for 8,848 and fighters for 1,228. Flying and other accidents damaged 3,159, of which 876 were write-offs.

After the early American daylight raids suffered some very heavy losses, the Anglo-American leaders changed tactics. The US Eighth Air Force was rested while the RAF night effort went into a higher gear and while long-range day-fighter escorts were developed. The pregnant pause paid off with the launching of the new daylight attack system in February 1944. By plunging deep into Germany the daylight attacks compelled the Germans to fight. Once they rose to the bait, they found themselves facing not only the close escort but also increasingly large roving hunter-killer groups who were not content to tackle fighters approaching the bombers, but who, by early 1945, were often willing to drop down on the deck and assault anything which moved, especially items with *Luftwaffe* markings. This decimated the German fighter force while badly affecting its morale. Moreover, the short range of German fighters meant that if they were withdrawn to airfields out of range of P-51s, which could escort bombers to Berlin and back, they could not reach bombers attacking targets in the Ruhr and the like. Attempts to resolve these

A German Fw-190 at high-speed with vapor trails from his wing tips. **USAAF camera-gun film**

P-38, long-range escort fighter.

B-17 in flight.

Buzz bomb.

B-24.

Arro Lancaster.

Lancaster with ground crew.

Halifax on ground.

Bombs for B-17.

difficulties by using parts of the famed *Autobahns* as airstrips were frustrated as Allied armies came into closer range so that even their tactical fighters could swarm over the defender's airfields, salvage depots, and supply trains. Through technological development and an indestructible arsenal in the US, as well as with the benefits of historical lessons, absorbed albeit with reluctance, the Allies were able to do to German air defence what the Germans had not been able to do to the British.

One interesting example of the power of the defence and the failure of offensive air power can be seen in the survival of Malta. Lying some sixty miles off the Sicilian coast and athwart the Axis supply routes to Africa, it instead of Crete should have been eliminated in 1941, as some Germans realized. The Axis powers failed to launch either an all-out air attack or an airborne invasion, even before the Russian campaign drained off the necessary forces. As a result, the British managed to maintain forces in Malta whose morale was from time to time raised by Spitfires flown in from British or American carriers. On one notable occasion, the new arrivals were just landing when radar picked up a German strike leaving its airfields in Sicily. The AOC Malta quickly decided to give them a surprise; every Spitfire was quickly unloaded, refuelled, rearmed, and scrambled in record time. The attackers received a nasty shock, and Malta gained a tremendous boost in morale, which helped carry the island through to its relief in 1943.

The one place in which the cordon defence worked fairly well was in the Allied defence of Britain against the V-1 flying bombs. An outer fighter belt was established in which the fighters had full rein, while inside this were fighter, gun, and balloon barrages. The speed of the defence system proved effective, but equally important was the over-running of the launching sites by advancing Allied armies after D-Day. On the other hand, no defence was found against the V-2, but in one sense little was needed. The V-2 rocket was spectacular, but as long as it was limited to a conventional one-ton warhead it was not exceptionally dangerous because it buried itself so far into the ground on impact before exploding. Nor did it pose a problem to civilian morale because unlike the V-1 it was not visible or audible until after impact. A more sustained barrage or attacks upon a population in a more jittery state might have had another effect.

Both sides engaged in operations which have since developed more significance. Intruding—mainly at night, but also with small fast aircraft by day—while not a major operation was one which was never given the emphasis it deserved. The Germans began the practice in 1941 and kept it up on a nuisance scale throughout the war. Intruders generally took advantage of the fact that night-bomber crews were tired after their long trips and so were not vigilant once they had reached the British coast. They also made use of the British Drem landing system which put an oval of lights around each airfield as a pattern which aircraft in the circuit followed. Counter-intruder work was made the more difficult by the number of aircraft in the area at the time, but was eventually helped by the installation of IFF in British aircraft. The RAF itself also engaged in both day and night intruder operations and fighter sweeps over northern France, which caused the Germans to draw back their aircraft to airfields out of range. Such operations were combined with train-busting and other nuisance work and the whole stepped up into a major assault in the transportation plan which preceded the D-Day landings. Night intruders, increasingly more active as radar became more sophisticated, harassed returning German aircraft and disrupted training. As Mosquitoes became available, they increasingly undertook special pinpoint raids to destroy key buildings and generally to keep the enemy defence on the *qui vive*. Their accuracy became legendary and they proved extremely hard to counter, for they often flew below radar level, hugging natural contours, and were for some time faster than enemy fighters.

In the Far East air defence was hampered by the lack of radar and by long distances over either jungle or water in which early-warning communications were sketchy, so that the defenders had little warning of approaching raids. It was not until spring 1944 that the Japanese high command realized that the B-29s would pose a threat to the homeland, and then they had only some 400 fighters on hand to deal with an aircraft which was much improved over the B-17 used in Europe. On top of this, rivalries between the Army and the Navy were such that home defence could not be properly co-ordinated, each service tending to keep its aircraft to protect its own bases and factories.

Like the Germans, the Japanese suffered from the decline in pilot training just when heavy, fast, well-armed fighters like the Raiden

The 1914 War had brought women back into the factories, the 1939 War put them in the cockpits. Here American WASPS ferry both a B-17 and a trainer. **USAF**

Bombers in the Pacific I

Waist gunners in the B-17 and the B-24 at 25,000 feet and minus 50 were hardly better off than the observers of World War I.

Growth in size of the bomber is seen in this shot of the Boeing B-17 of 1935 and its big brother the B-29 of 1943.

The Baka was a manned glider bomb, another suicide weapon.

The atomic bombs finally gave air forces deterrent capability.

Bombers in the Pacific II

Crew in the Aleutians.

B-29 cockpit.

B-29's dropping bombs.

B-29 overhead view.

Low-level bombing.

B-25 - 75mm gun.

B-25 attacking ship.

(Jack) were coming off production lines. The result was that training and operational accidents took a greater toll than did American gunnery. The Navy's new Shiden (George) fighter did well as long as a nucleus of aces were left to fly it, but they were soon killed. Thus by the end of 1944, General Curtis LeMay, commanding the American Twentieth Air Force, was in a position to consider a gamble—to remove almost all the armament from his B-29s so that they could carry the maximum load of incendiaries to Japanese cities. The country had never expected or planned for air attacks; the Japanese lacked the radar-controlled flak of the Germans, and most of their buildings were of highly inflammable materials. In 1945 the whole problem was intensified by the arrival of the American carrier task forces off the coast of the main island with their combat air patrols equal in strength to the whole Japanese fighter defence. Japan was defenceless before the atom bombs appeared.

4. Strategic Air Offensives

No discussion of the use of air power in the Second World War can avoid that emotion-packed topic, strategic—or more correctly, grand-strategic—bombing.

The Germans never really developed a doctrine of grand-strategic-bombing, and after the *Luftwaffe* failed in its attempted grand-strategic campaign against Britain, it reverted largely to a purely strategic and tactical role as an adjunct of the surface forces. In some cases German airmen struck at capital cities as strategic and grand-strategic objectives of surface attacks; such targets were bombed because their destruction could have an immediate effect upon the battle in progress and hasten victory. The 1940 German attack on London had started as a strategic bomber offensive, an extension of the tactical strikes against British airfields which were intended to prepare the way for an invading German army. But Hitler had decided by November to attack the Soviet Union and had withdrawn the invasion troops, and the Battle of Britain gradually degenerated into a grand-strategic campaign. German tactics shifted to night attacks on industrial centres and ports, but German intelligence was bad and it paid little attention to photo-reconnaissance materials (in contrast to meticulous use of such intelligence in land campaigns). Slightly more effective bombing of the ports, particularly the London and Liverpool docks, in the spring of 1941 might have brought British surrender at fairly small cost, by preventing the unloading and dispersal of the incoming supplies, and might thus have brought off the airmen's dream of victory through air power alone. Docking facilities were in short supply, railway junctions were vulnerable bottlenecks, and industrial centres were being attacked, in raids that received much critical attention in English propaganda. If the Germans just missed winning the war in the late summer of 1940 when they almost had Fighter Command down, they also again just missed in the spring of 1941 when their grand-strategic bombing of industry was having its effect, and they had almost jammed the docks to a standstill. At that critical moment the bombers were switched over to the attack on the Soviet Union. Yet the Germans had nearly won victory in Britain without a single 'strategic' bomber.

The *Luftwaffe* had been compelled in 1940 to wage a limited war both because its units were well below strength and because orders from on high limited targets to shipping in the Channel. The Germans also claim that the real reason lies in the fact that the *Luftwaffe* had no heavy bomber and that its best machine, the twin-engine Ju-88, had been made over into a dive-bomber. Ironically, having for the usual public relations value developed the Ju-88 into a record-breaking aircraft, military experts then loaded it down with so much operational equipment that its speed dropped from close to that of a Hurricane to some 100 mph slower, and its range from a 1,100-mile radius of action to about 600.

It is true that the Dornier Do-19 and Junker Ju-89 heavy bombers had been abandoned after Wever's death in 1936, but even if these aircraft or the He-177 had been available there is no guarantee that they would have enabled the *Luftwaffe* to beat Britain in 1940. Neither the intellectual make-up of Hitler and Goering nor the targeting system used could guarantee success. The German economy was not geared to produce the number of heavy bombers or engines that were needed; providing the crews for them would have taxed other airborne operations; and night-flying tactics and techniques were not developed.

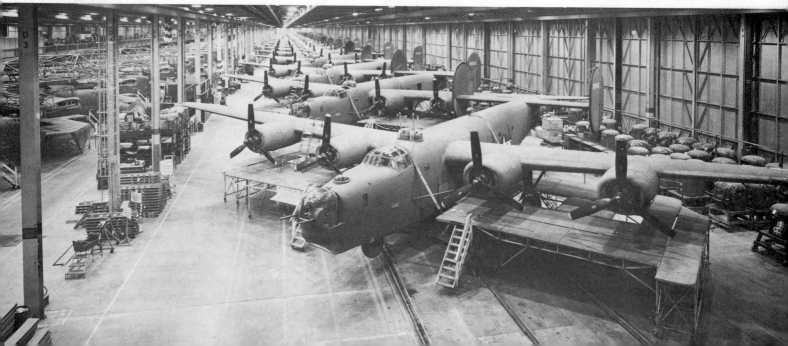

Aircraft production was a vital part of the American arsenal in WWII. Here B-24's are seen under mass-production in a plant in which the fuselages start down the lefthand side and come back down the right, gradually becoming complete aircraft, but even at this stage still riding the rails. **Convair**

In a rare 1944 daylight raid, an RCAF Halifax attacks LaHavre on the French coast, a port within fighter range of England. **Canadian Forces**

The British grand-strategic bomber campaign had its roots in the air mythology of the nineteen-twenties, although from Munich on the High Command knew how weak was the British counter-strike deterrent, and fear of retaliation led to its being used only for leaflet-dropping in the 'phoney war' period. But by the end of the summer of 1940 the British should have faced up to the basic question of what was to be their grand strategy. And the answer to this should have considered making the best use possible of the available and foreseeable air power according to the principles of war, especially protecting the lines of communication, securing the base, concentration, surprise, and economy of force. War calls for hard, clear decisions; too often they are not made.

The wave pattern found the British some way back in rearmamental instability when the war began. The heavy bombers needed for an independent bombing campaign were still in the prototype stages and would not be available to squadrons until 1942. Both tactically and in terms of technical developments, wartime equilibrium was not reached until well after the thousand-bomber raid on Cologne in May 1942. Demobilizational instability set in late in the war when the number of possible targets began to shrink rapidly and it became more and more difficult to employ the force by then in existence. This introduces, then, an additional facet of the model, that demobilizational instability may be brought about in part simply because there is no longer a job for a particular force to do.

The British deterrent in 1939 had not proved credible, except to the British themselves. By September 1940 it had obviously failed and the immediate necessities were defence of the United Kingdom, full production in the island arsenal, security for the lines of communication, victory in the overseas wars, containment of Germany, and neutralization of the neutrals. After the Battle of Britain, defence of the country demanded primarily air defence against night raids. Full production could be assured only if the sea lanes were secured, so that raw and manufactured materials, including machine tools, could reach Britain. This meant that as much air power as possible had to be diverted to winning the Battle of the Atlantic before the Germans had enough U-boats at sea to make really effective use of their newly won bases in France and Norway. Security of the sea lanes was also coupled to the problems of ending the campaigns overseas, notably in North and East Africa, advancing

political stability in the Middle and Near East, and bringing Italy, as the weaker partner in the Axis, to her knees. To secure these overseas areas and ultimately to defeat Italy would contain Germany and frustrate her westward ambitions, while ensuring British strength to meet any eventual return to the west by Hitler. Lastly, it was necessary to win victories in order to impress neutrals, so as to keep them either benevolently neutral or at least passive. Of these the most important were Turkey, Spain, Portugal, Sweden, and the United States. The six tasks demanded of British grand strategy were formidable enough without taking on another First-World-War-style continental war of attrition, which is what the air offensive against Germany became before 1944.

The qualification 'before 1944' is essential.

Only 17 per cent of the tonnage of bombs dropped on Germany by the British and American air forces was delivered before 1944. If the object had been to stimulate the German war economy and to encourage the Germans to fight, no better technique than the clumsy air offensive of 1940-1943 could have been devised. It is historically akin to the methods used at Gallipoli in 1914-1915 to prepare the Turks for an assault; and it had little adverse effect upon the German war effort, which did not begin to go into high gear until 1942 and did not reach its peak until 1944. With the benefit of hindsight it is clear that the German hit-and-run tactics should have been used. The Mosquito was an ideal weapon. Fast, cheap, using fewer engines (2:4) and a smaller crew (2:7) than heavy bombers and devastatingly accurate in its attacks, it also had a very low loss rate (2 per cent *vs* 5 per cent on average) and a much better availability on the morning after a raid (95 per cent *vs* 75 per cent). Moreover, it was a precision bomber able to strike at exactly the key targets which the economic planners most wanted to hit, such as oil and communications bottlenecks, and it could be used as a guerrilla to strike when and where the enemy least expected it. Unfortunately, Churchill, itching for action, sanctioned a large-scale, heavy bomber offensive.

The history of the bomber offensive against Germany is both difficult and simple to describe. Difficult because of the immensity of operations and their technological impedimenta, and simple because the patterns when seen from a distance are quite clear.

The first operations in 1939 quickly produced lessons which be-

As insurance against the B-29 not proving successful the USAAF also ordered the Consolidated B-32 Dominator with four 2200 hp engines, a 250 mph cruising speed and a bombload of forty 500 pounders. With 5,460 gallons of high-octane gasoline, it had a range of 3,700 miles. The crew of eight could man ten .50 caliber machine guns in five power turrets. **Convair**

cause they were wrongly interpreted had a lasting effect upon the war. The Wellingtons sent by the RAF contained only power-operated turrets, and the theory was that if the aircraft flew a properly tight formation enemy fighters could not attack effectively. Unfortunately, theory overlooked the fact that even the Wellington's tail turret contained first only two .303 machine-guns with which to face the 20-mm. cannon of the attacking fighters which quite outranged it. Moreover, the Wellington was vulnerable to attack from abeam, as German pilots quickly observed. At first higher RAF commanders were simply convinced that the pilots had failed to maintain formation. But they soon learned differently, and the immediate result was the limitation of heavy bombers to night operations.

With the 1940 attack in the West, bombers were put onto oil targets and transportation, in hopes of slowing the *Blitzkrieg,* making the *Luftwaffe* pull back fighters to defend the Fatherland, and compelling it to divert bombers to attack Britain. But as little damage was done by these very light raids, the German High Command sensibly ignored what protests there were and concentrated on quick victories in the land campaign. It is highly doubtful whether, in spite of the wishful thinking of their opponents, German morale would have cracked at this stage in a police state with a skilful and well-financed internal public-relations machine in control of the media. In fact, belief that a nation's morale can be cracked has to be analysed dispassionately and without inbred prejudices about political and other systems.

Following the German attack on Croydon, the British Cabinet desired retaliatory bombings of Germany, starting with a token raid on Berlin. This compromised the limited strength of the RAF by diverting it from oil targets. The Commander-in-Chief of Bomber Command in May 1940 had suggested limiting attacks to special targets in heavily populated areas in order to save bombs, and after the German attack on Coventry on 14 November 1940 the policy of a twin attack on oil and morale was accepted. But the damage done was minimal; these early raids were capable of delivering only about one hundred tons of bombs at a time; a bomb was only about two-thirds explosive and one-third casing; some 60 per cent of the bombs dropped on cities such as London landed in open spaces, and another 10 per cent were duds. The inaccuracy of British bomb-

ing began to be revealed by PRU photographs in November 1940, and eventually it was decided to follow the German precedent and make use of incendiaries with just enough high explosive to keep the firefighters in their shelters until the flames took hold. The effectiveness of these early raids was further blunted, however, by the desultory way in which the bombers reached the target area; while a raid might drag on for several hours, it violated the principles of war by not concentrating force in accuracy, weight, or time. And the whole effort was enfeebled by the constant necessity to call off aircraft for the Battle of the Atlantic, which was after all the fundamental conflict.

Bomber Command proposed in early 1941 that it go back again to attacks on transportation and morale, since it could not hit oil. The Cabinet agreed, but a month later a special study of the PRU claims, the Butt Report, showed the Cabinet that the aiming error was something like five miles; under those conditions there was little hope that Bomber Command could hit anything smaller than a city. The immediate response was to sanction area attacks. Again, the comment must be made that the whole grand strategy was wrong. Area attacks, while perhaps justifiable as retaliation, were a complete violation of the principles of war strategically. They vitiated forces rather than concentrating them against the decisive point, they were uneconomical of force, and they strengthened the enemy will to resist and innoculated him against later onslaughts.

The best solution to the effective use of Bomber Command in the bombing of Germany or, for that matter, elsewhere with the same aircraft and crews was the development in 1942 of the Pathfinder force. Leadership was given to D. C. T. Bennett, a sometime RAF pilot turned professional navigator. The author of one of the standard air navigation textbooks and the holder of a long-distance record, Bennett was a professional airman rather than a professional officer. The Pathfinder Force (PFF) went through many of the usual problems associated with establishing an élite organisation. Many commanders jumped at the chance to dispose of not their best but their worst crews. While some of the latter proved to be bright and were simply regarded as trouble-makers by sluggish commanders, others were duds who were promptly returned to their units. Gradually Bennett built up a force of élite crews which were specialists in locating targets and who could handle the new electronic

Passing lower over the Rumanian countryside north of Bucharest, B-24's of the USAAF depart the burning Ploesti oilfields after they had attacked the principal source of German oil supplies, 1 August 1943. **USAF**

gear which enabled them to place their pyrotechnic markers accurately at night. In addition the Master Bomber concept was instituted, according to which the bomber stream was commanded by a senior Pathfinder orbiting the target area who could call for new markers and give radio corrections to the arriving aircraft so as to keep bombs falling as close as possible to the aiming point. A nucleus of adept and experienced crews enabled a large number of inexperienced ones to concentrate on the target; thus, by vastly improving Bomber Command's aim the arrangement enabled it to develop economy of force.

At the same time, the Butt Report led to the appointment of Air Chief Marshal Sir Arthur Harris as Commander-in-Chief of Bomber Command. Harris, who had many of the solid qualities of Haig, assumed command at a time when Bomber Command was at last building up to a force of 500 bombers of the Wellington and Whitley types. In addition to the beginning of Pathfinder operations, Harris had two other advantages. He enjoyed close relations with Churchill, with whom he occasionally spent the weekend, thus by-passing the usual chain of command, and his experts began to work with those in the Ministry of Economic Warfare concerned with the German economy. In the spring of 1942 Bomber Command began to recover its reputation with a series of raids on German cities culminating in the massive attack on Cologne on 30 May. If not an outstanding military success, this was at least of considerable propaganda value.

It was in mid-1942, just as the RAF was working up its strength, that the first elements of the US Army Air Force's Eighth Air Force arrived in Britain to join the fray. Equipped with the much-vaunted Norden bombsight, their accuracy was reduced by European weather, while the necessity for a long straight run-in at a fixed altitude increased the vulnerability of the bombers to flak. Though they made a small attack on Rouen in northern France on 17 August, the necessity of building up for the 'Torch' attack on North Africa in November prevented the force from being effective until mid-December. It was at last allowed to move from attacks on the French coast to Bremen and Kiel, as P-47s arrived in Britain in January 1943, though they did not become fully operational until late summer in an escort role due to engine and radio failures.

At the Casablanca Conference in January 1943 the Allied heads

of state called for a round-the-clock air offensive against Germany. This was a great political gesture, but the means of carrying it out were still unavailable—not an uncommon dilemma facing military commanders. In theory the attack was to be a combination of massive RAF night area raids and precision USAAF day attacks. In fact, apart from the destruction of Hamburg in the fire-storm raids of July 1943, the scheme fizzled not so much on the inability of the Eighth Air Force to gain air superiority over Germany as on its intolerable losses when its bombers moved beyond the range of their escorts. The most disappointing of these raids were those on Schweinfurt of 17 August and 14 October 1943. That time elapsed before both these raids was due to the fact that if used intensively neither the bomber force nor its fighter escort was able to operate for more than about a week at a time. This meant that targets could not usually be demolished, only damaged, and the Germans were warned as to which targets needed to be dispersed and given time to undertake this.

For the twin attacks on the Schweinfurt ball-bearing plants and the Messerschmitt works at Regensburg of 17 August, 376 B-17 Flying Fortresses were dispatched, of which 315 attacked the target and dropped 724 tons of bombs. But sixty of the attacking force, or 19 per cent, were lost. The claim that 288 enemy fighters were shot down was greatly exaggerated; the Germans actually only put up some 300 fighters—a number far below the 4 : 1 ratio they believed necessary to defeat the American bomber force—and they lost only twenty-seven. Attacks in the second week of October cost the Eighth Air Force 148 aircraft and about 1,500 men. But the German fighter leaders, at least, now realized that they had to prepare to meet the long-range escorts which the Allies would now be bound to introduce. Hitler was still insisting that the bulk of fighter production go to the Eastern Front and the Mediterranean, and he and Goering opposed Adolph Galland, the German fighter leader who urged that the new jet Me-262 be pushed rapidly. Thus when in February 1944 a much augmented USAAF returned to German skies with P-51 escorts, the beginning of the end of German air power was in sight; the Germans, weakened by the 1943 attacks and with inadequate defensive aircraft, could not thwart the bombers, let alone the fighters.

The Battle of Germany was, however, virtually halted in the

Vietnam was not the first war in which aerial spraying and defoliants were used. Though this picture shows a C-123 in Vietnam, such activities took place in Burma in late WWII to clear routes of march of insects and cover. **USAF**

spring of 1944 by the need to deal with targets behind the proposed Allied beachhead in France. After some very strong political infighting within the Allied High Command, it was finally agreed that General Eisenhower, as Supreme Commander, should have control over not only the Allied Expeditionary Air Forces but also over Bomber Command and the Eighth Air Force. The plan to destroy transportation targets in France was the work of Eisenhower's Deputy, Air Chief Marshal Tedder. The directive Eisenhower issued in March essentially used the Allied air forces independently, as had been intended in 1918. Bomber Command attacked cities, and also transportation in France with an accuracy that surprised its Commander-in-Chief; the Eighth was assigned the destruction of the *Luftwaffe*, and the Allied Expeditionary Air Forces generally softened up northern France and German supply routes in the Low Countries. The end result was virtually a dislocation of the German ability to respond. Heavy bombers were even used over the battlefields and so churned up the ground that German tanks found themselves impotently isolated by craters. Thereafter, the bombers provided on occasion extra punch for tactical forces until released by the Supreme Commander in September.

At that time they went back to oil and morale targets, but the feeling existed, nevertheless, that Berlin should be demolished to aid the Soviets. The arguments between the oil group and the morale-busters lasted into 1945, when it was finally decided to make Dresden a psychological object lesson, with tragic consequences for the many refugees packing the city. The validity of that target has been argued ever since.

Both the British and American so-called strategic air offensive against Germany and the US Army Air Force attacks on Japan suffered from a lack of proper economic intelligence. At first highly inaccurate and consequently seriously damaging to areas surrounding military targets, strategic bombing was used as a sledgehammer, often wastefully and blindly. The reason for this can be found partly in the misinformation or lack of information concerning the capabilities and actual performance of the bombers, partly in the argument that war workers were combatants in a modern industrial conflict, partly in the fact that once a vast heavy-bomber force had

been built up its leaders were unwilling to keep it idle, and partly, in a sense on the part of the air forces that they had a 'mission' to smash evil. For some two years the British refused to believe photo-reconnaissance evidence that their average bombing error at night was five miles, and in any case economic intelligence was only gradually assessed as indicating that the key targets were small, compact, specialized industries such as ball-bearing plants, synthetic fuel refineries, and transportation bottlenecks. In Japan, as the United States' own Strategic Bombing Survey pointed out, the vital and easily broken rail network was largely ignored, although destruction of its few vital tunnels would have been decisive.

A technological argument could have been made for grand-strategic strikes against Russia which was related to the rate of Russian industrial development and to the Stalinist Five-Year Plans. This was that, because the Russians industrialized late, they had the advantage of being able to utilize large power plants and other complexes, whereas in the West the slower growth over a longer period of technological innovation resulted in smaller, scattered plants. Thus, ironically, while the Russians benefitted from the lateness of their modernization, conversely they were more vulnerable to precision attack. Fortunately for them, no one in the German air force appreciated this, or so Speer claims.

Thus though it is important not to overlook the seesawing technical battle between the attackers and the defenders, it must be recognised that the grand-strategic air offensives against Britain, Germany, and Japan resulted from intellectual political battles fought out at the higher-direction levels throughout the campaigns. In a scientific war oral evidence was no longer acceptable; airmen had to justify their claims by photographic and other means, and these were tested by economic and other intelligence units not under their control. In this respect it should be noted that Allied intelligence assessments of German aircraft production were highly inaccurate. Until mid-1942 they estimated the average German monthly aircraft production at 1,575, while the actual rate was 880; by 1944 they erred too far the other way—1,870 compared to the actual 2,811.

One of the great things about the P-51 was its range, so that when the B-29's opened the offensive from the Marianas against the Japanese home islands, the bombers could be escorted. Here a B-29 acts as lead navigator for its Mustang escorts. **USAF**

5. Land-based Air Power at Sea

Further to complicate the matter of choosing targets during the last nine months of the European war were the many parties to targeting, from Tedder at the tactical end to the Commander-in-Chief of the USAAF in Washington, not to mention the Admiralty, faced again with another new U-boat menace technically far more serious than any heretofore. And in a sense this brought home again the fallacy of not winning the Battle of the Atlantic before tackling Germany itself. While Harris, appointed Commander-in-Chief of Bomber Command in 1941, can be lauded for his single-minded devotion to the bombing of Germany, he can be condemned for his unwillingness to recognise the need to win the Battle of the Atlantic first. He fought constantly with the Admiralty over targets, always resenting the diversion of his force from what he regarded as its prime goals. While naval men may have argued that the way to defeat the U-boats was to let them attack well-defended convoys, proper use of air power also dictated attacks upon U-boat assembly slips and servicing pens, nearly all of which were easily identifiable targets because they were located on shorelines. That these attacks were not decisive till late in the war was due to the lack of effort, the lack of concentration, and the inadequacy of the attacks before 1944.

There are many unities between the Battle of the Atlantic and the Battle of Germany. Both were three-dimensional. In one, convoys faced U-boats; in the other, escorted bombers faced fighters. In each, the method by which a battle was won was to lure the opponents to the cargo carriers to be destroyed. This tactic failed when the defenders were too weak but was successful once the close escort was supplemented with hunter-killer groups and with direct attacks on the enemy's bases. Just as the convoys benefited from direction-finding wireless fixes locating their chattering enemy, so the bomber groups also depended on intelligence which located defending fighter formations. And just as the convoys began to benefit from long-range air patrols or planes flown off from escorting carriers, so the bombers over Germany benefited from pathfinding and other activities, even to the extent at times of decoy raids. While the problem of locating and destroying the U-boat was

a slower one, an interchange between night-fighter and anti-submarine warfare crews might well have proved highly rewarding, and still might. The problem remains essentially the same: protect, seek, find, and destroy.

The destruction or harassment of shipping by land-based air power was a constant feature of the war around Europe and was practised with varying success by German, Italian, and British airmen. The sea has marks for those who can see them, and crews learned to get the feel of the weather and to read the surface. The Germans, after some successes in the North Sea, settled down to make Luftflotte X the major anti-shipping force, and the personnel who manned its torpedo-carrying He-111s became highly efficient. While they quickly learned that attacks on British coastal convoys were often risky if fighter escort was present, they soon found profitable targets in the Mediterranean and then in the Russian convoys, which they mauled so badly in 1942 that between July of that year and March 1944, when air escort became available, only one convoy was run. Though the Ju-87 Stuka was effective in the English Channel and even more so in the clear Mediterranean, it remained highly vulnerable to fighters. In general the Germans used the He-111 and the Ju-88, especially when the weather was bad and the attack had to be made at low altitude. Nobody found the high-level bomber of much use except as a diversion.

The British at first used a twin-engine torpedo-bomber, the Beaufort; but, as it was as vulnerable as most medium bombers to the increasingly heavy flak which German coastal convoys threw up, as well as to fighters, its place was taken by its stablemate the Beaufighter. The latter was both heavily armed and highly manoeuvrable; it could also carry both a torpedo and rockets, when these came into use in 1943. Thus it had a punch like a light cruiser at ten times the speed.

The response of all sides was not only to arm convoys and their escorts heavily, but to develop other defensive devices such as kite balloons, towed in the First World War also, and flame-throwers, as well as looser steaming formations better suited to violent air-sea battles. It was in attacks on shipping that the Italians proved most brave and very adept, but they dropped out of the war just as their equipment became obsolete. From 1941 there was an increasing tendency to use fighter-bombers or rocket-firing fighters against the

The Consolidated Catalina or PBY was built in both the United States and Canada as a long-range patrol bomber for maritime operations. Though it cruised at only 117 mph with two 1200 hp engines, it could stay airborne for more than 28 hours. This one was built under license by Boeing in Canada for the British.

Flying-boats were floated onto beaching-gear and drawn out of the water when not on operations or when needing repairs. Here an RCAF Catalina is beached in Ceylon in WWII. **Canadian Forces**

many small coastal vessels which dotted the European shipping lanes. These were not worth a torpedo and were too hard to bomb, but were vulnerable to rocket and cannon fire. Moreover, offensive sweeps by fighter-bombers flying low were hard to spot on radar and harder to defend against. The one curse, apart from an opponent's air escort, was the inaccuracy of the attackers. Torpedoes were tricky to drop, had to be aimed carefully, and depended for their accuracy on the guesses and calculations made by the attacking crew, who had also to resist the tendency to jink on the approach. Rockets only required that the aircraft be held steady for a few seconds and could be aimed by firing the guns until hits on the target were observed. A similar advantage had been conferred on the heavy bombers when the British Mark XIV gyro bombsight became available, allowing the bombs to be dropped while the aircraft was taking evasive action.

The use of land-based air power at sea was perhaps best demonstrated by aircraft based on the island of Malta. PRU Marylands and Spitfires from there kept watch on Italian shipping, and it was their photos and reports which enabled the RAF and the Royal Navy to attack Italian supply ships almost constantly. Though the cost of maintaining Malta was high, the damage its ships and aircraft did was more than worth it.

But from the German and the British standpoints in the Battle of the Atlantic, land-based air power played yet another role, that of longer-range air patrol. German Fw-200 Condors scoured the Atlantic shipping lanes after the Fall of France seeking British convoys. The British retaliated with fighters shot off catapults on merchant ships, then with escort carriers, and by 1943 the U-boats were largely left to seek for themselves or relied on radioed intelligence. On the other hand, the British started the war woefully inadequately equipped to patrol the lifelines by air in spite of the lessons of the First World War. Though Coastal Command, which controlled land-based air power at sea out of Britain, was established in 1936, it had few suitable aircraft in 1939 or 1940. Even machines it could have had were squandered in ferrying supplies to Norway or in the bomber offensive against Germany. Its Sunderland flying-boat had only an 800-mile radius of action in an ocean three thousand miles across. On top of that, Britain's Irish bases had been largely given away in 1938 by a well-meaning Prime Minister. Air

patrols with Whitleys and Hudsons were started from Iceland, but it was not until 1942 that long-range Catalina flying-boats and VLR (very long range) Liberators began to become available, and not until an air base was established in the Azores in conjunction with greatly increased escort-carrier and hunter-killer forces was the air gap over the middle of the Atlantic closed. Before that, aircraft proved invaluable in patrolling close to convoys, thus keeping U-boats down so that they could neither sight shipping nor send out intelligence.

In May 1942 the RAF established a radar offensive against U-boats in the Bay of Biscay. This was a strategic air offensive properly designed to harass and destroy U-boats in transit between their own bases and operating areas along the convoy routes. To counter it, the Germans developed long-range patrols of Ju-88C heavy fighters but these had less effect as faster and better-armed aircraft, such as the VLR Liberator and Mosquitoes, were introduced over the Bay. The battles developed in intensity in 1942 and reached a climax in 1943. Once British aircraft equipped with radar and Leigh lights located U-boats on the surface at night, charging their batteries and attempting to make a quick passage, they dropped down, illuminated the surfaced submarine, and attacked. When the Germans countered by developing a radar detector, the British switched wave-lengths. In July 1943 aircraft sank six submarines in the first twenty-one days of the month, and destroyed nine more in the last seven days, in a combined offensive with hunter-killer surface forces. For all of this to be possible, well-trained crews and the right weapons were required. At first anti-submarine warfare suffered from a lack of suitable bombs and depth-charges, from poor aiming techniques which failed to allow for the movement of the U-boat while the depth-charges sank to their pre-set level, and from the general paucity of aircraft. By 1943 aircraft were available in sufficient quantities that, as soon as a sighting was reported, additional aircraft could be vectored in. Thus when U-boats took to travelling in company and fighting back on the surface, their defence could be disoriented by attacks from various directions simultaneously. The U-boat's 20-mm guns could also be stymied by the fire from the .50-calibre guns on Liberators and Fortresses, and eventually silenced by the arrival of the Mosquito with a 57-mm cannon and rockets. The submarine only had to be holed once for it to be fatal.

The Battle of the Atlantic was in its last two and a half years dominated by Allied air power. Of the German and Italian submarines sunk during the six years of the war, surface forces alone sank 285½, land-based aircraft 245½, ship-based aircraft 44, and a combination of surface and air forces 53. In addition, 64 were destroyed by bombing at their bases. But these figures alone do not tell the whole story, because the escalation of air effort was such that while in the first three years of the war surface vessels sank sixty-one and assisted in seven cases, aircraft accounted for only nine. In 1942–1943, when the Battle of the Bay of Biscay was on, aircraft accounted for eighty-eight and a half kills compared with seventy-five and a half for ships and sixteen combined sinkings. And in the last two years of the war aircraft destroyed well over half the submarines sunk in the European theatre. Bombing raids steadily grew more accurate and concentrated: after destroying two U-boats building in the first three years of the war, they disposed of twenty-six in the next two years and thirty-six in the final year of the war. In other words, attacking assembly plants was only effective when the raids were continuous and the aiming of sufficiently destructive bombs accurate. Air attacks at sea were less costly in losses of aircraft and highly skilled crews, and far more effective, as the onslaught on the U-boats was continuous, while they were only able to retaliate when surfaced. Even the adoption of the schnorkel, enabling them to travel submerged, did not shield them fully from the better radar by then in use.

The air war at sea was at all times strategic or grand-strategic and dependent for its effectiveness upon the tactics, equipment, training, and flexible response of the leadership. In the case of the Battle of the Atlantic it was for both sides a grand-strategic campaign vital to victory or defeat. The British won a definite victory because they were able to mobilize and concentrate their forces and because the Germans had not developed the concept of air cover and long-range reconnaissance for their navy, which Hitler did not favour.

6. Analysis

In answer to the airmen's complaint that they were never allowed to use air power properly, the critic is tempted, after considering the Second World War, to reply that the trouble is that they *were* allowed to use it *improperly*. The victor in most campaigns was he who could move most rapidly and who observed the principles of war in regard to protection of the base and the lines of communication, concentration, economy of force, and surprise. Many opportunities for airmen to have won the war went unrecognized or unheeded. In most cases, decisions affecting these opportunities had been made in peacetime. As noted earlier, actual declarations of war seem to come part way through the period of rearmamental instability, so that the force which is better prepared at that moment has the better chance of winning quickly. But the Second World War showed all too clearly that preparation must include the gathering and use of intelligence. The Germans, tactically oriented, were prepared to deal with Poland and France, and even Norway, but they were insufficiently educated where England and the Soviet Union were concerned. As continual campaigns eroded the German momentum, when wartime equilibrium set in late in 1942 the *Luftwaffe* suffered from the fact that the German economy was still not in high gear; the air force was trying to win with designs that came from the early years of rearmamental instability. Though the British put a temporary stop on their own developments for some months during the Battle of Britain, they continued to balance quantity with quality so that they kept the technical edge sharp. The Japanese made the mistakes of the Germans, while the Americans and the Soviets followed the British pattern. Yet good equipment without intelligent doctrine and qualified crews was not enough. Modern war requires the mobilization of manpower, management, and methodology. It is an organizational business in which the human problems can become paramount. Thus on the German side

One of the most useful vessels in closing the patrol gap at sea in the war against submarines was the baby flattop or escort carrier, generally built, as here, upon merchant hulls. In this case she is being used to ferry P-38's and P-47's to the war zone. **Lockheed**

Anti-shipping strikes were heavily used by both sides in the maritime war. Here a Douglas A-20 of the USAAF in the Southwest Pacific skip bombs a Japanese transport from masthead height. **USAF**

there were the problems of Goering, Udet, and Hitler; the British had Churchill and Harris; the Americans, the heirs of Mitchell.

The war showed the effectiveness of tactical air forces over land and sea and the ineffectiveness of the deterrent weapon. Early bombing offensives were highly inaccurate and costly, and since tactical air forces, operating at much lower altitudes over both land and sea, were much more accurate, it can be argued that they were a far better investment than high-level bombers. Yet operational research helped to increase accuracy; and, in fact, when high-level bombers were employed in tactical roles their accuracy surprised even the Commander-in-Chief of RAF Bomber Command, who had come to believe that they could only hit cities.

The war showed also that no weapon could be used continuously without modification in tactics and that senior commanders had to understand a weapon's limitation. Thus the Stuka had its heyday, but it soon became the victim of fighters unless moved to less well-defended targets. Paratroopers and airborne operations were acceptable only so long as they achieved a *coup de main* with minimum losses and were not expected to fight against fully equipped ground forces for more than about twenty-four to forty-eight hours. Another lesson was the extreme value of a transport service which had sufficient useful aircraft to be able to resupply an army on the move. Moreover, as aircraft ceased to be first-line they could be usefully employed in both training and tactical roles. Bombers which became too vulnerable for offensive operations were used in operational training units and as glider tugs or transports, or were assigned to ocean patrols. Fighters became fighter-bombers and personal transports. An aircraft designed for one task might be more successful in another; or conversely equipment that seemed wonderful in peace might prove of more limited use in war.

The problem in war was to make the most effective rather than the most showy use of what was available. To this end the work of the boffins was enormously useful, and their contributions, foreshadowed in the 1914 war but generally neglected in peace, became manifold. And behind them were experts in the laboratories, who developed better theories and better weapons, and the factories which produced the equipment. But even though this was a techno-

logical war, outside the main European theatre much of it was fought with the equipment at hand. In more distant theatres, as even in the Soviet Union, the side which did not have air superiority was not necessarily the side which caved in at once. In several theatres neither side had aircraft to cover the battlefield, let alone the back areas, so even if defenders had no air cover, unless it was in a naturally channelled area such as Greece they could counter with dispersion and anti-aircraft fire. Tactical air forces were ordinarily at their most effective when they could make continuous attacks upon an enemy caught by geography in a pass, at a river crossing, or in some other bottleneck, but in Italy and Burma geography could frustrate air power.

At almost no stage of the war was air power alone decisive. It was most effective when combined with surface forces, except in those cases where it had a distinct advantage over its opponent as in the war at sea, and it excelled in its capacity for continuous observation and destruction. It was used at its best in fast and sometimes repeated thrusts at a vital target, thus clearing the way for surface action, but at some other times its use was superfluous. Ironically, the economic effect of bombing cities was in the long run the opposite of that anticipated. By destroying German and Japanese urban areas and initially forbidding the defeated nations to rebuild armed forces, the victors forced them to start afresh and concentrate their energies; their very modernization has created economic nations that increasingly challenge the victors. Tactical air power created no such bogeys.

Since 1974 much has been revealed about the British decoding of the German Luftwaffe signals. These intercepts are in general known as ULTRA from their secret classification. It is true that the British through them had access to German intentions during the Battle of Britain, but such entry was not continuous. Not did it apply overseas immediately, so great care must be taken in assuming that older accounts are invalid because they were written before ULTRA as there were many other sources of intelligence. Conversely, neither British nor American codes were safe all the time. In the Pacific the American had cracked the Japanese code before Pearl Harbor and material from this source was and is known as MAGIC.

Noted Designers

Barnes Wallis

Ed Heineman

Willy Messerschmitt

The Regia Aeronautics was one land-based air force which was effective at sea. One of its most trusted weapons was the Savoia-Marchetti SM-79 torpedo bomber. **Source unknown.**

PART FIVE

The Second World War: Seaborne Air Power

1. The General Nature of Air Action at Sea

It must not be overlooked that the air war campaigns in Europe were characteristically long and drawn out; the strategic air offensive against Germany, for instance, dragged on for nearly six years. Even the operations of tactical air forces consisted of a fairly endless series of raids and sorties. Rarely, if ever, was there a clearly defined air battle in which it was clear to both sides that one had won and the other lost. The situation at sea was very different. Naval battles rarely lasted over four days and on most occasions much less than that. Clearly one side thought it was the winner, and generally it was right. But it is the very shortness and decisiveness of battles at sea, as well as the fact that the carrier actions meant a new kind of warfare, that makes these conflicts of such interest that a number have to be described in some detail. They must also be examined in order to draw up a balance between the coverage generally given by historical analysts to separate air forces and that given to naval air arms. Though naval aircraft used fewer bombs, the task forces wielded by carrier admirals were often as powerful as the armadas commanded by airmen over land.

Land-based air power played a significant role throughout the war at sea, and in Chapter IV some of the lessons of the Battle of the Atlantic and the early Mediterranean conflicts were analyzed. By 1943 the Battle of the Atlantic had reached the plateau of wartime equilibrium, and the use of aircraft carriers had become an accepted tactic. Although air forces flying from shore bases continued their important operations at sea until the end of the war, the discussion in this chapter will turn largely to seaborne air forces, or the naval use of naval air power.

The Atlantic-Mediterranean area and the Pacific theatre were on the whole scenes of entirely different naval aviation operations, and analysis of them provides different historical lessons. In the Atlantic-

Mediterranean area, which included the North Sea and the route to the Soviet Union, allied naval air power contended with Axis submarines and shore-based aircraft, but not with Axis carriers. In the Pacific there was little Axis submarine activity, nor did the Japanese respond in the air to the devastating US Navy underwater craft; but the Pacific was the scene of much carrier action between rival fleets. In both oceans escort carriers were employed for amphibious operations, and this was perhaps the greatest unity between the two theatres.

2. The Atlantic-Mediterranean Area

All through the inter-war years Liddell Hart and others had been stressing that the appropriate British role was not to fight on the Continent, where England did not have the manpower to compete, but rather to make use of maritime mobility to strike at times and places of her own choosing, forcing the enemy to expend his energies guarding against threats which might materialize in any one of a dozen or more places. As Captain Roskill, the official British naval historian, has noted, it was a blessing in disguise when the British were thrown off the Continent. Unfortunately, many of the advantages thus gained were frittered away by the Prime Minister's insistence on *action*, which led to the wasteful Greek campaign, the loss of an advanced base in Crete, and the virtual impotence of Malta, not to mention the diversion of resources in the air offensive against Germany.

A really effective British naval strategy was handicapped by the pre-war resistance to air power, a prejudice which was reinforced by the traditional outlook towards both submarines and aircraft displayed in the writings of the Navy's one influential pre-war thinker, Admiral Sir Herbert Richmond. The Admiralty was reluctant to develop aircraft-carriers at all, and particularly unwilling to build

The Fairey Swordfish, "the Stringbag," was on active service for a decade which included the whole of World War II, including the epic raid on Taranto. Slow, docile, and sturdy, it could be used to launch torpedoes or to chase E-boats. This is the FAA Museum's flying display aircraft complete with white ensign, hook down, and crew saluting during a flypast. **British Airways**

them instead of battleships. More than this, until three years after serious rearmament started it was the Air Ministry which controlled the design, development, and production of naval aircraft. As a result of such attitudes and organization, the British Fleet entered the war with too few carriers carrying too few aircraft of too old designs.

In addition, British tactical doctrine was more attuned to peace-time manoeuvre displays than to the facts of battle. The umpires and commanders on manoeuvres were usually gunnery officers, yet because the power of the air arm was so heavily discounted—and British ships were therefore not equipped with strong anti-aircraft armament—flyers had not been compelled to evolve new tactics which would distract the gunners. Moreover, despite the fact that torpedoes were regarded as the principal ship-killing weapon by both the Fleet Air Arm and the RAF, little work had been done to develop gliding or homing torpedoes (the latter in part because submarines were also distasteful to gunnery officers) or 'black-boxes' which would enable torpedoes to be dropped accurately with the minimum run-in.

A further limitation was Richmond's idea that if there were but a few vessels of any one type available, they should not be hazarded. Thus carriers should be used in anti-submarine and anti-raider sweeps in the open sea but kept out of the narrow seas in which they might be attacked by shore-based aircraft. Since naval aircraft would thus only be employed against ships at sea, not enough thought was given to fighter defence.

The continental powers were not much interested in carriers. The Italians really had no need for them within the confines of the Mediterranean because they had bases on both sides of it as well as in the Dodecanese. Moreover, in Italy the Air Ministry came into being in 1922, and aviation was thus placed firmly in the hands of a third service. The Italian Navy was not able to free itself, and perhaps did not entirely want to, from an air ministry which enjoyed the close support of the dictator. In 1939 France had one aircraft carrier, *Béarn*, but little concept of what to do with it. In Germany a start was made towards a carrier with the laying down of *Graf Zeppelin*, but as aviation was under the control of Goering's *Luftwaffe* no aircraft were developed to the operational stage for naval use other than those for catapulting from cruisers and capital ships.

It is fair to say that in the European theatre at the beginning of the war those who had carriers had little doctrine, while other naval powers had not yet come to appreciate the significance of the use of air power at sea. By the time France fell in June 1940, only the British were left with operational carriers.

On the whole, European naval aircraft were inferior to those of the United States and Japan at the outbreak of war and generally remained less efficient than American aircraft, although by 1944–45 many of the aircraft in British carriers were of American design. The reason for this was that only in the United States and Japan were there major naval air arms free to purchase designs specifically manufactured to meet their own requirements. In Britain until 1937 purchasing for the Fleet Air Arm was handled by the Air Ministry; naval officers lacked experience in writing specifications, and the three or four companies that had specialized in naval aircraft had received so few orders that they lacked the necessary expertise to produce new types quickly at a time when aeronautical technology was going through the revolution from fabric-covered biplanes to all-metal monoplanes. Even more than the RAF, the FAA suffered from the fact that its operational requirements, which had to be included in specifications, lacked farsightedness; and there was no encouragement for designers to risk limited resources on advanced conceptions. The creation and acceptance of new equipment require imagination both within and without the services.

The Royal Navy entered the war with a force largely composed of biplanes, a number of which were conversions of RAF models. It had a relatively new, though already obsolescent, torpedo-spotter-reconnaissance machine in the single-engine Swordfish biplane, which remained operational throughout the war, and a small quantity of modern machines in the form of the Skua and Roc monoplane dive-bombers and fighters. Later the Fulmar and Firefly were added. The first single-seat monoplane fighters to reach the FAA were ex-Battle of Britain Hurricanes converted in 1941 for use off merchant-ship catapults and also from carriers. These were followed by Spitfires and by the delivery of Martlets from America, and later by Corsairs and Hellcats. On the whole in European operations what British carriers needed were fighters to provide a defensive umbrella over the Fleet and other convoys. Offensive striking power was less important, but also less available. Most British torpedo-bombers were not successful in attacks on surface ships with air protection, and they could generally be used against ships in harbour only by exceptional tactics, such as in the night attack at Taranto in November 1940. At the end of the war suitable aircraft were just beginning to come from British manufacturers but, apart from the Barracuda, the majority of these never saw action.

In other European air arms the same problems arose. Naval aircraft were in most cases standard types adapted for work at sea as torpedo-bombers and in mine-laying duties.

Three important changes took place in the equipment of naval aircraft in the European area. The first was the increase in gun armament from two machine-guns to eight or to 20-mm cannon, or in the case of American aircraft to .50-calibre machine-guns instead of .303s. The second was the introduction at the end of 1941 of radar (then called ASV) in naval aircraft; and the third, the introduction of rockets in 1943. To these might be added the development of escort aircraft carriers and such other improvisations as merchant vessels fitted with a fighter on a catapult and flight decks on grain, and other 'MAC' ships (merchant aircraft carriers) which enabled aircraft to be carried to sea for local patrols near convoys.

The increase in gun armament paralleled that ashore and gave naval fighters a better chance against their shore-based opponents. It had been decided early in the 'thirties that the speed of air combat gave aircraft so little time to fire that with two machine-guns of the type then used they could not destroy an opponent. The British solution was to increase the number of guns; the American, to use the .50-calibre machine-gun; while most European nations favoured the installation of cannon, which, while firing at a slower rate, could use explosive shells, any one of which could cause severe damage. The British eventually followed this trend, but it was not until 1943 that cannon-armed naval Fireflies became operational. In the meantime the FAA's opponents were usually cannon-armed German Me-109s or Italian Macchi 202s, or the less well armed Fiat G-50 or the biplane CR-42s.

In multi-seat aircraft of all European powers, the rearward defensive armament had failed to keep pace with the increase in fire-power of fighters. Most aircraft used over the sea had a single machine-gun fired by the observer. The only aircraft which were hard to attack were the British Sunderland, though it only had .303-calibre machine-guns, and the American Liberator and Fortress, which were used on long-range patrols by Coastal Command, and possibly the German Ju-88C. The German Fw Condors and Heinkels, the Italian Savoia-Marchettis, and the British Beauforts and Hampdens were all easily shot down from the rear, as was the British Fulmar fighter-reconnaissance machine, which carried no rearward guns. On the whole more formidable was the American Avenger with its power-operated .50-calibre turret and ventral gun position, but few of these aircraft saw air-to-air combat in the Atlantic-Mediterranean theatre.

Experiments with airborne radar had started as early as 1939, but when the war broke out there was an acute shortage of experimental and production facilities. It was only in late 1940 that radar began to appear at sea on ships, let alone aircraft, and it was not until early in 1941 that aircraft on patrol could use it to spot both submarines and surface ships. As time went on it came increasingly into use, thus stripping vessels on the surface of the veil of darkness or fog. At the same time the installation of radar on ships prevented aircraft from making surprise attacks and gave defending fighters a chance to scramble and gain altitude to intercept attacks. This was particularly important in the case of defence against the German Stuka dive-bomber, which was very vulnerable when not in its dive. The early sets with a range of under fifty miles only gave less than a five-minute warning; in such cases fighters could only be scrambled if they were already spotted for launching. Forunately for the British carriers the Germans had not had experience with carrier operations and failed to time their strikes so as to catch the carriers at their most vulnerable, with aircraft landing on. British carriers were also saved on a number of occasions both by skilful handling and by their armoured flight decks. By the time small carriers were being used to support amphibious assaults in late 1942 and afterwards, even these smaller carriers were equipped with radar and casualties were light. No British carriers were lost to enemy air attack in European operations, and only the old carrier *Hermes* to Japanese. Five others were sunk by U-boats and one by an internal explosion.

Experiments with rocket projectiles for aircraft began in 1941 in Britain, but it was 1943 before tests were completed and naval aircraft began to use rockets at sea. They had a number of distinct

In the European theater the problem for naval fighters was that they constantly faced land-based aircraft of superior quality. The Macchi 205 was the developed version of the 202 Italian fighter. **Stato Maggiori Aernoautica**

advantages. They carried as much explosive as a three-inch or five-inch shell. They had no recoil so that they could be fitted to almost any aircraft, and they were simple to use with the pilot merely aiming the aircraft. After their adoption, the torpedo, with its need for intricate calculations and a perfect low-level approach, was much less often employed. Moreover, rockets allowed older aircraft, such as Swordfish and Albacores, to be used against E-boats and other small craft that were either not worth a torpedo or of too shallow draft for one to be effective. In addition, the weight of eight rockets was not as difficult for the less experienced new pilots to handle as was a torpedo, and they also cut down the training required of aircrew. Less use was made of them in the Pacific than in the Atlantic because in the former area naval aircraft were employed not so much against coastal shipping and submarines as against enemy fleets with their well-armoured ships.

In the European theatre the carrier, in spite of increases in the power of the aircraft in its striking force, remained of small potential as compared to land-based forces. The fleet carrier, even when equipped with American naval aircraft, could generally only launch a maximum striking force of some thirty-six to forty aircraft. In the case of *Ark Royal* in 1940 this meant eighteen fighters and eighteen torpedo-bombers. In the Pacific larger forces were operated, both because the carriers were bigger and carried sixty or more aircraft, and because doctrine and availability caused them to be operated in company. Thus striking forces of a hundred or more aircraft were common at the beginning of the war, and a combat air patrol might number well over 400 by the end of the war.

In both theatres carrier actions were few and far between, but they could be of great significance, especially when surprise was achieved. But as carriers became more effective striking forces, so their targets developed better protection.

Warship defence also underwent a change during the war as a result of experience. The traditional interwar view in navies that were largely dominated by gunnery specialists had been that aircraft were not a great menace, and as a result the anti-aircraft armament of most warships was quite light. In the Royal Navy some obsolescent light cruisers were fitted with high-angle guns, but these were not of a rapid-fire model and their crews were exposed to enemy strafing as were the crews of the multiple pom-poms, or batteries of

short-barrelled AA guns. Not envisaging the potential of air attack, designers provided insufficient stowage for the large quantities of anti-aircraft ammunition needed, nor was enough attention paid to fire discipline in this sort of action. The result was that for some time, especially in the Mediterranean, ships ran out of ammunition within forty-eight hours if kept under continual attack, and cruising formations did not allow sufficient room in which to manoeuvre and clear fields of fire. As the lessons began to be learned, new gun designs provided semi-automatic high-angle fire from turrets that fully protected the crews, larger magazines with a higher rate of delivery were incorporated, the number of anti-aircraft guns was increased, and new formations were adopted, including those which kept the carrier covered while operating her aircraft. Most of these developments were British, for they were then the only ones using seaborne aircraft. But their opponents also learned. High-level bombing was largely abandoned, because so few hits were obtained, except as a diversion for low-level torpedo- or dive-bombing attacks. Land-based units became far more skilful, and attacks on merchant ships in particular became much more of a menace as new techniques were developed.

Operationally the Atlantic-Mediterranean war can be divided into two major phases. In the first Italy was an opponent, and the period is characterized by fleet-carrier actions while surface forces achieved most of the U-boat kills. In the second phase, from the opening of the Mediterranean to the Allies to the end of the war, there were hardly any spectacular naval actions; even the *Tirpitz* was eventually sunk by RAF Lancasters. Naval air work was limited to convoy escort, amphibious support, and attacks on enemy coastal shipping.

In terms of the wave pattern, the war against Italy to the end of the North African campaign was the period of rearmamental instability for Britain, in which innovation and organization for war were still taking place. Wartme equilibrium set in well before Italy left the war in September 1943, and it can be suggested that the instability of demobilization began as the major British fleet units were transferred to the Far East in late 1944.

In the early days of the war, Churchill, newly returned as First Lord of the Admiralty, decided that the carriers then available could play a critical role in the trade war at sea by acting as the core of a hunter-killer group of four destroyers which would be stationed at

The British aeronautical artist Coulson's impression of the last attack on the German battleship **Tirpitz**, *12 November 1944, when she was struck by a direct hit from a 12,000-lb. armor-piercing bomb designed by Barnes Wallis and based upon the shape of the rigid airship* **R-100. Hawker-Siddeley**

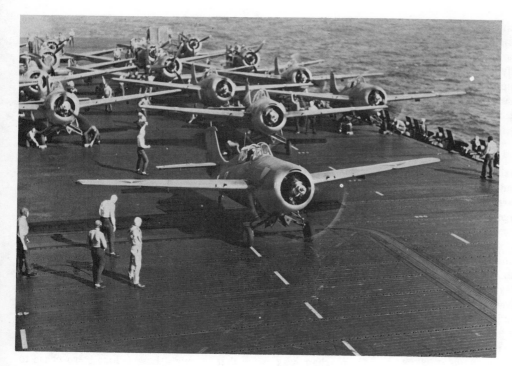

F4F's were known as Martlet's in the Fleet Air Arm and as Wildcats in the USN. In a typical USN scene deck crew in different colored T-shirts and helmets to denote their functions are starting Wildcats on their take-offs while Dauntlesses are being manned further aft. Note the wooden deck of the carrier with tie-down slots and the heavy 20-mm A/A armament just outboard of the deck in this May 1942 picture. **US Navy**

the great junctions of the sea lanes where large masses of shipping passed on their way to or from home ports. This was starting from where things left off in 1918. It was a logical development which was later on gradually taken up elsewhere, especially by the US Navy when escort carriers became available from 1941 onwards. But on the first occasion the result was a dismal failure, for *U-29* struck first and sank the large old carrier *Courageous*. At the same time the new *Ark Royal* was on anti-submarine patrol in the North Sea where she was attacked by *U-39*, who missed and was sunk for her pains. Meanwhile her aircraft attacked *U-30*, but two of the three dived too steeply and the crews ended up as prisoners on their intended victim, who escaped to Germany. A few days later *Ark Royal* barely evaded a 2,000-lb. bomb. Shortly thereafter the Admiralty detached her to join the force hunting raiders in the South Atlantic. Some time later, after the sinking of the *Graf Spee*, she returned to the Home Fleet in Britain.

The invasion of Norway illustrated the possibilities and the hazards of naval air power. The British Commander-in-Chief decided to make an attack on the German cruiser *Königsberg* berthed at Bergen. His original intent was to use aircraft from the carrier *Furious*, but she was attacked by land-based bombers that morning and instead he ordered Skua dive-bombers based in the Orkneys to strike at the limit of their range. This they did and with four bombs put *Königsberg* on the bottom. Other dive-bomber attacks were not so spectacular, but were equally useful. *Furious* and *Glorious* tried to provide fighter protection for units ashore, but, with only a squadron of Gladiator biplane fighters and one of Swordfish torpedo-bombers apiece, their obsolescent aircraft were spread too thin to accomplish much. Far to the north the battleship *Warspite's* Swordfish spotting aeroplane did invaluable work in detecting German destroyers lying in ambush in Narvik fjord. One further achievement preceded the final disaster. *Glorious* was sent to fetch off two RAF squadrons from Bardufoss. The Gladiators successfully flew on, but it was proposed to abandon the Hurricanes because no modern high-speed monoplanes had yet been landed on a British carrier. However, the pilots, with the typical love of airmen for their aircraft and disciplined reluctance to abandon them to the enemy, asked to be allowed to try to land on *Glorious*. They were successful, but this most important achievement was merely the prelude to mis-

fortune, for shortly afterwards *Glorious* ran into German battle-cruisers and was sunk.

The Norwegian campaign showed that carriers could be operated along an enemy coast that was not too heavily defended by airmen trained in naval tactics. But a carrier unescorted by a surface force at least as strong as any that might be sent against her was extremely vulnerable, especially if she was unable to fly off a strike against her tormentors. Moreover, the complement of aircraft in general was too small, and British carriers were at this date operated not as a task force but rather as ferries.

In fact this was a role they continued to play in the campaign in the Mediterranean and Middle East. The older carriers made a number of trips to the West African coast with Hurricanes, which were then flown on in a series of hops over three thousand miles across Africa to Cairo. On other occasions carriers penetrated the Mediterranean until they were just west of Sicily, when they flew off RAF fighters to reinforce Malta. The risk was justifiable in view of the imperative need to defend that base, a permanent thorn in the Italians' side, but indirectly these reinforcing operations cost the Royal Navy the carriers *Eagle* and *Ark Royal*, both sunk by U-boats.

The fall of France caused the British to attack the Vichy-French Fleet at Mers-el-Kebir, near Oran. When the battleship *Strasbourg* with a destroyer escort escaped, *Ark Royal* sent Swordfish in pursuit. The six aircraft failed to score any hits, and after a skilful approach the still inexperienced torpedo-bomber crews in the second group dropped their six torpedoes at dusk from outside the screen and also did no damage. The next morning they redeemed themselves with a perfect attack in line astern out of the sun—there was no radar yet—upon the beached battleship *Dunkerque*. Through surprise more than six hits were obtained.

By far the most spectacular and successful British naval air attack, confirming the success against *Königsberg* in Norway, was undertaken by aircraft from the new carrier *Illustrious* with a few additional machines from *Eagle*, forced to remain behind by a leaky fuel system resulting from near misses. The plans for the attack on Taranto had been laid before Italy entered the war on 10 June 1940, but time was needed for practice and reconnaissance and for fitting long-range tanks to the Swordfish so that they could make the round trip from their launching point 180 miles south of the Italian naval base. Then *Illustrious* had a hangar fire that damaged some aircraft, and the next date chosen proved to have no moon. With better trained crews this would not have been a hazard but, as it was, the safety of flare-dropping was questioned. Finally 11 November 1940 was chosen. There were six Italian battleships at anchor in the harbour. *Illustrious* was detached from the main fleet and sailed to the launching point. The first force of twelve Swordfish set out at 8:30 pm, followed by nine others, an hour later. In the first wave six aircraft carried torpedoes, four bombs, and two flares. Cloud split up the formation, but the flare-droppers accurately lighted up the eastern edge of the harbour, and then dive-bombed and fired the oil-storage tanks. The leading torpedo machine was shot down, but the rest evaded the barrage balloon cables, dropped their loads, and damaged the two large battleships and one smaller one. The second wave was equally successful, and *Illustrious* withdrew without being molested. On the next morning RAF photographs showed two battleships beached, and a third and two destroyers damaged, for a loss of two Swordfish.

Spirits in the Fleet Air Arm soared, and its officers hoped that at last the Navy would recognize its worth and stop confining its operations largely to the enemy in the open sea. But even the new British carriers had only a small striking power. When *Indomitable* joined the fleet at the end of 1940, she carried only ten Albacore biplane torpedo-bombers and thirteen Fulmar eight-gun monoplane fighters.

Late in March 1941 various units of the Italian fleet sortied in three groups, one of which contained the battleship *Vittorio Veneto*. The British fleet, including three battleships, the aircraft carrier *Formidable* and four cruisers, put out from Alexandria and a dawn air search was launched on the twenty-eighth. It was apparent that the advancing British cruisers were about to be caught between two powerful enemy groups, and a strike of six Albacores escorted by two of the new Fulmar fighters was launched by *Formidable*. Just as the enemy was sighted, the Fulmars were forced to break off and attack two German Ju-88s which appeared on the scene, but the Albacores dodged to within 800 yards and managed to make one hit on *Veneto*. The enemy ships turned for home, but the British commander was not going to let the Battle of Cape Matapan peter out. He dispatched another strike to slow down the Italian battleship, successfully achieving surprise because *Veneto* had stopped

evasive action, believing the attack to be over. A third attack was sent in at dusk, but by then the Italian cruisers had closed on their wounded comrade, and the anti-aircraft fire was so intense that the British were forced to abandon their traditional peacetime tactic of attacking in formation and to let every aircraft approach on its own. While *Veneto* was not again damaged, the cruiser *Pola* was hit and stopped dead, and the Italian admiral departed with *Veneto*, leaving two cruisers to guard her. All three cruisers were destroyed by the British fleet later in the night.

To prepare for an expected night surface action, the carrier *Formidable* was detached to operate off to the side of the line, and after destroying the Italian cruisers a British ship suddenly illuminated her with a sweeping searchlight; it was only quick action by a gunnery officer that prevented her destruction by eager gun crews, who assumed that any vessel out of line was an enemy. The incident illustrates the danger inherent in carrier operations in confined waters. The decision to keep *Formidable* in company may have been influenced by paucity of escorts, the presence of numerous enemy units, the short range of the FAA aircraft of the day, the fleet's fear of lack of air cover in daylight, and the traditional military principle of not dividing forces. She should, however, have been detached with escorts for the night, with orders to cruise safely to the east and rejoin at daylight. But it is also valid to note that Admiral Cunningham was aware that he might have a long stern chase to sink *Veneto* and that by morning he would be so far to the west that the carrier could not have caught up; in the meantime she would have been exposed to surface attack during the night.

The Grecian and Cretan campaigns which followed in April through June 1941 saw a complete change in the situation in the eastern Mediterranean. The British were expelled from their ill-advised Balkan intervention, and the Germans and Italians under the fresh leadership of Rommel were able to sweep them out of Cyrenaica, leaving them only the bridgehead at Tobruk, which was a naval liability. Crete might have been held if sufficient carriers and naval aircraft had been available to supply fighter cover over the island and strikes against the German air bases in Greece, but at this point the only carrier in the eastern Mediterranean was *Formidable*, and she was short of aircraft. So Crete was lost because the British lacked the means of defeating an airborne invasion in the

The ultimate British naval fighter of the war, the Hawker Sea Fury, a design based on the Tempest, but with folding wings for below-deck stowage on carriers. Sea Furies saw operations in the Pacific and later in Korea.
RCAF

air, they were unprepared on the ground, and had insufficient naval striking power.

Meanwhile in the western Mediterranean *Ark Royal* had been involved in the battle of Cape Spartivento. There the situation was similar to that at Matapan, but the less experienced naval aircrews were not as effective. A more important example of the use of naval air power took place, however, in May in the North Atlantic.

Alerted to the fact that the new German battleship *Bismarck* and her escorting cruiser *Prinz Eugen* had sailed for Norway, the RAF attempted to locate them. After one successful PRU effort, low cloud and fog enshrouded the powerful task force, but the news that they were at sea was finally signalled by a FAA aircraft which crossed the North Sea and made a detailed reconnaissance of the Norwegian fjords at 200 feet. On 22 May the Home Fleet sailed. The carrier *Victorious* was just working up with a cargo of crated Hurricanes for Malta. These were hastily off-loaded and the only naval aircraft available, a squadron of Swordfish and two flights of Fulmars, were taken aboard. *Bismarck* was sighted in the Denmark Strait northwest of Iceland and shadowed by a radar-equipped cruiser. The battleship *Prince of Wales*, still with builder's crews on board, and the battlecruiser *Hood* attacked. *Hood* was sunk and *Prince of Wales* damaged, but not before a shell had ruptured one of *Bismarck's* fuel tanks. The only hope of slowing her down was now the Swordfish in *Victorious*. Smashing through miserable weather associated with a cold front, the carrier launched her aircraft at ten at night. The Swordfish sighted *Bismarck*, swung out to make a good approach, and lost her. Redirected by *Prince of Wales* they flew in cloud until their radar indicated a ship. They dropped down, only to be facing a still-neutral US Coast Guard cutter. However, *Bismarck*, visible a short distance away, at once opened up with her radar-controlled guns. Each of the three flights then made separate attacks, strafing the ship with their machine-guns as they passed over her on their way back to *Victorious*. One hit had been achieved. As the aircraft approached, the homing beacon on the carrier broke down and they passed her. Her captain took the risk in U-boat waters of using direction-finding radio to home them and a searchlight as a visible beacon.

Prinz Eugen had already left *Bismarck* to refuel, and shortly after the attack *Bismarck* shook off the shadowing cruisers. A search

of the area was begun by the Home fleet and another force, including *Ark Royal*. By 26 May *Bismarck* had entered an area in which Catalina flying-boats from England could search, and it was one of these, guided by orders from Coastal Command, who found her. Fourteen minutes after the Catalina was driven off by gunfire, the first two *Ark Royal* Swordfish and another Catalina took up shadowing. Again as in the case of *Vittorio Veneto* at Matapan, the prey was too far ahead to be caught by the fleet, especially as the British battleships and cruisers were running low on fuel and fighting heavy seas. Once more, therefore, an air strike had to be laid on. While the aircraft were being ranged on deck and armed, the cruiser *Sheffield* was detached from Force H and sent to close the forty-mile gap between *Ark Royal* and *Bismarck*. Unfortunately, this move was not given to the pilots, so when the fourteen Swordfish were literally tossed into the air from their carrier's heaving deck they expected the first ship they would see would be German. Because of cloud they were using their ASV radar, and when a ship appeared on the screens they manoeuvred, dropped out of the overcast in line astern, and attacked. Eleven dropped their torpedoes before *Sheffield*, an unmistakably British design, was recognized. She just managed to evade these 'tin fish' and in response to the last aircraft's 'Sorry for the Kippers' sent a reply which caused some marvel at her signalman's ability to spell!

With aircraft on shadowing duty and three crashes when the first strike returned (*Ark Royal's* stern was pitching some fifty-six feet), a second strike was readied. Fifteen aircraft were flown off with strict orders to contact *Sheffield*, who would give them the course to the target. Dusk was approaching, cloud cover over *Bismarck* was at 700 feet, and there was danger of icing. By accident rather than by design, the attack was split up and the Swordfish approached in bunches from various points. As at Matapan a hit was scored by a straggler who came in after *Bismarck* had stopped firing. Another hit aft crippled the steering gear. To be sure of her, Swordfish fitted with long-range tanks were flown off to relieve their consorts, and she was kept under surveillance until after two the next morning, when a destroyer flotilla took over. At dawn *Ark Royal* again flew in a strike, but by then British battleships were in action and *Bismarck* was on her way to the bottom.

Within a matter of months Fleet Air Arm crews, flying obsolescent

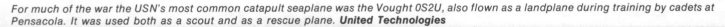

For much of the war the USN's most common catapult seaplane was the Vought 0S2U, also flown as a landplane during training by cadets at Pensacola. It was used both as a scout and as a rescue plane. **United Technologies**

aircraft with bravery and distinction, had materially contributed to victory in important battles. But in both the Matapan and *Bismarck* engagements they had not been opposed in the air. When they were, the story was not so happy, for pure bravery is no substitute for competitive equipment.

Late in 1941 the damaged *Ark Royal* was torpedoed and sunk in the Western Mediterranean while on tow to Gibraltar. The aircrews were sent back to Britain to re-form, and they were doing so when the Germans staged the daring dash up the English Channel of the battlecruisers *Scharnhorst* and *Gneisenau*, which had been sheltering in Brest together with *Bismarck's* consort *Prinz Eugen*. On 11 February 1942 the Germans left Brest at night, contrary to Admiralty assumptions. Radar breakdowns and other lookout failures left the British ignorant of the move until the vessels were well up the Channel under an umbrella of shore-based fighters, and even then Intelligence reported a convoy rather than warships. By now the Germans were passing through the Straits of Dover, but the ex-*Ark Royal* Swordfish squadron had moved to Kent. With six aircraft it hurriedly took the air and formed up under a Spitfire escort, which had trouble keeping contact because of the differences in speed. Within twenty minutes the enemy was sighted, but the Swordfish had to face not only the intense, radar-directed naval anti-aircraft fire but also Me-109 and Fw-190 fighters which the small Spitfire escort was unable to overcome. Despite their immense gallantry, none of the Swordfish scored a hit and less than two complete crews survived as all the aircraft were shot down. It was not until the Germans reached the Dutch coast that *Scharnhorst* struck twice and *Gneisenau* once on mines laid by aircraft.

The Channel Dash clearly indicated, if the actions in the Mediterranean had not, that warships could operate within range of shore-based aircraft if plans for their use were skilfully made and if they had adequate fighter cover. It also clearly indicated that the neglect of naval aircraft in the interwar years had come home to roost in Britain. After a public inquiry the Admiralty was granted greater priority in production of naval equipment and some Spitfires were converted to Seafires for use on carriers. But it takes time to pro-

duce a good aircraft, and no one in Britain had time. The solution was to get American aircraft: the US Navy had been consistently developing carrier types, and production lines were swinging into

Dauntlesses going into attack in the Pacific. **US Navy**

men, who had much earlier won a major position in their Navy. The exceptions to this latter rule, and they are few, would be the Royal Navy's raid on Taranto and attacks on the *Bismarck*. Later in the Far East the FAA was used more aggressively.

3. The Pacific Theatre

The proximity of land and the U-boat menace in the European theatre conditioned attitudes towards tactics and equipment; the vastness of the Pacific produced a different kind of naval air war. The forces were much larger, the distances much greater, and the engagements, though fewer, were usually of more significance. Submarine attacks on Allied convoys were few, and Japanese response to American submarines came from surface craft rather than aircraft. Perhaps equally important, the Pacific air war was fought by teams trained in carrier-versus-carrier concepts.

The opponents in the Pacific had modern carriers and aircraft, skilled personnel, and doctrine which had been evolved for nearly two decades. And, if the Japanese did score brilliantly in their carrier-based pre-emptive strike against the United States at Pearl Harbor, they failed to find any of the American carriers. Both sides, therefore, started with something like parity, to which has to be added the immense American advantage of holding the key for Japanese coded messages. Both sides rapidly developed their tactics, but in the long run the superiority of the American arsenal proved decisive. Industrious as they were, the Japanese were unable to turn out carriers to match those of the US Navy, and they made the same mistake as did the Germans in freezing aircraft design too soon, letting the development of the next technical generation lag and thus sacrificing quality to quantity.

The Pacific was a vast oceanic area in which naval forces steamed and flew with the same sort of freedom from restrictions that armoured forces found in the Western Desert in 1940–1943. And in this great spatial combat zone, the Japanese attempted a cordon defence. This failed, resulting in the defeat of an island naval power by a continental one, a reversal of the situation in Europe. It might be argued, of course, that the Anglo-American alliance was in many ways a continental one. And it can also be argued that Japan, Britain, and the United States were all maritime powers. In this case, Mahan's factors discussed in Chapter 1 also apply, and in the Second World War only the United States did not have to worry about home defence.

The Pacific Ocean theatre, besides being many times as large as the European area, was sparsely inhabited. Apart from the Southeast Asian peninsula and the East Indies and their adjacent archipelagoes, what land existed was mostly in the form of islands or atolls whose names are far larger on Pacific Ocean maps than their physical being. But just because of the sparseness of land, it was an ideal war theatre in which defenders could hold fortified atolls and attackers could sweep the ocean reaches. It was an area which the Japanese were rumoured and indeed believed to have fortified, though we now know that they had not. They relied instead on delivering a *coup de grace* which would leave them invincible behind great oceanic reaches, just as the Russians hoped to use space to save themselves.

top gear. Thus the Royal Navy was at last, as a result of a national humiliation, to be equipped with competitive aircraft. At the same time, the Admiralty finally recognized the importance of carriers. It now demanded fifty-five, and since neither resources nor time was available to produce that many immediately in Britain, again the solution was in part to obtain them from the United States under Lend-Lease.

After the Channel Dash there were really no more fleet actions in the European theatre, if attacks on *Tirpitz* and the sinking of *Scharnhorst* are overlooked. British escort carriers operated in support of amphibious operations in which they were equipped with modern aircraft, or with convoys where they met little air opposition.

If the air war at sea in the European theatre was largely a British story, it was because it was only they who operated carriers there in fleet fashion. British carriers were not employed, as Japanese and American ones were on occasion, to lend support for ground operations. The explanation for this lies both in geography because of the close nature of Europe and the fact that most European naval aircraft were inferior adaptations of land-based equivalents and in psychology because the Europeans were much more conservative than the more aggressive and better-equipped American naval air-

Later in the war the philosophy became to combine bombing, rocket-attack, and torpedo dropping in one attack aircraft which could then even defend itself as a fighter. One line of that development was the Douglas Skyraider, which went on to serve through the Vietnam War, another was the Martin AM-1 Mauler (above and below).

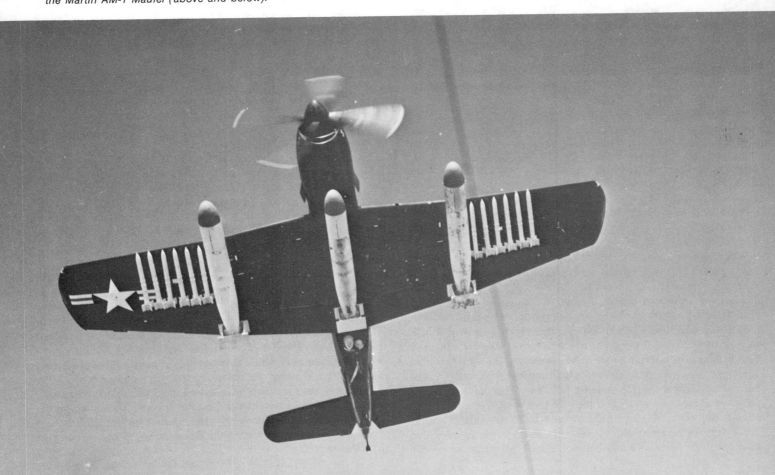

But the weakness of this strategy was the same in the Pacific as that which the Germans found in the Soviet Union and which Vauban had discovered two and a half centuries earlier on the borders of France: that forts are traps unless mobile forces exist to plug the gaps between them. So the vastness of the Pacific became a liability rather than an asset for the Japanese. Elements which particularly contributed to this disadvantage were inadequate aircraft

squalls happen to have played a fair part in the great air actions of the oceanic war, this is in part, perhaps, because commanders deliberately sought to use them as cover until at the end of the war radar negated such tactics. But it must also be remembered that the radius of action of American carrier aircraft was only 175 miles at the start of the war and not over 300-odd at the end; and even though long-range patrols could be flown from land, it was

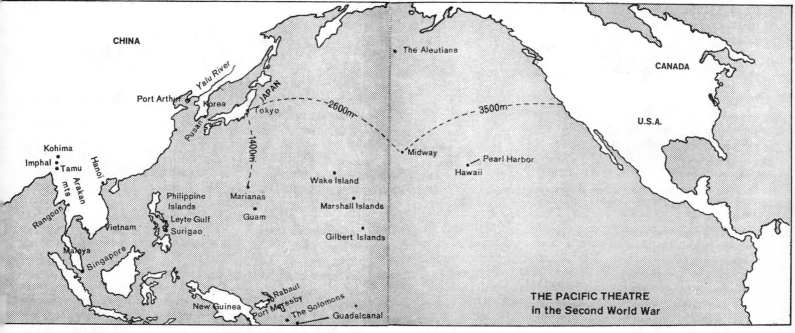

and facilities for refueling and resupplying at sea. These were available to the Japanese, but they failed to exploit them sufficiently because they failed to foresee the kind of war they were going to have to wage.

The Pacific was particularly suited to air operations, for the weather, while occasionally breeding typhoons, is rarely as severe as that in the stormier Atlantic. Carriers in particular did not have to fight ice or green water on the flight decks, and while clouds and

impossible to scout over anything like the whole area as was done in the Mediterranean and the Atlantic.

The size of the theatre and the fact that the Allies agreed that success there was secondary to winning the Hitler war, made progress in it slow. The Japanese strategy was what might be called a '*judo blitzkrieg*', based on the land and travelling light, a strategy they could follow by staging as they did down the mainland and island chains to the southeast, under an air umbrella. The very nature

USN Curtiss SB2C Helldivers form up after a bombing mission late in the war in the Pacific. The Helldiver was bigger, but not better than the Douglas Dauntless in the opinion of those who flew them. **USN**

Early in the war peacetime reliables still soldiered on, especially in distant theaters which were the last to get replacements if not attacked. This **Vickers** Supermarine Stranraer prototype, on beaching gear, was elegant in its day.

of the road from the American continent dictated an American football approach by a series of power plays, often passing, but backed by a formidable logistic bench and training system. And these national approaches and philosophies are reflected in the equipment employed.

Throughout the Pacific war there was surprisingly little change in equipment. The Japanese, long used to operating unopposed over China, had not been forced to think of technological change, and this especially affected their naval aircraft and carriers. By the time it became clear that their aircraft, which had been successful in the opening phases of the war, were becoming obsolete, the loss of experienced pilots, shortages of materials, and the bombing of the home islands prevented production of new models.

The US Navy entered the war just at a period of change-over in equipment, so that most of the aircraft in service in 1941 either represented a new generation or were shortly due for replacement. The standard American shipboard fighter was the Grumman Wildcat, slower and heavier that the Japanese Zero but faster in a dive. It was replaced in 1943 by the Hellcat, which was under development when war was declared, but which with the benefit of combat-experienced pilots' advice was rushed out to the fleet in some fourteen months and remained the major fleet fighter for the rest of the war. The Vought Corsair was also in the development stage in 1941, but it took thirty-two months to reach combat and was at first regarded as unsuitable for carrier operations. Both of these fighters used 1,850 or higher horsepower engines and while the Hellcat was very manouevrable, its speed was only about 380 mph compared to the Corsair's 420-odd. The Japanese Zero could never match this high speed and suffered from a lighter armament and lack of self-sealing tanks. The Japanese made a fatal mistake in not developing a replacement for it until 1945, when it was too late. Nevertheless, Allied pilots retained a healthy respect for the Zero, which was a first-class dogfighting aircraft.

War at sea quickly showed that level bombers were useless. Thus the attack machines soon fell into two types and were even in the prototype stage at the end of the war moving into a single type. Basically the US Navy was equipped with the Douglas Dauntless dive-bomber, which was just coming into service in 1941 and which remained the principal dive-bomber until 1943 when the heavier

Curtiss Helldiver appeared. The Japanese equivalent was the Type 99 Val, which had a fixed undercarriage, and was succeeded by the Kate with a retractable one. Again in terms of torpedo-bombers the US was lucky in its timing. The old Douglas TBDs were wiped out at Midway, as were the first of the new Avengers, but the latter were so modified as to remain standard throughout the war. They owed some of their longevity, of course, to the fact that the Hellcats controlled the air. The mainstay of the Japanese attack forces were the twin-engine Betties, which could not be operated from carriers. Here, too, as in other fields, a lot was due to American production. The US Navy started the war with 514 fighters and ended it with 13,940, out of a total of some 40,400 serviceable aircraft. At the same time it might be noted that its loss rate was remarkably low. Of 2,360 planes lost by all causes, only 664 were to enemy aircraft, while the US claimed to have destroyed over 8,600 of the enemy craft.

In terms of carriers the United States again enjoyed the advantage. Japanese carriers were generally lighter and smaller, though those of neither side were well armoured, or even well armed at first. What gave the US its particular edge apart from a highly efficient production and training system at home was the fact that it was just shifting to new carrier designs in the early 1940s and that many of these were able to benefit from combat experience while still building. While each battle seemed to reduce the strength of the Japanese aircrew pool, it had the opposite effect on the Americans. After Midway, moreover, the US Navy enjoyed the advantage, and though not operating on interior lines it could choose the time and place to strike. It was able to wait and to train its personnel, and after it managed to get through 1942 its technical advantages in terms of new aircraft, carriers, radar, and rockets constantly widened the gap over its opponent. The standard 27,000-ton, 30-knot *Essex*-class fleet carrier was indeed a formidable ship, with its eighty aircraft capable of striking some 200 miles.

The wave pattern of war can be seen in the Pacific even more clearly than in the Atlantic-Mediterranean. US rearmament was in full swing at the time of Pearl Harbor and continued until after Midway. Even for some time after that, the US Navy was still building up; neither tactically nor in terms of equipment did it enter the period of wartime equilibrium until the middle of 1943. On the other hand, the Japanese had already been prepared by their experience in China, entering the Second World War with an experienced fighting force. For them, wartime equilibrium began earlier, but it contained so many disasters that instability and defeat followed soon after. The US Navy, preparing to assault the Japanese home islands, did not enter the instability of demobilization until Japanese surrender became likely.

The Japanese at first could claim prestige as anti-imperialists who had defeated the white colonialists; they possessed the power that comes from war budgets; and they started the war with a wealth of combat experience, not only in the air but in logistics as well, which the Americans had yet to acquire. In a country on a war footing, whose government was controlled by military factions, it was easier to conceal intentions than it would have been in the United States at that time. The result was that the planning for the attack on Pearl Harbor was conducted in great secrecy. The Japanese fleet was able to assemble out of public sight, to study the models of Pearl Harbor, and finally to sail off across the unused reaches of the Pacific to the launching point for the attack without being spotted. Thanks to their intelligence agents in the Hawaiian Islands, the Japanese were well informed of the state of the US Navy and knew its habits well enough to know that a Sunday morning attack was most likely to catch it unprepared. The attack itself was a brilliant combination of the use of three-dimensional capabilities of the modern navy such as the German Admiral Scheer had tried to develop in the raids which led to Jutland in 1916. But in this case the main fleet was composed of carrier task forces rather than of battleships. The success of the strategy and the tactics which the British had tried to develop in the First World War of attacking the enemy in his own harbours was much enhanced by the relatively poor anti-aircraft defences both at Pearl Harbor and on the ships themselves, not to mention difficulties caused by the Sunday closing of ammunition lockers and early-warning radar sets.

In tactical evolution, the Japanese attack was well coordinated. Six aircraft carriers escorted by two battleships, three cruisers, and nine destroyers comprised the task force ahead of which were deployed in the Hawaiian area twenty-seven submarines. Intelligence relayed to the Japanese on 6 December showed that eight battle-

ships were in harbour, but that the carriers *Enterprise* and *Lexington*, the real prizes in the mind of carrier-commander Nagumo, were not. He decided to risk an attack, nevertheless, and at 6:15 a.m. he launched 183 aircraft (a sharp contrast to the eleven lonely Swordfish that attacked Taranto!). A study of history would have reminded commanders of the 1904 surprise Japanese attack on Port Arthur, but in spite of a war warning from Washington the Hawaiian commands were on nothing more than a sabotage alert. Nor was complacency ashore dispelled when, half an hour after Nagumo had launched his pre-emptive strike, a patrolling destroyer sank a midget Japanese submarine. And insufficient attention was paid to a radar sighting because the sets were new and those in charge too junior to assess the significance of their information, or to demand access on a Sunday morning to those who should have been able to evaluate the radar message.

Although December 1941 was a time when visual recognition was still a prime requisite of safety, as the war in Europe had already demonstrated to those who cared to note its lessons, the arrival of formations of aircraft from the north was ignored until at 7:55 am bombs began to spatter battleship row. The easily spotted high-level bombers and dive-bombers were sent in first, in a ruse already practised in the clear Mediterranean skies; before they came into action, but while lookouts and gunners still concentrated on them, torpedo-bombers skimmed in over the calm surface of the anchorage and unloaded their deadly 'fish' straight into the anchored battleships. The first combined Japanese attack was a perfect surprise, and in less than thirty-five minutes it effectively knocked out the US Navy's Pacific battleship fleet. The second wave of 170 fighters and bombers did far less damage and received the brunt of the casualties. The loss of US aircraft on neighbouring airfields was devastating, since they were mostly drawn up in neat rows. For a loss of only twenty-nine aircraft plus some which crashed in landing on their carriers, the Japanese destroyed 311 American aircraft, leaving only seventy-nine serviceable, sank two battleships outright, and caused three to need major repairs.

Looking back on it now, it can be seen that the raid was both a success and a failure. Tactically it was a partial success in that it did put the American battleship fleet out of action for a while and

The **Franklin D. Roosevelt** of the Midway class was originally to have been named **Coral Sea**. The first US Navy carriers to have armoured decks, the **Midway** and the **FDR** were commissioned in 1945 just too late to see action in World War II. At 45,000 tons they were a considerable improvement over the overloaded 27,000-ton **Essex** class, already by 1945 becoming top-heavy with the heavy loads of wartime aircraft and armaments. Photograph taken in 1965 when an angled deck had been fitted. **US Navy**

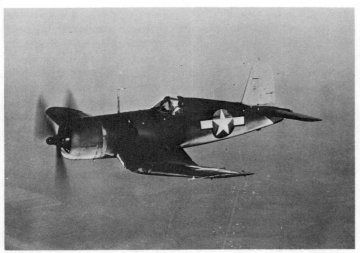

The gull-winged *Vought Corsair* was flown by the Marines and off British carriers long before in 1944 the USN decided to use it at sea. Some regard it as the equal of the famed Mustang as a WWII fighter. **United Technologies**

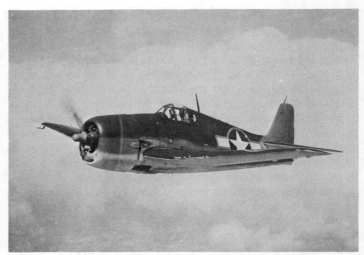

Just right in the replacement cycle was the Grumman F6F Hellcat which entered service late in 1942 with the benefit of the first combat experiences. Grumman worked closely with the Navy and that rapport down through the years led to a happy series of aircraft. **Grumman**

it did seriously weaken the air forces at Hawaii. But Nagumo can be faulted on tactical grounds and the Japanese high command on strategic and grand-strategic counts. Nagumo's fault lies in his failure to reflect upon his own actions. If he could carry out a successful strike with only two battleships in a force of carriers, why should not the Americans do likewise? By failing to hit the cruisers and destroyers in harbour, he left the basis for a future American task force. Moreover, he still had after the two strike waves some 300 aircraft available, and, since Japan was risking all to prevent America from interfering with her expansion into southeast Asia until it was a *fait accompli*, he should have risked more than he did. His intelligence people should have been able to provide him with some information on the whereabouts of *Enterprise* and *Lexington*. And even if they did not, *Enterprise's* planes came in to land in the midst of the attack on Pearl Harbor, so he knew she was somewhere around. In fact, she was returning from supplying aircraft to Wake Island. He had at least a three-to-one ratio of aircraft over her and about a two-to-one margin with his six carriers over both American carriers. Moreover, he had two battleships in company, where the Americans had none. If he had flown off scouts, they should have located *Enterprise* alone and he should have destroyed her, especially as she had flown off her planes to Hawaii earlier in the day and they had suffered casualties.

As a result of his omission, Nagumo did the US Navy a number of services. He removed the older battleships from the main fleet, and forced the Americans to go over to a carrier strategy, divorcing their striking forces from the lethargic and under-armed battleships; the battleships were relegated to the much more efficient role of fire-support for amphibious operations, thus sparing aircraft from a task for which they were really not as efficient, especially at night. It was only later in the war that the new fast battleships of the 1936 and later programmes joined the carrier task forces as floating anti-aircraft batteries and as command ships, a role for which they were suited because their heavy armour made them far less vulnerable than the volatile carriers to bomb and kamikaze hits. Further, the Japanese attackers neglected repair facilities and oil tank farms, thus leaving the recuperative ability intact. Nagumo's staff were not able to persuade him to pass through the islands and deliver additional strikes to finish the job.

From a strategic point of view, the attack on Pearl Harbor can be faulted because the commander was not briefed on the need for sacrifice to achieve the desired political end. The Japanese did not need carriers for their conquest of south-east Asia as much as they needed absolutely to destroy the American power to retaliate. Moreover, having decided upon what important segments of world opinion would regard as an immoral blow, the aggressor had to succeed or be placed in double jeopardy. Nagumo hit the mule-like American people over the head with the proverbial two-by-four. He got their attention, but not in the way he had intended. This was ill-considered grand strategy on the part of the Japanese High Command, for it aroused a people hitherto divided internally and united them.

In terms of the use of air power in the Pearl Harbor attack, it must be admitted that the conception was excellent. Air power is at its most economical and effective when used in a pre-emptive strike which abides by the principles of war. But war entails risks, and the impression is left that the Japanese were, like Jellicoe at Jutland, unwilling to take the risk of being decisive. Midway is often regarded as the turning point of the war. It may be suggested that it only made obvious the failure of Japanese grand strategy. The fate of Japanese expansion was settled at Pearl Harbor, after which the Japanese proceeded to jump down through the whole of southeast Asia to New Guinea and up the Indian Ocean to the Burmese gates of India in a campaign which was in many respects perfectly conventional. Air support was only of decisive importance because the Allied material facing the enemy was either scarce, badly out of date, or ill handled.

During this time the Americans made a number of basic decisions which were to govern the whole of the war in the Pacific. Most important of these was that which installed Admiral Chester Nimitz as Commander-in-Chief of the Pacific Ocean Areas, while General Douglas MacArthur became Commander-in-Chief of the Southwest Pacific. The basic strategy decided before the end of 1941 was to hold the line Hawaii-Midway-Fiji and to strike at the Japanese when possible. As a consequence of this, the US Asiatic Fleet, combined into the Allied ABDA organization in the Netherlands East Indies, was sacrificed. Its loss is of interest to the history of air power only in so far as it demonstrated the dangers of operating within range of enemy airfields without fighter cover and without means of undertaking aerial reconnaissance, especially in waters unfamiliar to the captains involved. At the same time, a very considerable blow was dealt British prestige in the Far East when, as a prelude to the loss of Malaya and Singapore, the battleship *Prince of Wales* and the battlecruiser *Repulse* were sunk on 10 December 1941. These two ships were the victims of indiscretion and of faulty pre-war planning.

It had largely been assumed in Britain that a Far-Eastern war would not be fought at the same time as a European war, and that in the event of war in the Pacific the main fleet would proceed to Singapore. Unfortunately, Admiral Jellicoe's astute 1919 recommendation that a Far Eastern Fleet should consist heavily of carriers had not been accepted. So when war did strike at a time when the Royal Navy was heavily involved in Europe, the Admiralty had only one carrier to spare. And to add bad luck to bad planning, *Indomitable*, then on trials in the West Indies, ran aground, and so there were none. Further complications compounded the problems. In the inter-war years political economy had dictated accepting the cheapest solution to the defence of Malaya. The result was that the naval defence of Malaya had been relegated to torpedo-bombers. But when war came the machines on hand were not only out of date, to put it mildly, but their reinforcement was to be from India (which had none anyway) via a series of airfields scattered down the Malayan peninsula and outside the army's defensive plan. The first Japanese move was to land near the neck of the peninsula and endanger the reinforcement airfields. It was in response to this threat that Vice-Admiral Phillips gallantly, but foolishly, took to sea. Shadowed early on by long-range Japanese aircraft, he had no air cover and was attacked in the classical manner, not in Royal Navy peacetime fashion. Whereas pre-war FAA attacks had been limited to formal formations, the Japanese were out to sink ships, not to impress visitors or gunnery-officer umpires. *Prince of Wales* and *Repulse* were quickly dispatched by aircraft which came in from all directions, making it impossible to employ the old naval counter to destroyer-type attacks generally delivered from abeam by swinging towards the enemy so as to comb the tracks and let the torpedoes slide harmlessly by.

Admiral Phillips' action gained him nothing but a grave and he took none of the enemy with him. He had failed to learn the elementary lessons well demonstrated by the course of operations in both the North Sea and the Mediterranean. But his error was greater than this. A commander has in the last resort two alternatives. He can ignore his orders, though when this means being accused of an unwillingness to fight it is a psychologically loaded choice. Or he can resign his command if his judgment is not acceptable to the higher command. Even allowing for very great pressures upon him psychologically, and knowing what the Japanese had done at Pearl Harbor, Phillips' action was unwise, and, more than this, it was bad strategy. Possessing the only Allied capital ships in the western Pacific, he should have preserved his force to provide punch for the ABDA fleet then being formed. In the series of surface actions which followed in early 1942 the weight of shells hurled by these ships should have been decisive in the engagements between Allied cruisers and Japanese forces protecting invasion convoys. Moreover, though in fact the Japanese sent Nagumo and his carriers to attack places like Rabaul during this period, the presence of a strong Allied force would have acted both as a greater deterrent and as a greater bait to the enemy and possibly have delayed the sweep down the East Indies. Of course it is perfectly possible that the Japanese would more swiftly have mobilized their strike forces and have dealt the same blow to the two ships at a different time and in a different place. But by then, if the two ships had been operating within the ABDA fleet they would have been surrounded by better anti-aircraft support. Lacking air power, Admiral Phillips should have beaten a strategic retreat and fought instead on another more propitious day.

It is ironical that the Japanese inflicted the damage they did upon the Royal Navy, because it was former RNAS officers who had gone out to Japan and given her naval airmen their initial training between the wars. And one of the major factors in the Japanese success was the reluctance of their opponents to admit to themselves that the Japanese were experts, or at least their equals. Not content with letting the Japanese prove off Malaya they had learned well, the British allowed them also to sink scattered units in the Indian Ocean including the old carrier *Hermes*, which was caught unescorted south of Ceylon. That no further disasters occurred was due to the withdrawal of both sides.

Before the initiative shifted to the Americans in mid-1942, several crucial battles took place while the US Navy was girding for the contest and before it had the ships, planes, and men to organize the decisive weapons which it employed to win the Pacific war. Besides

Pearl Harbor, 7 December 1941.

LCDR Minoru Genda **USNI**

the submarine force, which did to Japanese shipping what German U-boats failed to do to Anglo-American shipping, the two great American weapons, wielded by Nimitz and MacArthur in coordination but in a sense under one supreme commander, were the fast-carrier task forces and the amphibious landing forces. The one employed air power as its striking weapon. The other used air cover to enable it to operate with impunity within range of enemy air bases. Both based their power on carriers, though the first objective of amphibious forces was generally to obtain an airfield ashore from which Marine and Army aircraft could operate. Both made use of mobility and surprise, concentration and economy of force, to penetrate the cordon enemy defence.

Although, as has been suggested, the Japanese had already passed the decisive point with their attack upon Pearl Harbor, they could still have retrieved the war. The Americans were desperately short of carriers, and, although *Yorktown* was ordered around from the Atlantic to the Pacific, shortly after she arrived, *Saratoga* was torpedoed southwest of Hawaii and put out of action for a crucial five months. Fortunately for the US Navy, the Japanese submarine fleet, to everyone's surprise, proved to be impotent. *Saratoga* was allowed to limp 500 miles back to Pearl Harbor without being finished off.

At this time, Nagumo's carriers were off in the southwest Pacific aiding landing operations. As a counter, and to protect Samoa, the first American offensive operations were launched with carrier strikes against the Gilberts and Marshalls. Though small affairs, employing only one carrier in each case, they were psychologically wise offensive operations, and their effect was more than might have been expected in that the Japanese home government promptly ordered two of Nagumo's carriers home for defensive patrols, thus reducing his strength by a third.

An examination of the distances from American bases and a war game should have shown that the US Navy was far too vulnerable to undertake large-scale attacks on the Japanese mainland, even though the famous Doolittle raid was launched from a carrier on 18 April 1942. One problem for the Japanese was that they had little means of gathering intelligence about an enemy whose main bases were so far away. But just as the Allies tended to underestimate Japanese abilities, so, too, the Japanese overestimated American power. Home governments and headquarters always seem to inflate

General Doolittle on the left and Admiral Halsey on the right in a brief ceremony before the Army B-25's left the Navy's carrier to bomb Japan in 1942. **USAF**

their own importance and the destructiveness of their enemy. At the same time, they fail to warn the population that some attacks are to be expected, but that results will be minimal. Instead, by making elaborate statements about the invulnerability of the homeland, they create alarm when attacks occur, and this rebounds upon them in terms of political pressure for greater security, which in its turn detracts from the concentration of resources for winning the war. So with Japan. On the other hand, Americans rejoiced at Doolittle's brilliant strike against the enemy's capital and have overrated its effects.

The Doolittle raid was followed by an attack by *Lexington* and *Yorktown* air groups against a Japanese landing force on the northeast side of New Guinea. Though surprise was achieved by launching from south of the island, few ships were found; as was so often the case, by the time news of the Japanese landings was relayed to the strike forces, the vessels had pulled back, their mission accomplished.

Much more important at this time was the Japanese reconsideration of their strategy, now that they felt they had achieved most of their objectives in much less time than expected and with far fewer casualties. They were still bogged down in China and now had a vast perimeter to defend. After arguments between the Army and the Navy and more importantly within the Navy itself between the admirals at sea and the Naval General Staff ashore, it was conceded that it was vital to destroy American carriers. The Doolittle raid supported the admirals led by Yamamoto, and it was agreed that strikes should be made against Midway and the Aleutians. But at the same time it had already been agreed to undertake a modest campaign to isolate Australia. Considering the resources of the day and the immense length of Japanese supply lines, it can be argued that the two strategies were incompatible when undertaken concurrently. On the other hand, reviewing their successes to date, the Japanese had reason to believe that they could do both.

The first move was an attempt to isolate Australia by taking Port Moresby, New Guinea, so as to neutralize northern Australian airfields, and at the same time to take Guadalcanal as a step towards seizing Samoa, thereby severing the route to the United States. For the execution of these plans the Japanese sent six naval forces, including a carrier task force and a covering carrier force southwest.

The ultimate development of the piston-engined flying-boat was the Martin Mars which equipped a number of Navy transport squadrons in the Pacific by late in the war. **Martin**

The Allies had the advantage of access to Japanese coded messages, but the air forces in the area were under two commanders-in-chief many thousand miles apart. MacArthur controlled land-based air from Sydney, while Nimitz controlled naval air from Hawaii.

Nimitz, as soon as he learned of the enemy's plans, dispatched *Enterprise* and *Hornet*, hastily rearmed after the Tokyo raid, to join *Lexington* and *Yorktown* already in the area. The latter two carriers were merged into one fighting formation with a single screen under a peculiar command arrangement: during air operations Rear Admiral Aubrey Fitch exercised tactical command; the rest of the time seniority gave control to Admiral Frank Fletcher. The Americans were lucky that on the evening of 6 May, when they finally merged and were refuelling the carrier groups, Admiral Takagi's task force turned back at dusk when only seventy miles away.

Such flukes were to be typical of the ensuing battle of the Coral Sea. Bad weather, fog, and poor inter-service communications hampered both sides. On top of this, a mistake in coding caused Fletcher to launch an air strike against a force which turned out to be only two cruisers and two destroyers, instead of the two carriers and their escorts that he had expected to find. However, as luck would have it, these ninety-three planes discovered the 11,000-ton carrier *Shoho* and sank her with one lightning blow. Fletcher flew no more strikes that day, awaiting enemy attacks and news of the other two enemy carriers known to be in the area. The Japanese, too, had their share of misreporting and in consequence mistook the US Navy oiler *Neosho* for a carrier, wasting some time in attacking it. The cruisers Fletcher had detached to stop the amphibious thrust aimed at Port Moresby were attacked not only by the Japanese but also by the US Army Air Corps, but they survived both strikes. Meanwhile, these diversions had cost the Japanese the best part of a day, and they decided to gamble on a night attack on the American carriers. Of twenty-seven aircraft dispatched, nine were shot down by American fighters vectored in by the new radar from the carriers lying invisible under low clouds. The six pilots who returned to Takagi reported the American carriers only fifty miles away (actually they were ninety-five), but neither side dared a night surface attack.

The next day each side spotted the other at 8 am, but Fletcher was under clear skies while the enemy were in the bad weather zone, and his torpedoes were less successful than those of the Japanese, which were remarkably accurate. Nevertheless, a well-coordinated dive- and torpedo-bombing attack put the carrier *Shokaku*, caught in the open between rain squalls, out of action. The Japanese air strike force was intercepted by only three fighters, however, and the independent manoeuvres of the two US carriers, not used to working together, split the screen and allowed *Lexington* to be struck by torpedoes and bombs. Though she recovered all her planes, and Fitch had forty-nine aircraft serviceable compared to Takagi's nine, ruptured fuel lines caused internal explosions and the 33,000-ton *Lexington* was abandoned and sunk. *Yorktown*, having recovered most of her own planes, was unable to take on those of her companion. Erroneous reports by pilots that both American carriers had been sunk caused the Japanese to retire, and Fletcher got safely away.

Though the Japanese had won a tactical victory, strategically they were now checked, as they lacked the forces to continue their drive southwards. Neither surviving Japanese carrier, owing to aircrew losses and bomb and torpedo damage, was fit for the important battle of Midway, which followed less than a month later.

The Coral Sea was the first true carrier battle in history, but Midway would surpass it in importance. Here again the Japanese undertook elaborate planning and made use of a number of forces and objectives. Such multiplicity helped confuse both sides, but the Americans kept a clearer eye on their objective of destroying their opponent's carriers. If their enemy did not, he can at least in part be excused, for he believed that he had sunk both *Lexington* and *Yorktown*; and, unaware that the enemy had their code, the Japanese did not of course know that the US Navy realized American carriers could be safely brought from other areas to counter the Midway and Aleutians operations. (The Japanese attack in the Aleutians at this time was part of a complex plan to engage American forces; although weather in the Aleutians was abominable, the Japanese detached two carriers for it, thus reducing their numbers to five at Midway. As an aerial operation in itself, it has little to add to a general history of air power.)

The Japanese planned to cause the US fleet to steam through lines of submarines, entice them into the air net, and finish them off with the main battle fleet. Yamamoto himself was to command the

Generals Chow & Chennault

Japanese Zero fighter captured in China in flight with a P-43. **USAF**

battleships, and it was a battleship admiral's plan. Deprived (or shed) of their battleships, the American admirals had to think differently.

What the Japanese did not achieve, and what frustrated their attempt to take Midway—which would have given them a base from which to maintain a surveillance of Hawaii—was surprise. Instead Nimitz was able to get three carriers (*Hornet*, *Enterprise*, and *Yorktown*) across the vital Japanese early warning zone before the submarine patrols were established, and these carriers assembled 300 miles to the northeast. On Midway itself were some thirty PBY Catalina long-range-patrol flying-boats, together with some seventeen B-17s, twenty-six obsolescent fighters, and thirty-four attack planes manned by pilots straight from flight school. The only really modern aircraft were six newly arrived Grumman TBF Avengers. In addition to an air search by PBYs with a radius of 700 miles, nineteen US submarines on lookout and ambush duty were stationed west of the island.

On 3 June the main enemy invasion force was spotted, but except for a night torpedo attack by radar-equipped PBYs it was ignored. American commanders suspected that the enemy carriers were coming in from the northwest under a weather front, as indeed they were, in a mobile force under Nagumo. Just after daylight on 4 June a PBY spotted the 108 attacking Japanese aircraft, which were shortly picked up on radar. Within minutes a PBY found Nagumo's carriers (*Kaga*, *Akagi*, *Soryu*, and *Hiryu*) and radioed a sighting report, which however placed the enemy forty miles southeast of their actual position. Because of the warnings, nevertheless, most aircraft based on Midway were in the air, either patrolling, on their way to attack the enemy, or providing fighter defence; the attack damaged ground facilities, and of the twenty-six fighters only two were serviceable after its conclusion.

Midway's counterattack hit Nagumo's force just as he was about to launch a second wave. The uncoordinated thrusts did no damage and expended almost all Midway's attack aircraft, but the delay imposed upon the Japanese enabled *Hornet* and *Enterprise* to close to within the 175-mile range of their torpedo-bombers. *Yorktown*, which had had to steam into an easterly wind to recover her planes, turned west and, half an hour after the others launched half her aircraft, two hours later sending out another search for more Japanese carriers. The attack by the Midway planes confirmed the Japanese

flight commander's report that another strike was needed against the island, and Nagumo ordered the torpedoes replaced by bombs on the planes for the second wave. While still in the midst of the changeover, he was attacked by an American submarine, and shortly afterwards his first-strike planes returned to be landed on. He had just started to retire northwards when the planes from the US carriers appeared.

Lack of coordination hampered this first attack by aircraft from *Hornet* and *Enterprise*. Many of the planes ran out of fuel, having had to search for the enemy. Some made it back to their carriers; others attempted to make Midway, and many were lost. Some never saw the Japanese, while the torpedo-bombers, of an obsolescent design, ran smack into the enemy fighters which had come down to destroy the TBFs from Midway. The American dive-bombers, however, arriving overhead during the melee, took advantage of the confusion below to bomb accurately. *Enterprise's* bombers caught *Akagi* and *Kaga* with flight decks loaded with aircraft about to be launched, while the *Yorktown* group, arriving later, hit *Soryu*. The Second World War carriers were extremely volatile because of the high-octane fuel used by their aircraft, and neither the American nor the Japanese ships had armoured flight decks. Caught at their most vulnerable, the three Japanese carriers were soon flaming wrecks; the fourth, *Hiryu*, was some distance to the north and remained unscathed. Now the division of Japanese forces proved fatal, for the two carriers in the Aleutians and the one that had been kept with Yamamoto and the main body of the fleet, though now called to the scene could not reach the battle in time to redress the balance.

Hiryu launched a strike against *Yorktown*, the one carrier reported, and her attacking force was spotted only fifty miles from the American ship. The latter at once launched all aircraft on deck and waved away those coming in to land. Though twenty-eight fighters were on hand, the Japanese made three hits on *Yorktown*, and in a second strike hit her port side with two torpedoes. Without power to shift fuel or counterflood, she was taken in tow towards a repair base. For once the Japanese did the proper thing: a submarine was ordered up, which, after a lengthy search, found *Yorktown* and sent her to the bottom on 7 June. Ironically, just as *Yorktown* was suffering her second attack, one of her scouts spotted

Hiryu only some 100 miles away. An attacking American force of bombers set *Hiryu* on fire and worked over her escorts.

Only towards evening on 4 June did Yamamoto, still not directly involved in the battle, learn that three American carriers were in action, not one, as he had thought. At this point he called off the invasions of Midway and the Aleutians. Admiral Spruance, now in tactical command of the US forces, was aware that heavy enemy units might be in the area, and of course did not know that Yamamoto was now retiring. He moved to be in a position to support Midway in case of invasion, but on 5 June there was little action. Two Japanese cruisers that had collided in the night were spotted and attacked, but with no damage, by dive-bombers from Midway, and later in the day B-17s dropped eighty bombs on a destroyer but missed it. Striking forces from *Enterprise* and *Hornet* had a fruitless day and had to be recovered after dark. (As most had never before landed on at night, Spruance ordered the carriers illuminated; he well recognized that the handful of experienced combat crews he now had were priceless leaders for the future.) One of the damaged Japanese cruisers was eventually sunk, but the day ended peacefully. Spruance retired to refuel and to rest his depleted aircrew, and so ended the battle.

Midway was the most decisive engagement of the naval air war in the Pacific. By conducting an offensive defence and by a judicious retirement Spruance achieved a major American victory. He enjoyed a certain amount of luck, from possession of the Japanese cipher to the timing of his strikes against the opposing carriers. The Japanese carrier commanders were unlucky in their timing and in their lack of radar, which even in its primitive 1942 form forewarned the American carriers and enabled them to fly off their combat air patrols.

Yamamoto made a number of crucial mistakes. His forces were dispersed in such a way that they were not mutually supporting. Dispersion is valuable in a case where forces of different types are present, especially in an amphibious assault force, but it can be argued that he should have used the main force of the fleet as a screen for the carriers, and that greater dispersion of the carrier forces, as in the American case, would have prevented an attack on all of them at once. The argument that Yamamoto should have been aboard a carrier is faulty. Both Fletcher and Nagumo were forced to transfer their flags from carriers, which were the volatile prime targets of attackers. Later in the war even 'Bull' Halsey shifted his flag to a battlewagon so as not to lose control when in action, though here it may be granted that the TBS (talk-between-ships) system enabled him both to interview returned pilots and to keep in constant touch with his captains.

Midway provided many lessons for the US Navy. It showed that the old attack bombers were far too vulnerable to fighters, and that the new TBFs could not continue to use the old peacetime tactics of the long run-in at low level. To remedy these defects, combat survivors, who knew the lessons of actual battle, could now translate them into new doctrines, and their experience could be useful in the design of new aircraft. At least one firm, Grumman, had specialized in close liaison with the navy; the TBF was one product of this and another was shortly to be the F6F Hellcat. Another important technological fact reinforced at Midway was that the torpedoes were faulty, as had been claimed by American submariners and others. From a doctrinal standpoint the battle emphasized again the lessons of the Coral Sea: the need for better scouting and communications, and for better early-warning radar and quicker interceptions, as well as for more powerful anti-aircraft batteries on the screening forces. It also revealed the need for better coordination in attacks so that dive- and torpedo-bombers could complement each other in distracting the enemy's aircraft, though it was obviously desirable to have a fighter escort if possible.

Midway was both a tactical and a strategic American victory. Not only did it cost the Japanese four carriers, 322 aircraft, and 100 first-line experienced pilots, but it gave them their first defeat in centuries, prevented their capture of Midway, and ended the expansive phase of the war in the Pacific. Nevertheless, the results did not usher in a dramatic change. Both sides had to lick their wounds, and operations in the southwest Pacific as well as in North Africa stretched American resources, so that at times up to the end of 1942 there was only one American fast carrier in the Pacific.

Thus in some ways airstrips ashore again became important, especially in the southwest Pacific, where PRU showed the Japanese building an airfield on Guadalcanal. That vital point was included in invasion plans for the Solomons, but in terms of the history of air power the operations around Guadalcanal, while hot and fierce,

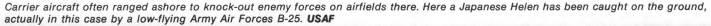

Carrier aircraft often ranged ashore to knock-out enemy forces on airfields there. Here a Japanese Helen has been caught on the ground, actually in this case by a low-flying Army Air Forces B-25. **USAF**

Airfields were vital in the Pacific islands campaigns. Here Royal Australian Air Force Kittyhawks watched by American GI's park at Noemfoor Island. **Australian Department of the Air**

offer no new lessons. Enemy submarines were for once very active, sinking the carrier *Wasp* and sending *Saratoga* home again for repairs. *Hornet* was sunk after the Battle of the Santa Cruz Islands, not by air attacks, torpedoes, or shells, but by the Japanese after she had been abandoned and they were unable to take her in tow. During this period the Japanese carriers operated from the main advanced base at Truk, a central position from which they could deploy on internal lines. But by the end of 1942 the US Navy was getting escort carriers that could provide air cover both for convoys in the battle zones and for amphibious landings, thus freeing the fast carriers to seek and destroy the main enemy forces.

At Casablanca in January 1943 it was generally agreed by the Allies that the Pacific would be an American war to which the British would contribute by driving the Japanese out of Burma and by teaming up with MacArthur in the Celebes Sea. Within the theatre it was decided that the main task would be to drive the Japanese out of the central Pacific by a series of offensives staged through Pearl Harbor. The Aleutians and the southwestern Pacific campaign were thus to be secondary. This strategy was undoubtedly correct. The Aleutians were neither in great danger nor of great military importance, and they were in fact abandoned by the Japanese in 1943. The southwest was twice as far from the US as the central area, and it appeared to involve a series of slow and costly island-clearing amphibious assaults. In fact, of course, MacArthur soon developed a by-pass system in the southwest, and Yamamoto's attempt to mount a special air offensive against the Americans and Australians, using shore-based naval aircraft, failed. Allied air power staged several successful operations in the southwest during 1943, shooting down Yamamoto himself in an action that made brilliant use of intelligence and timing, sinking convoys and their escorts, and attacking from carriers with better radar, better anti-aircraft fire, and better-trained crews than the Japanese could provide. Apart from improved equipment, better communications and control, and accurate concentration of aircraft in support of tactical forces, however, the southwestern campaigns offer no new lessons once the patterns were set.

Even in the central Pacific, where the fast-carrier task forces played a major role in the disruption of Japanese defences, techniques and tactics quickly became stabilized. American success was due to well-trained personnel manning a plethora of equipment, while directed by some of the best brains in the business, more than to innovation. To tackle this area of small atolls in an immense sea, the Fifth Fleet (so officially named in early 1944) was organized, beginning operations in the fall of 1943. Essentially it was composed of two classes of fast carriers, the 38,000-ton *Essex*, which included the new modification of a port-side elevator, and 14,000-ton light fleet carriers of the *Independence* class, which were converted light-cruiser hulls. By the time operations began, the Fifth Fleet consisted of six heavy, five light, and eight escort carriers, twelve battleships, fourteen cruisers, fifty-six destroyers, and a support force of twenty-nine transport and supply vessels, the whole comanded by Spruance of Midway. At its head was the Fast-carrier Task Force of four task groups each containing two heavy and two light carriers, escorted by about twenty surface vessels. Apart from the amphibious element of the Fifth Fleet was its land-based air force, drawn from Army, Navy, and Marines, which was used for advanced PRU and bombing missions and then for operations ashore after an airfield was captured.

The key to the whole concept, apart from the American industrial production, was logistical management through the Service Force. It provided mobile bases for repair and resupply and ultimately extended refuelling at sea to a full replenishment service that enabled the carriers to stay in the battle line for weeks on end. By 1945 the system was so refined that every day one of the four carrier task groups withdrew from the task force to be resupplied. The replenishment group was itself rotated on station.

The central Pacific campaign began in the fall of 1943 with American carrier strikes against the Gilberts and Wake which caused the defenders to fire off a lot of ammunition they could not replace and to withdraw their bombers which had been annoying Allied bases in the Ellises. On the whole, attempts to fend off American attacks on the Gilberts and Wake and against Rabaul in late 1943 cost the Japanese too many carrier aircraft and crews, so that when the amphibious attacks in the central Pacific came, the Japanese defenders were severely cramped.

By 1944 American carrier task forces were being used like panzer units in a sort of judo *blitzkrieg* warfare which reached out in thousand-mile jabs through the Japanese-held Pacific atolls. And in many ways the Japanese made the same mistakes in the oceanic areas that the Allies had made in Poland and France four years earlier. They assumed that natural barriers were on their side and they failed to organize a highly efficient, well-trained counter-attacking force. At first American strikes were simply designed to destroy as much enemy air power as possible, but in each case this was only the prelude to a later attack. In the oceanic campaigns, as in Europe, it was not necessary to occupy all the space; control of key routes and key points was sufficient. Time and again the Americans merely occupied certain single islands, causing the Japanese to pull back to a new line. Moreover, the US Navy was not hampered by a formal command structure as rigid as that of the Japanese, so that flexibility was possible: in the latter part of 1944 complete forces were shifted from the central to south Pacific commands while en route, and the attack on Leyte was moved up after Halsey's discovery that the Philippines were not heavily defended, and after President Roosevelt listened at Pearl Harbor to the arguments of Nimitz and MacArthur. And some of the planned island-hopping campaigns as well as the invasion of Leyte were eventually abandoned.

The battle of the Philippine Sea, commonly known as 'the Marianas Turkey Shoot', took place in the spring of 1944, and it afforded important lessons. The successful American seizure of the Marshalls, aided in part by the 750-plane Task Force 58 under Mitscher, followed by the effective neutralisation of Truk by carrier strikes, had shown that the US Navy's roving panzer forces could effectively operate well within the enemy's defensive perimeter. It was decided in March, therefore, that the central Pacific forces should jump 1,000 miles to the west and take the Marianas. This would open up a direct route to Japan, provide air bases from which the new long-range four-engine B-29 bombers could attack the Japanese home military-industrial complex, provide bases for other forces to attack economic communications within the Nipponese empire, and, hopefully, pose such a threat that the Japanese would be forced to come out and fight.

The ensuing battle was a classic case of a siege, for that is what on a condensed timetable the amphibious assaults were. The Japanese called for a relief expedition, but heavy attrition of their naval air power in previous campaigns, together with a chronic

Grumman *F7F Tigercat night-fighter.*

Martin *PBM Mariner patrol and rescue flying-boat.*

shortage of fuel and the American domination of the air, prevented the relieving force from getting the additional support it might normally have expected and left it unable to crush the American besiegers in a vice, as planned. At this stage of the war the lighter, less complex, and less heavily armoured Japanese aircraft had about a 300- to 200-mile range advantage over their American counterparts. However, their airmen were badly trained, for like the Germans at the same period they did not have the fuel to spare for flying training and the constant presence of American submarines off Borneo, where fuel was available, kept them in the harbours. Also, the Japanese central Pacific commander was lost in an air crash shortly before the campaign started, and his replacement insisted on the old tactics of a divided force. While it was true that the American TF-58s under Spruance cruised in five sections, no one group was more than fifteen miles from any other, so that they were mutually supporting, whereas the Japanese forces in five groups were 100 miles apart; attacks on the van could therefore not be beaten off by forces from the main body.

Every commander hopes to solve all his problems in one brilliant coup; the mature realize it is very unlikely to happen that way. Mitscher's task as commander of the carriers was basically to destroy enemy carriers, but he also knew he must recover as many of his own trained crews as possible, since carriers without aircrews would be merely empty symbols of power; deciding between the two courses was to give him some difficult moments. Spruance as over-all commander understood Mitscher's desires to pursue the Japanese carriers but correctly over-ruled them, because his primary mission was to secure Saipan and Guam for strategic reasons. Both Spruance and Mitscher knew they might be shuttle-bombed by Japanese planes operating from the carriers to Guam and back again.

Tactically, the battle was a display of what properly handled carriers combined with radar-vectored fighters could do under bold, mature leadership. The two commanders fought a classic offensive-defensive battle while at the same time containing the besieged. Hellcat fighters on 19 June shot down aircraft which attempted to take off from Guam and destroyed arriving reinforcements. When radar reported the approach at 150 miles of the first Japanese striking force, the American carriers first flew off 450 fighters as a massive combat air patrol, somewhat reminiscent of Lloyd's use of the

Japanese Sally III heavy bomber flying low over the jungle. **USAF**

The backbone of the US Navy's dive-bomber fleet throughout WWII was the Douglas Dauntless, easily identified by its "Swiss cheese" perforated flap/dive brakes. **McDonnell Douglas**

newly arrived Spitfires at Malta on 10 May 1942, and then launched the bomber and torpedo planes to orbit out of trouble and attack the defenders on Saipan. The result was that the attackers were driven off with losses while the defenders were able to use the carriers as Dowding had used forward airfields in the Battle of Britain so that fighters could be refuelled and rearmed in series. When the enemy paused to regroup, radar-vectored fighters were stacked above them and sent in for the kill. Of 430 Japanese attackers, 330 were shot down or suffered operational accidents. At the same time two American submarines got into the Japanese van and torpedoed two carriers, both of which eventually blew up and sank. The one thing that was in the Japanese favour at this point was the wind, which forced Mitscher to turn his carriers away from the enemy every time he wished to launch or recover.

Spruance was as yet unable to verify that the two reported enemy fleets had joined, and it was not until 4 pm on the twentieth that a reconnaissance plane spotted the enemy again. After a strike was launched, it was discovered that the position he had given was sixty miles out, and because of heavy radio traffic the correction was delayed. Mitscher, however, having taken one bold decision followed with another. Rather than recall the first strike, he cancelled the second and headed at full speed up the track of his flyers so as to recover as many as he could. The strike found the enemy, sank one carrier, and set fire to two others, but by then low on fuel it set course for the fleet. Mitscher turned on all lights and fired starshell. Pilots with poor fuel discipline landed in the sea, but many made it aboard any carrier they could reach. Mitscher then searched further back up the attack track and in the end recovered 160 of the 209 airmen in the strike. The combination of patience and boldness paid off. The Japanese eventually lost three more carriers and most of their trained air crews, a blow from which they never really recovered.

Though American carrier-borne aviation would eventually operate off the very coasts of Japan and would engage in strategic attacks against naval bases, airfields, and military-industrial targets, these operations were in most respects similar to those conducted from Britain as a kind of fixed aircraft carrier off the shores of Europe. The last great battle of interest in the naval air war in the Pacific was that of Leyte Gulf, with its famous 'Bull's Run', in October.

By autumn 1944 the Japanese were confused by a trick of American organization. When Halsey commanded the fast-carrier Task Force it was known as the Third Fleet; when Mitscher commanded, it was the Fifth; its subdivisions were accordingly TF-38.1 or TF-58.1, 58.2, and the like. But the Japanese, no doubt confused also by the ability of the US Navy to keep the seas for weeks because of its mobile replenishment system, thought they were facing two major fleets.

The Japanese response to the seizure of Saipan and Guam in the Marianas was to prepare another plan similar to the one which had led to the battle of the Philippine Sea. The Sho-Go plan called for land-based planes to devastate enemy forces while surface and air fleets were held ready for the *coup de grâce*. In fact, the plan failed before it could be properly launched. Halsey's raids in the China Sea and other attacks had destroyed over 1,000 planes in the two months preceding the Leyte landings, while submarines had concentrated on Japanese tankers to such an extent that the fleet could not operate as a unit from the Home Islands, but had to be based where fuel was available, with all the consequent problems of disunity, distances, and disoriented communications. Battleships were at Singapore, light forces in the Ryukyus, and carriers in the Inland Sea. Yet Toyoda, the supreme Japanese naval commander, had to fight, because if the Philippines were lost the empire would be cut off from Japan itself. Forced this time by economic geography and logistics to operate initially in three groups, the Japanese still failed to combine for one concentrated thrust. The two main attacks were to be made by surface forces, and the carrier force, with hardly any pilots well enough trained to be able to land on, was simply to be a decoy for Halsey's Third Fleet. As a gamble to seriously damage the American fleet, the Sho-Go plan almost succeeded, but it could not have stopped the overall American offensive. By this stage of the war there was getting to be a super-abundance of material on the American side, while the Japanese did not have the air power left to exploit a victory if they achieved one.

The battle essentially consisted of three parts: the classic defeat of the southern Japanese force in Surigao Strait by American battleships under Oldendorff, the confrontation between Kurita's centre force and first Halsey's and then Kinkaid's carriers, and the success of the decoy by the Japanese carriers which pulled Halsey away from

San Bernadino Strait and uncovered Kinkaid. In terms of the history of air power, the first phase can be ignored. In the opening of the second, Halsey's scouts discovered Kurita heading into the Sibuyan Sea in the central Philippines. Third Fleet carrier task forces were ordered to close formation, and strikes were launched at once on 24 October. Kurita's battleships, without air cover, were forced to retire, and the super-battleship *Musashi* was sunk. When darkness fell, it looked as if Kurita was beaten. Meanwhile, by launching all fighters and retiring under a rain squall the one American carrier group spotted by the Japanese avoided damage, while its experienced pilots shot down all but twenty of the attackers. Halsey was now aware of enemy carriers in the area.

Unfortunately, this was the first time the central and southwest Pacific forces had operated in conjunction, and a certain lack of clarity in orders became evident. Nimitz's operations plan specified that Halsey's primary duty was to protect the invasion forces *unless a major* portion of the enemy fleet could be destroyed, when that was to become his primary target. Kinkaid, however, to whom a copy of the orders had been sent, was under MacArthur's direction, and he had armed his ships simply for the support of invasion forces and not for a possible naval engagement. Thus his carriers had large supplies of anti-personnel bombs but few heavy bombs or torpedoes. He was convinced that Halsey's role was entirely to protect him against enemy naval forces, and when he intercepted Halsey's preparatory signal for the formation of a battleship group to be detached from TF-38 in case a surface engagement developed, he incorrectly assumed that such a group had been formed and was being left to guard the exit from San Bernadino Strait. This was to lead to subsequent trouble and to a post-war verbal battle.

On the evening of the twenty-fourth the main force of Japanese carriers was located, Halsey construed their appearance as part of a plan to make a pincer attack on Leyte Gulf, and he was at once determined to break it up. The southern Japanese force could obviously be handled by Oldendorff, and Halsey's pilots assured him that Kurita in the centre was retreating after being badly damaged. To avoid being shuttle-bombed, Halsey, who could not close the Philippine airfields as Mitscher had shut down those on Guam, elected to move out to meet the enemy carriers. Thus he was sucked out of position, as the Japanese desired. He took with him the battle-ships which Kinkaid mistakenly assumed were to be left on guard as a separate Task Force 34, and the message informing Kinkaid of his decision to go north was unfortunately ambiguous to the reader. No thorough air coverage of San Bernadino Strait was maintained, therefore, for fear that during the night Kinkaid's planes would be shot down by Halsey's. And Kinkaid's patrols, like the RAF's at the time of the Channel Dash in 1942, just happened to miss the enemy ships as they sortied. Halsey for his part, convinced that Kurita was no threat and that the carriers were, continued north despite new evidence that came in during the night that Kurita had turned about. As a consequence, when early on the twenty-fifth Kurita sailed out into the Pacific, Kinkaid's only shield was a force of light carriers providing close support for troops ashore. Halsey's Task Force 34 had in fact been formed by now, but it was to be a clean-up group to pounce on cripples left after air strikes against the northern Japanese carrier force.

Halsey finally received a message sent off two and a half hours earlier by Kinkaid, asking for confirmation that TF-34 was backing his light forces at the mouth of San Bernadino Strait. Halsey's 'Negative' was a real shocker. Receiving further cries for help, he ordered McCain's group, then refuelling, to proceed at once to Leyte Gulf, while he kept on after what he believed to be the bigger threat. To add to Halsey's difficulties, and to illustrate a commander's problems in modern war, Nimitz had been listening in from Hawaii to the flow of signals. He now asked Halsey, 'Where is, repeat, where is Task force 34? The world wonders.' The latter sentence was the enciphering padding, but Halsey did not know this; he now made the difficult decision to turn TF-34 about and dash south in the infamous 'Bull's Run', taking with him one carrier group as air cover. Mitscher continued his attack on the northern Japanese force and finished off all but one of the enemy carriers there.

Meanwhile Kurita, never able to establish radio contact with the northern group, did not know that he had a clear field. With a force that still consisted of four battleships, eight cruisers, and eleven destroyers, he was more than a match for the escort carriers and amphibious support vessels of Kinkaid's right flank, but mistakenly thinking he had come upon fast fleet carriers, he failed to destroy the slow small force which should have been at his mercy. Instead, attacks by defending destroyers and continuous harassment by car-

The Consolidated PB4Y-1 was the Navy's version of the Army's B-24J fitted with an Erco turret and used primarily for low-level patrols and attacks. **Convair**

rier planes caused Kurita to sheer off after sinking only one small American carrier for a loss of three cruisers. Almost simultaneously kamikazes made the first of their attacks, sinking *St Lo* and damaging two other escort carriers. Faulty intelligence lured Kurita away to tackle a non-existent American force, and he then came under attack from McCain's carriers, just then coming into reach. He sensibly retired.

The battle of Leyte Gulf was frustrating for both sides. Neither got the chance to annihilate the other; the Japanese were plagued by faulty intelligence, and the US Navy proved to be susceptible to misunderstandings on the command level in a joint operation by two major forces. Leyte Gulf also emphasized the need for clear communications, especially when commanders have been actively engaged in major operations for several days. If Halsey had been allowed to follow his plan to the north, Japanese military leaders might not have continued to resist civilian and imperial pressures for peace, because they would have had nothing left with which to resist.

4. Analysis

Although not all US Navy admirals in the Second World War were airmen, they grasped the significance of the carrier because Pearl Harbor gave them no other choice. The British Admiral Phillips demonstrated only too clearly off Malaya in 1941 what happened when air power was discounted, and the Japanese provided the lesson of the fate of a service whose chief is shot down. All of these things can be seen behind the strategic and tactical lessons. The Americans in the Pacific fought essentially an offensive war and from Midway on sought to use sea and air power strategically, as Liddell Hart and Fuller had urged Britain to do with a maritime rather than a continental policy.

On the tactical level, the war at sea showed how formal peacetime tactics are tested by the accidents of weather and war. Peacetime manoeuvres should at least periodically be structured only to the extent that an 'enemy' is delineated for planning purposes, so

that new tactical methods or lessons can be discovered. The Pacific conflict was a flexible air war in which it was possible to employ *blitzkrieg* and even judo tactics to win dramatic victories through imaginative planning and timing. An ability to take a calculated risk and the sense to withdraw on occasion to fight another day were also essential. Like the war in the Western Desert, this was truly unlimited mobile war in which air power was used essentially as a tactical striking force to obtain strategic and grand-strategic ends.

The largest Japanese flying-boat was the Kawanishi H8K, seen here at the USN's Patuxent River test station in 1946. **Source unknown**

By 1945 the second generation, the H-5, was operational and beginning to be deployed all over the world on rescue missions. **USAF Museum**

By 1943 the practical helicopter was becoming operational from the hands of Igor Sikorski and the Vought-Sikorsky division of what is now **United Technologies.** *The assorted crowd of service and civilian officials is watching an early model land on a platform over the forward hold on a Liberty ship.*

Between the past and the future — 1945. The German V-2 rocket developed in World War II presaged the coming of the missile and space age.

Below, from the XB-70 upper center to the B-17 lower right, the development of air power on display at the old USAF Museum at Wright-Patterson AFB.

The Swedish Air Force: Another Look

As a neutral Sweden well represents the dilemmas of the country which wishes to remain independent in the days of increasingly expensive technology. Some types were designed and built at the Saab factory at Linköping, some were constructed there under license, and others simply bought abroad. During the 1939-45 War a certain amount of equipment simply fell into Swedish hands.

(1 & 2) The SK-14 was the North American NA-16 manufactured under license as an advanced trainer. It was replaced in 1947-48 with SK-16's, Harvards built in Canada.

(3) When the country was almost totally cut-off during the war it produced aircraft with steel-tube fuselages covered with birch plywood and powered with improved American Wright radial engines without a license, for which however, a compensatory payment was made after the war. Here J-22's are under construction at Stockholm.

(4) Immediately after the war the De Havilland Vampire was bought as both a fighter and as a trainer and was the basis of jet experience.

(5) This led to the development of the Saab J-29 or "Flying Barrel" which saw action during the Congo peacekeeping affair, the only hot war in which Sweden has been engaged since Napoleon's time.

(6) The next Swedish machine was the Draaken, which is still in service in 1983. Most RSAF bases have underground hangars deep in the rock in which the aircraft can start their engines as in this picture.

(7) But the RSAF also flies small American Cessnas when on peacekeeping missions as over Lebanon in 1958.

(8) Also in the current Swedish inventory as both a homebuilt trainer and in wartime a ground-attack aircraft is the SK-60, of which Austria has also bought some. It is powered by two American GE J-85 engines.

1

2

3

4

5

7

6

8

A common Cold War scene — two RAF Lightnings intercept and escort a Soviet Bison approaching the British coast. **MOD (Crown Copyright reserved)**

PART SIX

Cold and Limited Warfare since 1945

1. Background: Strategic and Technological Reactions to Nuclear Power

August 1945 marked a watershed in aeronautical history. The two atomic bombs dropped on Japan had far more destructive power than any used before—although the damage they actually did was not as great as that done by incendiary raids—and one aircraft could now carry enough power to obliterate a city. The moral issue had not changed: the bombing of cities continues to be a topic for fervent national and international debate, and the extent to which the ordinary citizen can be considered a combatant when his country is at war has of course not been determined; if he makes munitions or raises food, is he a legitimate target for enemy aircraft?

The atomic bombs ushered in a revived burst of thinking about strategy, in which much of the published work came from the hands of American civilians either in quasi-private establishments such as the USAF-sponsored Rand Corporation or in academic institutions. Belatedly in 1958 the Institute of Strategic Studies was set up in London to concentrate British and other brains on international strategic problems. And within governments, the work of military pundits, whose position papers never reached the public, began to assume more and more significance as technological decisions were made which committed a nation to a certain course years before the public could speak to the point. By the late sixties a tendency appeared to be emerging, in the United States at least, to recognize the real dangers of such procedures, and to call for public discussion of such imensely expensive and potentially dangerous systems as the anti-ballistic missile (ABM). That such discussion could take place was due in part to the rise to power of politicians who had served in the Second World War, and to the enormous increase in interest in these matters taken by the mass media and to the genuine and lobbyistic attempts of both to explain the problems to the general public. Economists, political scientists, sociologists, and other academicians, not always for purely professional reasons, found themselves concerned with the subject of defence. Even more importantly, suffering from guilty consciences over the atomic bomb and the secret consumption of vast government funds for defence research, and perhaps horror-stricken at the destructive powers they had created and doubtful of the rational nature of man, scientists themselves were talking in public about the consequences of their work. The debate began with the Oppenheimer-Teller squabble in the United States over the hydrogen bomb, and it gradually coalesced with many other problems whose side effects, such as air pollution and lack of safety in the cities, were becoming too evident to be ignored.

But for the history of air power 1945 marked a watershed in many other than atomic ways. The jet engine posed new problems in aerodynamics and metallurgy, public relations, and expense, though it simplified that of fuel. And the jet engine pushed the whole aircraft, not just the tips of the propeller blades, up to and beyond the sound barrier. Demands for far more sophisticated metals, for much more exacting flying procedures, for better electronic aids, and for noise suppression for better public relations created greatly increased costs. While weights and costs had risen about six-fold between the two world wars, in the twenty years after 1945 weights increased about six-fold, but costs rose thirty-fold. And costs rose very largely because the old rule-of-thumb design methods and handcrafting simply could no longer be risked.

By the Second World War aeronautical manufacturing had become one of the major defence industries; it remained a key economic factor after 1945, for, although military orders fell off drastically in Britain and America for a few years, they were revived for the Cold and Korean Wars. The air budget peaked in 1962 in Britain, and it has continued at a very high level in the United States. In the Soviet Union spending on air defence and deterrents remained high from 1945 onwards. In all three countries, the demands of civil aviation provided the industry with a better basic market than had existed before the war, but with rising costs and limited design staffs the problem increasingly—for both nations and companies—became one of choosing the correct economic course. After 1945 such choices required teamwork: success or failure depended not only upon astute analysis of the future, in political, economic, social, diplomatic and military, even ideological terms, but also as much upon correct technological intelligence and projections, cost analysis, and market research.

These procedures were slow in coming. Neither firms nor nations could afford to make mistakes, though it can be argued that even mistakes provided employment and useful technological spin-off. The critical stage at which the cost of developing and producing a single product could bankrupt a firm was reached by the mid-fifties, when a major British firm (Bristol) had to be rescued by Cabinet order. The difficulties into which some of the aerospace industry, as it began to call itself, fell came from long domination by individuals and failure to reinvest profits in research and to merge into larger groups with stronger capital structures. Manufacturers who had long relied on government financing found they could not get airlines to bankroll them during the years it now took to develop a new airliner and ready it for service. And the airlines could well argue that there was no reason why they should when they needed to turn over their own limited capital at least every ten months in order to make enough money to pay for the new aircraft they had on order. Operating in a growth industry with a 14 per cent per annum general rate, they had enough difficulties of their own to solve.

The impact of nuclear bombs precipitated a very costly expansion of the aviation-electronics defence industry, not to mention certain naval aspects. This tended to force attention on almost impossibly expensive projects to the neglect of possible ones. The power of the hydrogen bomb in particular became such that by the end of the 'fifties it was becoming apparent even to policy-makers that it was not likely to be used, but would remain a stand-off *éminence grise* which, however, might, as the film *Dr. Strangelove* showed, lead accidentally to an atomic holocaust. Doubts about the use of nuclear ballistic missiles, which by the end of the 'fifties were replacing

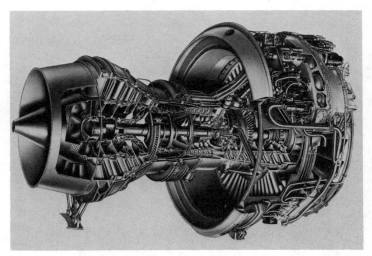

The Rolls-Royce RB-211 42,000 lb. thrust jet engine of the late 1970's, a by-pass fan engine. **Lockheed**

manned bombers, remained and were intensified by the development in the 'sixties by Red China of its own nuclear weapons system. Nevertheless, the principles of war still applied—and would even if the whole system were moved into space.

No government could afford to be so imprudent as to neglect the protection of its national vitals, or at the very least the creation of a dependable deterrent.* Under any circumstances, the arsenal base, the deterrent, and certain lines of communication have to be protected, even if this function is left to another friendly power. Circumstances, of course, change, and the end of the sixties saw European nations outside of Russia, and possibly France and Britain, becoming less concerned about the chances of an all-out war and consequently limiting defence in reality to frontier protection. It has, unfortunately, been a rule of human behaviour that nations have only agreed to disarmament in terms of those weapons which have become obsolete or thought to be so, or which have become too expensive to operate. When this concept is coupled to the sixty-year cycle of technologically acceptable performance mentioned above in Chapter III, the question is raised whether grand-strategic bombardment may be fading from the political scene as a viable weapon, and the emphasis shifting to more acceptable means with less costly ends.

What nuclear theories of war did do initially was to cause the western powers, notably the United States, to overlook the vast possibilities for escalation of guerrilla warfare in the underdeveloped areas of the world, where latent social problems could easily be made kinetic by effective leaders backed with small cadres of properly equipped personnel. Having tried the use of massive pressure over Berlin and been foiled by the Allied Airlift, and having failed again in Korea, the Communists gave up appeals to force in favour of appeals to the people in which the odds against them were almost reversed by the inability of western powers to use their superior

The Pratt & Whitney R 4360 Wasp Major, an example of the well-developed radial piston engine with its multitude of moving parts. **United Technologies**

*Wide recognition of the deterrent concept is at least as old as Machiavelli's doctrines, and it was understood by leaders well before that. The concept was sound as long as it was credible to the potential aggressor, convincing him that the cost of an attack would not be justified by the potential gain. The problem with the nuclear deterrent was that when it existed only in massive form, not balanced by conventional forces, the opponent was encouraged to look to a nibbling strategy which has been much harder to combat, even in psychological or propaganda terms.

The New Look in the Jet Age

The jet age demanded G-suits to keep the blood from flowing away from the brain in maneuvers and better helmets to protect the head from the jars of high-speed flight. New materials made these possible. At the same time the shape of the jet quickly changed from the straight-winged monoplane of only a little over a decade earlier to new swept-wings and deltas.

The crew of an English Electric/**Martin** Canberra dressed for flight.

In the air and on the ground the first American jet aircraft, the Bell XP-59 Airacomet was still rather conventional though fitted with Whittle jet engines of British design. *USAF*

The very rapid and sharp change to the future is to be seen in the **Boeing** B-47 Stratojet bomber which could outrun contemporary fighters.

Dressed for flight in anti-G suits.

Bell XP-59

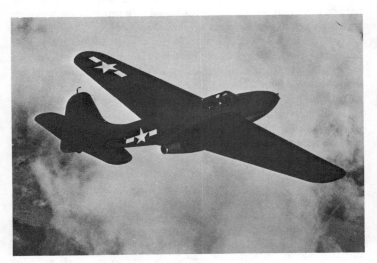

Bell XP-59 Airacomet

Boeing B-47

Dassault Mystère

MiG-17

Lockheed P-80

Supermarine Attacker

McDonnell Banshee

North American F-86

Republic F-84

Convair F-106A

technology against packets of guerrillas, by their failure to understand the nature of the wars being fought, and by their lack of rapport with the people who wished to liberate themselves. For the Communists, the cost of such actions was usually negligible.

The decision-making machinery tends to be too slow in its response to realities, especially in peacetime. Thus nuclear policy-making in Britain was just reaching its peak in 1957, with the publication of the White Paper on the three-day war (*Cmnd. 124*), which emphasized nuclear rockets. But in fact, Suez had made it obvious that what were needed were conventional forces able to deal with minor powers. Even before that the retreat of the French in Indochina had shown the way wars were likely to go. It was a misunderstanding of the nature of modern civil wars (which are essentially negative pre-emptive operations) and of insurgent ideological rebellions or revolutions linked to local grievances, which caused the American over-involvement in Vietnam.

2. Military Policy, Organization, and Equipment

It is against this paradoxical background that air power has developed since the Second World War. Thus on the one hand the so-called American strategic bomber developed into an eight-engine jet monster of 500,000 lbs all-up weight which ended by being used for strictly strategical or tactical missions in Vietnam; whilst on the other the fighter-bomber was developed from a tactical weapon into a respectable (by 1945 standards) heavy bomber which was sent on grand-strategic missions. Moreover, since no enemy possessed carriers after 1945, the US Navy found its air power diverted into two un-naval operations—long-term use of expensive carrier aircraft in tactical support for the army ashore, and nuclear grand-strategic warfare. The former, while effective, is not necessarily justifiable in terms of the wear and tear on specialized forces which may better serve national interests by being used elsewhere. The latter has meant cluttering carriers with large aircraft with a questionable mission, while they might better be armed with strike forces suited

In the new age the helicopter became commonplace and by Vietnam had moved from a rescue and communications tool to the role of attack weapon. This is a standard Sikorsky HUS-1.

for anti-submarine warfare or suppression of brushfire wars until regular army and air force units can become operational from shore bases.

The post–1945 period also saw the rapid development of the air-support arms, both maintenance and air transport. Owing to vast distances and the accelerated pace of modern diplomatic and military events, the use of air transport became more and more important. Moreover, the airlines were able in the early 1950s to sell the armed forces and merchant shipping companies on the economies of sending personnel by air, as opposed to having them out of action for weeks while travelling by train or ship. At the same time maintenance became more of a problem as usage rose, demanding skilled mechanics at a time when the armed forces found themselves hard put to meet the competition from civilian life. Aircraft were becoming increasingly complex and needed specialists to adjust their increasingly sensitive and sophisticated gear. Those nations faced with a real national shortage of manpower, such as Israel for example, realistically and sensibly opted for much simplified aircraft flown by less highly-trained but nonetheless highly skilled pilots, and with maintenance problems reduced by the removal of over-sophisticated equipment.

One of the curses of peacetime in most air forces tends to be the escalation of the age of responsibility and a consequent growth in the requirements for command to justify its retention in the hands of an aging *élite*. Such a system leads to greater turnover in the lower ranks and an over-expenditure on education not really needed by those whose real proficiency should be in the flying arts. A large proportion of the budget is thus expended on salaries and education rather than on training. This is not to suggest that war is good, or that armed forces should be composed of automatons. It is to suggest that leadership becomes ossified during long periods of peace, while the tendency is to over-educate junior officers in nonessentials rather than to over-train them for the essentially straight-forward business of operations.

The effects of peacetime could be seen in the problems facing the USAF in Vietnam as opposed to Korea. In the latter there were still plenty of Second World War pilots available, but in the former these had shrunk to a group largely composed of lieutenant-colonels who were flying simply as squadron pilots because of a shortage of some

*By the late 1960's radar had become both vital and impressive and, indeed, photogenic, as in this picture by staff photographer Sgt. Ruth Heeler, **USAF**.*

Just as the B-29 had dwarfed the B-17, so the postwar B-36 intercontinental bomber had the same power, being 22 feet longer than the span of the '29's wings. **USAF**

4,000 pilots. And retention rates were way down because by the mid-sixties the airlines—with nineteen new jets a week joining commercial fleets in America alone—were desperate for aircrew; they could pay better salaries and offer married men a career of very little risk. Another peacetime curse, generally eliminated in wartime equilibrium, is the constant modification of equipment and routinization of methods and techniques. In the sixties the armed forces and the airlines benefited from the development of a methods branch closely allied to the computer, but at the same time the mere volume of business, space, and paper tended to clog the system, which was run by people unwilling to abandon old methods. The advantage of occasional wars, or of losses instead of profits, is that they allow a quantum jump forward towards solving accumulated problems by the use of an efficiency sword on the Gordian knot.

The revival of deterrent theory with the nuclear bombs once again put the bomber leaders back in the saddle, if indeed they had ever left it in the American and British air forces. The first evidence of this came with the battle over the B-36 in the United States between the newly independent USAF and the USN, now both subordinate to the new Department of Defence. The airmen took the view that the atomic bomb could solve any difficulties which diplomacy could not handle. The Navy was supported by the Secretary of Defence in its view that while a deterrent was important, eventually ground troops would have to be committed, and this would require both a tactical air force and protected logistical support. Moreover, naval officers, with their long years of experience in quasi-war situations, recognized the need for forces to cope with brushfire wars, and they regarded as unsound the air force demand for control over all aviation. But in budgetary battles the air force panacea seemed so simply logical that it won many supporters. After all, was it not cheaper? The battles of 1946 were revived again in 1948. The Navy asked for newer and larger carriers, in part so that naval aircraft could carry atomic bombs. The Air Force took this as an attempt to usurp some of its powers and responded with a journalistic campaign in favour of the B-36. The new Secretary of Defence sided with the Air Force, refused the carriers, and fired the Chief of Naval Operations. The battle continued in the corridors of the Pentagon, however, until the Korean War brought liberalized budgets.

Some of the arguments were affected by the fact that the Russians,

extremely conscious after the Second World War that they did not have adequate air defences, proceeded to put a maximum effort into the development of both radar and other air defences, and the atomic bomb. The result was that on May Day 1949 the Russians were able to display MiG-15 jet fighters which vitiated the argument that the B-36 was impervious to hostile defending forces. In fact, for those who were not blinded by their faith, the lessons of the 1943 Schweinfurt and Regensburg raids were plainly written on the wall of history: bombers cannot always get through with acceptable loss rates. The British had jets which could reach the B-36 in eight minutes from radar-warning scramble and could do 540 mph at 30,000 feet to the B-36's 370. At the same time Congressional hearings caused charges of influence to be bandied about where the six-million-dollar B-36 was concerned. Despite all the controversy, the B-36 remained in service until 1958. But better solutions to the delivery of grand-strategic strikes appeared in the all-jet Boeing B-47, which was as fast as current fighters and could operate from the bases acquired around the Soviet Union either by NATO or SEATO treaty or by arrangements opened up by Korean war spending.

Even before the B-36 controversy had fully run its course, the declining order-book situation in the American aircraft industry had begun to worry manufacturers and political leaders. In 1947 President Truman appointed the Finletter Air Policy Commission to study the whole business of America's place in the air age. In its 1948 report, entitled *Survival in the Air Age*, the commission pointed out that a scientific-technological revolution was endangering the safety of the United States and that it was imperative that the USAF start immediately to build a modern force. (It was claimed that in 1947 44 per cent of US Navy aircraft were obsolete and that in 1948 95 per cent of USAF aircraft were Second World War types; these figures were played for effect). The commission was unhappy about recommending a seventy-group air force, but it felt it had to do so while at the same time urging that other roads to peace be explored. After considerable discussion, by mid-1948 Congress and the President had agreed to a sixty-six group force, which was just being built when the Korean War started.

The British also were concerned with the grand-strategic bomber and developed three aircraft, all jets, eventually to replace their piston-engined Lincolns, which had entered service in 1945 and remained operational until 1955. The new V-bombers—Valiant, Victor, and Vulcan—showed a progression away from conventional aircraft. The Vickers Valiant was the first into service and, while it had swept wings, it was reasonably conventional. The Handley Page Victor had a crescent wing and a high-altitude performance equal to that of a fighter, while the most radical of all was the delta-winged Avro Vulcan. But what was often overlooked by those discussing strategic bombing was that, though these aircraft were under development in 1947, neither the Victor nor the Vulcan joined squadrons until 1956, the year of Suez. The Valiants after flying only 2,500 hours each were withdrawn in 1965. Yet strategists talked as though the bombers existed long before in fact they were operational. And distance restrictions were still a serious factor. While it was true after the Second World War that the major air powers benefited from the British development of aerial refuelling, for this range-extender to be effective, safe refuelling rendezvous had to exist; at one time there was a British proposal simply to send crews on suicide missions into the Soviet Union, because there seemed no other way of reaching vital targets. Another common fallacy was to credit the Soviets with a whole force of a type just because one or two were flown over at the annual Tushino display. Fortunately, containment rather than conflict was the rule until suitable striking forces were developed.

Much more speculative for a long time were the roles that France and China were to play. After De Gaulle once again took the reins of power in 1958, France moved to develop her own *force de frappe*, a nuclear capability which would give her a say in international affairs. Her aircraft industry had been quietly working to produce fighter-bombers and small strike aircraft able to deliver nuclear weapons. Yet where it stood as a military-diplomatic force remained in doubt in the sixties. At the other end of the world the Chinese appeared to have developed nuclear bombs, but, rather than going in for long-range bombers, they appeared to be moving directly towards ballistic missiles. As to Chinese intentions, analysis of these rather depended upon whether the foreign observer believed that China was essentially a paper dragon, more afraid of others than intent on aggression, or a real one.

The advent of ballistic missiles, foreshadowed by the German V-2s of the Second World War, started arguments in both the techno-logical and military communities. The discussions ranged around the solid- versus the liquid-fuelled rocket, with the solid-fuel spokesmen gradually winning out in the early sixties for both airborne and seaborne missiles, and even for those in silos, because the rocket could be fired instantaneously without going through a time-consuming topping-off process. The arguments also revolved around the morality of using nuclear weapons. Whether or not people liked to think about the unthinkable, pundits like Herman Kahn argued that they had to do so and to decide just about how many millions of people could be sacrificed in a nuclear battle. By the end of the 'sixties this had shaded off into a new argument over whether the Soviets were deploying, and the Americans should deploy, the ABM. What made the argument particularly difficult to resolve was the prospect of a battle in space between two robot systems each of which was now capable of polluting the atmosphere with deadly fall-out which might kill millions, while still leaving the chance that at least one warhead would get through, especially if MIRVed.

There was a long gap between the evolution of nuclear deterrent theory and the availability of the hardware. Second World War rocket developments and subsequent advances made in aircraft design, gyro-stabilizing systems, radio, and radar made ballistic missiles possible; but developments in the immediate post-war period were restricted by several factors, among them relocation of the German expert teams in the United States and the USSR, and restricted budgets. And, in the United States at least, the core of the German team went to the Army rather than to the Air Force. But the lag was also due to the fact that air-breathing missiles were more popular with military decision-makers. Not until 1954 did the miniaturization of inertial guidance systems and the arrival of the thermo-nuclear warhead, which provided greater punch for a smaller space and weight, make it possible for unmanned missiles to strike with fair accuracy a target some 5,000 miles away. Even so, in spite of the impetus given the American programme by the Soviet launching of the Sputnik I satellite, it was 1958 before the first Atlas was test-fired; and the missile situation was one of the issues in the American presidential election of 1960. Meanwhile the Soviet Union and the United States had developed intermediate range missiles (IRBM), with a range of about 1,600 miles. The intercontinental missile (ICBM) became operational in the 1960s, and the Navy's Polaris

Comparative design approaches to the heavy bomber can clearly be seen in this shot of a British Avro Vulcan V-bomber and an American **Boeing** *B-52.*

Workhorse of the grand-strategic bombing program in the Vietnam War was the Republic *F-105 Thunderchief, "the Thud."*

*The first of the British V-bombers was the **Vickers** Valiant. When changed from high to low-altitude approach patterns by new strategies, fatigue caught up with it and it was withdrawn after about 2500 hours in service after ten years in 1964. Stress was a subject not adequately understood when the aircraft was designed in the late 1940's.*

missile enlarged its range by its ability to be moved into firing positions closer to the targets. Starting with a range of 1,200 miles, the improved Polaris A-3 was credited with 2,875 miles by 1969. As a counter to this development the Russians accelerated their sophisticated oceanographic research, concentrating on anti-submarine warfare measures and developing missile-carrying submarines.

Other nations engaged in experimental rocket programmes and atmospheric and spatial exploration, but only the British attempted to rival the two major powers in the 'fifties. Their Blue Streak was cancelled before it was test-fired, however, and instead some attempt was made to use American Thor IRBMs; but by the end of the 'sixties the British had dropped out of the race.

In the USSR and the United States, work on anti-ballistic missiles continued, and whether they would be successful would depend upon the amount of money expended in research and upon the political forces their supporters could muster, as much as upon the technical know-how of the manufacturers and operators involved. History has shown, however, that an antidote to any weapon can be found if enough effort is put into the task.

To some extent the two super-powers had recognized by 1961 that the dangers of nuclear war probably outweighed the advantages; thus they established the 'hot line' between Moscow and Washington and used it effectively during the 1962 Cuban missile crisis and the 1967 Arab-Israeli War to neutralize a conflict, even between themselves. The original impetus for the hot line came, however, from a political scientist's observations that a nuclear holocaust could be started by an unknown, or *nth*, power, lobbing a missile from a submarine into one of the major cities of the two super-powers, in the hopes that they would, like the two sleeping giants, knock themselves out and leave the world to others.

The hot line was in addition, of course, to elaborate peripheral radar defences set up by both sides, including the well-known Canadian-American DEW line across the Arctic facing Russian missiles launched on a great-circle route. By the later sixties these systems had been extended to satellite surveillance, yet ironically the warning time remained about the same fifteen minutes it had been in 1939, until 1969, when the United States claimed its Midas

spy-in-the-sky would give it thirty minutes. The USAF Strategic Air Command developed an airborne-alert system under which some of its aircraft and a command ship were always airborne. Another deterrent invention was the Skybolt stand-off bomb, essentially an airborne missile, which could be fired as far as 1,500 miles away from the target; this system was abandoned, with some Anglo-American repercussions, when the Polaris submarines became operational at the beginning of the 'sixties, and solid-fuelled rockets were emplaced in silos in the continental United States.

Both the Soviet and the American air forces pressed for the development of new manned bombers. Various attempts had been made to develop an atomic ship and then when that proved not to be very practical to produce a large supersonic bomber to take the place of the aging B52s as well as of the supersonic B-58 Hustler. By 1960 two prototypes were under construction, but the XB-70 programme was held to a testing level and in early 1969 the survivor was given to the Air Force Museum at Wright-Patterson Field. The manned-bomber lobby still continued in action, but with ballistic missiles able to reach any target in the world the arguments for a manned super-bomber other than a very expensive test vehicle for a supersonic transport began to appear unsupportable. This was no longer the field in which manned air power could make the most meaningful and economic contribution. But early in the seventies the US evolved the Triad concept of land- and sea-based missiles given added flexibility by a low-level supersonic strategic bomber, the B-1.

By the end of the 'sixties Vietnam was showing that the wars of the future were increasingly likely to be local affairs in under-developed areas, in which tactical aircraft would be able to carry sufficient force to do the job if properly assigned. Even more importantly, Vietnam and the Arab-Israeli War of 1967 showed that it was how conventional aircraft were handled that counted, and that generals needed a really sound understanding of the strengths and weaknesses of air power and of the limitations under which it operated. These wars began to show, as did limited budgets in the smaller powers, that more attention needed to be paid to simpler, less sophisticated, but more usable aircraft than to B-52s and F-4s. In a sense war had come full cycle to another aspect of the Second World War, the tactical. What were needed were aircraft like the old reliable AD-1 Skyraider which had a remarkable bomb- and rocket-load, great endurance, and the ruggedness to operate off relatively primitive fields. Built at the end of the 1945 war, the Skyraider

*Wind-tunnel testing became much more important in World War II and has increased in the years since as design has become far too complex for rules-of-thumb approaches. **Lockheed-Georgia***

The Changing Airliner, 1945-1975

Brabazon

Stratocruiser

C-124

Valetta

DC-7

R4Y

Britannia

Viscount

Changing Shape of the Airliner II

Comet I

Convair *990*

BAC-*111-500*

Tupulov Tu-134

Boeing 747 and 707 of **Pan Am**

Vickers *VC-10*

Boeing 737

Lockheed *1011 Tristar*

The Evolving Aircraft, 1945-1984

Convair F-106

Lockheed C-5A unloading helicopter.

Fuselage "plugs" to stretch a Lockheed C-130.

A 1983 four-pound powerless computer for aircraft data and flight planning. Lockheed

Workers inside a C-5A wing. Lockheed

British Rolls-Royce. RB 211-524 turbofan engine with thrust in 1983 of up to 53,000 lbs. for Boeing and Lockheed airliners.

Naval Aircraft, 1960-1980

Lockheed P2V

Grumman S-2D

North American RA-5C Vigilante

Douglas A-4 Skyhawk

Vought A-7 Corsair IIs

Lockheed WV-1 Super Constellation

Grumman E-2A Hawkeyes

McDonnell F-4 Phantoms

proved to be irreplaceable in the latter 'sixties. In its stead were flown aircraft which lacked its basic qualities in one way or another. Eventually a number of replacements were accepted, including the twin-jet light Freedom Fighter, the F-5, sold originally to air forces which could not afford the F-4 Phantom and adopted with reluctance and then enthusiasm by the USAF, whose fighter side tended to be dominated by the 'air superiority' group. Others in the same economic fix such as the Australians and the Israelis opted for French Mystères and Mirages, though the Australians were also talked into a few expensive F-111s which the British finally quite rationally cancelled as unsuitably expensive for their needs.

Navies, too, underwent changes. Almost all carrier improvements were confined to the American and British navies, as these were the only ones developing advanced equipment. In both, the battle against the rival air force caused the adaptation of technology to become 'cost effective'. In the US Navy the yardstick by which performance was measured was ability to hit Russia, and traditional roles were neglected. Larger and stronger flight decks as well as better handling facilities were required for post-war jet fighters, and the steam catapult, the deck-edge elevator, the angled deck, and the mirror landing system, all British innovations, were produced, followed by the radar lock-on approach tracking and television supervision through island- and deck-mounted cameras. The old and the new carriers were now vastly more efficient: a 60,000-ton *Forrestal*-class carrier was able to launch four aircraft a minute, while keeping tankers overhead to refuel returnees short of fuel. Jets meant that strikes were faster and that deck-handling had to be more precise on the part of ground crews and pilots. The first American operational jet squadron roosted aboard USS *Saipan* in May 1948 flying McDonnell FH-1 Phantoms. With a top speed of 479 mph, a weight of 10,000 lbs, and a ceiling of 41,000 feet, they were the precursors of the F-4 Phantoms of the Vietnam war, which in turn were aircraft the size of a DC-3, weighing 50,000 lbs and capable of 1,400 mph. The latest development in carriers, apart from helicopter ships, was the nuclear-powered *Enterprise* class, with a flight deck 1,040 feet long (twice the 1922 *Langley's*), an extreme beam of 252 feet, and a full-load displacement of 85,350 tons. There have been some, indeed, who have wondered if the super-carrier was not a case of putting too many eggs in one basket. The Russians also began to undertake carrier development, but by the late 'sixties the nucleus of their force was still the helicopter ship *Moskva*, useful for brushfire wars.

B-58

The development of helicopters after the Second World War showed no startling innovations until 1968, when the rigid rotor machine capable of aerobatics and speeds of close to 300 mph was demonstrated. Much neglected was the convertiplane, which should have played a major role in anti-submarine warfare, as it had considerable range advantages over the conventional helicopter. But even more significant was the general failure to exploit the new gas-turbine engines for the development of short take-off and landing (STOL) aircraft, which were basically machines that used modern power and construction techniques to deliver the same short-field performance as aircraft in the twenties but with much greater safety. Ironically, one of the reasons for the slow development of the STOL aircraft was that it was unsaleable to air forces whose leaders had their eyes focused on the bigger and better sonic boom. Yet for both airlines and the military in many parts of the world the STOL aircraft was the most practical solution to a roadless area filled with small clearings. Of all the aircraft manufacturers, it was De Havilland of Canada who most realized the possibilities. Two further ironies were evident: by the early 'sixties it was becoming hard to find any engineer with experience of propellers for STOL work, yet at the same time an active, working market was found for fibreglass copies of such an old reliable as the Ford Trimotor, an aircraft at least thirty years old.

3. Airlines and Aircraft Industries

The evolution of airliners until recently followed ten years behind military developments, just as operational aircraft entered service a decade after record-breakers. Two innovations were basically British: the first efficient turbo-prop airliner, the Vickers Viscount, which entered service with BEA in 1951, and the ill-fated De Havilland Comet I jetliner, which BOAC put into service in 1952. Turbo-props proved to be ideal for intermediate routes with a large number of stops, but when developed into larger, prestige aircraft

Mystere IV

F-84 cockpit.

F-111

XB-70 Valkyrie

F-80 engine change.

Mirage V

The Changing Aircraft (cont.)

F-104's and F-4

Dassault Etendard

De Havilland Caribou

Saab 37 Viggen

Farchild A-10 Warthog

North American B-1

General Dynamics F-16 Falcon

KC-135 and C5-A

USS **Forrestal**

they ran into difficulties because they could not compete against jets, which entered service to stay in 1958. The Lockheed Electra was caught in the latter dilemma, but continued to offer satisfactory service into the 1970s, while the Bristol Britannia suffered from the fact that it was four years late entering service and so was a bare six months ahead of the big jets on the highly competitive North Atlantic routes. Turbo-props were developed by the Russians and the Canadians for over-water patrols and for freight services, and were gradually adopted by the fighting services of other countries for supply-dropping and anti-submarine warfare (ASW).

The major problem for the aircraft industries after the Second World War was that the cost of research and development rose so drastically that companies could no longer play with several projects but found themselves increasingly limited to as few as one, and then able to undertake that only with massive government financing or the guarantee of orders of up to at first fifty and then 100; by the time of the big jets, the break-even point had risen to around 300 aircraft each, with a price tag of some $5,000,000. Such staggering figures meant that companies which did not very carefully estimate markets, costs, inflation, and research and development times found themselves dangerously close to bankruptcy.

By the seventies, the world had three supersonic civilian transports (SSTs) flying or on the drawing boards, apart from military supersonic aircraft. Little was known about the politics behind the Russian Tu-144, but in the west the Anglo-French Concorde faced airline resistance on its economics and severe cost recovery problems; its basic development cost estimates had skyrocketed from £150 million in 1962 to £1,000 million in 1971. In the United States a lengthy competition for the SST design contributed to the financial troubles of Lockheed and Boeing, and Congress in 1971 proved unwilling to continue spending on the development of a commercial SST. In fact, these planes appeared to bear out the hypothesis that technological development continues for three generations, or fifty to sixty years, before it hits a plateau caused by political, economic, social, and ideological, not to mention military and diplomatic, resistance. How long the plateau lasts depends upon the development of both a new climate of opinion and a more economically appealing technology.

At the end of the 1939 war only three large national aircraft industries remained intact, the American, the British, and the Soviet. All

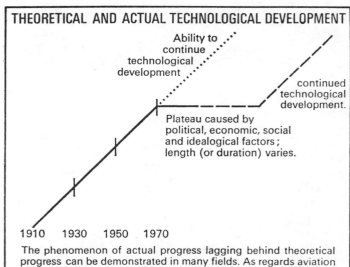

THEORETICAL AND ACTUAL TECHNOLOGICAL DEVELOPMENT

The phenomenon of actual progress lagging behind theoretical progress can be demonstrated in many fields. As regards aviation the American STT is one predictable victim of the uncertain financial and political climate of the early seventies.

three suffered in varying degrees from the immediate post-war demobilizational insecurity and benefited from the coming of the Cold War and the Korean conflict. Though demobilization hit the American industry, the demands of consumers for other goods coupled with a government programme of selling off wartime factories for a dollar apiece accelerated the move out of the industry of temporary wartime manufacturers, while the demand for airliners and private planes soaked up the capacity the services did not need. Then the Cold War and Korea created a new expansion; this was coupled to the American demand for the best technological developments, so that much that was war-surplus was junked or sold abroad. British industry suffered a severe demobilizational insecurity and was still sliding downhill, in spite of the Brabazon programme of planned post-war airliner production, when the Korean War started. Britain was forced to borrow American aircraft for the RAF until production could be restarted in 1951. In the early 'sixties demobilization again found the British aircraft industry in increasing

Transport Aircraft Transition, 1941-1956

C-47

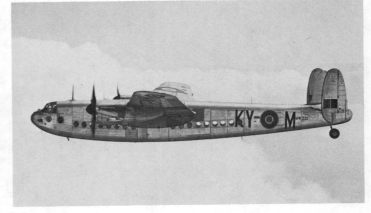

Avro York

C-54

C-54 interior.

C-69

Constellation cockpit.

Convair XC-99

Constitution

Lockheed lengthening Hercules.

difficulties, and government-directed mergers and joint international projects did not compensate for the loss of both the RAF market and overseas customers.

In the Soviet Union the aircraft industry passed along a rather different path, because the Second World War had shown that the Soviet Air Force possessed a number of serious weaknesses. In particular it was vulnerable to the sort of grand-strategic attack which Anglo-American forces had been using. So the Russians set out first to build a defensive fighter force and then to develop strategic bombers. In this work they were greatly helped by the fact that four-fifths of the German aircraft production facilities fell into their hands, including crates of brand-new but short-lived (10-12 hours) axial-flow jet engines of poor metallurgical quality, together with the specialists to design, produce, and maintain them. The British engines they obtained were high quality centrifugal types which provided the MiG-15 over Korea with its highly competitive performance, to mention but one example. More than this, they managed to get most of the German rocket scientists with their experience in high-speed aerodynamics. In 1946 the strategic bomber force was once again reactivated and given copies of American B-29s until turbo-prop and four-jet bombers were available to carry the atomic weapons the Soviets produced in the 'fifties.

The Soviets also knew they needed to develop air transport, for they had seen how successfully the Germans had switched their air power on the Russian front through the use of air transport; and Aeroflot had the routes upon which to employ transport aircraft, ironically in part because industry had been scattered east of the Urals as well as rebuilt in traditional areas, thus necessitating bureaucratic travel. While the usual struggles for financial allocations went on between groups favouring one particular type of aircraft or style of fighting, as they did in other air forces, the Soviets had the advantage over the United States in that there were not two almost equally matched services carrying on an annual battle for the financial pie.

The supply of Soviet aircraft to Communist China and the satellites, while at times of benefit in keeping the aircraft industry employed, also saw a number of types manufactured abroad under licence agreements alone. Central control over the aircraft industry appears to have provided somewhat clearer direction than in the West, though in the latter countries the close ties between industry and government suggest that the interlocking military-industrial complex may in effect be centrally controlled. In a nation dedicated to State management, however, allocation of resources, including manpower, are clearly centralized, and there has been little place for rival projects; permanent design teams have been kept grouped about a few successful designers such as Tupolev and Ilyushin and Antonov. While it is noticeable that many Soviet civil aircraft appear to be virtual copies of those produced in the West, this is not true of its fighters or bombers.

By the late 'sixties the Soviets were feeling the loss of the Chinese market as the latter had shown themselves capable of stealing the latest Soviet designs such as the MiG-21s sent in 1966 to North Vietnam, or of producing new aircraft themselves. The repercussions of the Sino-Soviet split on the aircraft industries of the two nations were only partially apparent by 1970. What was clear was that as the needs for the defensive fighter and the grand-strategic bomber were replaced with missiles, the Russians began once more to pay greater attention to ground-attack aircraft and to helicopters. On the other hand, the Chinese, who started virtually from scratch after their success in 1949, except for one ex-Japanese factory in Manchuria, soon learned from the Korean War that direct air battles with a first-class air power were highly expensive. Even the 1954 contests with the Nationalists off Formosa were not without casualties. Thus the Red Chinese concentrated on building up both defensive fighter and tactical bomber forces, while developing their technological know-how as rapidly as possible. The result has been a regeneration whose significance must not be overlooked. The Chinese tradition of craftsmanship together with patience appears to be creating an efficient modern force manned by young personnel who are not being lured by Nationalist cash offers. Periodic battles over North Vietnam and South China seem to support this thesis, although there are reports, too, that there is a struggle within the air force between the 'professional' officer corps and the militia officers.

In the twenty years after the Second World War various European manufacturers came back into business, in an attempt to grasp those sectors of the world market in which the Americans lacked a competitive aircraft. But timeliness and reputation, compatibility, and interchangeability of parts are realities and headaches which the

DC-8

DC-10

DC-9

A-300

companies have had to face in addition to personality and political problems. In seeking the solution of all of these, there has constantly loomed in the background the possibility of merging into American consortia, if the local government would allow such action. The German, Italian, and Dutch industries seem likely to be locked into a European consortium for survival, though much of the success of that appears to depend upon whether or not European politicians can face facts and leave technical negotiations and agreements to those who understand them and have to carry them through.

Outside of Europe the most successful manufacturers are likely to be the Japanese, who have the traditions, skills, capital, and dedication to make their industry viable. Japanese aircraft industry was by 1971 turning to defence contracts as the country became more independent. Whether this tendency will lead to the kind of suicidal spiral of costs that was engulfing Lockheed and Rolls Royce in the west in 1971 remains open to speculation. Attempts to create an Indian aircraft industry have largely fallen upon the same stony ground as in Britain—the ability to design but the inability to produce. After the 1945 war a number of leading German experts emigrated to Argentina, but there, despite a friendly society, little appears to have been done. An aircraft industry is expensive, complex, and highly sensitive; it must be managed both by its owners and directors and by the government with great perspicacity, and it must be well supplied with capital, research facilities, and markets. Few countries can meet these requirements. Some at least fail because they pursue the prestige rather than the practical aircraft.

Closely associated with the aircraft industry are many ancillary firms. The complexity of modern aircraft is reflected in their weight growth. In Britain in the late 'fifties, at a time when there were sixteen airframe and four engine firms in the Society of British Aerospace Constructors there were 540 ancillary firms. Electronics, pressurization and air conditioning, navigation equipment, and the like have all caused their spawning, and the very existence of these creates military-industrial-complex problems in each country desiring to build its own aircraft. Governments are highly unwilling to be dependent upon outside sources for vital parts, so pressure is applied to have home-manufactured equipment fitted, even if the airframe and engines have to be bought abroad. But this makes for uneconomical maintenance problems. The costs of spare parts, for

instance, rose so rapidly when the big jets came into service that Boeing set up a pooling organization around the world. Further moves to cut the costs of holding large inventories of spares are being pursued, for who can afford to hold some 40,000 for just one type of aircraft? The country which wishes to build its own aircraft is faced with either giving them only simple equipment or relying for many parts on outsiders. The decision gambles security with economics, not to mention challenging the pilots' unions. But lesser powers are most likely to continue to be supplied by greater allies; they will have to judge which one is most likely to be able to deliver the goods at a crucial moment. Perhaps a study of the Turkish air force in the Second World War provides the best equivocal answer!

4. Operations

Though there have been a number of aerial conflicts since 1945, in general they have done more to sharpen the lessons of the Second World War than to provide new ones in themselves. Thus once studies are available of the use of air power in colonial conflicts by the British and the French in the inter-war years, the student will probably find that many of the things that he has thought to be new in anti-guerrilla warfare were there earlier, with only the jungle and helicopters providing a partially different setting and timing. Instantaneous communication has affected operations, it is true, enabling the Press to query the President before the pilot returns from a mission and letting armchair generals see the edited battle on their fireside TV sets. While this means that the officer on the spot is more open to instant criticism, it also means that he will get the benefit of better informed, yet still detached comments.

Air Intelligence. On and off throughout the Cold War period incidents developed over lost and snooping aircraft. Many aircraft, ships, and permanent stations have been employed in intelligence gathering, a favourite means of which has been electronic eavesdropping. The most spectacular of the episodes involved the shooting down of an American U-2 spy plane over the heart of the Soviet

Lockheed's SR-71 Supersonic photo-reconnaissance plane is another product of "Kelly" Johnson's "Skonk Works" in Burbank — unusual and sophisticated.

Union in May 1960, an incident that was used by the Soviet Premier as an excuse for calling off a Paris summit conference. Though in this case the pilot was employed as a civilian, the President of the United States took the unprecedently honest step of admitting that he knew of the overflight. Yet such flights were not new. The Germans overflew Britain before the Second World War and the British sent a specially equipped civilian aircraft over Germany. The *Graf Zeppelin* was used to scout British radar defences. Nevertheless, airborne spying has become big business, with the latest planes such as the American SR-71 reputed to cost $24.7 million apiece. The real question is whether the destruction of a spy plane costs the victor more than he gains, and whether the system, 'illegal' as it may be called in an area of international relations which is still in a predatory state of nature, is not in fact a safeguard rather than a liability.

Berlin Airlift, 1948–1949. Though spyplane incidents have occasionally indicated what air forces were doing in a routine way, the post-1945 period has been punctuated with a number of hot wars that are of interest to the history of air power. The first of these cannot perhaps be truly called hot, but it was a diplomatic incident in which power was exercised and a struggle of wills ensued. On 24 June 1948 the Soviet Union decided to close the surface routes to West Berlin, with the apparent intention of taking the area by

*That this was possible was in part due to the plethora of air transport companies flying war-surplus machines for whom the airlift was a shot in the arm. In the mid-fifties the supply of these aircraft dwindled away, but gradually in the 'sixties a surplus jet capacity became available which could be chartered when needed and whose working capacity was many times greater than that of the aircraft used in the Berlin airlift.

starvation. To their surprise, the Western Allies responded at once with an airlift. Here the training of the RAF and USAF in the Second World War paid dividends, especially as the commander of the airlift was the same General William Tunner who had managed the American Hump operation to China. Apart from Soviet harassment, the major problem was the weather; but new radar developments, especially the radar Ground Controlled Approach, enabled aircraft movements to reach 1,000 daily at the three fields in use. By the time the airlift was withdrawn in October 1949, 2.3 million tons had been carried in 277,728 sorties.* The operation showed that the western Allies were prepared to stand their ground and not to be intimidated.

Korean War, 1950–1953. Only some nine months later the Korean War broke out. It presented a number of novel features, as the first war in which jets tangled, but did not really contribute very much to air-power concepts other than proving once again that slow bombers cannot operate in daylight in the face of fast fighters and that speeds in a dogfight remain relative. What was new and frustrating was the sanctuary from which the Communist air force flew and the tacit stand-off between the Chinese and the Americans that limited the war to the airspace over the peninsula south of the Yalu River and north of the Pusan perimeter. Grand-strategic bombing was ruled out because both sides were vulnerable.

The United Nations forces were caught badly off balance at first, but their quick recovery resulted in the destruction of the North Korean air force at a time when the Soviets were just reorganizing the Red Chinese Air Force. The result was that the Soviets got *carte blanche* and a chance to test their planes and pilots against Americans. Quickly finding in November and December 1950 that MiG-15 jet fighters were more than a match for the Second World War F-51s and the jet F-80s, the USAF threw in the F-86 Sabre. The Soviets and the Chinese had the immense advantage of early-warning radar that allowed them to climb from airfields north of the Yalu to 50,000 feet and then to swoop from out of the sun onto USAF planes attacking targets just south of the Yalu. USAF tactics had to be short and sharp, as even with long-range tanks their aircraft were low on fuel. But their pilots had the benefit of radar gunsights and the kill ratio for the remainder of the war rose to nearly 10:1 in their favour. The Chinese air force was badly beaten.

American strategic bombers, mostly B-29s, plugged away at Communist targets while tactical aircraft, many from carriers off-shore, carried out the usual interdiction raids along and behind the front. One lesson that had to be learned, and it should have been learned earlier, was that the multitudinous Asian peasants with messianic leadership had the perseverance to rebuild bridges and railways, or to make by-pass embankments, overnight. Moreover, inefficient as it might be by western standards, the peasants were willing to pad along all night to bring supplies forward. Western Intelligence offi-

Douglas DC-9 production line — notice man in circle and look at page 59 (Hudson).

F-86 in action.

cers, in fact, took some time to understand that conventional assessments meant nothing when made about people who used feudal methods. (A continuous problem was the over-optimism of USAF zealots who believed they could cause the North Koreans to retreat to the Yalu without ground loss.) But the North Koreans and their Chinese allies became willing to sue for peace when they found that they could not maintain air bases south of the Yalu and thus could not, at least with the equipment then available, launch attacks against the UN beachheads and ports, and keep enemy air forces from dominating the air over North Korea.

The Korean War showed the USAF that it had to relearn from past experience. It was lucky in 1950–1953 that its leaders and fliers were still largely those who had fought the Second World War. But there was obviously a need to accelerate the production of its histories and special historical studies so that future generations would not overlook past lessons. Included in this was the need to document current experiences so that future lessons could be disseminated. Interestingly in view of the Vietnam conflict the USAF concluded that Korea was a fluke and that it was only possible to use strategic air power for tactical purposes because this particular situation demanded it, that lavish tactical air support would not be available to ground troops in the future because tactical air forces would have to spend most of their time fighting for air superiority, and that the navy would never again be as free to use the seas for mobile air bases. Therefore, it would be fatal for the USAF to model itself on the successful mix used in Korea: that would lead to global suicide in an air force without a massive grand-strategic bomber force and without an air-superiority force with which to hold the skies.

In these concepts they were right, within limits. For Korea showed that interdiction behind the battleline was most effective because it caught the enemy when he was both concentrating his forces and engaged at the front. Strategic bombing had to take the place of grand-strategic, because industrial targets lay beyond the Yalu, and thus the war had to be fought over the army's battleground. Air superiority lessons had to be modified because the narrowness of the battlefield enabled sweep tactics to be employed against the Com-

munist air force, whose pilots did not really understand or exploit the advantages of their machines. The USAF can complain that neither MacArthur in proceeding northwards nor Ridgway in maintaining a static position appreciated the limits and the advantages of air power. MacArthur was defeated when he attempted to range beyond the area in which air power could control the enemy's logistical system and give sufficient direct tactical support to troops at the limits of their supply lines. Ridgway failed to allow the UN air forces their freedom over North Korea in mid-1951 for fear of disrupting truce talks, which in fact dragged on for two more years, without recognizing that interdiction without a ground battle could not win. In other words, as the air power people themselves now admit, air forces alone cannot win wars.

The USAF has been most concerned about another war in Europe, yet history has ironically forced it to fight in the Far East, where both the opponents and the geographical conditions are quite different. But precisely because the USAF was prepared to fight on its preferred battlefield, and in part because its strategy called for a massive nuclear retaliation if it did so, it was most unlikely that a conventional war would break out there. Yet the USAF had taken its doctrine from the European area, and it expected the army to use its artillery to the full. The US Marine Corps, on the other hand, had derived its doctrine from the Pacific campaigns in which light infantry was thrust ashore with the support of its own tactical air forces while the Navy flew high cover; the operation could expect little artillery support other than that supplied by naval guns afloat. In Korea the army demanded the marine system, and it worked because of the air superiority enjoyed by the UN forces as a whole. (When after the war the USAF denied the concept, the army went ahead and developed, especially in Vietnam, its own air force of helicopter gunships and tactical aeroplanes.) A Joint Operations Centre was devised in Korea which effectively concentrated all the air units available to handle crises on the front. The adoption of the 'Mosquito' forward air controller system was considered impractical for the future, and it was assumed that the identification of targets would be placed in the hands of jet fighter-bomber pathfinders or be done by radar. Yet in Vietnam the use of light planes for Forward Air Controllers remained vital and effective.

The most dramatic and long-range effect of the Korean war was the expansion of the USAF from forty-two wings in 1950 to ninety-five by 1953, with a goal of 143, while at the same time the budget

F-100 heading down to the right.

was allocated on the basis of the role to be played so that the air force came out with the biggest chunk. The Eisenhower 'New Look' at defence only reduced the number to 137 wings in view of the nuclear ratio with Russia. Backed up with a 'massive retaliation' strategy, this expansion deterred the Communists from overt actions.

Vietnam, 1950 onwards. Effectiveness of covert action was well demonstrated in the way in which the French were ousted from Vietnam. Granting the French strategy was wrong and that the military commanders on the spot for political and economic reasons worked with one hand tied behind their backs, the operations there showed that the mere use of air transport alone could not counter guerrilla tactics in a civil war. The fall of Dien Bien Phu amply demonstrated that the French had learned nothing from Crete or other Second World War battles. From 1950 onwards paratroopers were dropped into hopeless last-ditch engagements. Attempts to counter the Viet Minh seizure of the jungled highlands with napalm and rockets meant useless shooting into the dark green foliage. When in April 1953 the French attempted to set up airheads in the Plaine des Jarres, 500 miles from Hanoi and 1,000 miles from Saigon, they mortgaged all their air transport. At Dien Bien Phu they repeated mistakes made in Burma by trying to maintain an airfield surrounded by a ring of hills dominated by the enemy and his antiaircraft guns. That the US got away with such an action later in 1968 at Khe San remains a puzzle, unless it is assumed that the Communists used their threat to the base as an attrition tactic or a feint.

In general the successful suppression of guerrillas demands a 10:1 manpower ratio and has to be done on the ground. Air power can only be effectively used if its power to spot and spoil is backed up by intelligent ground support which both denies the guerrillas sustenance and wins over the local population and ultimately the dissidents by honest political and economic reforms. The object is peace and prosperity, and massive destruction is not an answer; air power cannot make reforms, as both Cyprus and Malaya demonstrated. Moreover, the jet is seldom the answer. Helicopters and STOL aircraft are needed, for the targets are small and relatively slow-moving, the expense of pacification continuous, communication essential, and

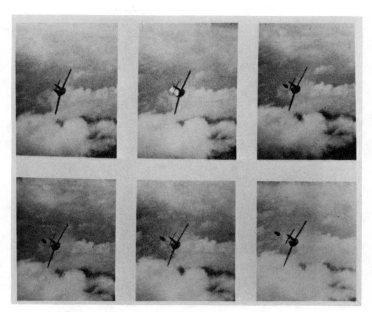

Mig pilot bailing out.

the patience of the taxpayers touchy. In other words, while air power can support such conflicts in a limited way, it is much better employed in open limited wars.

The Vietnam war in many respects bears out these points. Though air power has been heavily used, the war has dragged on because the targets are not large enough or concentrated enough for it to be really effective. The few genuine targets, largely contained in the Hanoi complex, were placed off-limits until the war was escalated, and such a technique destroyed the value of air power's physical and psychological impact. Moreover, as in Korea, a sanctuary was created, north of the demilitarized zone, which by order of the American President was off-limits after it appeared peace talks might begin. A second sanctuary existed in Red China itself. As in the Spanish Civil War, outside military leaders appear to have seen the Vietnam War as a great place to test equipment and theories. Certainly the war has shown that the air-superiority fighter when used for tactical purposes has many disadvantages. Designed for high-speed combat at high altitudes against missile-equipped opponents, USAF jets have been found highly vulnerable to small-arms fire, as almost the whole of their cubic content contains critical equipment and is unarmoured. The result has been that North Vietnamese peasants armed with automatic small arms with simple sights have been knocking down or damaging Mach 2 fighters and fighter-bombers. In many cases the lessons of the Second World War had been forgotten: unarmoured aircraft with vulnerable fuel tanks and hydraulic control systems were put out of action by random hits. Fleas have killed elephants.

In many ways Vietnam was a colonial war reminiscent of British operations in Iraq with cumbersome ground forces gradually superseded by air forces. Ironically part of the original escalation of ground forces was to protect massive air bases made possible themselves by the lack of enemy air opposition. The lack of an opposing air force shows starkly in the figures for enemy aircraft shot down: between July 1965 and February 1968 they could confirm claims for only 61 MiG-17s and 25 MiG-21s. Interestingly, 25 of these credits went to single-seater F-105s, the rest largely to two-seater F-4s.

US air raids against the north, which started with retaliation for the Tonkin Gulf attack on a USN destroyer, were escalated into a full-scale offensive in March 1965. But rather than using air power

Fairchild C-82 Packets.

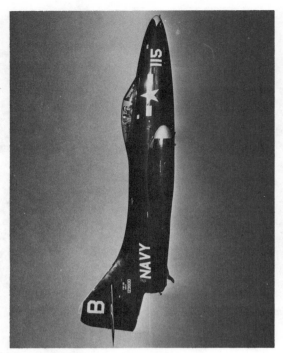

Grumman *F9F*

as it should have been used in a series of short, sharp grand-strategic strikes at Hanoi and the critical war-making industries, airfields, and docks elsewhere in North Vietnam, the air offensive was launched as a drawn-out series of raids by fighter-bombers which were gradually stepped up until attacks on Hanoi itself were allowed. By then, of course, the Reds were ready. Nor did the bombing slow down the flow of men and supplies to the south. The rate in fact almost doubled from 4,500 men a month in 1965 to 7,000 in 1966.

By the end of 1967 the US had lost 3,000 aircraft in all areas including 1,401 planes and helicopters in action and 1,555 to various operational causes. Though this loss rate was only 2.18 planes per thousand sorties as opposed to 3.5 in Korea and 9.5 in the Second World War in both the latter cases there was air opposition. The Communists increased their surface-to-air (SAM) missile forces and at first saw increased successes, but US airmen discovered that by keeping low and taking evasive action they could avoid the missiles, though this often placed them within range of effective ground fire. The USAF developed SAM-detection and jamming gear, and pilots found that SAMs could not follow when they made sharp turns. The Soviets claimed the SAMs were 50 per cent effective; the US that only 2 per cent made kills. Much of the use of F-105s to bomb North Vietnam has been dependent upon aerial refuelling, and there is a danger that such dependence may critically endanger strike forces in a war where they are faced with enemy interception of the vital but highly vulnerable tankers.

The use of carriers off Vietnam gradually began to be seen as expensive and wasteful, and in 1968 they were ordered to slow down their operations when the USS *New Jersey,* the only battleship in commission, arrived off the coast. Hard use of the carriers had been costly, if useful in ironing out the 'bugs' and enabling the Navy to realize that it needed the slower, longer-ranged, more heavily armed LTV F-8 Corsair for many roles rather than the sophisticated and expensive F-4, which should essentially have been reserved for air-superiority roles. Moreover, there was less need to use carriers with many airfields now available ashore.

As in Korea, grand-strategic bombers were used for strategic missions. By February 1969 some 105 B-52s from the Strategic Air Command were flying about 1,800 sorties a month from Guam

(2,000 miles from the battlefields), Okinawa, and Thailand. Most of the raids were spoiling attacks in which large tonnages of bombs were dropped over suspected areas of enemy concentration to hinder organization of enemy divisions for battle. The 750-pound bombs used created hazards to both health and the economy. The craters could not easily be filled in, and the stagnant water in them bred malarial mosquitoes, while bomb splinters so damaged trees as to cause the lumber industry to lose two hours a day repairing saws at the mills. This was hardly the way to win over the populace. And the high cost of such operations, which amounted to air-freighting high explosives over great distances, raised sound arguments for a larger tactical air force operating from local fields.

The credibility of bombing operations in Vietnam coincided with a growing public interest and awareness in Anglophobe countries of the attacks upon Germany and Japan in the Second World War. By 1971 an argument was raging as to whether or not the six million tons of bombs dropped upon an area the size of Texas (this was three times the tonnage dropped upon Germany) was either effective or justifiable. Interestingly more than half this tonnage was dropped by fighter-bombers such as the F-105 which carried as much as a B-17 of 1944. Opponents of bombing cited the ecological and physical devastation, proponents the disruptive effect upon enemy operations and the salvation of friendly ground troops especially at places such as Khe San where 6,000 marines held off 25,000 attackers.

The most interesting development of the Vietnam War was undoubtedly the successful employment of helicopter air-cavalry tactics, first suggested by General James M. Gavin, an airborne commander of the Second World War, in August 1957. Helicopter fuel systems were vulnerable to ground fire, but the casualties to helicopters were at first surprisingly light. The US Army estimated in 1969 that about 18,000 combat sorties were flown per helicopter lost. The air-mobile concept was based upon an acceptance of a certain degree of vulnerability, and it succeeded because of surprise and flexibility, enabling troops to be moved around even in actual battle without long vulnerable supply lines. Both men and artillery could be airlifted to the tops of ridges from which they could interdict or enfilade the enemy. Moreover the removal of casualties to base hospitals was quick, helping to raise the morale of even isolated units. The army viewed the Vietnam experience as equivalent to a nuclear war, in that pockets

A-7 refueling.

Two views of Royal Navy carriers still in service long after World War II. The upper view shows Westland (Sikorsky) Wessex helicopters over HMS **Bulwark**, which has her forward elevator lowered, and the lower shows Blackburn Buccaneers over HMS **Eagle**, a ship modified postwar with an angled deck. **Crown copyright reserved.**

of the enemy and not the seizure of terrain would be the objective, and the helicopter was adapted to carry out fire-power, mobility, logistics, and communications roles. Helicopters gave the army the mobility and concentration with which to hit a numerous enemy with limited forces; and provided the air force could keep enemy fighters out of a twenty-mile area behind the battlefield, the air-cavalrymen were convinced they had a battle-winning weapon.

By 1971 this began to look less certain, for the Viet Cong and the North Vietnamese had at last realized that helicopters were vulnerable to small anti-aircraft fire and rockets. Vietnamization offered them a greater chance to lure in or decoy helicopters by broadcasting commands in pidgin English on helicopter frequencies. And in the ten years in which 'choppers' have been used in Vietnam the operations have not been cheap. By early 1971 more than 4,200 had been lost; 45 per cent of them had been shot down. At that time helicopter losses were running at the rate of three a day, out of a force of 3,500 machines. Losses ran at about a 4:3 ratio to losses of fixed-wing aircraft, and helicopters accounted for 71 per cent of the aircrew and passenger casualties.

Helicopters provided great mobility and enabled infantry and artillery to be switched quickly from one area to another. And in a manner reminiscent of the picquets used to guard hilltop flanks on the North-West Frontier of India, fire-support bases were established on hilltops rather than around airfields as the French had so fatefully done at Dien Bien Phu. It can be argued that helicopter losses were light considering their intense use, but a case can also be made that this was only possible because of the lack of enemy air opposition. However, helicopters may prove to be the best anti-guerrilla weapon armies possess because in most such operations the enemy is unlikely, unless supported by an outside power, to have aircraft which can challenge control of the skies. Anti-aircraft guns and rockets are another matter.

Another aspect of the Vietnam War that caused comment was the use of herbicides. The technique of airborne spraying of the countryside with defoliants so that movements and ambushes could be seen could be supported on military grounds, since air surveillance was certainly far cheaper and quicker than ground patrols, if less accurate. But herbicides caused damage both to rubber trees and to the ecology generally, and their use raised again the problems of

Helicopters in VN.

public relations, not so much in the battle area as at home (by December 1968 the subject of defoliants split the membership of the American Association for the Advancement of Science) and in neutral countries. And this has become an important consideration when so many states have voting rights in the United Nations.

The assessment of the use of air power in the Vietnam War has been made the more difficult by the fact that at the time of writing the war had not ended and emotional factors could not be eliminated from any estimation of its results. Evidence from the enemy side is not available; and in any case, if written, it is likely to be just as biased as some of that from the Allied side. And the use of air power has been entangled with the whole war strategy in such a way that it will be hard to unravel what is valid air historical experience and what is invalid because of political overtones and considerations, if not blunders.

The use of air power in Vietnam was vastly complicated by the political position. On the American side while the view will be different than it was in 1965, when the Rolling Thunder campaign of air attacks on the North was initiated, on the whole honest men were trying to make honest decisions. The slow escalation of Rolling Thunder can be attributed, perhaps, to too much political science and not enough military realism. The spraying programmes, which later came under ecological criticism, were originally scientific solutions to battlefield problems. Perspective on the whole war has been distorted by complex political and emotional responses, yet it seems quite clear that the old political lesson should have been heeded that involvement by outsiders in a civil war is a kindness to no one.

As too often has happened in the past, the military feel that political policy was decided, and then the generals were asked how it could be carried out. Unlike the balance of military and political objectives achieved in the Second World War, there was an incompatibility of objectives in Vietnam. It can be argued that while airmen found themselves involved in the concensus process which is modern American policy-making, there was no airpower myth because airmen who had grown up in the First World War were well aware that airpower alone cannot win wars, especially counter-guerrilla ones.

One of the legacies of the conflict in South Vietnam is the US-trained VNAF. It has had to take over the role of lavish air-support

Helicopters in VN.

Folland Gnat.

for ground forces now accustomed to massive USAF help. The provision of defence against North Vietnamese MiGs and helicopter support made the American air forces the last to withdraw under the Nixon phasing-out from the Asian land war.

India-Pakistan, 1965. One curious war of the post-1945 period was the armed clash between India and Pakistan in September 1965. Essentially a Second World War campaign, it was fought without grand-strategic purpose, without much imagination, and in the end without effect. The air role was strictly limited to ground support, and the results were on the whole misconstrued owing to the fact that reporters generally failed to divide claims of aircraft downed by at least a factor of three. As in other battles earlier, once this was done, the losses on each side came close to the figure acknowledged by the loser. If any lessons can be drawn, they are that countries entirely dependent for their supply of arms upon the outside world should very carefully weigh the odds and the objects of going to war. Both sides suffered severe wastage of their ammunition and fuel, as well as other equipment. Fighting was largely brought to a halt by supplier powers imposing an embargo on arms shipments.

Tactically aircraft of both sides flew under radar screens. The Pakistanis, having only one enemy, were able to concentrate their aircraft and thus ease their maintenance problems; the Indian air force, with more kinds of aircraft and the possibility of Chinese opposition, faced more complex problems. Yet both in the air and on the ground the Pakistanis found that the Indians had the advantage in numbers, though both sides found that it was the simpler, older and more familiar equipment which was easier to maintain and operate. Air forces especially tend to become over-sophisticated to the extent that the equipment exceeds the abilities of the humans assigned to it; this is a kind of technological 'Peter Principle'.

Though a good deal was made of the fact that Pakistan had American F-104s (it actually had only twelve) and that the Indians had MiG-21s, they never met in combat, and air superiority was never made an issue; what did happen after the war was that, with American aid cut off, the Pakistan air force had to buy French and Soviet aircraft and thus become more polyglot than was desirable. Nevertheless it appears that the Pakistan air force, with its more aggressive spirit, emerged with a strengthened ego from the conflict, while India, already upset by the Chinese invasion of 1962, was left

with losses of some seventy-five aircraft to the Pakistanis' nineteen. As in the case of the Arab-Israeli conflicts, the smaller and of necessity better trained air force, proved once again that it could stand up to a much larger force, and, if pilot morale was high and maintenance good, inflict disproportionate losses. The whole so-called war was so short that no more lessons can be drawn from it than from one annual manoeuvre, nor with any more safety.

Arab-Israeli War, 1967. The historian of air power is much happier dealing with the very clear-cut lessons of the 1967 Arab-

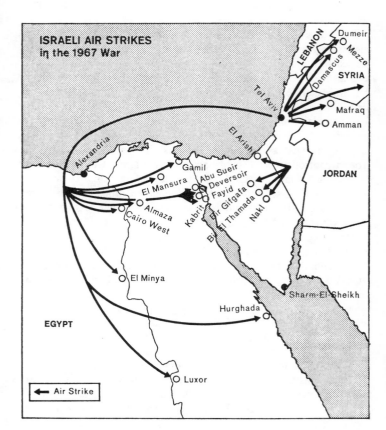

F-104's coming and going.

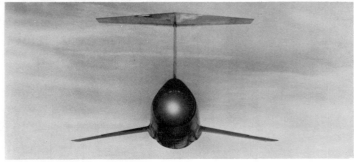

Israeli War. Here the failure of the United Nations allowed the Arabs to make aggresive moves in the hopes of either cutting Israel off from access to the eastern seas or forcing the Israelis into attacking. The Israelis chose to make a pre-emptive strike in June 1967. The vulnerability of the Arabs was revealed by the drastic way in which Israel improved upon the 1956 Sinai campaign, one in which British and French efforts to seize Suez were hampered by irresolution at the top in the face of American threats. The whole Israeli plan in 1967 was based upon precise timing, hard training, accurate striking power, understanding of their own limitations, and proper intelligence, including an accurate psychological assessment of their opponents.

The dawn Israeli strikes were launched before the Egyptians customarily were ready for work, and they swept in low from over the sea to the northwest. Within three hours they had attacked sixteen airfields with special bombs and cannon fire; within two days the Arabs had lost 333 aircraft on the ground and ninety-five in the air so that the Israelis had no need to fear either bomber attacks on their homeland or tactical interference with their armies. The strikes employed the principles of concentration, economy of force, and surprise, as well as simplicity, yet flexibility was maintained by ground controllers who could have switched aircraft to new targets as needed. All targets were hit from as low and as close as possible so as to avoid misses and decoys. Thus concrete dibbler bombs were dropped from 100 feet and cannon used at ranges of about 100 yards, yet speeds of 500 knots were employed. (Prior to battle, training had been limited in order that virtually 100 per cent availability of aircraft could be achieved.) The aircraft were then switched to direct support of the army. The result was *blitzkrieg* at its best. No attacks were made on civilian centres, so that Arab politicians had the least cause for creating a general will to war. In fact, the Israeli forces in general have inherited a legacy from the Second World War and polished it to perfection in an arena that is still in many ways the Western Desert. And they have maintained an initiative by the acquisition of US aircraft when French sources were closed, and by refusing to sign the nuclear non-proliferation treaty.

The Israelis won a classical campaign, but they found themselves facing a guerrilla war, the logical reaction of the Egyptians and their Soviet advisers. When Israel countered sneak infantry raids with jet strikes against guerrilla bases and deep into Egypt, the Russians shifted from fighter defence to the development of SAM sites. Israeli strikes at these were effective until a ceasefire was imposed which allowed the Egyptians to carpet their side of the Suez Canal with SAMs. By 1971 it looked as if a stand-off had been reached which in turn might lead to a peace settlement if the defence had made the offence too costly. But knowing Israeli determination and tactical ingenuity and given the religious nature of the nationalistic conflicts in the area, nobody could bet on it.

5. The Legacy

What can be learned from the study of the use of air power since 1945? Certainly air forces themselves have been left with many puzzles, because the wars which they have fought have not, with the exception of the Arab-Israeli incident, been the wars for which they have trained. Yet paradoxically, it is perhaps exactly because they prepared for a massive war that it has never taken place. Each side knows that it has more to lose than to gain. The communists, because their aggressive doctrine concentrates on alternatives, were the first to realize after Korea that if they could not succeed overtly, they would have to operate covertly, but even this resolution became entangled in the socio-political-economic problems of the areas in which they chose to work, thus making it the more difficult for western statesmen to understand what were the realities of the situation in any one country at any given time. Perhaps all military men like to keep things simple, while politicians like to keep them ambiguous; and, above all, airmen prefer a clearcut shooting war, if a war there has to be. But such an approach does not accord with the facts of modern wars, as events since 1945 have all too clearly revealed.

The Berlin Airlift and the Korean War showed that the United Nations was prepared to counter aggression as in the thirties the League of Nations and the democracies had not been. In both cases western air power turned the tide, but in neither did the air leaders believe they were fighting the correct type of war. Bomber-deterrent

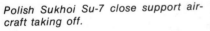

Polish Sukhoi Su-7 close support aircraft taking off.

Phantom I head-on.

Phantom I cockpit.

P-3B

P2V

AIRCRAFT ACCIDENT COMPARISON
AT FIRST 650,000 FLIGHT HOURS (CUMULATIVE)

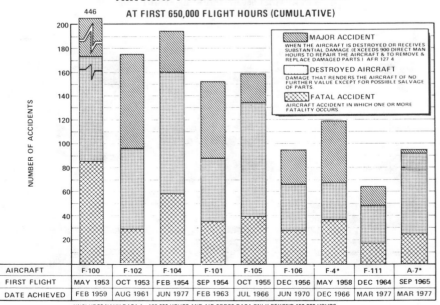

446

MAJOR ACCIDENT
WHEN THE AIRCRAFT IS DESTROYED OR RECEIVES SUBSTANTIAL DAMAGE (E EXCEEDS 900 DIRECT MAN HOURS TO REPAIR THE AIRCRAFT & TO REMOVE & REPLACE DAMAGED PARTS) AFR 127 4

DESTROYED AIRCRAFT
DAMAGE THAT RENDERS THE AIRCRAFT OF NO FURTHER VALUE EXCEPT FOR POSSIBLE SALVAGE OF PARTS

FATAL ACCIDENT
AIRCRAFT ACCIDENT IN WHICH ONE OR MORE FATALITY OCCURS

NUMBER OF ACCIDENTS

AIRCRAFT	F-100	F-102	F-104	F-101	F-105	F-106	F-4*	F-111	A-7*
FIRST FLIGHT	MAY 1953	OCT 1953	FEB 1954	SEP 1954	OCT 1955	DEC 1956	MAY 1958	DEC 1964	SEP 1965
DATE ACHIEVED	FEB 1959	AUG 1961	JUN 1977	FEB 1963	JUL 1966	JUN 1970	DEC 1966	MAR 1977	MAR 1977

*INCLUDES NAVY DATA 1st 150,000 HOURS AND AIR FORCE DATA ONLY BEYOND 150,000 HOURS.

theory left over from the twenties still remained in favour and led through the nuclear stand-off to the establishment of missile arsenals and satellite spy systems. Expensive though these systems were, they provided domestic benefits in a high rate of national expenditure that created both employment and technological spin-off. In addition, they made for over-all peace and saved the world from self-destruction.

The grand-strategic air forces thus became the silent partners of peace, but the new kind of localized, limited, often guerrilla conflicts call for a tactical air force well endowed with transport and schooled in an understanding of the problems involved. Other people's civil wars are wonderful places in which to try out theories and weapons, but commitment beyond the level of supply and advice is dangerous. The Russians and the Chinese seem to have understood this better than the western powers. Discretion is not only the better part of valour at times, it is also the better part of international diplomacy. Air power is so spectacular that its real role can easily be lost sight of in the swift passage and thunderous roar of a jet. Unable to afford mistakes, the Israelis have perhaps understood this better than anyone else; other nations still have to learn from history.

Skyraider 1965

Carrier lift with F3H.

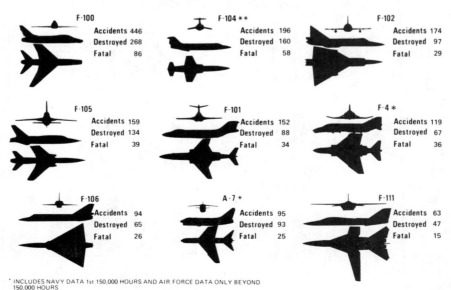

ACCIDENT COMPARISON
AT FIRST 650,000 HOURS OF FLIGHT TIME

F-100		F-104 **		F-102	
Accidents	446	Accidents	196	Accidents	174
Destroyed	268	Destroyed	160	Destroyed	97
Fatal	86	Fatal	58	Fatal	29

F-105		F-101		F-4 *	
Accidents	159	Accidents	152	Accidents	119
Destroyed	134	Destroyed	88	Destroyed	67
Fatal	39	Fatal	34	Fatal	36

F-106		A-7 *		F-111	
Accidents	94	Accidents	95	Accidents	63
Destroyed	65	Destroyed	93	Destroyed	47
Fatal	26	Fatal	25	Fatal	15

* INCLUDES NAVY DATA 1st 150,000 HOURS AND AIR FORCE DATA ONLY BEYOND 150,000 HOURS

** 600,000 FLT. HRS. (HAS NOT ACHIEVED 650,000 FLT. HRS.)

Soviet Li-2, a Lend-Lease C-47, though some were also built under license in the USSR.

Mig-19 called Fresco by NATO shown both flown by Soviet Naval forces and in Polish service.

TC-616 is a special Mig-15 in that it was flown in 1953 by a North Korean pilot to South Korea, dismantled there and taken to Okinawa, where US pilots test flew it. Then it was again dismantled and taken to Wright-Patterson for further testing before ending up in the **USAF** Museum.

The Mig-21 Fishbed is a short-range delta-wing fighter. This one belongs to the Yugoslav Air Force. **US Navy**

A Soviet Tupulov Tu-114 Moss AWACS aircraft on patrol over the Mediterranean. **US Navy**

Soviet Aviation

*The Tu-20 Bear is probably the best known long-range Soviet reconnaissance aircraft, its turboprop engines and speed blisters giving it great range for oceanic reconnaissance. Escort is a **USN** Phantom II in 1971.*

*The Tu-28B Backfin is a long-range missile armed fighter which entered service in the early 1960's. **US Navy***

Soviet Aviation

The Bison was in 1964 the main Soviet long-range jet bomber. **US Navy**

*Above: The Soviets have considerable helicopter forces. Here a USN Sea King flies formation with a Soviet MA-25 Hormone from a Soviet destroyer leader. Below: The Soviet development of carriers in the 1970's, a new thrust, is represented by the **Kiev,** a helicopter ship.* **US Navy**

1971-1983

Author's Note

In rereading the text more than a dozen years after it was written, I was pleased to feel that more harm than good would be done by tampering with the original text and that, moreover, apart from adding illustrations for the benefit of readers unfamiliar with aviation, the most useful thing that could be done was merely to add a short section indicating what had happened in the intervening dozen years while at the same time attempting to strike a better balance in the overall story by including some material not covered earlier.

Though it seemed that for a while in the 1970's relations between the two superpowers would warm somewhat, by the early eighties they were again heading for the freezer. That this was so was due in part to the see-saw of technological advantage. The U.S.S.R. unveiled the Backfire swing-wing long-range bomber at a time when the USAF's XB-70 had been sent to the USAF Museum and the Carter administration had cancelled the B-1 follow-on in favor of cruise missiles, so at first those with their eyes only upon prestige failed to see the flexibility provided by the cruise missile and its almost guerrilla threat to as vast a land-mass as the Soviet Union. Conversely, the Russians, having witnessed the ease of movement of the U.S threat from one sea to another began to demonstrate their usual ability to copy from the West not merely in ICBM missile submarines, but also in the development of the helicopter carriers *Moskva* and *Kiev* with evidence that full Fleet carriers might appear in the eighties to challenge U.S. domination of the high seas. The election of Ronald Reagan in the U.S. put defense back into the saddle and the B-1 was reinstated, but at the same time together with a willingness to resume disarmament negotiations.

In the meantime, Soviet and American equipment continued to be tested at the tactical level in the Middle East. The Israelis were surprised in the Yom Kippur War in 1973 which followed on the period of Arabic electronic guerrilla war. In this encounter, the Egyptians started with the advantage of surprise, but the Israelis reacted with their usual battlefield flexibility on top of their rapid mobilization. The Egyptian SAMS were cleared out by surface forces and then the IAF was unleashed, resulting once again in a rapid victory for a country which cannot afford a long war. Gradually over the next few years the Israelis not only made peace with the Egyptians but were supplied with ever more sophisticated US air-

craft and systems until by the 1980's they had the F-16 Falcon. Then they once again showed that surprise could be achieved in launching a daring strike across Arab territory to destroy what they claimed was an Iraqui nuclear bomb plant. The small force of F-16's flew a very tight formation which gave a radar signature of an airliner and its spokesmen chattered in Arabic for a complete deception. Partly out of fear of other such attacks and partly because of the Iranian Revolution, the United States became involved in loaning AWACs aircraft to Saudi Arabia and in the sale of F-15 Eagles to Arab countries as well as to Israel. In 1982 Israeli air power again proved its competence in the invasion of Lebanon when drone decoys were used to enable Syrian SAMS to be taken out, thus once again giving the IAF freedom to operate in support of the ground forces. But when they reached Beirut and the Palestine Liberation Organization refused to surrender, the IAF was largely powerless and the war reverted to a tank and infantry house-to-house affair.

The war in Vietnam was still continuing in 1971, though it would shortly come to a conclusion. The long Rolling Thunder campaign in the South had not proved particularly successful. There was too much political interference from Washington at the end of a telephone line. Air power as an instrument of policy cannot be used successfully if it is escalated gradually for that deprives it of its psychological shock value and violates the principles of war. The heart of the will to war lay in Hanoi, which should have been struck by surgical air strikes. When President Nixon decided on the Linebacker II strategy, grand strategic airpower was at last used properly and B-52's flew in from Guam and Thailand and hit targets in North Vietnam and quickly brought serious peacetalks. At last mass was used to strike offensively at the decisive point while at the same time demonstrating economy of force in pursuing a clearly defined objective. As in World War II not only were iron bombs dropped, but evasive routings were employed so that maneuver helped achieve surprise and maintain security.

The story of the Vietnam war is still in 1983 shrouded in emotions and media as well as national security problems, making it difficult to complete a fully rational analysis. Nevertheless it seems clear that over the long run of the war airpower was hampered by the fact that three important U.S. Presidents considered themselves qualified to play the role of Commander-in-Chief and that modern communications allowed them to do so. Eisenhower, Kennedy and

*Soviet helicopter carrier **Moskva** in the Mediterranean, 1969, realizing the old Russian dream of a warm water fleet and the new one of an air navy.*

Johnson were determined not to lose to the Communists, but also to do this at the least cost, and under Secretary McNamara, the Chiefs of Staff acquiesced in the political decisions, and that allowed the politicians to make military decisions as to targets. The result was a quasi-air war in which aircrews were endangered for the advantage was given to the enemy defense by order of the U.S. C-in-C. Secondly, the American manner of waging war in SE Asia was imperial — they took over — and this destroyed the confidence of the Vietnamese in their own abilities, including in that of their own air force. Moreover, when a victory was achieved over the enemy's Tet offensive in 1968, for domestic political reasons the American leadership threw it away to win the elections at home. The best grand strategic weapon the U.S. had was the B-52, but it was held on a tight leash until President Nixon made the decision to use it against Hanoi, seven years after U.S. involvement began in 1965.

It can also now be pointed out that the American approach was the normally profligate one so common to U.S. activities before the Arab fuel embargo of 1973 and sharply escalating fuel prices. There were essentially four air forces operating in Vietnam — the USN from carriers at Yankee Station in the north for grand-strategic raids with tactical aircraft against Hanoi and from Dixie station in the south in tactical support; F-105's and later F-111's from Thailand also in grand-strategic roles, jet and piston-engined aircraft flying from bases in-country, and the Marines' and the Army's helicopters. It is true that enemy attacks on the enormous bases that the landbased forces in-country occupied did require large garrison counter forces, but nothing to what might have been needed if the North Vietnamese had had an offensive air force. This lulled the Americans into two false senses of security which the Israelis have never been able to afford. Too many aircraft on the ground in vulnerable dispersals and too great reliance on operations in which aerial refueling was a key ingredient.

Much like other wars, the war in SE Asia also showed that the

Modern command and control functions for both military aviation and civil air transport are carried on from electronic command centers such as this one located beneath SAC Headquarters in Omaha, NE.

most reliable weapons may well not be the most modern, but old tried-and-true friends. Still much valued was the C-47, a 1936 design, as both a cargo carrier and a gunship and the Navy's old A-1 Skyraider, which the USAF found so useful that it seriously investigated putting it back into production again for its weight-lifting, reliability, simplicity, and loiter time. Links with past wars could also have been found in programs which reinvented the wheel such as defoliation and the Axon (TV-guided) bombs.

It is possible that eventually Command posts may be located in space and supplied by reusable space shuttles such as **Enterprise** seen here on the back of its 747 used for local shuttles within the United States.

Backfire

highly successful 707 and 727 lines, the latter after selling over 1800.

In part the future of the American manufacturers is linked to that of the domestic airlines, and since 1978 they have had rough weather. The decision to deregulate after years of control by the Civil Aeronautics Board and a recently stimulated expansion period following on the losses caused by the sudden surge in fuel prices from 9¢ a gallon to 99¢ and rising labor costs as a result of aging pilots and mechanics and non-discrimination against stewardesses and others, meant that airlines could only make increased productivity pay if guaranteed stability. Instead deregulation brought chaos. Braniff went bankrupt, Continental filed under Chapter 11 of the Bankrupcy Act, and Frontier became a holding company and then set up a non-union airline, Frontier Holdings. Part of the cause of all this turmoil was the entry into the field of a rash of new airlines not burdened with regulatory costs and requirements of serving unproductive markets or of providing social servies, but free to operate only on lucrative routes from which they could skim enough cream using second-hand older aircraft to damage seriously established airlines with large financial commitments for new airliners. Just as the demise of the international Laker Airways brought in its wake international lawsuits, so the domestic pattern may well follow that of earlier times when the new lines will be forced out either by the older companies in fare wars or by the costs of replacement equipment or by poor commercial judgment.

The third part of the manufacturing community has produced the largest number of units, but the smallest by weight — the general-aviation companies. In the United States Beech and Piper had by the eighties moved from the leadership of the founding dynasties to other corporations, while Cessna had changed management. They and Cessna had followed in the steps of Lear in introducing either turboprops or pure jets for executive use. Their products were also finding increasing acceptance on commuter airlines, a growing fraternity. However, in that field they faced competition especially from DeHavilland of Canada whose turboprop Twin Otter and DHC-7 proved highly fuel efficient.

By the eighties, too, another development with significant potential was appearing, and this was the miniaturization of navigation equipment thanks to advances in the computer business which made Loran available, for instance, to small private aircraft at an affordable price and at an acceptable weight. Coupling this to the development of plastics and carbon fibres and aerodynamic expertise, the future appeared to be exciting and quite likely of unusual form. In these areas, of course, as in so many others in aviation, international linkages played an important part as did the fact that aviation continued to reflect the societies in which it thrived as well as opening new ones.

In any war, an air force is only as good as the mix of all its parts including its commanders, especially when the service is being used as an instrument of policy. This involves political, diplomatic, military, economic, scientific, technological, medical, social, and ideological questions.

Between war and peace lies the aircraft industry. In the more than ten years since 1971 three patterns in aircraft production can be noted. In Russia the trend continues to produce aircraft to keep design teams and factories busy, since costs are not as important as full employment. But one result is that the aircraft turned out are not as saleable abroad as those of the West, and it is also noticeable that the Soviets are more hesitant to make their most recent military types available to even their satellites. In the West, the number of manufacturers has sharply declined. In Britain and France moves have been made to consolidate the companies into national enterprises. One strong result of this has been the emergence of Airbus Industries as a multinational conglomerate with the strength and products to challenge Boeing in the battle for the world's large and medium airliner markets, a head to head struggle in which sometimes the deciding factor is ancilliary equipment and sometimes financing. In the United States Lockheed dropped the TriStar and appears to have left the passenger aircraft business while still producing the C-5B and the C-130 turboprop. McDonnell Douglas gave up the DC-10 after failing to win a large USAF order and has decided to concentrate its passenger efforts solely on the DC-9 series, renamed the MD-100. Boeing successfully launched the narrow-bodied twin 757 and the wide-bodied 767, while closing down its

F-16

*United Air Lines **Boeing** Stratocruiser of the late 1940's, a derivative of the B-29 bomber, but much more comfortable.*

6. War on the Airways 1945-1988

Just as Clausewitz said that war is the continuation of peace or diplomacy by other means, so, too, peace is the continuation of conflict, by economic, political, and diplomatic methods. Nowhere in aviation has this been more true than in the airline business.

Since World War II, aircraft have grown in size, complexity, and sophistication, their crews have enlarged proportionately until labor cost limits have been reached, gender divisions aboard have fallen, and their range has extended to a record 8,000 miles non-stop. All of these factors have created both human and geo-political consequences. Also to be taken into account is the sheer growth of travel by air. In 1986 U.S. domestic airlines carried 418 million people, or roughly twice the population of the country. Several common bonds have joined the competitive airlines together — from 1945 to 1975 the dominance of U.S.-built airliners, engines and ancillary equipment, computers (especially for reservations systems from the 1960's onwards), and the English language.

Fifth-ranked Northwest Airlines with 300-odd planes is an air force by today's standards. Every day it despatches 1,600 sorties with 98 percent on-time departures in contrast to a USAF F-15 squadron which still has only 75 percent of its aircraft available — the same percentage of the RAF's Spitfires and Hurricanes in the 1940 Battle of Britain.

Airline history is the source both of the plateau theory, which is based upon the SST's and of the barbed-wire strand, which came from observation of airline capacities. But the latter could equally well apply to the projected and actual supply of qualified pilots, which at the end of the 1980's loomed as a 400,000 world-wide shortage in spite of mergers and lay-offs due to the increasing numbers of pilots needed by new aircraft.

The story of the wars of the airways is also one of pooling and alliances, mergers and purges, all inevitably leading to larger corporate bodies less and less dominated by visible giants such as Juan Trippe of Pan Am, and more and more controlled by financiers such as Lord King of British Airways. And as the great have grown, their feeders have been either absorbed or spun off or died, to be replaced by new feeders with more reliable, larger equipment and more business-minded managers. Thus Central merged into Frontier which was bought by People's Express. And when People's went to the wall, it ended within the Continental empire of Frank Lorenzo of Texas International. This was part of the predatory deluge of changes following the 1978 deregulation in the USA. In 1988, the freeing of European air transport was announced for 1993. In spite of the European Economic Community (EEC), the question remained how nationalism and the national airlines would be accommodated when SAS was not allowed to buy British Caledonian in 1987-88. The answer appeared to lie in the pooling precedent.

In the Far East, a Pacific consortium appeared to be a voluntary solution, a natural evolution also from pooling. In the USSR, of course, there was no problem as Aeroflot was *the* only airline. Nevertheless, the winds of *Glasnost* (the policy of openness) swept it, too, in early 1988 with massive reorganization and much more autonomy to its divisions in order to create self-reliance and economy in its massive fleet of 3,500 planes, from cropdusters to jets.

Other major changes which affected airline development after 1945 included World War II, decolonialization, the jet and turboprop engines, the introduction of tourist then economy and finally one-class service, cargo, and the interrelationship of air transport and society at the airport, especially in the areas of noise, the environment, and crime.

Just as in the airlines there has been consolidation as a result of the relentless pressure of competition (*i.e.,* war), so, too, in the aircraft industry the nature of the product and of the national sales determined survival. In 1945 the Americans were dominant but the British were reviving, while the Russians were an unknown and the Germans, French, Italians, and Chinese were ravaged victims of wars.

In the first twenty postwar years, the British followed the will-o'-the-wisp of prestige aircraft, hypnotized by the twin concepts that there were types suitable for the North Atlantic and those able to operate on Empire routes. The Americans had learned during the war that any aircraft which could fly across the United States and operate from its hot and high airfields could also span the oceans and fly anywhere in the world. Moreover, because the country was the underdog in aviation from before the war, American salesmanship was determined to grab the world market. American airliners were designed and tailored to be adaptable to the most airlines possible. British aircraft manufacturers were still hampered by getting their orders through the Ministry of Supply, the successor to the Air Ministry in procurement, and thus their focus was only on what the nationalized airlines thought they wanted. And for some years, they did not have to pay for changes. Moreover, there was a lack of coordination of limited resources, so that while the RAF led the way to three jet V-bombers, there was little coordination with BOAC to develop the V.1000 derivative of one of these into a long-range airliner. If there had been, this derivative might have been the necessary stop-gap when the Comet I had to be withdrawn from service in 1954. Instead, the V.1000 was cancelled and eventually replaced by the VC-10 and Super VC-10, fine aeroplanes, but commercially unnecessary and too noisy for the environment in which they found themselves in the 1960's.

In the meantime, the British had made a success of the turboprop Viscount with its Dart engines, even breaking into the U.S. market. At the same time, the cockpit nose section of the ill-fated Comet was supplied to France for the French aircraft industry's first jet success, the long-lived twin-jet Caravelle. And then in the early sixties the British and the French agreed to their historic collaboration on the supersonic transport, the SST, known as the Concorde, which would enter service in 1976 and raise the cruising speed from 585 mph to 1,340. But the SST proved to be the perfect example of the plateau effect. Public outcry over damage to the environment, take-off and landing noise, and especially the sonic boom basically came to limit the machine to trans-Atlantic routes. There there was a sufficient growth of traffic to support a luxury surcharge fare.

The real story behind the Concorde, of course, was that in many ways it was a smokescreen for two important happenings. On the one hand it represented the decline and fall of the major British airframe industry from lack of private and government foresight and on the other the determined recovery of French technical supremacy from the ashes of World War II.

In 1940 not only was France defeated, but its aircraft industry was stripped and made the servant of the German. It emerged upon liberation in 1944 years behind the leaders. But fortunately, certain members of the industry and the governments of France, in spite of their coming and going at half-yearly intervals, determined upon a series of five-year plans to recreate the industry as a sinew of great-power status. Just as in Britain Rolls-Royce and Bristol-Siddeley saved the jet engine business, so, too, in France determined companies such as SNECMA worked on engines and Dassault on fighters, and eventually in the seventies a new consortium called Airbus emerged after thirty years of patient work to challenge the American dominance of the airliner field. The French success was carefully orchestrated. It also fitted the country's socio-economic patterns in which there are close links between the polytechnical colleges, the armed forces, bureaucracies, and industry in such a way that passage from one to the other is regarded as natural and beneficial. Moreover, because the French aircraft industry has been an underdog, like the Swedish, it has been innovative — the A-320 being, for instance, the first airliner to fly with sidestick controls and a fly-by-wire system.

Not unnaturally the French have emulated the successful American companies. Airbus is building a family of airliners as has Boeing. Given the fact that airlines fly a variety of routes and need a mix of long-, medium-, and short-range aircraft, the more compatible these types can be, the less expensive the spares inventory and the smaller the work force and the greater the savings on labor. Thus Boeing's first family of jets included the 707, the 727, and the 737, all with the same cockpit and fuselage cross-section providing up to 60 percent commonality amongst the 40,000 spare parts required. And starting in 1960, many of these were kept in Renton, WA, at Boeing's headquarters, to be shipped upon teletype request or in world-wide spares pools, thus cutting down everyone's inventory and money tied up unproductively.

As prices have risen, the number of aircraft manufacturers has declined. How many major manufacturers there will be outside of the USSR and China by the year 2000 will probably be able to be counted on the fingers of one hand. Lesser airframe companies will continue to come and go, for a while depending upon breakthroughs in materials, manufacturing methods, size of aircraft produced, and propulsion used: Exchange of technology is such that the four major engine manufacturers and their ancillaries in the Western world all have or have had some commercial relations.

In the years since the big jets came into service in 1958, the public

*The downstairs cocktail lounge on the **Boeing** Stratocruiser relieved boredom on transcontinental and trans-Atlantic trips.*

has tended to overlook not only the enormous commercial influence they have had in shrinking the world by moving people and goods, but also the way in which they and their associated equipment, services, infrastructure, and the like, have really come to supersede military procurement as the backbone of the aviation industry. The most prominent example is the Boeing Commercial Airplane Company of Seattle which has produced more than 5,000 jetliners, a number exceeding that of F-4 fighters produced by McDonnell Douglas. The significance lies in the cumulative weight, size, and cost of these machines, the newest and latest of which, the 747-400 in its fully developed 1988 model, sold for $129 million vs the North American Rockwell B-1B at $278 million. But only 100 of the latter were ordered in contrast to more than 1,000 747's. Moreover, as the new jets have come into service, their fuel economy has been improved to the point where the 747-400 is capable of carrying a full load of passengers with below deck a cargo equal to the capacity of a 707 non-stop from New York to Tokyo westbound against the headwind or on another leg non-stop from London to Singapore. And for these sectors the aircraft's two-man crew will be relieved en route by additional pilots who will sleep aboard in a special bunk area.

In the race to control the world's airliner markets, Boeing bought the successful shorthaul manufacturer De Havilland Canada from the Canadian government. In Britain the government privatized, or denationalized, British Aerospace, once more a profitable company.

Though not new in 1988, a significant emerging force in aircraft sales had come to be the leasing companies who were placing orders for as many as 100 jet airliners at a time. The game being played was to give airlines flexibility in the seat market with aircraft which would last twenty years while the markets could change more rapidly.

In the USA, where 65 percent of the free world's aircraft by number have long been produced, Cessna, a leader in general aviation, saw its sales go from 551 in 1951 to 3,116 in 1961, to 3,847 in 1971, peak at 8,400 in 1979, and then drop back to 187 in 1987. The umbrella GAMA (General Aviation Manufacturers Association) sales for the same years were 2,302, 6,778, and 7,466, peaking in 1978 at 17,811 and dropping to 1,495 in 1986. The fifteen companies of 1947 had shrunk to 9 by 1987, but they were producing bigger and more expensive aircraft such as the Cessna Citation.

In 1980 pilots on the FAA rolls peaked at 827,071, but by 1986 had dropped to 709,168. Significantly, airline pilots showed a healthy increase, as did non-pilots, rising from 304,747 in 1973 to 410,079 in 1986.

Nor has it been just in airframes and engines that great progress has been made. Electronics is a field which was in its infancy in World War II to such an extent that the word itself was unknown. But from radar, Gee, Loran, and their derivatives, it progressed rapidly to GCA (Ground Controlled Approaches) to by the late sixties the fully automatic landing in which the aircraft is automatically flown down the glide-slope and landed. Coupled with these advances have been those in communications which allowed the dropping of the radio-operator from the flight crew because by the mid-1960's the Single-Side-Band radio enabled captains to communicate with company headquarters

*Forty years of **Air France** trans-Atlantic service is symbolized by the propeller-driven DC-4 and the supersonic Concorde. In 1946 the Paris-New York flight against the prevailing headwind required two stops and 21 hours, 30 minutes cruising at 217 mph. Today the Concorde makes the same trip non-stop in 3 hours, 45 minutes at a cruising speed of 1,350 mph.*

from anywhere in the world while airborne. Then it became possible to dispense with the navigator even for over-ocean flights as Inertial-Navigation Systems (INS) became sophisticated out of the World War II plot-keeping developments to the point that when set correctly an airplane can fly a complex course from take-off in Alaska to landing in Seoul (though if it did not do it accurately, it might get shot down as happened to KAL 007 on 1 September 1983).

Electronics, of course, has also been at the heart of air warfare in the Middle East where drones have replaced manned aircraft in the deadly SAM-belt reconnaissance flights or as decoys there to enable the SAMS to be destroyed. The cost of military electronics equipment for offense and defence of stealth as well as coatings is what makes a B1-B cost $280 million vs the $130-odd million for a 747.

Simulators, which began to come into use with the Link Trainer before World War II, have in the last forty years matured as much as the pilots from that conflict who had been flying them as airline pilots to the age of 60. By the 1980's companies could use simulators for much proficiency work including in recent years attempts to fill the pilot shortage by retraining engineers. Alitalia in 1983 found this not a success. However, TWA, taking its flight engineers back into the righthand seat, had more success when it treated them as *ab initio* students. Having drained their own pilot pools, the majors then started on the 173 commuters in the USA. As a result, the latter were by mid-1988 experiencing up to a 70 percent annual turnover in spite of employing female cockpit crews. To deal with this new problem, Flight Safety International embarked upon a $100 million program to build simulators for commuter aircraft. These machines cost $4 to $5 million, much more than commuters can afford.

Related to the airline simulator program is also that of the world's air forces. Flying safety has always been emphasized, even in wartime, as dead airmen do not win wars. Moreover, the services operate high performance aircraft in demanding roles. Yet the RAF's accident rate per 10,000 hours flown dropped sharply from 12 fatal accidents in 1983 to 5 in 1986, but rose to 7 in 1987. The normal proportion of cause has been aircrew error 40 percent, technical defect 17 percent,

servicing error 0, natural operating and medical risks 10 percent, other (unknown) 6 percent, and not positively determined 27 percent. Each year about 700 RAF aircraft have been hit by birds, with anywhere up to 36 minor accidents a year, necessitating a civilian-operated anti-bird program at 36 airfields in the UK. The services now release accident data, if only in limited form, making the seriousness of the topic obvious, as do the data recorders now carried in both military and civilian aircraft. This data also provides clues as to non-combat wastage rates.

Union busting, whether via negotiations for greater productivity, by mergers, or through bankruptcy proceedings, has also become prominent in the airline management's war on waste, deficits, and costs. With companies losing millions in any currency, savings had to be made. UTA gave its pilots and cabin staff in 1988 the choice of productivity higher than flying 34 hours a month on Pacific routes, for instance, or lower pay. Ground crews have faced the same hard choices — break old habits, stop feather-bedding on new labor-saving, more maintenance-free machines, or retire. Or even more bluntly, grant concessions or lose the company and a job. In a few cases, such as United, the pilots have fought back and sought to buy the company. Others such as Frontier, People Express, and British Caledonian have been merged and purged.

The impact of high oil prices stimulated production after 1973 and resulted in an oil glut that reduced fuel prices and then held them steady, while at the same time the much more significant long-term result of the 1973 Arab oil embargo was the technical refinement of engines to give a vastly reduced fuel burn altogether. And another unforeseen development has been that the growing age of airliners has been countered by a new wave of fatigue, corrosion, and noise problems at a time when the independent feeder airlines have been forced to opt for more fuel- and noise-efficient medium airliners. Thus the early 1988 miraculous descent of a topless Aloha 737 with 89,000-plus 24-minute flight cycles meant the grounding of older planes and more orders for new ones.

The aircraft industry has increasingly paid less attention to military

*The well-known **Douglas** DC-6B was part of the famous DC-4-DC-7C series of great piston-engined airliners which dominated the world's air routes until after the 707 and the DC-8 jets came into service in 1958-60.*

Wichita Mid-Continent Airport is typical of the medium-sized airport of the 1980's, capable of handling jets and large numbers of passengers as well as freight. (Wichita Airport Authority & Wolpert Consultants)

orders because these, though valuable, are few, far between, and onerous. Airline orders have begun to be in quantities at least as large as the 100 B-1's ordered, and the customers are much more reasonable due to continuity of management and contacts.

And even though some U.S. airlines have lost staggering sums, most are now run by financiers and can tap large fiscal resources. They also judge all purchases by their contribution to productivity, whether buying aircraft or labor contracts.

Lessons
Spares and maintenance and safety

The Germans in World War II pushed production, but did not supply adequate spares, and thus units were never up to strength and in retreat had to abandon unserviceable aircraft which added to overall losses. The British had the same problem in France in 1940, compounded by lack of ground transport, and in the Middle East by want of a repair infrastructure in the theater.

A rough rule of thumb is that approximately 20 percent above the cost of an aircraft has to be allowed for spares which must be positioned within 24 hours of the required installation facility.

In the period since 1945 a gradual evolution in aircraft maintenance has taken place accelerated in the late fifties by the arrival of the jet airliner. First came "lifing" of the airframe to 30,000 hours, re-buildable to 60,000 hours, and then this was expressed in either pressurization cycles or landings. Next components were also lifed so that progressive replacement of parts could coincide with annual overhauls. And finally as the "C" Check interval extended from the 2,000 hours of the mature 707 to the 4,500 hours of the 747 and of all the A-300 series, the system was changed in 1984 to be in accord with the C of A certification category, so that the Airbus A-310 came on service with a "not to exceed one year" maintenance check, rather than an operational limitation. Concurrently engines went from a time between overhaul (TBO) of 1,200 to 1,800 hours of the pistons to the 14,000 hours of the Rolls-Royce Darts with their inspect and replace as

The shape of the early jet-age airliner — the swept-wing **Boeing** *707.*

needed philosophy, to the big jets which have now passed 15,000 hours in service or almost five years on the airframe. Airframes and engines as well as other parts reflect the growing reliability of late twentieth century aeronautical technology.

Related to serviceability or availability is safety-consciousness on the part of all personnel. Remarkable studies have been made in the last three decades with the USN, for instance, reducing accidents from 3,348 per 100,000 flying hours in 1956 to 3.4 in 1987. And airlines have in the same period improved reliability by blind-landing systems which allow aircraft to actually touch down in Category III conditions when the pilots' heads are literally still in the fog. This has been an economic necessity with planes carrying tons of cargo and 400 to 550 passengers on tight schedules, all the while depreciating at the bank by the minute. Much more than air marshals, airline executives are constantly at war winning victories on the bottom line. Economics is their driving force, and the natural forces of the market place something that must always be reckoned with.

This economic drive helped allow the commuters to flow in to fill the vacuum as the trunk carriers pulled out of the regional airports in favor of settling into hubs from which they sent out their spoke routes. In the U.S., by 1988 most of the major commuters had been either taken over, become affiliated with, or at least operated in the wing of major companies, and had gates next to them in the terminals, joint fares, and access to their computers. The commuters were not as safe as the majors, but nevertheless remained far safer than automobile travel.

The smaller airlines generally since 1978 moved up in size from twin-engine general aviation aircraft to commuter machines. In the meantime, the major general aviation manufacturers in the U.S. went into a nose-dive in the eighties. Where in 1983 they delivered over 17,000 units, by 1987 that number had dropped to just about 1,000. Cessna and Beech had stopped production of their single-engined piston types, and although undoubtedly liability lawsuits were a contributing factor, so, too, were rising prices, FAA regulations, and stagnant designs versus exciting small cars and VCR simulations of flying at pennies a flight.

At the very low-powered end of the scale, manpowered flight

became a reality and began to follow the age-old patterns: first, successful flights, then across the English Channel, and in 1988 from Crete to Santorini (74 miles). Then, too, the round-the-world unrefuelled record was broken by Yeager and Rutan in the unconventional piston-powered *Voyager* in 9 days. At the other end of the spectrum, a Boeing 747SP circled the world in 36 hours and 54 minutes with two refuelling stops in 23,000 statute miles, only to be beaten a few weeks later by a Grumman Gulfstream IV with 36 hours and 8 minutes and four stops. The difference would have been less if a pressure refuelling system had not failed the 747 at one stop, again emphasizing the importance of immaculate ground support.

The Gulfstream represented the best in modern corporate jets and proved a point that they can compete with both long- and short-haul airliners with careful route planning. The 747SP now has as a stablemat, the 747-400, capable of 8,000-mile sectors with a two-crew cockpit. But with 14-hour flight times, not to mention 18-hour duty times, new aircraft such as this and the Airbus 340 may well require bunks and a total of four cockpit crew on long hauls, posing new labor and productivity questions.

A world-wide shortage of 400,000 cockpit crew loomed, which had begun to arise before 1988. This in turn was already impacting the world's air forces, with a severe drain on the smaller ones. The Royal Australian Air Force had lost nearly one-third of its pilots and had been forced into a high bonus scheme to retain aircrew — which made ground staff unhappy. The Dutch were borrowing pilots from the RAF. This more than anything else appeared likely to make NATO air forces inferior to the Warsaw Pact regardless of how modern their aircraft.

In the meanwhile, development time, which for a fighter just before or during World War II had been from 90 days to four years, had by 1988 stretched to the point where the newest European fighter prototype had just flown, but was not expected to enter service until 1996, eight years hence. And the lightweight Northrop F-20 Tiger II, designed to be available in quantities for medium-budget powers, was shelved because the USAF would not buy it — and thus no one else would.

This same attitude killed the Israeli Aircraft Industry's Kifir, an advanced fighter based on a U.S. engine and Middle Eastern combat experience.

Combat experience in Vietnam as well had proved the gun still essential and fighter vs fighter dogfights still possible in spite of missiles. The latter have become much more reliable, but identification problems, counter-measures, and skill have negated them. Electronics have become much more reliable, miniaturized, and computerized. By 1988 simulators could be used not merely for flight training, but also for air-to-air combat scenarios. And though none of this was cheap, it was safer and less costly than losing personnel in accidents or combat.

Computers have been a hidden loss-leader in the airline business as well. Introduced in the reservations systems in the early 1960's, they have become both world-wide facilitators and slave-drivers as well as a means to monopolistic control. What has killed one airline was not the cost of new aircraft, but that of locking into a computer reservation system, probably on a shared basis. Computers also manage aircraft in many ways, from fuel to crew rostering, to maintenance.

Computers also have become vital in world-wide air traffic control, especially in the highly concentrated corridors such as the airways in North America, across the Atlantic, and in Europe. But these wonder calculators have themselves been undergoing revolutionary changes, especially when coupled to radar. The result has been built-in obsolescence at a time of escalating budgets, leading to political sleight of financial hand in the U.S. to keep trust funds unspent so as to appear not to be going deeper into national debt. The not unfamiliar result has

The wide-body **Douglas** DC-10 developed at the end of the 1960's was designed to fill the gap between the DC-8 and the 747. It could handle up to 300 passengers at ranges comparable with the early models of the 747. The **Boeing** 737-100 (below) used the same cockpit and fuselage as the 707 and 727, but started as a low-density, short-haul aircraft. By 1988, however, the 737 had superseded the 727 as the -300 was capable of flying Seattle-Philadelphia non-stop with a full load of passengers and required fuel reserves.

The **Fokker** F-50 is a modernized F-27 with hushed Rolls-Royce Dart turbo-props. The airframe design is over a quarter of a century old while the engines are close to the half-century mark.

been a deterioration of the air-traffic environment, especially following the Reagan government's firing of striking controllers. While undoubtedly, as the fuel crisis of 1973 showed, waste could be eliminated and the whole made more efficient, to do so required some capital expenditure and education of personnel from management down.

At the same time, the growth of air traffic with the new hub-and-spoke concept of airline operations required tidal flow at airports not necessarily capable of handling such massive arrival and departure flow whether on the runways or at the toilets. The first new airport to be voted in by the public since Dallas-Fort Worth is the new $1.5 billion replacement for Denver's mile-high Stapleton with four north-south take-off and two east-west landing runways, forty miles from downtown. With the new hushed jets, noise should not be a factor, but convenience will be until people build houses around the new field.

What has happened to airports in the last forty years can be seen in the brief story of Chicago's O'Hare and Wichita's Mid-Continent airports. The former with approximately 40,000 people employed in 1988 had 94,682 arrivals and departures in 1950 and handled 176,902 passengers. In 1987 the number of movements had risen to 792,897, carrying 57,543,865 passengers. Or the average of 1.86 passengers per movement of 1950 had become 72.6 thirty-seven years later, but the number of movements had not increased proportionately because the size of aircraft had jumped instead from the 21-seat DC-3 to the 400-seat 747. At Wichita, the city employed by 1988 101 people while another 4,000 worked at the airport, not one of whom was paid less than $20,000 a year. It had an operating budget of $10 million from which, thanks to grants and the like, it spent $25 million a year. The revenues from the parking lot paid for the reliever airport, while cost accounting was used to determine landing fees. On the other hand, revenues were being hurt in the latter eighties by tax reform, by oil prices which affected the companies based in the area, and by the hasty reactions of the FAA to terrorism which caused Wichita-based general aviation aircraft to seek other, less-controlled bases. The government paid the airport authority not to plant a good deal of the 3,500 acres of the airfield, and tenants rented 1,500 acres. Firefighting and snow-removal were not nearly as costly as at O'Hare, but still a considerable part of the budget. Wichita Mid-Continent's direct economic impact on the community is $192 million and its multiplier effect is estimated at $482 million more.

Hub-and-spoke systems have not only become an idea whose time has come for passenger airlines, but also for freight and parcels services. United Parcel Service got into business in 1953 and went overnight in 1982 when jets became available; it now flies a fleet of 115, of which 11 are turboprops. (UPS, for instance, uses Louisville,

The **North American Rockwell** B-1B in the low-level, high mach mode is highly sophisticated, but at lower altitudes it has been vulnerable to a 15-lb pelican.

*The early jet engine of 1950, derived from the British Whittle model, powered most British, US, and Soviet jet fighters, as well as some early bombers, and airliners. This is a **Pratt & Whitney** of about 10,000 lb. thrust.*

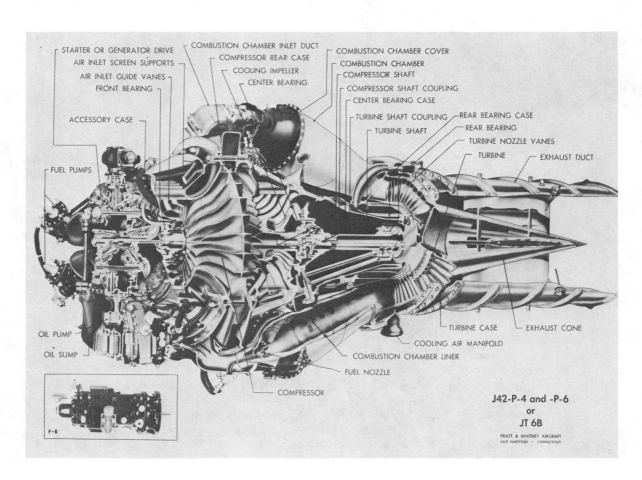

STARTER OR GENERATOR DRIVE
COMBUSTION CHAMBER INLET DUCT
COMBUSTION CHAMBER COVER
AIR INLET SCREEN SUPPORTS
COMPRESSOR REAR CASE
COMBUSTION CHAMBER
AIR INLET GUIDE VANES
COOLING IMPELLER
COMPRESSOR SHAFT
FRONT BEARING
CENTER BEARING
COMPRESSOR SHAFT COUPLING
ACCESSORY CASE
CENTER BEARING CASE
TURBINE SHAFT COUPLING
REAR BEARING CASE
TURBINE SHAFT
REAR BEARING
FUEL PUMPS
TURBINE NOZZLE VANES
TURBINE
EXHAUST DUCT
OIL PUMP
TURBINE CASE
EXHAUST CONE
OIL SUMP
COOLING AIR MANIFOLD
COMBUSTION CHAMBER LINER
FUEL NOZZLE
COMPRESSOR

P-6

J42-P-4 and -P-6
or
JT 6B

PRATT & WHITNEY AIRCRAFT
EAST HARTFORD · CONNECTICUT

Since the arrival of the jet aircraft, cargo of all sorts has grown steadily, and in recent years the overnight parcels industry has blossomed. **United Parcel Service** Boeing 757PF all-cargo aircraft criss-cross the United States and the Atlantic every night, their holds filled with fifteen containers efficiently packed off conveyor belts at central handling facilities.

Four Smaller Jets

Fokker *F-100*

British Aerospace *BAe 146*

Cessna *Citation II*

Cessna *Citation III*

The **Boeing** *737 production line in Seattle. Compare the lack of clutter and the few workers versus the size of the aircraft and the facility with the picture on p. 30.*

A Small Airliner
The Saab SF 340

*Both the **Saab** SF 340 from Sweden and the **Embraer** Brasilia from South America have been developed for the commuter market. The four pictures at the top show the clean lines, accessibility, and efficient cockpit layout of the SF 340, while the bottom shot gives a good idea of the pleasing looks of the modern turboprop engine and airframe.*

*The **British Aerospace** Hawk won the USN contest with McDonnell Douglas teamwork in a joint venture to produce an undergraduate jet pilot training aircraft. The Hawk is also used both as a trainer and as a light attack aircraft in a number of foreign air forces.*

KY, for domestic and Cologne/Bonn, West Germany, for international operations).

The critical factor for airlines will remain efficient ground handling for minimum turn-around time in order to get 11 to 12 hours airborne daily out of each aircraft. Even so, the bottleneck is still loading people into an aircraft at the gate.

At the time of writing, the future of the unducted fan (UDF) engine as a commercial proposition for use on the MD-90 series (DC-9's) and other aircraft has started along the classical path of technological innovation. Greatly acclaimed as cutting fuel costs 30 percent, it appears to increase maintenance by 19. The developed high by-pass ratio jets already reliably in service with an airframe time before check inspections of 15,000 hours (or roughly four to five years) seem a safer bet. Only tried and true turboprops, such as the Rolls-Royce Dart with nearly 40 years in service and just starting a new cycle on the Fokker F-50, or the well-tried Pratt & Whitney Canada PT-6 and the like, seemed in 1988 to have an assured future.

As for military engines and aircraft, some new shapes have been emerging, but in many cases performance seems to indicate that bigger may not be so much better as reinventing the wheel. Numbers and training may still be the real clue unless a stealth paint as much as stealth technology makes a real breakthrough. Certainly it is true that the B-1B has a radar signature less than .016 percent that of the B-52, while the stealth bomber is calculated at only .003 percent of that of the 30-year old SAC warhorse.

What the Soviets and the Chinese may now do is not yet clear, but neither Soviet performance in the case of the Tu-144 supersonic transport nor in Afghanistan should be weighted to assume that they cannot produce surprisingly sharp results when they wish. Aviation technology has always been linked internationally, and if enough manpower and money is managed correctly on the same topic, similar or ingenious solutions are likely to appear.

The Soviet war in Afghanistan (1979-1988) was the continuation of a long series of British and Russian forays into that hostile region and with no better results in nine years than to prove that guerrillas can still beat technology to a draw in suitable terrain, especially if supplied with weaponry from a safe refugee in Pakistan.

The Falklands/Malvinas War of 1982 in the South Atlantic was a most interesting affair in that both sides fought at the limits of their range. In theory the most dangerous weapons were Exocet missiles, but this might be disputed if thicker-sided ships had been engaged. Moreover, the results for the British might have been quite different if Israelis with their flair for adaptive tactics had flown the Mirages and A-4 Skyhawks against the Harriers and the Royal Navy's last armored World War II carriers.

As it is, the Soviets like the Americans in Vietnam have swallowed their pride and withdrawn, while the British are stuck with a sheep pasture that is a hostage to Argentine fortune.

The long, dragged out Iran-Iraq war of 1978-1988 seems to be repeating the lessons of the past. On the Iranian side the highly sophisticated air force was largely deprived of its pilots and command structure by the Revolution which ousted the Shah, ran short of spares, and has been unable to maintain and operate sophisticated weaponry. On the other hand, it has countered the lack of airmen by creating a missile force and returning to the tactics of the Germans of 1944-45 by aiming long-range rockets at Bagdad, the Iraqi capital, for psychological effect. On the other side, Iraq with a trained air force and with access to new aircraft and spares has used its limited air power sparingly, though it, too, has engaged in raids against the enemy capital and other cities. In a stalemated war reminiscent of the First World War, air power has given neither side the advantage for victory.

All in all as the twentieth century draws to a close, it is obvious that the commercial and peacemaking side of aviation is far outstripping the military in power and value, so much so as to suggest the future of the world's air forces lies as training establishments and keepers of the peace. The nuclear shield seems increasingly likely to remain in its silo or merely as an unusable threat unless accidentally used, perhaps by a minor new member of the club. Public reaction to the costs of weapons systems is causing their number to shrink and the incentive for new ones to melt away in favor of more civilized human services.

It appears that the long-standing airman's claim may at last be realized — that air power's great gift is to bring mankind closer together in peace.

Taking off on its maiden flight, the Boeing 747-400 represents the ultimate in long-range airliner development in 1988 with its winglets, 400 passengers, and 8,000-mile range.

This Junkers Ju-88D carries within its own story a capsule history of the air war. Built in Germany, it was delivered to the Rumanian Air Force in June 1943, but on 22 July a defector flew it from Novorossysk, USSR, to Cyprus. There the RAF took it over and flew it to Cairo, where it was turned over to the USAAF, which painted on the American markings and flew it to Wright Field, where it remains preserved at the USAF Museum today.

PART SEVEN

Patterns and Philosophies: Some Lessons

1. The Ideal

THE early apostles of air power were full of idealism, but the attitudes of airmen have from the first contained the thread of a quick, clean, mechanical, impersonal solution to problems with which others have struggled for years. Airmen have become more professional and more realistic, and air transport possesses great potential for peace through cultural exchange among nations. The military use of air power has sometimes tended to prolong wars and threaten peace, but at the same time the industrial apparatus needed to support air power in all its phases has been a stimulant to progress and employment. In the twentieth century air power has become a part of the political, economic and industrial, social and ideological life of almost all peoples, and any interpretation of it must take into account the national characteristics and state of development of each nation studied. Much as electricity was a symbol of prestige in the second half of the nineteenth century, so air power became such a symbol in the first six decades of the twentieth, perhaps to be replaced by nuclear rockets or spacecraft.

Aviation has demanded a linking of technology and manpower, and as aircraft have become more and more mechanical to operate, and more and more technologically sophisticated, it has been natural to concentrate on the machine, while the importance of the human beings controlling it has appeared to shrink in proportion. Yet it must be remembered that almost all aircraft only obtain their impact from human control, whether it be by a national leader or by the pilot alone. Aircraft are the visible symbols of air power, and it

is not easy to think of air power without envisaging warplanes or airliners, agents of destruction and construction.

Theories concerning the use of air power in war grew up as the service itself expanded. Ideally an air war calls for the quick seizure of air superiority, or control of the air, and consequent ability to attack any target within range and prevent the enemy from making any use of his air power. The victor can undertake grand-strategic bombing in such a way that he can break the enemy's will to fight before surface forces meet in a decisive engagement. At the least the victor can hold air superiority over a limited area so that his strategic and tactical forces can proceed unmolested and with air support as needed. His reconnaissance aircraft and his forward air controllers are free to come and go, and his movements are concealed. These ideals were set forth as early as 1915 by the English aeronautical engineer, F. W. Lanchester. As an engineer he was a realist and knew that the realization of many of these concepts was years in the future. Before the end of the First World War P. R. C. Groves and Sir Frederick Sykes in Britain and Mitchell in the United States carried these theories to their logical extreme of expecting the next war to be won entirely by a pre-emptive air strike. In Italy General Giulio Douhet and Count Caproni set out a more concrete theory of war based upon Italian geographical considerations.

In post-1918 debates over the role of aviation airmen tended to make exaggerated claims about what they could do, claims which would not become reality until the advent of the atomic bomb. In the meantime, the more practical theorists were those in the American and Japanese navies who developed the tactical carrier air forces, and in the German and Soviet armies who created air-supported mechanized armies. Even after the Second World War, air-power leaders failed to learn that war cannot be won by arid theories which concentrate on only one aspect of human relations. History has long shown that capital cities are not the only sources of national power, and that frontal assaults, perhaps the most obvious way in which to attack, are less successful than more indirect approaches.

Industrial and transportational ideals are as important as military goals in the use of air power; certainly there are lessons to be found in these two civil facets of air power which cannot be overlooked. The cycles of war and peace are observable in air transport activity

RADM William A. Moffett, USN, shown in the good old days when the admiral actually still flew his flag on his aeroplane. Note also the standard seat-pack parachute, disallowed by some air forces in World War I because it was likely to bring out the white feather in aircrew. **USN**

as much as in military-industrial operations. In a sense competition in air transport means that it is continually at war; the airlines are continually in combat, and the cycles within the airline industry are shorter and sharper than in military combat, where wars are occasional disturbances of the norms of peace. (It must be noted, however, that the enormous and necessarily long-term expense of jet aircraft has caused a lengthening of the cycles or distances between wave crests.)

The aircraft used by the airlines have reflected military developments and have usually been governed by the same cycles of obsolescence, although the controlling criteria have been passenger demand or acceptance and financial practices, rather than theoretical or actual conflict. The airlines have paralleled the military services, too, in their need for equipment and facilities that are economically viable and that best suit a particular route and traffic system. Since 1945 the American dominance of the air transport market has tended to provide a uniformity of equipment, but the exact numbers required and the patterns in which they have been used have been determined by a mixture of domestic and international political and capital considerations, International Air Transport Association rules and fare structures, scheduling requirements, and labour contracts and maintenance schedules. For both airlines and manufacturers planned guesses about the future have played a vital role in their selection of equipment and in the stimulation and development of traffic to turn projects into viable realities. Success or failure has been measured in a long-term assessment of profits and losses rather than in any narrow conception of victory: an early write-off of major new pieces of equipment may result in paper losses that must be countered by adequate profits. In a continuous war there should not be any such thing as a final victory or a conclusive defeat; even if an airline is run as some form of a national social service, the airline president is still a general, a manager, who must keep the confidence of his backers or stockholders.

2. Realities

History makes it clear that the realities of time, place, equipment,

airfields, logistics, higher direction, money, and national character must be taken into account, together with the principles of war, in the application of air power. And these realities are often governed by the progression of the wave theory hypothesized in Chapter I.

The First World War was the first large air war, but the production of official histories of its air aspects was delayed, or in some cases not provided for at all. As a result almost all of those who wrote about it before the Second World War ground their own particular axes and nobody looked at it impartially. If they had done so they might have learned some significant lessons. The Germans observed some of them because they had been defeated; control of their air forces was largely kept in the hands of the army in its covert stage, and those who were to lead the air forces later were soundly indoctrinated with basic rules of warfare.

One lesson for nations that possessed air arms was that, unless the enemy possessed the power to do irreparable harm at any time and place, air superiority was only worth fighting for when it was needed to cover a particular operation on the ground, or to protect reconnaissance sorties. Far more significant than the heroic fighter aces were the forward air controllers who in that war directed artillery shoots, and much more attention needed to be paid to their equipment, morale, and protection. Fighting for air superiority merely for the sake of fighting used up men and machines and resulted in high casualties that led to deficiencies later when the pressure was on. Training was as important as fighting. Unnecessary wastage meant that lesser theatres could not be supplied with air support from trained crews, yet it was in just such indirect approaches to victory that the greatest chance of success might lie.

The use of long-range grand-strategic bombing paid dividends where home defences were not organized and populations unused to facing war. Relatively small forces could be used to effect in tying down enemy air power that might have been used elsewhere. The mere threat acted as a deterrent and an inhibitor. But it was a violation of the principles of war to continue such attacks in the face of mounting opposition, for the defence eventually always got the better of the attack as long as the attacking forces pursued repetitive tactics.

The war also provided an example of the see-sawing technical battle that could be expected in any air war and made clear the need for repair and salvage units. Lastly, the use of air power at sea was worthwhile both offensively and defensively and might, in fact, be more vital than continual fighting over a fixed battlefront.

The Ethiopian campaign in 1935–1936 showed that air power could dominate but could not win a war in unsuitable territory, and that the use of bombs, and even gas, might produce significantly adverse reactions among neutrals.

But it was in Spain and China that the lessons of war were again written clearly. The performance of fighters and bombers was tested and their weaknesses observed. In China, attacks on enemy airfields which obeyed the rules of concentration and economy of force were apt to produce quicker results than grand-strategic raids against distant industrial targets. The war in China also showed that aircraft carriers could be used as mobile airfields which enjoyed relative immunity to land-based aviation, while naval air arms were particularly effective because of their training in long-range navigation and in striking pinpoint moving targets.

Many of these same lessons were reinforced by experience in the Second World War but with some new twists. The opening phases showed that air power was a gambler's weapon, and that co-ordinated air and ground forces used in a *blitzkrieg* could punch their way to victory; in such dynamic campaigns grand-strategic bombing was too slow to be of any use unless the defender had to pass through blockable bottlenecks. Events in Spain, China, Poland, and France demonstrated that even a technologically superior air force was no match for attacking air forces supported by ground forces that could over-run airfields and facilities.

The Battle of Britain reinforced the lesson that the defence could master the offence if enough time and money were devoted to the problem, while also making it apparent that an indirect approach might be the most effective even in air warfare. Because there were no boundaries in the air, strategists were sometimes misled by the ability to switch air power from one part of the war zone to another, sometimes finding themselves trapped by that very flexibility. The Germans were over-confident of flexibility and came to grief in the Soviet Union, because in spite of their transport force they could not make *blitzkrieg* work against a foe who could trade space for time.

A grand-strategic bomber force was no substitute for dynamic tactical victory when actively engaged with the enemy in the field; but on the other hand, when the armies were not in action, grand-strategic bombing, such as attacks on British ports, was mistakenly neglected. Both in the Soviet Union and in the Middle East air forces with partly or wholly obsolescent equipment but professional morale were able to stay in the field and harass the enemy because neither side had sufficient forces with which to eliminate the other.

Gradually the tide of victory in any particular theatre turned in favour of that side which could muster the largest air force and maintain it in top flying condition. Ultimately this meant a combination of industrial might, economic and military planning, training, maintenance, and morale. The Germans could have won the Battle of Germany if they had concentrated on it rather than dissipating the *Luftwaffe* over too many theatres, but they did not grasp the lessons of their own campaign against Britain in the First World War.

Additionally, the nations that won were those able to field highly-trained forces, and that they were able to do so depended upon their recognition of the importance of instructors and fuel supplies and their ability to keep these beyond the range of the enemy. Both the Germans and the Japanese flew their trained units too hard, failed to re-circulate personnel from them through the instructional system, and ended up with too few well-educated pilots at a time when their fighter forces faced both sophisticated new aircraft and seasoned enemy pilots.

The Burma campaign showed that air supply could free an army of traditional support, thus giving it a new speed of movement in difficult country.

The war at sea from 1939 to 1945 emphasized the need for equipment designed for naval work, for viable carrier doctrine in both attack and defence, and for an understanding of maritime strategy. Carrier doctrine could only succeed when supported by trained airmen and modern naval aircraft. The use of air power at sea in the Second World War established techniques which the Japanese had used to a lesser extent off China, as carriers were used to provide air

Boeing's 727, up to 1984, the world's most successful passenger jet airliner with about 1,800 sold. **Western Airlines**

Japanese Kawanishi Shiden (George) fighter — too few, too late, and too few pilots to handle them and too little fuel for training. It was an excellent example of a private-venture land-based development for the Japanese navy started in 1941, but dragged out so that, though the equal of the Hellcat in combat, it made little impact during the war. **USAF Museum**

cover for landing forces and even strategic attack against shore targets. Since 1945 the technique has been refined and in fact over-used off Korea and Vietnam, in that expensive carriers were kept continually engaged in a land war. In the later Second World War campaigns carrier forces were used successfully as *blitzkrieg* weapons to strike through the line of defensive atolls to the vital centres, but up to the latter part of 1942 the outcome of a battle in several cases hung in the balance and was decided as much by luck and fate as by admiralship or equipment. Later in the war American massed forces were skilfully employed, and the long periods between major actions enabled training to be undertaken. Replenishment at sea helped make the US carrier task forces vitally effective, and the Allies bene-fited from new equipment constantly updated.

The lessons from the post-Second-World-War period are largely a repetition of those which should have been learned by that time. Air power has a vast potential for peace as long as it is seen as a balanced system and its massive application is quick; it cannot be dribbled out, because it costs by the second, and its strength dissipates after its first sudden impact. Thus to escalate its use on a gradual basis is akin to subjecting a body to steadily increasing doses of poison at a rate not exceeding its tolerance to absorb the toxic agent. In anti-guerrilla warfare air power's supply and propaganda functions are the most important.

Intercontinental bombers and ballistic missiles, if used only in a negative manner, can create a stand-off that will prevent the world's self-destruction. Once the deterrent or the karate blow has failed, then, assuming the situation does not escalate into nuclear war, air power becomes tactical. As such it is an extension of surface forces and must be used to enable them to fulfil their roles on land and at sea. And this is likely to remain the job of a manned rather than a missile force for some time to come.

3. The Wave Pattern over Fifty Years

The wave pattern of peacetime equilibrium, rearmamental insta-bility, wartime equilibrium, and demoblizational instability, provides a quantitative and qualitative means of examining the course of air power history. It varies with each air force or airline examined, but general conclusions can be drawn from an examination of the history of air power in terms of the cycle.

In peacetime equilibrium a nation's leaders emphasize economy. Before the First World War neither politicians nor the highest military leaders were willing to spend much of their limited funds on aeronautics, which was then in its ineffective infancy. Major industrialists were not very much interested either, although occa-sionally one might be attracted by the hope that air power would become important in the near future and make many sales for his firm. Designers were often virtually the whole of a firm, and air-lines were non-existent. The military establishment was generally hostile to new developments, although in each country one or two influential people saw the need to explore the new arm. As inter-national rivalries sharpened and others appeared to be developing their air arms, each nation tended to follow suit in fear of being left behind.

In the early peacetime equilibrium career patterns were affected to the extent that most officers were discouragd from associating with the new arm. A few did strive to get attached to it, some because they wanted the challenge and desired to move ahead faster than the peacetime establishment would allow, and some because for various reasons they had little hope of promotion within the older systems. Some, of course, joined simply because they liked adventure. Strategy and tactics were also limited because of uncertainty in the high command as to what air power could and could not do, and by the technical weaknesses of the equipment itself. Procurement, design, and development were either experimental or governed by established procedures which did not apply to a nascent arm.

The second period of peacetime equilibrium, that between the two world wars, was not unlike the period before the First World War, but the limitations were different. The threat of a war was more imagined than real, air power had partly proved itself in its first war and was showing itself economical for colonial policing, the equip-ment was still fairly simple to maintain, and flying speeds were slow enough to keep casualties low. Again, however, politicians were unwilling to spend on defence unless there was public pressure. The bombing of Britain in the First World War led to the creation in

1922 of the British Home Defence Air Force, because it could be argued that the only service that could provide air defence was an air force. But the logic of this was not extended to placing anti-aircraft guns and searchlights under air force control. Moreover, the inter-war years were dominated until 1934 by the hope of disarmament, a hope that caused postponement of needed re-equipment. Airmen preparing to take over the anti-invasion role did little about developing ship-killing weapons and effective doctrine or tactics.

Conversely, navies that had had contrary attitudes towards air power in 1918 found themselves forced to support their airmen or lose control of naval aviation to a land-based air force. Forced to take back their air arms, navies found themselves developing carriers and the tactics that went with them, especially since the Washington disarmament treaty banned the building of battleships.

The impact of a new period of peace upon careers was to make promotion slow and seniority a dominant factor. Services found themselves cut back to pre-war levels and budgets. With increased pay scales resulting from wartime inflation and fewer officers with private incomes, the pressure was on to cut the numbers in service. The concentration upon strategic plans and goals tended to be neglected in favour of the tactics of public display, though some nucleus 'think-tanks' were maintained at places such as Randolph Field for the US Army Air Corps. Racing and record-breaking not only made headlines but also developed material and techniques, and the second period of peacetime equilibrium saw extensive technological developments. With limited budgets the new airlines demanded economy of operation and reliability, while air forces curbed procurement in favour of development. Peace and the Depression cut the number of manufacturers drastically. Banned from engaging in military aviation, the Germans concentrated on airlines and upon training other air forces abroad as a means of developing their own. Thus the new *Luftwaffe* started with some advanced aircraft and engines, as well as with important political backing.

The third period of peacetime equilibrium, after 1945, was stimulated by both the Cold War and recurrent limited wars. In the major air nations, America, the Soviet Union, Britain, and France, military orders stimulated and sustained the aircraft industry, and the whole cost of what came to be called the 'aerospace' developments increased rapidly from the springboard of the Second-World-War

scientific, technological and operational research. Added to demands for military equipment were substantial airline orders and a steady demand for civilian aeroplanes. By 1945 the public had become 'air-minded', and the question was no longer whether air power would survive, but how much of it should a country have. Nuclear weapons and ballistic missiles made every nation vulnerable. Politicians and the air marshals, generals, and admirals, could now argue for air appropriations along grounds of keeping the peace, home defence, and stimulating the economy. While this third period of peacetime equilibrium saw the maturity of the major air powers, it also saw new states, such as China, just entering the field and some older ones, notably Britain and France, moving towards retirement, and yet another, West Germany, being reincarnated in more restrained form.

The new stability in aeronautical affairs affected career patterns. The Korean War and the Cold War called for larger air forces, as did other tensions in international relations. US carriers spread about the world as peacekeepers, while both America and the Soviet Union sent advisers to other air forces. Airlines, too, helped new companies with money, management, and maintenance. As for both airmen and officers their air force training opened roads to new civilian careers in electronics, automotive and aeronautical maintenance, and airlines. At first, Second World War veterans kept pace with the needs of the airlines, but after the introduction of jets the demand for new pilots became so great, at least in the United States, that it had the effect of robbing the air forces of potential career men. In Britain, on the other hand, as the air force entered the downward curve towards retirement it ceased to supply men for the airlines, so a national scheme for civilian aircrew training had to be developed.

The introduction of better simulators than the wartime Link trainers meant that through intensive gaming and more realistic training better strategy and tactics could in theory be worked out, in some cases by organizations outside the military establishment. More than in the previous periods the emphasis was upon strategy, while tactics were tested in periodic encounters between various air forces and improved by the much greater availability of aviation literature in both public and official publications.

No period of peacetime equilibrium in the past had seen such

Boeing Model 299, the prototype of the B-17 grand-strategic bomber, being wheeled out when the automobile was only making the transition from the Model A to the V-8. **Boeing**

North American B-25 Mitchell displaying its characteristic gull-wing.

great technological changes, but the operational life of aircraft remained about the same as it had been earlier. Types changed less frequently and costs rose dramatically. Unmanned ballistic missiles began to play a greater part in military thinking, leading to a reassessment, in those air forces having big bombers, of the role of the manned aircraft. At the same time economic factors forced attempts to create once again a general-purpose aircraft. In the major air forces spasmodic war led to an occasional rearmamental instability with hectic periods of modification, intensification of servicing and maintenance, and the elimination of 'bugs' not detected even in sophisticated modern testing programmes.

Rearmamental instability has, in general, occurred also three times, in 1912-1916, 1934-1943, and 1948-1955. In the middle of each of these periods nations have passed from peace into war, but, as was noted earlier, the outbreak of war rarely sees an air force fully ready for combat. Squadrons are under strength, aircraft and aircrew are in short supply, and the logistical machinery is at the most only warmed up, while civilian priorities still take commercial precedence. Wartime equilibrium, when many of the basic problems have been solved, is usually not established until two or more years after the conflict begins.

Instability is generally triggered by a feeling of international uneasiness and a domestic belief that the nation is endangered. Political demands for a crash programme cannot be fulfilled, because drafting specifications takes time, while manufacturing facilities are usually inadequate. The training of management for an expanded programme is complex, and factories are not properly equipped. Production of aircraft that are already obsolete will be continued, as they can be reported as 'aircraft produced' or 'available for front-line service'. The mental transition from peacetime to the expansion of rearmamental instability may lead to such procedures as adding a zero or two to all appropriations and orders without much thought about the implications. Traditionally it has been a period in which air forces have found themselves being exhorted to expand and at the same time accused of spending recklessly and allowing manufacturers great profits. Increased air activity causes a rise in accidents and more noise, bringing more complaints. Faced with a real possibility of war, planners are forced to look at their plans once again,

yet strategy may not be properly linked to grand strategy because the statesmen themselves are ignorant of war and of the world.

All of these things directly affect the military establishment during rearmamental instability. Officers used to leisurely peacetime schedules find themselves working long hours on crash programmes, intensive training, or planning, and until the crisis becomes acute it may be very difficult to recruit the mature managers needed to handle modern expansion. Technologically the period is equally difficult. Old ideas have to be discarded, specifications must be flexible to allow for changes, while a prime consideration is that the items needed be mass-produceable. Salvage and repair may be overlooked or ignored because of a shortage of the necessary manpower.

The first period of rearmamental instability saw the introduction of the aeroplane itself and all the problems of learning to fly; the second was a time of innovations in fuels, engines, airframes, propellers, undercarriages, and flying techniques, not to mention radar. The third coincided with the widespread introduction of the jet, computers, and nuclear weapons. Progress was often sudden and could produce personal crises for individuals faced yet again with a new challenge to their skills and comprehension.

All of the things that happen in pre-war periods of rearmamental instability become intensified in wartime. Time becomes too short, the enemy breaks rules and preconceptions, civilian and military organization is diluted, if ultimately strengthened, with civilians who challenge established procedures. Coupled to losses in action or accidents, there is a rapid change of personnel, promotional ladders are uncluttered, and the future provides an exciting challenge to younger officers and men. Realities test doctrine, leaders, men, and equipment. Emphasis has to be laid upon recovery and restoration of men and machines, bringing them up to date with fresh training programmes and technological modifications.

Once all these processes have taken place wartime equilibrium exists. It differs from peacetime mainly in that change and expense are accepted; almost everything is being done on a more massive scale while at the same time there is an intense concern about quality. Wartime equilibrium may be of short duration, turning quickly into demobilizational instability. In fact, it can be suggested that wartime equilibrium for air power has not been reached until roughly

Sikorsky S-44a taking off. One of the last of the great flying-boat classes in the world, Excalibur is now preserved at Hartford, CT. **United Technologies**

Fw-190 in flight. **USAF**

thirty-odd months after the start of a war and that it has rarely lasted as long as that, partly because demobilizational trends have begun up to a year before the end of the war. Training of new recruits took about a year by the middle of the Second World War, and governments were anxious not to be caught with a lot of surplus material at the end of the conflict; therefore, planners began warning that programmes should be cut back well in advance of the end of the war. Both the First and the Second World Wars left masses of surplus aeronautical goods that had to be sold for scrap or left to rot. The danger exists, too, that supplies of stocks will be cut back too low to support another conflict.

Demobilizational instability covers a period in which political, military, and industrial planners are concerned with the future. It means a mental and physical conversion to peacetime standards, attitudes, and values in a civilian-dominated world. Designers work on civilian products, and research staffs are ordinarily cut back. (In fact, developments since the Second World War have seen a gradual escalation of research teams to such an extent that the 140,000 personnel engaged in backing up the launching of the Apollo moonshot of July 1969 were the equivalent of the United States Army in 1940 or the British Army of 1935). In the military services, temporary personnel are phased out and soon squadrons consist of at most a few caretakers.

After each war the question for air power has been, Would the future be better? Optimism after the Second World War had a sounder basis than that after the First, but it was a bit more cautious. After the Korean War the picture looked brighter, and after the Vietnam conflict, with the vast expansion of the airlines and the public acceptance of flying, it looks better still. But it will not be the peacetime equilibrium most flyers like to remember, but a tough workaday world of controlled airways and expensive sophisticated aircraft stacked into neat, close, deadly holding patterns.

The century has seen two world wars and several limited ones. Nuclear and broken-backed wars have not changed the picture very greatly from what it was in the first five decades of air power development. While the new weapons systems have made awesome destructive power available, they have brought with them increasingly sophisticated machinery for their control, while at the same time more discussion has taken place and more understanding of the problems of war has come about than existed before 1960. It can be argued that the secrecy that tended to shroud developments in pre-Second-World-War days was a bigger handicap than the complexities of the weapons systems and the choices today. Further, it can be suggested that as long as modern leadership understands its own dilemmas, the options are greater than before. The unknown remains, of course, in that there will always be some unpredictable human beings, or misinterpreted intentions. There will always be gamblers. Yet air power, whether viewed conventionally in terms of aircraft or less so in terms of ballistic rockets, is ultimately controlled by political leadership.

The USAF now refers to itself as an aerospace force. Just as the principles of war, the wave patterns, and history itself have recurred in the unfolding of air power, so the same laws will apply as space becomes the newest technological and military frontier. Yet it is the mundane rather than the dramatic aspects of air power, the STOL aircraft and the helicopters and crop-dusters, that will enable the gap between the rich nations and the poor nations to be closed, and thus strike at the root causes of war.

Until air power is understood in terms of all its facets, both military and non-military, it will not be a real factor for peace.

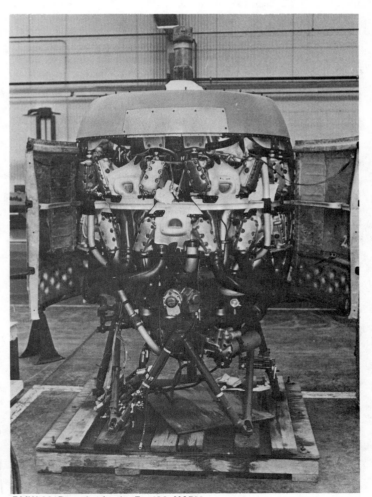

Concorde. **BAC**

BMW-801D engine for the Fw-190. **NASM**

Bibliographical Essay

Preface to the Bibliography

The author's work and interests have been largely in the area of British aviation. It is not surprising then that the bibliography is slanted also in this direction with the aim, however, of indicating the kind of sources which are available so that others who wish to do some of the basic work which yet remains to be done to tell the story of the non-English-speaking air forces, airlines, and aircraft industries can see the sources which may be used.

So great is the out pouring in this field that a whole cupboard full of new books has appeared since this bibliography went to press in 1970.

1. General Background

It would be foolish to try and cover the whole history of air power in one short bibliographical essay. Instead all that is attempted here is some indication of the kinds of sources which exist, the majority of those cited being in English. Though the latest work on the subject is not always the best, if a recent work cites most of the existing literature, it has been used rather than lengthen the list unduly.

For those who would gain an understanding of the continuity of military history in its broadest sense, the following provide a general introduction. Field Marshal Viscount Montgomery of Alamein, *A History of Warfare* (1968) is a lavish work with the emphasis upon combat, while Lt/Col. David H. Zook, Jr., and Robin Higham *A Short History of Warfare* (1966 and later editions) is just that, with half the book devoted to the period since 1914. A general introduction of a different sort, but with an excellent list of sources in the footnotes is Theodore Ropp, *War in the Modern World* (1959). Bernard and Fawn Brodie's *From Crossbow to H-Bomb* (1962) provides a quick survey of weapons development; David Eggenberger, *A Dictionary of Battles* (1968) is a useful reference tool. Early in the Second World War, E. M. Earle edited *The Makers of Modern Strategy* (1943), which has become a classic, though much of it is now out of date in the light of new scholarship and interpretations. Bernard Brodie's *Naval Strategy* (1942 and 1965) and his *Strategy in the Missile Age* (1959) are both basic, as is Morton Halperin's *Contemporary Military Strategy* (1967). John Garnett's reader, *Theories of Peace and Security* (1970) is worth noting. Richmond's *Statesmen and Sea Power* (1946), Julian Corbett's *Some Principles of Maritime Strategy* (rev. 1918), and Alfred Thayer Mahan's *The Influence of Sea Power upon History 1660–1783* (1890) provide a basic grounding, as does Machiavelli's *The Prince* (1531 and many editions) and Liddell Hart's *Strategy* (1929 and later editions). Melvin Kranzberg and Carroll Pursell's second volume of *Technology in Western Civilization* (1967) is complementary to Brodie. Eliot Janeway, *The Economics of Crisis: war, politics, and the dollar* (1968) suggests other avenues of approach. Terence Qualter, *Propaganda and Psychological Warfare* (1962), Frederic J. Brown, *Chemical Warfare: a study in restraints* (1968), and David Kahn, *The Codebreakers* (1967) provide introductions to yet other phases of warfare.

Cyril Falls, a sometime official historian of the 1914 war has two introductory volumes, *The Art of War* (1961) and *A Hundred Years of War* (1943) which together with Alistair Buchan, Director of the Institute of Strategic Studies' *War in Modern Society* (1966) and Louis C. Peltier and G. Etzel Pearcy's *Military Geography* (1966) provide a broad background. The best general history of naval affairs is the US Naval Academy's E. B. Potter and Fleet Admiral Chester W. Nimitz, *Sea Power; a naval history* (1960).

The entwined aspects of policy making are tackled in a variety of forms the background for which is revealed in works such as Samuel P. Huntington's *The Soldier and the State: the theory and politics of civil-military relations* (1964). while the military themselves are the subject of Morris Janowitz's *The Professional Soldier: a social and political portrait* (1960), and his *The New Military* (1964). I. F. Clarke's *Voices Prophesying War, 1763–1984* (1966) is weak on air power, but otherwise fascinating. J. F. C. Fuller, *The Conduct of War, 1789–1961: a study of the impact of the French, Industrial and Russian Revolutions on war and its conduct* (1962) is a provocative work by a master pundit. George H. Quester's *Deterrence before Hiroshima: the Airpower Background* (1966) must be used with care and compared to more detailed research. F. C. Iklé's *The Social Impact of Bomb Destruction* (1958) suggests more studies of the impact of bombing, as does Milton P. Goss's, *Civilian Morale under Aerial Bombardment, 1914–1939* (1948), while J. M. Spaight's *Air Power in the Next War* (1938) is a contemporary view, and Harry Howe Ransom's "The Politics of Air Power: a comparative analysis" (in *Public Policy . . . 1958)* is a useful synthesis.

The best guides to aeronautical periodicals are the USAF Air University *Periodicals Guide* to current literature starting in 1949 and the listings of aeronautical periodicals published in the JOURNAL OF THE AMERICAN AVIATION HISTORICAL SOCIETY in Vol. 6, No. 1, Spring 1961, 64, Vol. 7, No. 2, Summer 1962, 136-139, Vol. 7, No. 3, Fall 1962, 220-221. The series of symposia sponsored in recent years by the USAF Academy and published starting in 1971 by the USGPO provide some fresh insights into general issues in military history. However, research in periodicals should be conducted with care. If possible the biases of the editor should be determined and especially those of the writer. While contemporary articles may be inaccurate, especially in wartime, they may also provide valid evidence for who said what when and also photographic materials which enable pictures to be verified. Also very useful are annuals such as *Brassey's* and national yearbooks, of which an example is the annual *Naval Review* published by the US Naval Institute since 1962/63 and in 1970 incorporated in the *Proceedings* in May.

Vast quarries of government materials remain untouched and something is said about these where each chapter is concerned. NASA in the USA provides a basic annual Chronology, for instance.

Oral history is currently the rage. It can make many valuable contributions if the interviewer is thoroughly knowledgeable, if the tone of voice is noted (The inability to determine whether or not a speaker meant what he is reported to have said can be a real handicap, especially in reading transcriptions and legislative records.) and if it can be checked against other evidence. Hindsight must be taken with a grain of salt. A large repository of oral history materials is available at Columbia University in New York City.

As far as the analytical history of air power itself is concerned, there has not been one. The reader who wishes to start with basic materials can use Eugene Emme's *The Impact of Air Power* (1959) which contains excerpts from many sources. Then he can move to J. L. Nayler and E. Ower, *Aviation: its technical development* (1965), and Charles Gibbs-Smith, *Aviation*, split in 1971 into two volumes in a much revised version of his earlier, *The Aeroplane*, and also the excellent new study by Ronald Miller and David Sawers, *The Technical Development of Modern Aviation* (1970), to R. E. G. Davies's *History of the World's Airlines* (1964) and the short supplementary volumes written independently by Kenneth R. Sealy, *The Geography of Air Transport* (1957), by Peter W. Brooks, *The Modern Airliner* (1961), and by the former Editor of AERO-NAUTICS, Major Oliver Stewart, *Aviation: the creative ideas* (1966), which is however, not altogether accurate. Air Marshal Sir Robert Saundby, who was Chief of Staff of RAF Bomber Command in the Second World War has written, *Air Bombardment: the story of its development* (1961), but it should be compared with Noble Frankland's *The Bombing Offensive against Germany: outlines and perspectives* (1965), Giulio Douhet's *The Command of the Air* (1921 and later) and the polemics by Alexandre de Seversky, *Victory Through Air Power* (1942) and *Air Power: Key to Survival* (1949) written to support greater air appropriations, and with Wing Commander Asher Lee's *Air Power* (1955), a useful book which is, however, based really on the author's observation of the Second World War as the RAF's expert on the German Air Force and some work on the Soviets, still leave us without a real study of air power as such.

For those who want to see surviving examples of the planes which made air power history, the best guide is the American Aviation Historical Society's volume by Stephen Muth, *Museum and Display Aircraft of the World* (1967).

The general history of air power suffers from a dearth of single-volume histories, certainly in English, of the various air forces. For instance, even the fiftieth anniversary of the RAF had not (at least by March 1971) produced a sound general history. Some histories have been written for the use of the various service academies, and some of these studies are most useful, though not without their biases, but they are not always available to the general public. Then there are the illustrated histories such as Martin Caidin's *Air Force: a pictorial history of American airpower* (1957) and his *Golden Wings: a pictorial history of the United States Navy and Marine Corps in the Air* (1960), which have wonderful photographs, but not much text, or anthologies such as those edited by Major Gene Gurney, *Great Air Battles* (1963), which are good reading, but not particularly valuable for more than a feel of the times. More useful are works like Geoffrey Dorman's now out-dated *Fifty Years Fly Past* (1951), a combination of reminiscences and dates and data on aerial developments as seen by a British journalist. Some others are mentioned in the various sections below dealing with particular periods. But better things are coming.

We can start with John Rae's *Climb to Greatness* (1969), a study of the development of the American aircraft industry to 1950, and in more detail there is William Glenn Cunningham's *The Aircraft Industry, a study in industrial location, Los Angeles* (1951), and the recent translation for NASA of A. S. Yakovlev's *Fifty Years of Soviet Aircraft Construction* (1970). Colonel Carroll V. Glines, Jr.'s *The Compact History of the United States Air Force* (1963) is very uneven; better is Wilhelmine Burch *et al.*, edited by Alfred Goldberg, *A History of the United States Air Force, 1907–1957* (1957). Scot MacDonald's *Evolution of Aircraft Carriers* (1964) brings together a series of articles under the sponsorship of the USN's Office of the Chief of Naval Operations; now superseded in depth by Norman Polmar's 250,000 word volume *Aircraft Carriers* (1969). One of the main problems confronting the author of any single volume, including this present writer's, is that until monographic studies have been done on all phases of aviation throughout its history, the detailed story is not available. Even official histories of wars may take twenty-five years to appear. So far little has been done about armed forces in peacetime apart from this author's own work of that title on Britain, so there are great gaps in the story. Many publishable doctoral dissertations might be made out of these long years of military history; a number of unpublished ones exist, of course.

The following represent the one-volume histories known to exist at present. A start can be made with the March 1959 issue of RIVISTA AERONAUTICA which was devoted to *I primi cinquant' anni dell'aviazione italiana* and which ought to be translated into English. To this can be added G. Bignozzi and B. Catalanotto's *Storia degli Aerie D'Italia dal 1911 al 1961* (1962), which is a combination of short historical summaries with detailed coverage of the aircraft involved, and Vergnano's *The Origins of Aviation in Italy* (1964). Then there are two works by Asher Lee on the Russians, the short *The Soviet Air Force* (1950) and the longer volume of the same title of 1962, in between which came Robert A. Kilmarx's *A History of Soviet Air Power* (1962), the Soviet's *Civil Aviation USSR, 1917–1967* (1968), Robert Jackson's *The Red Falcons: the Soviet Air Force in Action, 1919–1969* (1970), and John W. R. Taylor, *The Soviet Air Force* (1970). For the Finns there is a short work by R. Ward and Christopher Shores, *Finnish Air Force 1918–1968* in the Aircam booklet series (1969). The story of the *Luftwaffe* was told in most detail by Asher Lee in his *The German Air Force* (1946), a hot-from-the-war assessment by a top intelligence man which starts in 1919; of wider scope but less sound is John Killen's *The Luftwaffe: a history* (1967), The French are ill-served, there being only Réné Chambé's *historie de l'aviation des origines á nos jours* (1958), a new series (*l'aviation française, 1914–1940, des escadrilles, ses insignes* by Commandant E. Moreau-Berillon (1969) on French Squadron Histories) contains a wealth of detail, and two recent journal issues: *Revue Mensuelle de L'Armée de l'Air*, "Forces Aeriennes françaises" (Oct. 1970, No. 273), and *Revue Historique de L'Armée* "L'Aviation militaire française" (1969). Surprisingly, almost the best served are the Canadians who have had Leslie Roberts's *There Shall be Wings: a history of the Royal Canadian Air Force* (1960), the official J. D. F. Kealy and E. C. Russell *A History of Canadian Naval Aviation, 1918–1962* (1967), and John A. Griffin's detailed tabulation *Canadian Military Aircraft* (1970). A sometime official historian, George Odgers is the author of *The Royal Australian Air Force: an illustrated history* (1965), which can be supplemented by a large number of articles on the RAAF in STAND-TO. Geoffrey Bentley *RNZAF: a short history* (1969) fills a gap and consolidates the official histories, while Louis de Jong with his *Onze Koninglijke Luchtmacht* (1970) and the anonymous *Vijftig Jaar Marine Luchtvaardienst, 1917–1967* provide some background on the Dutch. A hostile study of the RAF is David Divine's *The Broken Wing: a study in the British exercise of air power* (1966); more sympathetic is Charles Sims, the longtime photographer for THE AEROPLANE in *The Royal Air Force: the first fifty years* (1968), and John W. R. Taylor and P. J. R. Moyes, three-volume *Pictorial History of the RAF* (1968–1970), while the Air Britain books, *RAF Unit Histories* (1969–   ) are useful for data. There is a clutch of books on British naval flying starting with Vice-Admiral Sir Arthur Hezlet's *Aircraft and Sea Power* (1970), Robert Jackson's *Strike from the Sea* (1970), Hugh Popham's *Into the Wind* (1970) and the older work by Lt/Cdr. P. K. Kemp *The Fleet Air Arm* (1954). Aireview's *The Fifty Years of Japanese Aviation, 1910–1960* (1961) is another picture history of which Volume II, however, is in English of a sort.

A lot of material is buried in the multitude of volumes dealing with aircraft ranging from Ray Wagner's full and usefully illustrated *American Combat Planes* (1960) through Fahey's *The Ships and Aircraft of the US Fleet* (various editions since 1945) and Jane's

All the World's Aircraft (annually since 1909) (supplemented in 1970 by Jane's *Weapon Systems, 1969–70,* the first of a new annual series), to the series by William Green published by Macdonald, the Putnam books, and the various Harleyford volumes, Len Morgan publications and the Profile series. In addition to works covering all the aircraft ever flown by any one service or any one country, these also include special volumes on individual aircraft, some of which are mentioned in the various sections below, and works such as Bruce Robertson's *Aircraft Camouflage and Markings* (1956) and *Aircraft Marking of the World* (1967). Unfortunately, there is a lack of consistency in the presentation of information in the series so that it is sometimes very hard to determine, for instance, exactly how many of any type were actually built. Yet these volumes often reveal policy as seen in specific actions, hesitations, and cancellations.

The history of the aircraft industry has largely remained a closed field owing to a variety of causes from wartime destruction of records to the more normal business sense of secrecy. In fact, as Eugene Emme once remarked, history is murdered by corporations. In contrast, official histories have become increasingly more honest and more carefully researched than any private work can afford to be as can be seen by noting the work done by the NASA historians Swanson, Grimwood and Alexander on *This New Ocean: A History of Project Mercury* (1966). The one firm which has had the unusual distinction of having had both its history and the autobiography of its founder published is de Havilland: C. Martin Sharp, *DH: an outline of de Havilland history* (1960) and Sir Geoffrey de Havilland, *Sky Fever* (1961), to which can be added A. J. Jackson's *De Havilland Aircraft* (1962). A few others have contributed similar volumes abroad as for instance Ernst Heinkel's *He 1000* (1956), and Harold Mansfield, *Vision: the story of Boeing* (1966) by its public relations director. In general, however, company histories have tended to be public-relations pieces done by journalists or employees. Boeing and Cessna, however, to pick two random examples, each have well done short illustrated booklets which include interesting scaled aircraft geneological tables; in Boeing's case there are also the volumes by Harold Mansfield.

Essays by editors, authors, directors and scholars on official military history since the Crimean War together with complete lists of the publications of military, naval and air historical services with the titles given both in the original language and in English will be found in Robin Higham, editor, *Official Histories* (1970).

2. The Beginnings

The pioneer years are chronicled in a number of books of varying value. L. T. C. Rolt's *The Aeronauts: a history of ballooning, 1783–1903* (1966) makes a good starting point, to be followed along this line by Douglas H. Robinson's *The Zeppelin in Combat* (1962 and later editions) and Robin Higham's *The British Rigid Airship, 1908–1931; a study in weapons policy* (1961). Specialist studies of early flying are dominated by the work of Charles H. Gibbs-Smith, a long-time student of the subject, such as *The Aeroplane: an historical survey* (1960) and *The Invention of the Aeroplane, 1799–1909* (1966) to which should be added H. F. King's *Aeromarine Origins* (1966) and R. Dallas Brett, *The History of British Aviation, 1908–1914* (1933) and Harold Penrose, *British Aviation: the pioneer years* (1967) in addition to some of the more general works mentioned above. More specialized, but also worth consulting are John R. Cuneo's two volumes of his unfinished study of the German air force, *Winged Mars* (1942) and *The Air Weapon, 1914–1916* (1947).

The tribulations of the pioneers are the subject of Fred C. Kelly's authorized biography *The Wright Brothers* (1943) and Peter Wykeham's *Santos Dumont* (1962). Air Commodore Allen Wheeler's *Building Aeroplanes for 'Those Magnificent Men'* (1965) is a useful look at what the aircraft of 1910 were like to fly as compared to the Second World War types. Admiral George van Deurs' *Wings for the Fleet* (1966) is by one of the American naval pioneers. Archibald D. Turnbull and Clifford L. Lord in their *History of United States Naval Aviation* (1949) carry that story into the interwar years; the British equivalent is the fourth volume of Arthur Marder's *From the Dreadnought to Scapa Flow* (1969).

Some early American Army problems are the subject of I. B. Holley's little classic, *Ideas and Weapons* (1953). The first air war is recorded in the official Italian Air Force publication, *I Primi Voli di Guerra nel Mondo, Libia, MCMXI* (1961).

3. The First World War

Sources for the history of the First World War are varied. There are, for instance, original narratives and diaries of personal experiences, most of which are now out of print, or have never seen the light of day. A certain mass of historical material is to be found in official files, but of these the Russian may not exist, the German were largely destroyed in the Second World War, the Italian were badly mangled in the same conflict, the French have never been fully explored, and the British, while open, are in the process of being weeded out and destroyed, though some official materials have found their way to the Imperial War Museum, to the Public Record Office, the Air Historical Branch of the Ministry of Defence, to the Royal Aeronautical Society and the Royal Aero Club. In the United States the National Archives, the Smithsonian, and the USAF Museum at Wright-Patterson Field, all contain some materials of interest, while bibliographies on both the USAF and on the location of sources are coming from the new office of Air Force History.

More useful, but not always reliable, are official histories. The largest and most accessible set is the British Sir Walter Raleigh and H. A. Jones, *The War in the Air* (1922–1937) which covers both land and sea operations. The French, the Americans, the Austrian Navy and the Russians have never published such narratives, but the Italians have a single volume and the Germans are still in the process of completing their series, which was somewhat deflected in the days of Hitler (see Higham's *Official Histories*).

For the reader or researcher who wishes to know more about the aircraft of the day there are several series of books in English which provide a wealth of detail. A good starting point are Charles Gibbs-Smith's books mentioned earlier, Douglas H. Robinson *The Zeppelin in Combat* (revised 1967), Robin Higham, *The British Rigid Airship* (1961), Owen Thetford, *British Naval Aircraft, 1912–1958* (1958), G. W. Haddow and Peter M. Gross, *The German Giants* (1962), and Raymond H. Fredette, *The Sky on Fire: The First Battle of Britain* (1966), not to mention Peter Gray and Owen Thetford, *German Aircraft of the First World War* (1962). The most comprehensive coverage of one group is J. M. Bruce, *British Aeroplanes, 1914–1918* (1957). The latest on markings is Heinz Nowarra's *Eisernes Kreuz und Balkenkreuz* (1968).

In addition to the Robinson, Haddow and Gross, and Fredette just mentioned, there are numerous accounts of the war in the air, some reprints of older classics such as C. Day Lewis' *Sagitarius Rising* (1936) and C. F. Snowden Gamble's *Story of a North Sea*

Station (1928) and others, newer works of a romantic sort. John Killen, *The Luftwaffe: a history* (1967) devotes some early chapters to the period, but his sources are mostly the well-known printed ones. Geoffrey Norris, *The Royal Flying Corps* (1965) somewhat supersedes Hilary St. George Saunders *Per Ardua* (1944), a condensation of *The War in the Air*. The romantic approach is to be found in Edward Jablonski's *The Knighted Skies: a pictorial history of World War I in the air* (1964). The more serious side is given in J. E. Johnson's *Full Circle: the story of air fighting* (1964), but his own Second World War account, *Wing Leader* (1956) is much better as he is no historian. For the French see René Chambé, *Histoire de l'aviation des origines á nos jours* (1958) and Etévé, *La Victoire des Cocardes* (1970), which gives another side of the story. Marshal of the RAF Sir John Slessor's *Air Power and Armies* (1936) is a study of the Western Front, while Alan Morris in *First of the Many* (1968) looks at the Independent Air Force of 1918. F. M. Cutlack's official *The Australian Flying Corps in the Western and Eastern Theatres of War, 1914–1918* (1953) is worth a look, as are W. A. Musciano's *The Eagles of the Black Cross* (1965), Bauer's *Wir Flieger 1914–1918* (1930) on the Austrians. For the Italian view, the best comprehensive coverage is the March 1959 issue of RIVISTA AERONAUTICA: *I primi cinquant' anni del l'aviazione italiana*, but see also Captain Contini's *L'Aviazione Italiana in Guerra* (1934), and Apostolo and Abata, *Caproni nella Prima Guerra mondiale* (1970) while the broader British picture is given in Harald Penrose, *British Aviation: the Great War and Armistice, 1915–1919* (1969). Some of the theoretical background is to be found in Robin Higham, *The Military Intellectuals in Britain* (1966), in Alfred Hurley, *Billy Mitchell: crusader for air power* (1964), and in Archibald D. Turnbull and Clifford L. Lord, *History of United States Naval Aviation* (1949), as well as George Van Deurs, *Wings for the Fleet . . . Naval Aviation's Early Development, 1910–1966* (1966), and in the documents in Captain S. W. Roskill's Naval Records Society volume, *The Naval Air Service . . . 1908–1918* (1970) which must be used with care.

The best new work on the First World War combats is undoubtedly James L. Hudson's *The Hostile Skies: a combat history of the American Air Service in World War I* (1968); Hudson, now a university professor, was a Second World War fighter pilot.

Material on the Russian air forces is very sketchy. There is D. P. Duz, *History of Flying and Aviation in the U.S.S.R. 1914–1918* (1960), an official Soviet publication, and a short section in the Carnegie Foundation for International Peace series, *The Russian Army in the War* (1931) by General Nicholas Golovine and in Igor Sikorsky's autobiographical *The Story of the Winged-S* (1939), but apart from the general histories mentioned earlier, that seems to be about it.

General von Hoeppner, who commanded German aviation, wrote his memoirs, *Deutschland's Krieg in der Luft* (1921) but they have never been translated into English.

The next best inside book is probably Maurice Baring's *Flying Corps Headquarters, 1914–1918* (reissued in 1968) which was written by Trenchard's secretary. More recently Andrew Boyle's *Trenchard* (1962) appeared as the official biography of the commander of the RFC. General Mason Patrick, USA, wrote his memoirs, *The United States in the Air* (1928). Equally useful is the official report of the Assistant Secretary of War and Director of Munitions in the United states, Benedict Crowell, *America's Munitions, 1917–1918* (1919) which is a more sympathetic and factual account than those stirred up later by the U.S. Senate's Nye Committee investigations of 1935.

For the spirit of the combat there are a number of both first- and secondhand accounts of which a small mixed bag are: Heinz Nowarra and Kimbrough Brown *Von Richthofen and the "Flying Circus"* (1958), Floyd Gibbons, *The Red Knight of Germany; the story of Baron von Richthofen* (1927), Colonel General Ernst Udet, *Ace of the Iron Cross* (1970), Captain René Fonck, the French ace, *Ace of Aces* (reissue 1967), R. H. Kiernan, *Captain Albert Ball, V.C.* (1933), Duncan Grinnell-Milne's autobiographical *Wind in the Wires* (new edition 1966), William Bishop *Winged Warfare* (1967 reissue) which is autobiographical and his son, William Arthur Bishop's biography of his father *The Courage of the Early Morning* (1965), and lastly there are two American accounts, Major Charles J. Biddle's *Fighting Airman: the way of the eagle* (1968 reissue) and the former president of Eastern Air Lines, Captain Eddie Rickenbacker's *Fighting the Flying Circus* (1919 and later). One special unit which attracted a lot of attention, romantically at least, was the Lafayette Escadrille, whose story in a book of that title has been told by Herbert Molloy Mason (1964). And lastly, historians, at least, might take a look at the little book by Sir Winston Churchill's physician *The Anatomy of Courage* (US edition, 1967) which contains some useful insights into psycho-medical problems fliers faced.

4. 1919–1939

The interwar years were the dull years and badly need more work. Much of the history of them is contained in books mentioned above which continue their story on beyond 1918. Apart from Higham's works already mentioned on British aviation, there is his *Britain's Imperial Air Routes* (1960) and *Armed Forces in Peacetime* (1963), and Roskill's sequel both to his *The Naval Air Service* and his two volumes on *Naval Policy between the wars*, of which the first appeared in 1969. In American history Edwin H. Rutkowski's *The Politics of Military Aviation Procurement, 1926–1934; a study in the political assertion of consensual values* (1966) not only explores a complex peacetime problem, but provides a useful guide to the sources on the period. In addition to the first volume of the US Army Air Force's history of the Second World War by W. F. Craven and James Lea Cate *The Army Air Forces in World War II* (1948–1955), the picture is filled in by a series of USAF Historical Studies of which the most useful for the period are No. 10 *Organization of the Army Air Arm, 1935–1945* (1956), No. 24, *Command of Observation Aviation: a study in the control of tactical airpower* (1956) by Robert F. Futrell, No. 89, *The Development of Air Doctrine in the Army Air Arm, 1917–1941* (1955) usually known as the Thomas H. Greer work, and No. 100 *History of the Air Corps Tactical School, 1920–1940* (1955). In addition a fair amount of information can be found in two works on Mitchell, the first *General Billy Mitchell: champion of air defense* (1952) by Roger Burlingame, who specializes in the popular history of American technology and the second by Colonel Alfred F. Hurley, head of the History Department at the USAF Academy, *Billy Mitchell, Crusader for Air Power* (1964). Following Mitchell, probably the next most influential Army airman was General H. H. "Hap" Arnold, whose autobiography, *Global Mission* (1949), contains many insights and much material.

There is as yet no full-length published study on Douhet. The chapter on Douhet and Mitchell in Earle's *Makers of Modern Strategy* (1943) is out of date and biased. But there are two unpublished doctoral dissertations, one by Cappelluti "The Life and Thought of Giulio Douhet" completed at Rutgers University in 1967 and the other by Raymond Flugel, "United States Air Power Doctrine: a study of the influence of William Mitchell and Giulio Douhet at the Air Corps Tactical School, 1921–1935", University of Oklahoma, 1968.

Material on the French Air Force between the wars is hard to come by as the FAF went into a sharp decline, but a start may be made with Alvin D. Coox's unpublished doctoral dissertation, *French Military Doctrine, 1919–1939: concepts of ground and aerial warfare* (Harvard 1951) and Robert W. Krauskopf, *French Air Power Policy, 1919–1939* (Georgetown 1965). A different sort of memoir is that of Group Captain F. W. Winterbotham, *Secret and Personal* (1970), who was the Chief of Air Intelligence, Secret Intelligence Service in Britain up to 1939, especially when read in conjunction with French Air Minister Pierre Cot's *Triumph of Treason* (1944?). John McVickar Haight's *American Aid to France, 1938–1940* (1970) adds another dimension. Angelo del Boca, *La Guerra d'Abissinia, 1935–1941* (1966), Jonathan W. Thompson, *Italian Civil and Military Aircraft 1930–1945* (1963), Hugh Thomas, *The Spanish Civil War* (1961) and Captain the Duke of Lerma, *Combat over Spain: memoirs of a Nationalist fighter pilot, 1936–1939* (1968), deal wth aspects of the employment of air power in the wars of the mid-thirties, while Richard K. Smith's *The Airships Akron and Macon: the flying aircraft carriers of the USN* (1965) is a well-illustrated account of a particularly interesting development. Constance Babington-Smith's *Testing Time: a study of man and machine in the test-flying era* (1961) is one of the few studies of that speciality.

Much of the other sides of aviation during the period must be gleaned both from the periodicals of the day and from the writings of the participants. For instance a number of Nevil Shute [Norway], the British writer and aircraft designer's, books describe the period. This is true both for his novels and for his autobiography, *Slide Rule* (1955). Another who set the romantic tone was Antoine de Saint Exupéry, the French aviator, whose *Night Flight* (1931) and *Wind, Sand and Stars* (1939) were literary prize winners. Sir Francis Chichester's *The Lonely Sea and the Sky* (1969) is the autobiography of an especially skilled pioneer pilot and navigator. Henry B. Palmer Jr.'s *This Was Air Travel* (1962) is a pictorial history which goes hand in hand with C. R. Roseberry's *The Challenging Skies: the colorful story of aviation's most exciting years, 1919–1939* (1966). The American admiral Richard E. Byrd was amongst those who sought the Poles by air, one episode of which he describes in *Skyward* (1928). The Italian General Umberto Nobile has written *My Polar Flights* (1961), while Alexander Forbes in *Quest for a Northern Air Route* (1953) and Clayton Knight and Robert C. Durham *Hitch Your Wagon: the story of Bernt Balchen* (1950) discuss wartime work, a part of which is mentioned in passing in Ernest Gann's enthralling autobiography *Fate is the Hunter* (1961). For an overall picture of polar flying see John Grierson's *Challenge to the Poles* (1964). Outside of polar flying the real routine work of establishing airlines was done by people like Air Commodore H. G. Brackley whose wife compiled *Brackles* (1952). In a period of aerial gambling, Lesley Forden's *The Glory Gamblers* (1961) provides details of one crazy venture, the 1927 West Coast-Hawaii race.

5. Scientific Developments

Linking the interwar years with World War II and beyond are the books telling the story of scientific developments, which often started covertly long before war began, as C. P. Snow showed in *Science and Government* (1962; later editions contain addenda). On radar see Robert Morris Page, *The Origin of Radar* (1962) an American account, Ronald W. Clark *Tizard* (1965) and *The Rise of the Boffins*

(1962), Dudley Saward, *The Bomber's Eye* (1959) on radar bombsights, F. T. K. Bullmore, *The Dark Haven* (1956) on radio aids to lost aircraft, the Air Ministry's *Operational Research in the RAF* (1963), Air Commodore Allen Wheeler, . . . *that nothing failed them; testing aeroplanes in war* (1963), to which should be added D. C. T. Bennett's *Pathfinder* (1958) which like Saward and Bullmore concentrates on wartime applications. Sir Frank Whittle's *Jet* (1953) details the frustrations on the British side of jet engine development, while Clayton Hutton's *Official Secret* (1960) gives those connected with the development of escaping devices. Edward Bishop in *The Guinea Pig Club* (1963) tells the story of the development of plastic surgery for RAF aircrews burnt and otherwise wounded. To it should be added the Rexford-Welch volumes on RAF medicine in the official history series. Then there is the development of the V-weapons. Here one can start with Basil Collier's *The Battle of the V-Weapons, 1944–1945* (1964) which gives the overall picture, and then turn to General Walter Dornberger's *V–2* (1954). Dornberger was the commander at the German experimental station at Peenemünde and he reveals how inefficient the Germans were due to political complications. The whole story is wrapped up in David Irving's *The Mare's Nest* (1964), which is the best overall account by a writer specializing in Anglo-German history, but which should be supplemented by James McGovern's *Crossbow and Overcast* (1964). On atomic bomb development David Irving in *The Virus House* (1967) describes the ill-fated German efforts which fortunately did not succeed, while Lansing Lamont in *Day of Trinity* (1965) and Fletcher Knebel and Charles W. Bailey II in *No High Ground* (1960) tell the American story. Knebel and Bailey's additional article in LOOK, 13 August 1963, should also be consulted because of the light it sheds on the long-term censorship exercised by General Leslie R. Groves. The British story is in Margaret Gowing's first volume (1955) of the official history of atomic energy in Britain and in C. P. Snow's novel, *The New Men* (1954).

The American search for the German atomic scientists is dramatically related by one of the leaders in Colonel Boris T. Pash's *The Alsos Mission* (1970); F. W. Chinock's *Nagasaki: the forgotten bomb* (1970) carries the story to the end of the war. A number of new books touch upon various aspects of military and civil aviation over a long period. Thus we have Brigadier-General George W. Goddard's *Overview* (1969), a history of the development of aerial photography in the USAF, Major-General Norris B. Harbold's *The Log of Air Navigation* (1970) and a forthcoming history of air navigation by Colonel Monte Wright of the USAF Academy faculty not to mention Stephen Barlay's *The Search for Air Safety* (1970), David Beatty, *The Human Factor in Aircraft Accidents* (1970), and G. M. Rickus *et al.*, *Comparison of Career and Non-Career Naval Aviators* (1968), and the US government report, *German Aviation Medicine in World War II* (1950).

The German side of some of these stories is contained in works like Cajus Bekker's *Augen durch Nacht und Nebel, die Radar-Story* (1964), Horst-Adalbert Koch, *Flak, die Geschichte der deutschen Flakartillerie, 1935–1945* (1954), Karl Hoffmann's *Geschichte der Luftnachrichtentruppe* (1965–66) on the GAF Signals branch, and other works listed in Bekker's *The Luftwaffe War Diaries* (1966) as well as in Leslie E. Simons's *German Research in World War II* (1948).

6. The Second World War

The history of the Second World War is now a vast sea of books, but a good deal yet remains to be tackled. Official histories of the various armies and navies and in some cases the separate air forces are all in the process of being completed. A complete list of those available with historical essays are in Higham's *Official Histories* mentioned earlier. Because of the all-pervading nature of air action in the 1939–45 war, material on air matters can be found in a wide variety of places, one of the most rewarding being the medical histories such as S/Ldr. S. C. Rexford-Welch's *Royal Air Force Medical Services* (1954–1958), with some information on naval aviation medicine in Surgeon/Commander J. L. S. Coulter's *Royal Naval Medical Services* (1954–1956). The effects of bombing are described in detail in other British medical and civil volumes as well as in the military ones. More detailed studies of the Allied bombing efforts against Germany and Japan are given in the many studies which compose the *United States Strategic Bombing Survey* (1945–1947), but it must be remembered that questions sometimes lead to answers and that interpretations of the answers can vary.

A general view of the conflict is supplied by J. F. C. Fuller in *The Second World War 1939–45: a strategical and tactical history* (1948) and in 1970 by Liddell Hart's posthumous volume, while Seymour Friedin and William Richardson's *The Fatal Decisions* (1956) gives the German whys of losing the war. S. A. Stouffer *et al.*, *The American Soldier: in combat and afterwards* (1949) is a mine of sociological information well worth the digging. Major General J. L. Moulton's *A Study of Warfare in Three Dimensions: the Norwegian Campaign* (1967) will repay a careful reader as will I. McD. G. Stewart's *The Struggle for Crete* (1966). The development of the American long-range fighter is the theme of Bernard Boylan's 1955 doctoral dissertation at the University of Missouri, while Ken C. Rust's *The 9th Air Force in World War II* (1967) is more of a combat history of an American tactical air force. In a class by itself is S/Ldr. D. M. Clarke's *What were they like to fly?* (1964) which tells a lot both about aircraft and attitudes. The most important air studies are the seven volumes of Craven and Cate, mentioned above, the four of Webster and Frankland, *The Strategic Air Offensive against Germany* (1961), Anthony Verrier *The Bomber Offensive* (1968) and Basil Collier, *The Defence of the United Kingdom* (1957), Postan, Hay and Scott, *The Design and Development of Weapons* (1964), I. B. Holley's *Buying Aircraft* (1964) in the U.S. Army series, Samuel Eliot Morison's *United States Naval Operations in World War II* (15 volumes) (1947–1962), Robert Sherrod's *History of Marine Corps Aviation in World War II* (1952), Dennis Richards and Hilary St. George Saunders, *The Royal Air Force, 1939–1945* (1953–1954), the Australian, New Zealand, and Indian official series, and the semi-official "Airpower Lessons of World War II" by Robert F. Futrell in AIR FORCE AND SPACE DIGEST, September 1965. German, Italian, Russian, and Japanese official histories have been slow in appearing for a variety of reasons, including loss of records or their impounding by the victors and the lack of any armed forces for which an historical section could work. Thus there is a certain weakness in that much of the story has been told from the point of view of the eventual victors. However, the United States Naval Institute has made available a number of volumes such as Vice-Admiral Friedrich Ruge's *Der Seekrieg* (1957), Commander Marc Antonio Bragadin's *The Italian Navy in World War II* (1957), and Mitsuo Fuchida and Masatake Okumipa's *Midway, the battle that doomed Japan* (1955). Then there are the special USAF Historical Studies No. 75 *Air Supply in the Burma Campaigns* (1957) by Joe G. Taylor, No. 97, *Airborne Operations in World War II, European Theater* (1956) by John C. Warren, No. 153, *The German Air Force versus Russia, 1941* (1965) by Generalleutnant Hermann Plocher, a commander on the front, and No. 189, *Historical Turning Points in the German Air Force War Effort* (1959) by Richard Suchenwirth. The Purnell (Britain) and Ballantine (USA) Illustrated History of the Second World

War Series is providing a variety of single-volume studies whose asset is clarity and some re-interpretation rather than depth. A slim, but useful book, is Alan S. Milward, *The German Economy at War* which should be read in conjunction with the memoirs of Albert Speer (1970). Kent Roberts Greenfield's little *American Strategy in World War II: a reconsideration* (1970) is provocative. Air Chief Marshal Sir Philip Joubert adds another dimension with *The Forgotten Ones: the story of the ground crews* (1961). Allen Andrews, *The Air Marshals: the air war in western Europe* (1970) assesses the leadership on both sides. Albert Merglen's *Geschichte and Zukunft der Luftlandtruppen* (1970) is a general history of paratrooping. 1930–1968.

More material on the *Luftwaffe* is becoming available, though some of it has yet to be translated, such as General-major Fritz Morzik's *Die Deutschen Transportflieger im Zweiten Weltkrieg* (1966). Then there is Roger James Bender's *Air Organizations of the Third Reich* (1967), Koehler's *Bibliographie zur Luftkriegsgeschichte* (1966), an official listing of material on air warfare, Feuchter's *Der Luftkrieg* (1964), Mano Ziegler's *Rocket Fighter: the story of the Me 163* (1963), T. J. Constable and R. F. Toliver, *Horrido: Fighter Aces of the Luftwaffe* (1968), and William Green's *Warplanes of the Third Reich* (1970). The recent reissue of the Air Ministry's *The Rise and Fall of the German Air Force 1933 to 1945* (1970) (originally 1948) makes available a detailed official account written right after the war. The Soviet victory in the East is explained in Earle F. Ziemke's official American monograph *Stalingrad to Berlin* (1968), while Oleg Hoeffding of the Rand Corporation provides another view in his *German Air Attacks against Industry and Railroads in Russia, 1941–1945* (1970).

A wide variety of individual volumes exist covering many aspects of air warfare in the Second World War. The following represent a cross-section with emphasis occasionally upon certain aspects. The memoirs of commanders range from Marshal of the RAF Sir Arthur Harris's *Bomber Offensive* (1947) through General H. H. Arnold's *Global Mission* (1949) and Marshal of the RAF Lord Tedder's *With Prejudice* (1966) to General Adolph Galland's *The First and the Last* (1954), and General Werner Baumbach's *The Life and Death of the Luftwaffe* (1960), to Anna Chennault's story of her husband, *Chennault and the Flying Tigers* (1963) to the autobiographical *The Wartime Diaries of Charles Lindbergh* (1970). In less important positions are Group Captain J. E. Johnson's *Wing Leader* (1956), Pierre Clostermann's *The Big Show* (1951), Colonel Gregory Boyington's *Baa Baa Black Sheep* (1958), and three by General Robert Lee Scott, Jr., *God is My Co-Pilot* (1943), *Tiger in the Sky* (1959), and *Flying Tiger: Chennault of China* (1959). The fighter war is further illustrated by Oliver Moxon's tale of Burma, *After the Monsoon* (1958), in the general accounts of aces and others in such books as Edward H. Sims, *The Fighter Pilots: a comparative study of the Royal Air Force, the Luftwaffe and the United States Army Air Force in Europe and North Africa, 1939–45* (1968), and General George C. Kenney, *Dick Bong, ace of aces* (1960). Hans Ulrich Rudel gives a unique look in *Stuka Pilot* (1958). A special class of men were those who fought at night such as Heinz Knoke, *I Flew for the Führer* (1953), and Wilhelm Johnen, *Battling the Bombers* (1958) on the German side, and J. R. D. Braham, *Night Fighter* (1961), Roderick Chisholm, *Cover of Darkness* (1958), and C. F. Rawnsley and Robert Wright, *Night Fighter* (1957) all of whom were British fighter pilots. Jean Calmel, *Night Pilot* (1955) tells of a bomber over Germany, while Jerrard Tickell's *Moon Squadron* (1956) is about supplying the underground in France. Ivan Southall *They Shall Not Pass Unseen* (1956) is an Australian account of Coastal Command, while Ralph Barker's *Down in the Drink* (1955) deals with Air/Sea Rescue; but escaping was also done on the ground as Kendall Burt and James

Leasor recount in *The One that Got Away* (1956), the story of the only German airman to escape from British captivity; P. R. Reid's *The Colditz Story* (1953) is but one of many British accounts.

Aspects of maritime warfare are to be found in Air Chief Marshal Sir Philip Joubert's *Birds and Fishes: the story of Coastal Command* (1960) by one of its C-in-C's, in Ralph Barker's *The Ship-busters: the story of the RAF Torpedo Bombers* (1957) Lawrence Cortesi, *The Battle of the Bismarck Sea* (1967), J. D. Potter, *Fiasco: the breakout of the German Battleships* [up the English Channel in 1942] (1970) and H. L. Thompson, *Aircraft against U-boats* (1950) as well as the official histories.

Apart from the official accounts, the Battle of Britain has been covered in numerous books which appeared for the 20th and 25th anniversaries. The largest of these is the heavily detailed Francis K. Mason, *Battle over Britain* (1969), which supersedes that older classic by the two air correspondents, Derek Wood and Derek Dempster, *The Narrow Margin* (1961); a more recent French account is Marcel Julian, *The Battle of Britain* (1967). The ground defences were commanded by Churchill's friend General Sir Frederick Pile who tells his story in *Ack-Ack* (1949). An important work is Robert Wright's study of Dowding because Wright was personally involved in the controversy; *Dowding and the Battle of Britain* (British title) *The Man Who Won the Battle of Britain* (USA title) (1970).

The Bombing of Germany (1963) by Hans Rumpf, a German civil-defence specialist, is a useful starting place as a counter to official military histories. It and David Irving's *The Destruction of Dresden* (1963) are both controversial. Roger Freeman, *The Mighty Eighth: Units, Men and Machines* (1969) is an excellent work on the American bomber force and can be supplemented with USAF Historical Division volumes, *Combat Squadrons of the Air Force, World War II* (1970), Jack Olsen's *Aphrodite: desperate mission* (1971) on the attempts to develop drone B-17s, and the United States Federal Civil Defense Administration Study, *Fire Effects of Bombing Attacks* (1952). James Erdmann's *Leaflet Operations in the Second World War* (1969) illuminates one special type of operation, while Robin Reilly's *Sixth Floor* (1969) describes one of the crack RAF Mosquito raids, this one against Shell House in Copenhagen. Other aspects of the story are told in Constance Babington-Smith *Air Spy* (1957) on PRU, Wing Commander Guy Gibson, *Enemy Coast Ahead* (1946) by a Pathfinder leader, Paul Brickhill, *The Dam Busters* (1955), Martin Caidin, *The Night Hamburg Died* (1960) and *Black Thursday* (1960), Bert Stiles, *Serenade to the Big Bird* (1947) James Duggan and Carroll Stewart, *Ploesti* (1962), Squadron Leader A. E. Haarer, *A Cold-Blooded Business* (1958) and Major A. B. Hartley, *Unexploded Bomb* (1958) together with two works on the bombing of Japan, Martin Caidin's *A Torch to the Enemy* (1960) and Major Gene Gurney, *Journey of the Giants* (1961) on the B-29s.

Various aspects of the airborne can be studied in books ranging from S. L. A. Marshall's *Night Drop: the American Airborne Invasion of Normandy* (1962), through R. W. Thompson's *D-Day: spearhead of invasion* (1968) to Major-General R. E. Urquhart's *Arnhem* (1958) Baron von der Hyde's *Return to Crete* (1958), and Brigadier George Chatterton's *The Wings of Pegasus* (1962) by the man who helped found the British Glider Pilot Regiment and the recent *The Champagne Campaign* (1969) by Robert H. Aldeman and Colonel George Walton on the airborne invasion of southern France in 1944. A semi-official unpublished monograph on American airborne forces which contains a wealth of background material is James A. Huston's *Out of the Blue: US Army Airborne Operations in World War II* (1969). Then there are two autobiographical works on air transport at war: General William Tunner's *Over the Hump* (1964) and Sir Hudson Fysh's *Quantas at War* (1968).

The war at sea in the Pacific has its own collection of literature

starting with Masatake Okumiya and Jiro Horikoshi with Martin Caidin's *Zero* (1956) and Saburo Sakai with Martin Caidin and Fred Saito *Samurai!* (1957) which both give background on the Japanese side and carry the story of the fighters through the war. The background to Pearl Harbor is given by Roberta Wohlstetter in her *Pearl Harbor: warning and decision* (1962) while the attack itself is more colourfully described by Walter Lord in *Day of Infamy* (1957); Gordon W. Prange, *Tora, Tora, Tora* (1963); James Leasor, *Singapore* (1968) and Masanobu Tsuji *Singapore, the Japanese Version* (1960) are both useful. Basic to the study of the Pacific War is Clark Reynolds, *The Fast Carriers: the forging of an Air Navy* (1968) and P. C. Smith, *Task Force 57: the British Pacific Fleet, 1944–1945* (1969), which should then be followed by Mitsuo Fuchida and Masatake Okumiya *Midway: the battle that doomed Japan* (1955) and Walter Lord's *Incredible Victory* (1967). Also worth looking at are *Admiral Halsey's Story* (1947) by the admiral and J. Bryan III, who also wrote *Aircraft Carrier* (1954); Lt. Frederick Mears was a young pilot whose life is described in his *Combat Carrier* (1944); Commander Edward P. Stafford's *The Big E* (1962) is the story of the USN's most famous carrier, a fighting ship also included in Captain Donald Macintyre's *Aircraft Carrier: the majestic weapon* (1968). And lastly there are three books on the suicide planes, Yasuo Kuwahara and Gordon T. Allred, *Kamakazi* (1957) and Captain Rikihei Inoguchi, Commander Tadashi Nakajima and Roger Pineau, *The Divine Wind* (1958) and Bernard Millot, *Divine Thunder* (1971), not to mention Stanley Falk's *Decision at Leyte Gulf* (1966) and Burke's Davis's *Get Yamamoto* (1969), and D. O. Woodbury's *Builders for Battle: how the Pacific Naval Air Bases were constructed* (1946); while Rene J. Francillon's *Japanese Aircraft of the Pacific War* (1970) includes material on the aircraft industry as well as on the air forces.

7. After 1945

In the post-1945 world the problems of air power tend to become entwined with those of grand strategy and more especially the nuclear debate. But the latter is really outside the scope of this volume. A starting point is Perry McCoy Smith, *The Air Force Plans for Peace, 1943–1945* (1969), and the more general works by Morton H. Halperin, *Contemporary Military Strategy* (1967) and R. N. Rosecrance *Defence of the Realm* (1968), while an older but still useful source is Gordon B. Turner and Richard D. Challener, *National Security in the Nuclear Age: basic facts and theories* (1960), and on a different tack, Gene M. Lyons and Louis Morton, *Schools for Strategy: education and research in national security affairs* (1965). Two who have contributed to strategic thought are Marshal of the RAF Sir John Slessor in *Strategy for the West* (1954) and Air Vice-Marshal E. J. Kingston-McCloughry in *The Direction of War* (1955), *Global Strategy* (1957) and *Defence* (1960). The views of American airmen have been expressed in General Nathan E. Twining, *Neither Liberty Nor Safety* (1966), General Thomas S. Power, *Design for Survival* (1964), in General Curtis LeMay's autobiographical *Mission with LeMay* (1965), and in earlier polemics such as Alexandre de Seversky's *Air Power: key to survival* (1950). See also, however, Marshall Andrews *Disaster through Air Power* (1950) and Vincent Davis, *Postwar Defense Policy and the US Navy 1943–1946* (1966) and *The Admirals' Lobby* (1967). Of a different sort is the history of aerial bombardment by the Canadian General E. L. M. Burns, *Megamurder* (1967).

Apart from general works mentioned earlier, Richard M. Bueschel, *Communist Chinese Air Power* (1968) describes one of the new post-war air forces. Its opponent in Korea is seen in Robert F. Futrell's *The United States Air Force in Korea, 1950–1953* (1961) and Arne Stade *"Operation Strangle", FN-flygets stora understödsaktion i Korea 1951–53* (1953). The Arab-Israeli Wars await something more than journalism and memoirs, so readers must do with such as General Moshe Dayan's *Diary of the Sinai Campaign* (1965) and William Stevenson's *Zanek! a chronicle of the Israeli Air Force* (1970), *Strike Zion!* (1967), an unbalanced example of instant history, M. Larkin, *The Hand of Mordecai* (1968) on the 1948 war, E. Stock, *Israel on the Road to Sinai, 1949–1956, with a sequel on the six-day war, 1967* (1967); Hugh Thomas, *The Suez Affair* (1967), the anonymous Israeli *Commanders of the Six-Day War and their battle reports* (1967) all make varying contributions to the picture, while A. Beg's *Seventeen September Days* (1965) and S. P. Baranwal's *India Faces War* (1966) are respectively Pakistani and Indian accounts of their 1965 fracas. Until the publication of *The Pentagon Papers* (12 vols., 1971), Lyndon Johnson's memoirs, *The Vantage Point* (1971), and John Lewallen's *Ecology of Devastation: Indochina* (1971), there was not much on Vietnam other than very contemporary materials. Frank Harvey's *Air War—Vietnam* (1967) is more impressionistic than historical. Some older material on the Vietnam air situation is to be found in the expert, Bernard Fall's *The Two Vietnams* (1967) and his other works. O. Hoeffding's *Bombing North Vietnam: An appraisal of economic and political effects* (1968) is a Rand Corp. study, while *Pro-communist Eye-witness Reports of US Bombings of Civilians in North Vietnam*, a Department of Commerce Report (1967), the US Senate's Committee on Armed Services *Air War against North Vietnam* (1967) and lastly Admiral U. S. G. Sharp and General William Westmoreland's *Report on the War in Vietnam* (1969) all add varieties of information and opinions. Capt. Moyers S. Shore II, *The Battle for Khe Sanh* (1969) is the official USMC account of the 1968 action; Colonel Jack Broughton's *Thud Ridge* (1969) is a very informative and strongly worded account of the frustrations of the F-105 campaign against Hanoi. Moving up again to the higher levels there are General Lewis Walt's *Strange War, Strange Strategy* (1971), a USMC view, Phil G. Goulding's *Confirm or Deny* (1970), an insider's story of the problems of Pentagon public relations, and Townsend Hoopes, *The Limits of Intervention* (1969.

The work of the RAF is sketched in Edgar O'Ballance's *Malaya: the Communist Insurgent War 1948–1960* (1966). The surveillance role is discussed by David Wise and Thomas B. Ross in *The U-2 Affair* (1962) and in Elie Abel, *The Missile Crisis* (1962), as well as in Francis Gary Power's *Operation Overflight* (1970)

Korea produced three novels and one autobiography. James Michener's *The Bridges at Toko-Ri* (1953) on naval jets, James Salter *The Hunters* (1957) on jet fighting, and Walt Lasly, *Turn the Tigers Loose* (1956) on night bombers; while the Reverend Colonel Dean E. Hess talks about his work with the infant Korean Air Force in *Battle Hymn* (1956). In addition to Futrell's volume mentioned above, General James A. van Fleet, *Rail Transport and*

the Winning of Wars* (1956), and Cdr. Malcolm Cagle and Cdr. Frank A. Manson, *The Sea War in Korea* (1957) deal with self-evident aspects of the struggle.

The development of jet transports is sketched by Derek Dempster in *The Tale of the Comet* (1958), Martin Caidin in *Boeing 707* (1959) and Richard G. Hubler's *Big Eight: the biography of an airplane* (1960). Douglas H. Robinson's *The B-58 Hustler* (1967) gives a well-illustrated look at one supersonic bomber. More serious is Frederick C. Thayer, Jr., *Air Transport Policy and National Security: a political, economic and military analysis* (1965). The Air Registration Board in London's *World Accident Summary* contains many facts, while the ARB's David P. Davies *Handling the Big Jets: the significant differences in the flying qualities between jet transport aeroplanes and piston-engined aeroplanes* (1967) is a useful technical treatise. Donald Whitnah *Safer Skyways: Federal Control of Aviation, 1926–1966* (1967) tackles an important aspect of the whole subject. John Stroud's *Soviet Transport Aircraft since 1945* (1968) contains a mass of information partially related to policy developments. The important linkage between science and aeronautics is discussed in such works as G. F. Meeter's, *The Holloman Story* (1967) about the USAF test centre and in the slim official USAF work by N. A. Komons, *Science and the Air Force: a history of the Air Force Office of Scientific Research* (1966). A different aspect is to be found in W. Henry Lambright's pamphlet *Shooting Down the Nuclear Plane* (1967), in various issues of the *Naval Review*, in M. Kamins's *Jet Fighter Accident/Attrition Rates in Peacetime* (1968) and D. M. Landi's *Positioning Recoverable Spares in Military Airlift Networks* (1967), both of which are Rand Corporation studies, D. Clay Whybark's, *Forecasting Pilot and Mechanic Requirements and Pilot Supply for Civil Aviation* (1968) and Roland Beamont, *Phoenix into Ashes* (1968) on test piloting. Hearings of the United States Senate Committee on Foreign Relations looked in 1967 at arms sales, always a touchy matter.

Other recent books on the above subjects include Berkeley Rice, *The C-5A Scandal* (1971) which should be read in conjunction with G. Williams, *et al., Crisis in Procurement: a case study of the TSR-2* (1969), Great Britain: Ministry of Technology, *Productivity of the National Aircraft Effort* (1969), Michael Armacost's brilliant *The Politics of Weapons Innovation: the Thor-Jupiter controversy* (1969), and Alain C. Enthoven and K. Wayne Smith, *How Much is Enough?* (1971), not to mention A. Chayes and Jerome B. Wiesner, editors, *ABM: an evaluation of the decision to deploy an anti-ballistic missile system* (1970), and Thomas J. Wilson, Jr., *The Great Weapons Heresy* (1970) on Oppenheimer and nuclear weapons policy.

The development of the SST has been generating a lot of articles, but books are scarce except for John Davis, *The Concorde Affair* (1969) and T. E. Blackall, *Concorde: the story, the facts and the figures* (1969). No doubt the highly controversial American SST will be the subject of works in the near future. On the Caterpillar Club there is Ian Mackersey, *Into the Silk* (1957). Lastly, the development of ejection seats is explained by one of the Martin-Baker "guinea pigs" in Doddy Hay's *The Man in the Hot Seat* (1969).

1984 Supplement to the Bibliography

As I noted (page 170) when the original of *Air Power* went to press in 1970, the presses were rolling at an ever faster rate with new aeronautical books. Under the circumstances it is much less easy than before to be anything like complete. The reader can only be referred either to those works which break new ground, to those which provide guidance, or to those which do an exceptionally good job of bringing up to date material which has heretofore been unavailable. As examples of what has happened the following can be considered. In the first place there has been a general opening of the official archives on the Second World War with the cutting back in Britain of the Fifty-Year Rule to Thirty Years and on top of that of the agreement in 1972 to open virtually all of the records for the whole of the war at once. Two years later Group Captain F. W. Winterbotham was allowed to publish his then sensational *The Ultra Secret*, revealing the existence of the British decrypts of the German Enigma codes. On top of this four years later came Ronald Lewin's *Ultra Goes to War*, then *Kahn on Codes*, and still in process the multi-volume official history *British Intelligence in the Second World War* (1979-   ) by F. H. Hinsley *et al*. Both Winterbotham and Lewin have to be read very carefully with especial attention paid to what they say about the early years of the war. Another aspect of the European intelligence story is unfolded in Winterbotham's later *The Nazi Connection* (1978) about his official trips to Germany before the conflict began. Gordon Prange deals extensively with the decoding of the Japanese signals known as Magic in *At Dawn We Slept* (1981) and the sequel on Midway. Other works breaking new ground are those about the Vietnam War just beginning to come from the U.S. Office of Air Force History in Washington.

Bibliographical guidance is to be found in the works of Myron J. Smith and in the series produced by Robin Higham starting with *A Guide to the Sources of British Military History* (1971), a similar Guide to the U.S. in 1975 with supplements in 1981 and 1985 edited by Donald J. Mrozek, all of which include chapters on the air force and materials on naval aviation, and the series being published by Garland of New York edited by Higham and Jacob W. Kipp which includes a volume on the Luftwaffe by Edward L. Homze. Each volume of the nearly thirty in the Time-Life Epic of Flight series contains a short bibliography. In addition Higham and Kipp edited *Soviet Aviation and Air Power* (1973), each chapter of which contains extensive notes.

Of special help in reading aviation works of all nations is *The Rand McNally Encyclopedia of Military Aircraft, 1914-1980*, edited by Enzo Angelucci (1981) which covers 800 types in all.

Contributing to our knowledge of special fields have been a variety of books. Douglas H. Robinson's *The Dangerous Sky: a history of aviation medicine* (1973) is a fine starting point in that field. Ronald Miller and David Sawers, *The Technical Development of Modern Aviation* (1970), deals with the technical and economic evolution of the modern airliner, but was published just before the fuel crisis which has caused some considerable changes of thought in the last decade. Herschel Smith in *Aircraft Piston Engines* (1981) provided an invaluable technical historical survey of which we need a jet sequel. The nearest work at the present is Edward W. Constant's fine *The Origins of the Turbojet Revolution* (1980) and the retrospective collection edited by the National Air and Space Museum's Walter J. Boyne and Donald S. Lopez, *The Jet Age* (1979) which contains reminiscent pieces by some of the pioneers from around the world.

In a class by itself is Lee Kennett's satellite view *A History of Strategic Bombing from the First Hot-air Balloons to Hiroshima and Nagasaki* (1982), which comes from an author steeped in the French literature.

The well-known Putnam series of reference books having just about exhausted the British companies and their ramifications has now moved into the American field with Peter M. Bowers, *Curtiss Aircraft, 1907-1947* (1979), and volumes on McDonnell Douglas and Lockheed, as well as R.E.G. Davies sequel to his world volume, *Airlines of the United States since 1914* (1972).

Not unnaturally the British have continued to benefit from the outpouring of books on air warfare. These now start with Bruce Robertson's fascinating *Aviation Archeology* (1977) on the identification and recovery of wrecks and other pieces of the air branch of industrial archeology, and his equally useful *RAF: a pictorial history* (1978). Guides to the squadrons of the RAF have now been completed with John W. R. Rawlings' volume on strike and transport units (1983). Peter Lewis has added to the Putnam series with *British Racing and Record-Breaking Aircraft* (1970). Though the First World War seemed to have been pretty thoroughly covered, two basic explorations of the evolution of bombing theory — Barry D. Powers, *Strategy without Slide Rule* (1976), and Neville Jones, *The Origins of Strategic Bombing* (1973), and Peter Mead's *The Eye in the Air* (1983) about reconnaissance, which leads up through the Second War and ties in well with Ursala Powys-Lybbe's *The Eye of Intelligence* (1983) about her own work in interpretation at Medmenham have appeared Denis Winter shows very well what can be done by a fresh inquiring mind who takes another look at the 1914-18 fighter pilots and gives a useful profile in *The First of the Few* (1983). F. J. Adkin's *From the Ground Up: a history of R.A.F. ground crew* (1983) is a personal reminiscence that provides a fresh slant. H. Montgomery Hyde's *British Air Policy between the Wars 1918-1939* (1976) should be read in conjunction with Captain S. W. Roskill's parallel volumes on the Royal Navy. H. R. Allen's *The Legacy of Lord Trenchard* (1972) is suggestive, Air Marshal Sir Victor Goddard *Skies to Dunkirk* (1982) is revealing, as is R. V. Jones, *The Wizard War: British Scientific Intelligence, 1939-1945* (1978), and Sir Maurice Dean's *The Royal Air Force and Two World Wars* (1978). Derek Wood's *Attack Warning Red* (1976) is a history of the Royal Observer Corps, long the eyes and ears of British air defense. Wing-Commander H. R. Allen's *Who Won the Battle of Britain?* (1974) is a controversial start on demythologizing the great British victory of 1940. For the post-war picture two official histories by Air Chief Marshal Sir David Lee, *Flight from the Middle East* (1980) and *Eastward* (1984), give a far different picture than his delightful interwar memoir of India, *Never Stop the Engine When It's Hot* (1983).

The official biography of Portal by Dennis Saunders (1977) lacks depth; this is a pity since Churchill thought he was the best strategist of the Chiefs of Staff.

Two recent Canadian contributions are important both as contributions on their own and for the light they throw on the history of the RAF. These are the first volume of the new multi-volume history of the Royal Canadian Air Force by Syd Wise, *Canadian Airmen and the First World War* (1980), which basically and concisely rewrote the older official British *The War in the Air*, and F. J. Hatch's *The Aerodrome of Democracy: Canada and the Commonwealth Air Training Plan, 1939-1945* (1983), a revealing story.

For the overall civil picture Harald Penrose's *Wings Across the World* (1980) is an illustrated history of British Airways, 1919-1980, but only tells the surface story. Various other aspects of recent history are to be found in such works as Keith Hayward's *Government and British Civil Aerospace: a case study in post-war technology policy* (1983), Ian Lloyd's long-delayed three-volume history of Rolls-Royce

(1977-78), which was completed in the late 1940's and contains a great deal on the development of the Merlin and the Griffon engines, and John Costello and Terry Hughes, *The Concorde Conspiracy* (1976). For two contrasting inside stories, one British and one American, see Sir Basil Smallpiece, *Of Comets and Queens* (1980), and General Lawrence S. Kuter, *The Great Gamble: the Boeing 747* (1973), and follow these with John Newhouse, *The Sporty Game* (1982).

The one overall cohesive view to appear has been R. J. Overy's solid *The Air War, 1939-1945* (1980) by a student of the German economy.

A work which falls in a class by itself is Colonel Roy M. Stanley II's *World War II Photo Intelligence* (1981), a careful, well-illustrated study of the aircraft, cameras, film, pictures, and the clues revealed from this work.

Linking together the airmen of all nations in World War II is the volume edited by Battle of Britain pilot "Laddie" Lucas, *Wings of War* (1983), which is both highly readable and full of items of interest as well as of glimpses of human emotion.

Crossing the Channel to the home of the largest air force in the world in 1918, we at last have a one-volume history to commemorate that nation's long prominence in the air with General Charles Christienne and General Paul Lissarrague *et al.*'s great tome, *Histoire de l'Aviation Militaire française* (1980). The next best thing are the individual issues of the magazine of the French airline pilots, *Icare*, which carries a book review section, as does that other French aviation periodical *Le Fanatique*.

For the reader wishing just a quick overview of the German air force, Tony Wood and Bill Gunston's illustrated history of *Hitler's Luftwaffe* (1977) has much to recommend it visually; for the more serious student Matthew Cooper's *The German Air Force, 1933-1945: an anatomy of failure* (1981) and Williamson Murray's *Strategy for Defeat: the Luftwaffe, 1933-1945* (1983) provide British and American views respectively. For a much deeper aspect of German developments, see Horst Boog's detailed official *Die deutsche Luftwaffenfuhrung, 1935-1945* (1983) and his article in the March 1984 *Aerospace Historian*. Edward L. Homze, *Arming the Luftwaffe: the Reich Air Ministry and the German Aircraft Industry 1919-1939* (1976) breaks new ground as does the work of John H. Morrow, Jr., on the Germans before (1976) and during the First World War (1982).

The Red Air Force is the subject of Bill Sweetman and Bill Gunston, *Soviet Air Power: an illustrated encyclopedia of the Warsaw Pact Air Forces today* (1978), which amplifies Higham and Kipp mentioned at the beginning of this section. In addition Von Hardesty's book, *Red Phoenix* (1982) provides a readable account of the Russians in the Great Patriotic War, while the Soviet official history is available edited by Ray Wagner (1973).

About the only useful book to appear on the Japanese side of the air war in the Pacific, in English, apart from the Gordon Prange volumes mentioned above, is Rene J. Francillon's *Japanese Aircraft of the Pacific War* (1970, rev. 1979). To this may be added the republication of the World War II British handbook, *The Japanese Air Forces in World War II: the organization of the Japanese Army & Navy Air Forces, 1945* (1979), and Bert Webber's interesting account of one of the most ingenious of all the long-range grand strategic bombing campaigns, that against the West Coasts of the United States and Canada described in *Retaliation: Japanese attacks and Allied countermeasures on the Pacific Coast in World War II* (1975).

For those wishing to do a little further reading on World War II and its aftermath, the Nazi minister, Albert Speer's, *Inside the Third Reich* (1970), details some of the impact of the Allied bombing as seen by a production manager; Bruce Myles, *The Night Witches* (1981), is a general account of Soviet women in combat, which includes pilots; General William W. Momeyer, USAF, has outspoken memories of *Air Power in Three Wars* (1978), while Tom Wolfe's popular *The Right Stuff* (1979) tells the story of the test pilots who became astronauts.

Aviation literature in the United States has in the last decade begun seriously to come of age with a new group of scholars devoted to the field both within and without the armed services. Thus Joseph J. Corn, concerned with values and technology in society has produced *The Winged Gospel: America's romance with aviation, 1900-1950* (1983). Roger E. Bilstein, an aeronautical historian, has produced *Flight Patterns: trends of aeronautical development in the United States, 1918-1929* (1984) dealing with the important incubatory period just before the technological revolution erupted and one on which Richard Hallion has also worked with his books such as *Legacy of Flight* (1975) on the Guggenheims and *Test Pilots* (1981), and William Leary has emerged to study the development of American sponsored airlines in the Far East in such works as *The Dragon's Wings* (1976). On the military side the Air Force Historical Foundation has sponsored two groundbreaking works by the journalist DeWitt Copp, *A Few Great Captains* (1980) and *Forged in Fire* (1982), which carry the story essentially from the First World War through the Second. Now the USAF's Office of Air Force History is picking up the story in more detail with LTC. John F. Shiner's *Foulois and the U.S. Army Air Corps, 1931-1935* (1983). Typical of the better type of writer working outside the service is museum curator Barrett Tillman, an expert on naval aircraft, with books such as *The Wildcat in WWII* (1983). In this respect a lot is to be gleaned from the works of Bill Gunston about various types of American aircraft, about how some of them were flown in the series edited by Higham, Siddall, and Williams, *Flying Combat Aircraft of the USAAF/USAF* (1975-1981), and from Ed Heinemann and Rosario Rausa's *Ed Heinemann: combat aircraft designer* (1980). One of those who participated in important decision-making as a junior and again as a senior policymaker was W. W. Rostow, whose *Pre-Invasion Bombing Strategy: General Eisenhower's Decision of March 25, 1944* (1981) poses questions about how such actions are taken.

The development of the USAF is a story now told in Herman S. Wolk's official *Planning and Organizing the Postwar Air Force, 1943-1947* (1984) and makes an interesting contrast to both the struggles dealt with by Copp and the way in which the RAF was created. Closely related to the emergence of the USAF was the development of a modern arms policy, and this struggle is well described by Fred Kaplan in *The Wizards of Armageddon* (1983). The other side of that development was the U.S. involvement in Vietnam, another classic tale of weapons development. Official and unofficial accounts from the air side are only just beginning to emerge. The place to start is with two overall assessments, Stanley Karnow's *Vietnam: a history* (1983), a spin-off from TV, and Colonel Harry G. Summers, *On Strategy: a critical analysis of the Vietnam War* (1982). Then it is possible to sample the official histories such as Jack Ballard's volume on gunships (19) and Ray Bowers' on tactical airlift (1984). For the naval side, the best introduction is Mersky and Polmar, *The Naval Air War in Vietnam* (1981).

Civil aviation has seen many changes since 1945 including on the technical side the introduction of jet engines and supersonic flight as recorded in Kenneth Owen, *Concorde: a new shape in the sky* (1982), which is a serious documented study, while Captain Ken Larson's *To Fly the Concorde* (1982) compares it with his Boeing 747 experience. But *the* work on aircraft handling is probably the British Air Registration Board's Chief Pilot D. P. Davies' later *Handling the Big Jets* (1967 and after). Airline histories have become quite a business recently. Many have been written by Robert Serling, whose latest in 1984 was *Howard Hughes' Airline: an informal history of TWA* (1983), while even the former commuters who have become regionals have begun to have their stories told, as in *Pioneer of the Third Level: a history of Air Midwest* by I. E. Quastler (1980). A solid effort by two aviation historians is W. David Lewis and Wesley Newton, *Delta: the history of an airline* (1979). And women have been long enough in the commercial cockpit that the WASP's of WWII are being followed by regular airline captains such as Bonnie Tiburzi, author of *Takeoff!: the story of America's first woman pilot for a major airline* (1984). The story of the makers of the military and big aircraft, as opposed to general aviation, has been told in Charles D. Bright, *The Jet Makers: the aerospace industry from 1945 to 1972 (1978).*

For insight into the ramifications of the design, development, and disintegration of an airliner see the *Sunday Times* investigative team of Paul Eddy, Elaine Potter, and Bruce Page's *Destination Disaster* (1976) and Lawrence Speiser's *Lawsuit* (1982). Part of the system which controls and handles airliners in flight is discussed in Frank Burnham's *Cleared to Land: the FAA story* (1977) and in Captain Brian Power-Waters, *Margin for Error: None* (1980).

Of the big three general aviation manufacturers in the US there are now histories of Beech (1970) and one of Piper by Devon Francis called *Mr. Piper and His Cubs* (1973).

This book does not deal with space, but the Shuttle is now not so much a rocket as an aircraft and so perhaps it is appropriate to suggest ending with two references to the greater leap off the earth documented in such detail in NASA studies. The easiest place to start is with Kenneth Gatland's *Illustrated Encyclopedia of Space Technology: a comprehensive history of space exploration* (1981) and then to follow that up with Richard P. Hallion and Tom D. Crouch's *Apollo: ten years since Tranquility Base* (1979), which contains an easy to find bibliography.

Lastly, the March 1984 issue of *Aerospace Historian* was devoted to an international overview of the state of aviation history and may even appear as a paperback in slightly enlarged form to cover also Latin America and the Middle East.

USAF Thunderbirds in their Northrop T-38's.

Additional Bibliography for the 1988 Edition

As time passes and aviation begins to be regarded as a serious historical subject and as authors emerge who are trained in the field, so it seems that at last from both official and private sources a better quality of work has begun to appear. What follows is no more comprehensive than the earlier listings and is primarily restricted to English, the common language of aviation.

A number of solid magazines appear abroad, such as *Icare* and *Le Fanatique de l'Aviation* in France which provide some access to the works in French, for instance, and *Aerofan* in Italy which has a summary in English. In the United States new magazines have also appeared which contain much detailed information — *Skyways* (1987-) and *Air Wars, 1919-1939* (1985-). Of a more fundamental nature for anyone engaged in research is Joan K. Haas, Helen Willa Samuels, and Barbara Trippel Simmons, *Appraising the Records of Modern Science and Technology: a guide* (Chicago, 1987).

Two of the volumes in the Garland series can prove helpful: Dominick A. Pisano and Cathleen S. Lewis, editors, *Air and Space History: an annotated bibliography* (New York, 1988), and Gerald Jordan, editor, *British Military History* (New York, 1988), which contains a chapter on the RAF. Robin Higham and Donald J. Mrozek, editors, have been providing supplements to *A Guide to the Sources of U.S. Military History* (Hamden, CT, 1975-) with chapters on the USAF and its predecessors as well as sections on the air arms of the other U.S. services. For doctrinal background, the revised edition of *The Makers of Modern Strategy*, edited by Peter Paret (Princeton, 1986), contains several chapters of interest, especially one by David MacIsaac on Douhet, Mitchell, *et al.* For a more general approach, take a look at *The Smithsonian Book of Flight* edited by Walter J. Boyne, late Director of the National Air & Space Museum (Washington, 1988).

More specifically dealing with the history of aviation are Laurence K. Loftin, Jr., *Quest for Performance: the evolution of modern aircraft* (Washington, 1985), a hefty, but readable introduction to the important subject of higher, faster, and farther. Very much linked to that volume which was heavily based upon the NACA/NASA records is James R. Hansen's *Engineer in Charge: a history of the Langley Aeronautical Laboratory, 1917-1958* (Washington, 1987), which is solidly based on the records and does not shirk from telling both the technical triumphs and the human tragedies of the pursuit of excellence. Then, too, some of the regional offices of USAF History have taken it upon themselves to produce respectable histories which they sell themselves. One such is Lois E. Walker and Shelby E. Wickam, *From Huffman Prairie to the Moon: the history of Wright-Patterson Air Force Base* (WAFB, 1982?), a well-done illustrated history which starts with the Wright Brothers and takes the reader through the trials of the F-15 and the A-10. A similar work concentrating on a somewhat later period is *The Air Force Communications Command, 1938-1986* (Scott AFB, IL, rev. 1987). On an individual city basis is James J. Horgan's *City of Flight: the history of aviation in St. Louis* (Gerald, MO, 1984).

With 75th anniversaries of flight rolling up these days, books are also commemorating those events. *Naval Aviation News* provided the 75th Anniversary of Naval Aviation Commemorative Edition, and Robert L. Lawson, the Editor of *The Hook*, produced *The History of US Naval Air Power* (London, 1985), a very well-illustrated coffee-table tome packed with information.

The relatively compact and intimate RNZAF has recently been portrayed in Geoffrey Bentley and Maurice Conley, *Portrait of an Air Force. . . 1937-1987* (Wellington, 1987), a well-presented text and photos book, to be accompanied by David Duxbury, Ross Ewing, and Ross MacPherson, *Aircraft of the Royal New Zealand Air Force* (Auckland, 1987), which provides a potted history in alphabetical order by manufacturer of each type used by the service. Originally published in Sweden in 1982, Klaus-Richard Böhme's *The Growth of the Swedish Aircraft Industry, 1918-1945* is now available in English (Manhattan, KS, 1988); it tells the fascinating story of the hothouse development in a cool climate of a small, high-quality manufacturing concern under many interesting influences and pressures.

The availability of materials on the French air force, French aviation, and the L'Armée de l'Air has recently been considerably augmented by a number of publishing events. First has come the translation into English of Charles Christienne and Pierre Lissarague, *A History of French Military Aviation* (Washington, 1986), by the former head of the Historical Service of the French Air Force and the Director of the Musée de l'Air et d'Espace at Le Bourget. Then there is Prof. Emmanuel Chadeau's *L'industrie aéronautique en France 1900-1950, de Blériot á Dassault* (Paris, 1987), which is a volume such as exists for no other country in which the industry is examined for the first half century, and all the parts put together by an economic historian into a comprehensive technological whole with organizational sense. Although it is in French, Claude Carlier's *L'aéronautique francaise, 1945-1975* (Paris, 1983) is well worth reading because it details the way in which the French government set out to put the French aircraft industry back on its feet and thus make France once more a power with which to be reckoned. And lastly there is one article by Chadeau and two by Claude Carlier in *Aerospace Historian*, 1986-1988, detailing the rise of the French to 1988.

Memoirs of World War I are still appearing, *viz*: Josiah P. Rowe, Jr., *Letters from a World War I Aviator* (Wellesley, MA, 1987). Perhaps more importantly, a trickle of the writings of aviation mechanics are also beginning to surface, as for instance, Geofrey Ellis, *Tool Box on the Wing* (Shrewsbury, UK, 1983), by an airman who started at Halton in the RAF and ended with a commission in the RNZAF. Along with that goes Malcolm Smith's much more scholarly look at *British Air Strategy between the Wars* (Oxford, 1984) which is solidly based upon the newly opened archives and revises some earlier research. A welcome volume adding to the very sparse materials until very recently on the interwar U.S. air arms in Maurer Maurer's *Aviation in the U.S. Army, 1919-1939* (Washington, 1987) which provides a solid base from which to judge the new biographies now appearing and to place on the shelf next to Shiner on Foulois mentioned previously.

A first-class view of the war over the trenches has been recreated by Denis Winter in his *The First of the Few: fighter pilots of the First World War* (Athens, GA, 1983).

Four important books on the USAAF side of the Second World War have been published. The intimate portrait by the general's aide, James Parton, *"Air Force Spoken Here": General Eaker and the command of the air* (Washington, 1986), is a fine look at one of the better leaders the USAAF has had and a revered father of the present USAF. A parallel biography also sponsored by the Air Force Historical Foundation is David Metz's study *Master of Airpower: General Carl A. Spaatz* (San Rafel, 1988). Two critical studies of the conduct of the air war are Ronald Schaffer's *Wings of Judgment: American bombing in World War II* (Oxford, 1985) and Michael Sherry's *The Rise of American Air Power* (New Haven, 1987).

Equally apropos to the study of air power in World War II is *Knowing One's Enemies: intelligence assessment before the two world wars*, edited by Ernest R. May (Princeton, 1984), which should be coupled with F. H. Hinsley *et al., British Intelligence in the Second World War*, four volumes (London: 1979-1988), which contains a wealth of information about air matters as well as upon ULTRA. In this connection one of the USAF Warrior Studies edited by Diane T. Putney is *ULTRA and the Army Air Forces in World War II* (Washington, 1987), an interview with Justice Lewis F. Powell, Jr., sometime ULTRA officer. Another side of the USAAF coin is represented by Martha Byrd's biography, *Chennault: giving wings to the Tiger* (University, AL, 1987), and by William Colgan's *World War II Fighter-Bomber Pilot* (Manhattan, KS, 1988) and Reginald G. Nolte's *Thunder Monsters Over Europe: a history of the 405th Fighter Group in World War II* (Manhattan, KS, 1986), both of the latter being by participants in P-47 operations in Europe.

Switching to the Pacific theater and the war at sea, the best new general coverage is Ronald Spector's one-volume *Eagle against the Sun* (New York, 1985). Behind that big picture is the work of one of the codebreakers, *"And I Was There" — Pearl Harbor and Midway — breaking the secrets,* by RADM Edwin T. Layton (New York, 1985); Layton was one of the key staff at the naval headquarters on Hawaii and his book has much to say about those first two crucial air-sea battles. His book should be read in conjunction with John B. Lundstrom's *The First Team: Pacific naval air combat from Pearl Harbor to Midway* (Annapolis, 1983) and Norman Friedman's *U.S. Aircraft Carriers: an illustrated design history* (Annapolis, 1984). See also Robert R. Rea's letters, *Wings of Gold* (University, Al, 1987).

Edward H. Sims, *Aces over the Oceans: the great pilots of World War II* (Blue Ridge Summit, PA, 1987), gives vignettes of actions which involved crossing the sea, not necessarily by naval airmen. On the other hand, former naval flyer Captain Eric "Winkle" *Brown in Wings of the Navy: flying Allied carrier aircraft of World War II* (Novato, CA, 1987) includes a number of oddball naval aircraft of the 1939-45 war as well as later machines. Alwyn T. Lloyd of Boeing in his Detail and Scale series *Superfortress: the story of the B-29 and American Airpower in World War II* (New York, 1988) make use of official and Boeing archives to tell how the war-winning bomber was created and put to use against Japan.

On the technical side, two notable sets of volumes have become available. From Britain, Ian Lloyd's three volumes of the history of Rolls-Royce, completed some time after the war but held until 1978 and then privately printed and released by the company, and a cluster of other RR memoirs including the important one by Sir Stanley Hooker, *Not Much of an Engineer* (Shrewsbury, UK, 1984), and Peter Stokes, *From Gypsy to Gem — with diversions, 1926-1986* (Derby, 1987), etc. The other important line of history starts with Jack Nissen with A.W. Cockerill's *Winning the Radar War, 1939-1945: a memoir* (New York, 1987). Much more comprehensive is the two-volume, Volume 8 of the History of Physics by Henry E. Guerlac, *Radar in World War I* (American Institute of Physics, 1987). This is a mine of information not only on how radar works, what the British, French, and Germans knew and how they transmitted that, but an enormous quantity of material on the developments in the United States and how they applied to air warfare. A different sort of work, but helpful, is Christopher Chant's *The Encyclopedia of Code Names of World War II* (London, 1987).

Although the RAF yet awaits a comprehensive overview history, as does the USAF and its antecedents, John Terraine, known for his work on the First World War on the ground, has provided a provocative start with *A Time for Courage* (in the UK as *The Right of the Line*): *the Royal Air Force in the European War, 1939-1945* (New York, 1985). And standing next to it, also based very much on the archives, is W.A.B. Douglas, *The Creation of a National Air Force* (The Official History of the Royal Canadian Air Force, Volume II), (Toronto, 1986). Brian Johnson and Terry Heffernan in *A Most Secret Place: Boscombe*

Down, 1939-45 (London, 1982) reveal the inner secrets of the wartime testing of British, Allied, and other aircraft in test reports. A rare novel which gives the feel for the times is Derek Robinson's *Piece of Cake* (New York, 1984) on the Battles of France and Britain. Something of the same heroic quality is displayed in Tony Spooner's tale of a romantic real-life PRU pilot in *Warburton's War* (London, 1987). The role of luck in air warfare, 1917-1966, is found in Laddie Lucas, *Out of the Blue* (London, 1985), while the tangled workings of the system in wartime are laid out in Robin Higham's description of the RAF in Greece in *Diary of a Disaster* (Lexington, KY, 1986). The life and death of a flattop in European waters is portrayed in John Winton's *Carrier Glorious* (London, 1987). The successful redevelopment of tactical air forces by the RAF in the Western Desert and the USAAF from then on have recently been the subject of two official American studies. Daniel R. Mortensen for the U.S. Army and the Office of Air Force History Historical Analysis Series, *A Pattern for Joint Operations: World War II Close Air Support North Africa* (Washington, 1987), and Kenneth A. Steadman of the Combat Studies Institute, Fort Leavenworth, KS, *A Comparative Look at Air-Ground Support Doctrine and Practice in World War II with an Appendix on Current Soviet Close Air Support Doctrine* (1982).

On the German side, Williamson Murray's Air University study has been published in slightly altered form as *Luftwaffe* (Baltimore, 1985). This version of *Strategy for Defeat* has been amplified with visual additions and contains provocative materials. For a detailed look at one of the first grand strategic Luftwaffe offensives as all parties saw it then and now, After the Battle's *The Blitz* (London, 1987-) is the first of several volumes which the noted British publisher will bring out tracing in detail not only the ebb and flow of the battle, as it has already done for the Battle of Britain, but also how the incidents affected the lives of the people involved. Additional volumes are in preparation which will carry the story through 1945. This means that they will overlap Norman Longmate's *Hitler's Rockets: the story of the V-2's* (London, 1987), which has a strong cast toward the social impact of war.

Turning to the postwar world after 1945 it is a pleasure to be able to note that the Putnam series now encompasses almost all the major U.S. aircraft manufacturing companies and that the long unavailable Peter Bowers volume on Boeing should be back in print as a revised reference shortly. Additionally Charles A. Ravenstein produced for the USAF *Air Force Combat Wings: lineage and honors histories, 1945-1977* (Washington, 1984), and Lloyd S. Jones has issued a fourth edition of his reference *U.S. Bombers, 1928 to 1980's* (Fallbrook, CA, 1984) which contains a good deal of information, and especially pictures and drawings of models of aircraft never built.

A fine place to start for an overview of the USAF is *Makers of the United States Air Force* (Washington, 1987), a volume edited by John L. Frisbee and sponsored by the Air Force Historical Foundation which contains essays on twelve leaders who played a significant role in founding and propelling the USAF from 1947. Herman S. Wolk's judicious study *Planning and Organizing the Postwar Air Force, 1943-1947* (Washington, 1984) provides a solid base from which further study of the USAF can be launched. On the other hand, the fortieth anniversary history of SAC, *The Development of Strategic Air Command, 1946-1986* (Offutt AFB, 1986), is more of a chronology than an analytical history. Alwyn T. Lloyd's *B-52 Stratofortress* in the Detail and Scale series (Blue Ridge Summit, PA, 1988) provides an excellent, brief technical overview of the backbone workhorse of SAC. Nick Kotz, on the other hand, gives a very different picture of the successor aircraft in *Wild Blue Yonder: money, politics and the B-1 bomber* (New York, 1988). The cheap competitor of the B-1 has its story told in Kenneth Werrell's, *The Evolution of the Cruise Missile* (Maxwell AFB, AL, 1985).

The most recent work on the assumed principal opponent of the USAF is that of the Englishmen R.A. ("Tony") Mason and John W.R. Taylor, *Aircraft, Strategy and Operations of the Soviet Air Force* (London, 1986), which is particularly valuable for its opening discussion of the nature of the sources for the study of Russian air power. The book is both history and current reference.

Douglas K. Evans, *Sabre Jets Over Korea, a firsthand account* (Blue Ridge Summit, PA, 1984), provides a fine way to get into the first of the limited wars that followed World War II for the USAF. Richard P. Hallion, a veteran historian, provides an overview of one aspect in his concise *The Naval Air War in Korea* (Baltimore, 1986). *Air Interdiction in World War II, Korea and Vietnam* (Washington, 1985) provides interviews with three general officers of the USAF who served in the different conflicts and relates their distilled observations for Project Warrior inquirers. A much different and more analytical approach is taken in Donald J. Mrozek's Airpower Research Institute volume from Maxwell AFB, *Air Power and the Ground War in Vietnam: ideas and actions* (1988). A more specific history is that by Jack S. Ballard, *Development and Employment of Fixed-Wing Gunships, 1962-1972* (Washington, 1982), which deals with that form of firepower which was under USAF control as opposed to helicopters which were an Army force. The naval side of the air war has been covered succinctly by John B. Nichols and Barrett Tillman in *On Yankee Station* (Annapolis, 1987), while the USAF's *Search and Rescue in Southeast Asia, 1961-1975* by Earl H. Tilford (Washington, 1980) deals with a vital work which sometimes also plucked up Navy fliers. And lastly, John Schlight, sometime of the Office of Air Force History, has edited the Army's paperback, *Second Indochina War Symposium: papers and commentary* (Washington, 1986), which provides a wider and more provocative background for viewing the air war. David J. Dean, *The Air Force Role in Low-Intensity Conflict* (Maxwell, AFB, AL, 1986), looks at a number of less intensive areas and suggests possible scenarios.

One development since 1945 has been of faith in the helicopter. That was partly the cause for the incautious *Iranian Rescue Mission*, whose failure is discussed by Paul B. Ryan (Annapolis, 1985).

After Vietnam, the fourth generations of jet fighters began to appear, a subject discussed by Christopher Campbell in *Air Warfare* (New York, 1984) and by Robert Jackson in *Flying Modern Jet Fighters* (Wellingborough, UK, 1986). The more arcane side of the debate is covered in Walter Kross, *Military Reform: the high-tech debate in tactical air forces* (Washington, 1985), and especially in the lively and interesting Robert W. Drewes, *The Air Force and the Great Engine War* (Washington, 1987), which hones in on the F-100 engine which powers several modern jet fighters.

Turning back again to the RAF, Terry Gander's *Encyclopedia of the Modern RAF* (Wellingborough, UK, 1984) contains a fair amount of historical material buried in its individual entries and references. Robert Jackson's *Avro Vulcan* (Wellingborough, UK, 1984) tells the story of the longest lived and most unusual of the RAF's V-bombers, and the one to see action in the Falklands War of 1982. In the British services helicopters have remained part of the RAF and thus some of their story is to be found in General Sir William Jackson's *Withdrawal from Empire* (London, 1987), a story that is amplified in the official history by Air Chief Marshal Sir David Lee in *Eastward: a history of the Royal Air Force in the Far East. 1945-1972* (London, 1984). (His autobiographical work on service on the Northwest Frontier in the interwar years, *Don't Stop the Engine When It's Hot* is a most amusing

and enjoyable look at a former era). Lorna Arnold's *A Very Special Relationship: British Atomic Weapon Trials in Australia* (London, 1987) gives the official story. Another side by the commanding officer of an earlier effort is AVM Wilfred E. Oulton's *Christmas Island Cracker* (London, 1987) by the commander of the task force.

The world's most active air force has been one in the Middle East and its history is told by Stanley M. Ulanoff and David Eshel in *The Fighting Israeli Air Force. . . 1948-1984* (New York, 1985). The other air war, fought with some of the same equipment, is described by Jeffrey Ethell and Alfred Price as *Air War South Atlantic* (New York, 1983) on the Falklands, and from the other side in broader perspective at the end of Robert L. Scheina's *Latin America: a naval history, 1810-1987* (Annapolis, 1987). The future in space is approached historically by Grover E. Myers with *Aerospace Power: the case for indivisible application* (Maxwell AFB, AL, 1986). This can be coupled then to the reading of two classic reactions to an accident, the *Report of the Presidential Commission on the Space Shuttle Challenger Accident* (Washington, 1986) and the far more critical book by Joseph J. Trento, *Prescription for Disaster: from the glory of Apollo to the betrayal of the Shuttle* (New York, 1987).

For those with an interest in what aircraft really looked like and who wish to be authentic in their modelling, William Green and Gordon Swanborough, two deans of the field, have compiled *Flying Colors* (Carrollton, TX, 1981) which contains more than 100 aircraft from the First World War to 1981 in various full-color paint schemes. Equally interesting is *Painting Planes: the aviation art of Don Connolly* (Stittsville, ONT., Canada, 1982) which tells how the artist became one and explains what aviation art is.

In the field of civil aviation there has also continued to be an increased quality of books since 1984. Edmund Preston's official *Troubled Passage: the Federal Aviation Administration during the Nixon-Ford term, 1973-1977* (Washington, 1987) deals with affairs at the center just before deregulation and the dissolution of the controllers' union. Nick A. Komons, *The Third Man: a history of the airline crew complement controversy, 1947-1981* (Washington, 1987), looks at something in which Bonnie Tiburzi, author of *Takeoff!* (New York, 1984), has been involved as a participant in the cockpit. George C. Eads of the Brookings Institution has studied *The Local Service Airline Experiment* (Washington, 1972), while I.E. Quastler in *Pioneer of the Third Level: a history of Air Midwest* (San Diego, 1980) tells part of the story of one which was bought out in 1988. North of the border the story has been a little different in that deregulation has not yet fully taken place. The story of recent years is in Garth Stevenson, *The Politics of Canada's Airlines from Diefenbaker to Mulroney* (Toronto, 1987).

Recent airline histories include Robert Serling, *Eagle: the story of American Airlines* (New York, 1985); Frank Borman and Robert J. Serling, *Countdown: an autobiography* (New York, 1988), by the astronaut turned fighting chairman of Eastern Air Lines; Philip Smith, *It Seems Like Only Yesterday — Air Canada, the first fifty years* (Toronto, 1986); John Gunn, *Challenging Horizons* (St. Lucia, Queensland, Australia, 1987), his second volume carrying Qantas from 1939 to 1954; and two of several books on the disastrous results of the straying of the Korean Air Lines flight into Soviet airspace — Alexander Dallin, *Black Box: KAL 007 and the Superpowers* (Berkeley, CA, 1985) and Seymour M. Hersh, *"The Target Is Destroyed"* (New York, 1986).

Index

— A —

Aden, air policing of, 48
Aeroplanes,
  A-4 Skyhawks, 175
  A-7, 150
  A-20, 99
  A-300, 146
  A-320, 164
  AD-1 Skyraider, 135, 140, 161
  Airbus 340, 168
  Albacore, 103-104
  Albatros D-1, 17, 18
  Aloha 737, 166
  Auster, 66
  Avenger, 102, 112, 118
  Avro, 24, 144
  B-1, 123, 142, 160, 167
  B-17, 33, 38, 87, 88, 89, 94, 103, 118, 119,
    150
  B-24, 82, 87, 91, 94
  B-25 Mitchell, 62, 74, 79, 90, 182
  B-29, 38, 62, 89, 90, 91, 95, 121, 145, 147
  B-32, 93
  B-36, 133
  B-47, 130
  B-52, 135, 150, 160, 175
  B-58 Hustler, 135, 140
  BAC-111-500, 137
  BAe 146, 173
  Backfire, 160, 162
  Baltimore, 74
  Barracuda, 103
  Battle, Fairey, 69
  BE, 16
  BE-2C, 18, 21
  Beaufighter, 71, 79, 85, 96
  Beaufort, 71, 96, 103
  Beech 18, 57
    cockpit, 57
  Beech AT-11, 62
  Bellanca, 56
  Betty, Japanese, 112
  Bf-110, 86
  Bison, Soviet, 129, 159
  Blenheim, Bristol, 69, 70, 74
  Bleriot, 50
  Boeing, 38, 162
  Boeing, B-17, 46
  Boeing, 226, 56
  Boeing 247D, 56
    cockpit, 56
    cabin, 57
  Boeing, 304, 57
  Boeing, 707-436, xi
  Boeing, 707, 137, 164, 168
  Boeing, 727, 164, 179
  Boeing, 737, 137, 164, 173
  Boeing, 737, 100, 169
  Boeing, 747, 137, 170
  Boeing, 747-400, 165, 168, 176
  Boeing, 747SP, 168
  Boeing, 757PF, 172
  Boeing flying-boat, 40
  Boeing P-12B, 38
  Boeing Stratocruiser, 163, 164

Brabazon, 136
Brewster Buffalo XP2A-1, 45
Brisfit, 25
Bristol Bombay, 53, 46
Bristol Bulldog, 45
Britannia, Bristol, 136, 143
Bucker, 133, 44
Bucker Jungman, 44
C-5A, 138, 142
C-5B, 162
C-47, 77, 144, 161
C-54, 144
C-69, 144
C-82, 149
C-123, 94
C-124, 136
C-130 turboprop, 162
Canadian Royal Mail, 56
Cant 2506B, 71
Caproni bomber, 27
Caravelle, 164
Catalina, 97, 107, 109
Caudron bomber, 15
Cessna, 126, 127
Cessna Citation, 165
Cessna Citation II, 173
Cessna Citation III, 173
Claude, Japanese, 118
Comet I, De Havilland, 49, 137, 164
Concorde, 143, 164, 165, 183
Consolidated PT-1, 44
Consolidated Vultee VII, 37
Constitution, 144
Convair 990, 137
Convair XC-99, 144
Convertiplane, 140
Corsair, Vought, 102, 112
CR-42, 103
Curtiss JN-4 Jenny, 24
Curtiss flying-boats, 6
Curtiss NSB-1, 46
Curtiss P-6E Hawk, 45,
Curtiss P-26, 45
Curtiss SBC Helldiver, 48, 49
Curtiss 75a, 45
Curtiss racer, 41, 42
Czech, 43
Dakota, 78, 79
Dassault Etendard, 142
Dassault Mystere, 131
Dassault, type 220, 57
Dauntless, Douglas, 109, 112, 122
DC-2, 57
DC-3, 38, 57, 140, 170
DC-4, 165
DC-7, 136
DC-8, 146
DC-9, 146, 147, 162
DC-10, 146, 162, 169
De Havilland Caribou, 142
De Havilland DH-4, 32
De Havilland Moth, 52
De Havilland Vampire, 126
development in WWI, 14-16
Devoitine D-510, 43

DH-2, 17
DH-4, 18
DH-51, 44
DH-88, 44
DH-89, 58
DHC-7, 162
Do-17, 43, 53, 62
Do-19, 91
Do-217, 86
Dornier flying-boat, 40
Douglas A-4 Skyhawk, 139
Douglas DC-3, 56
Douglas Skyraider, 110, 156
Douglas TBD, 108, 112
Draaken, 126, 127
early manufacture, 23
Electra, Lockheed, 143
Ellsworth expedition plane, 56
Embraer Brasilia, 174
Excalibur, 36
F-2b, Bristol, 18
F-4 Phantom, 135, 139, 140, 142, 149
F4F, 105
F-5 Freedom Fighter, 135
F-8 Corsair, 150
F-15 Eagle, 160
F-16 Falcon, 142, 160, 162
F-50, 175
F-80, 141
F-86 Sabre, 131, 147, 148
F-100, 148, 173
F-104, 142, 153
F-105, 134, 149, 150, 161
F-106, 138
F-106A, 131
F-111, 135, 141, 161
Fairchild Cornell, 1
Fairey Fox, 43
Farman, 16
FE-2 pusher, 17
FE-2b, 17, 18
FH-1 Phantom, 140
Fiat, 62
Fiat BR-20, 46
Fiat CR-42, 43
Fiat G, 103
Firefly, 102, 103
flying boats, 16, 22, 36, 40, 48, 107
Fokker D-VII, 18, 19
Fokker Dr-1 triplane, 18
Fokker E-1, 16
Fokker *Eindecker*, 17
Fokker F-7, 56
Fokker F-50, 170
Fokker triplane, 15, 16, 18, 27
Folland Gnat, 153
Ford Trimotor, 65, 140
FW-190, 86, 109, 183
FW-200 Condor, 44, 97, 103
Fulmar, 102, 103, 106, 107
George, Japanese, 91
Gladiator, 67, 105
Gotha, 25
Grigorovich seaplane, 19
Grumman E-2A Hawkeyes, 139

Grumman FU-4F, 45
Grumman F7F, 121
Grumman F9F, 150
Grumman Gulfstream IV, 168
Grumman S-2D, 139
Grumman TBF, 108
Halberstadt D-11, 17
Halifax, 87, 92
Hampden, 69, 103
Handley Page O/100, 24
Harvard AT-6, 63
Havoc, 85
Hawk, 175
Hawker Hart, 28, 43
Hawker Sea Fury, 106
He-51, 53
He-111, 53, 62, 68, 69, 96
He-177, 91
Heinkel HD 36, 52
Heinkel (long-range), 103
Hellcat, Grumman, 62, 102, 112, 114, 119
Helldiver, Curtiss, 62, 111, 119
HP Heyford, 46
HS-123, 43
HS 2L, 36
Hudson, 71, 94
Hurricane, 69, 70, 74, 85, 91, 102, 105, 107, 163
I-15, Russian, 53
I-16, Russian, 53, 75
Il-2 Sturmovik, 75, 76
J-22, 126
Jack, Japanese, 91
Johns Multiplane, 33
Ju-52, 38, 44, 58, 67, 68, 70, 73
Ju-52/3M, 53
Ju-86, 44
Ju-87, *see* Stuka
Ju-88, 86, 91, 96
Ju-88C, 97, 103
Ju-88D, 177
Ju-89, 91
Junkers, W-13, 56
Kate, Japanese, 112
Kawanishi H8K, 124
KC-135, 142
Kettering Aerial Torpedo, 20
Kittyhawk, Curtiss, 74
L-33, 22
La-4, 76
La-5, 76
Lancaster, 62, 87, 104
Liberator, 97, 103
Lightnings, 129
Lincoln, 133
Lockheed C-130H Hercules, v
Lockheed 1011
    Trister, 137
Lockheed P-80, 131
Lodestar, 57
Lysander, Westland, 74
Macchi, 62
Macchi 202, 103
Macchi 205, 103
Malmen J-23, 51   Martin AM-1 Mauler, 110
Martin B-10, 46
Martin Marauder, 71
Martin Mars, 116
Martin PBM, 121

Martin PM-2, 36
Martlet, Grumman, 102
Maryland, 74, 97
McDonnell Banshee, 131
Me-109, 53, 62, 66, 69, 80, 85, 86, 103, 109, 76
Me-110, 67
Me-163, 86
Me-262, 86, 94
Me-323, 74
MiG-15, 147
MiG-17, 131, 149
MiG-19, 157
MiG-21, 157, 212, 225, 145, 149, 153
Mirage, 135, 141, 175
Mitchell, 71
Mohawk, Curtiss, 78
Mosquito, 62, 66, 79, 85, 88, 92, 94
Mystère, 135, 140
NA-16, 126
naval aircraft armament, 103
NC-4, 36
Nell, Japanese, 49
Nieuport, 9, 13, 17, 18
North American RA-5C Vigilante, 139
North American Rockwell B-1 bomber; vi
Northrop F-20 Tiger II, 168
PB4Y-1, 123
PBY, 96
P-3B, 155
P-26A, 45
P2V, 155
P-38, 87
P-40, Curtiss, 49, 78
P-47 Thunderbolt, 67, 86, 94
P-51 Mustang, 66
PAA Twin Boom, S-62534-M, 36
PE-2, 71, 75
PE-8, 75
Pfalz D-III, 18

problems of development, 9
pusher aircraft, 15, 17
R4Y, 136
R-34, 22
R-38, 23
reconnaissance plane, 14
Republic F-84, 131
Roc, 102
Rockwell B-1B, 165, 170, 175
Round-the-World Cruisers, 29, 30
Saab 37, Viggen, 142
Saab J-29, 126
Saab SF 340, 174
Sally III, 121
Savoia-Marchetti, 101, 103
Savoia S-55 flying-boat, 48
SB-2, Russian, 53
SBD Dauntless, 48
SE-5, 18
SE-5A, 20
Seafire, 109
seaplanes, 22
Short flying-boat, 40
Short S.23 Champion, xi
Shturmovik, 62
Shuttleworth
    Rumpler C IV, 24
    SE-5A, 26

Sikorski, 16, 19, 35
Sikorsky flying-boat, 40
Sikorsky 0S2U Kingfish, 80
Sikorsky S-42, 36, 58
Sikorsky S-44a, 182
Sk-14, 126
Sk-16, 126
Sk-60, 126, 127
Skua, 102, 105
Sopwith Camel, 18
Sopwith Pup, 17, 20, 22
SPAD, 18, 21
Spitfire, 66, 67, 74, 78, 86, 88, 97, 102, 109, 122, 163
Spitfire VIII, 78
SR-71, 147
STOL, 140, 149, 183
Storch, Fieseler, 74n
Stratocruiser, 136
Stuka, 30n, 67, 69, 96, 99, 103
Su-7, 154
Sunderland, 97, 103
Supermarine S-6b, 42
Supermarine Spitfire, 45
Swordfish, 102, 103, 105, 107, 109
tactical formations in WWI, 17
Taube monoplane, 16
TC-616, 157
Thulin K, 50
torpedo-bombers, 22
Tu-28B, 158
Tu-114, 158
Tu-134, 137
Tu-144, 143, 175
U-2, 146
Val, Japanese, 49, 62, 112
Valetta, 136
Valiant, 134, 135
Vickers FB-9 Gun Bus, 18
Vickers Supermarine S-6B, 42
Vickers Supermarine Stranraer, 112
Vickers Valentia, 46
Vickers VC-10, 137, 164
Vickers Vildebeeste, 54
Vickers Vimy, 16
Vickers Wellesley, 46
Victor, 134
Viscount, 136, 140, 164
Voyager, 168
Voisin, 16
Vought 0S2U, 107
Vulcan, 134
Vultee BT-13, 61
Wellington, 69, 78, 92, 94
Whitley, 69, 94, 97
Wildcat, Grumman, 112
Wright Military Flyer, 4
Wright Model B Flyer, 1, 3
WV-1 Super Constellation, 139
XB-70, 135, 141, 160
XP-59, 130
Yak 1, 76
Zero, 49, 78, 105, 112, 118
Air Board, 26
Aircraft production, 39
Air forces: before 1917, 9; importance of independence for, 31, 32; inter-war colonial actions, 32; in 1939, 59; aging of commanders, 132; Soviet, 76. *See also* individual countries

Air France, 40
Air intelligence, Cold War, 146-147
Air Ministry, British, 5, 30
  formed, 26
Air power: theorist, 5, 178; will to fight, 5-6; maritime use of, 6, 96-98; as *coup de main*, 8; classic use in Palestine campaign, WWI, 98; gradual build-up in WWII, 62; Allied over-use of, 77; use in Burma, WWII, 77-79; and national defence, 79-91; analysis of use of, 98-99; seaborne, *see* Atlantic/Mediterranean area and Pacific theatre; development since WWII, 132-156; ideal, 177-178; realities of, 178-180; wave pattern in, 180-183; instrument of policy, 160-162
Air/Sea rescue, 61; tactical, 75
Air transport, 40: destruction of German in Holland, WWII, 68; and in Crete, 73, 77; use in Burma, WWII, 78-79; Allied forces in 1944, 74; post-WWII developments, 132, 145
Airborne operations, WWII: troops, 73, 94; Crete, 70, 73; Middle East, 74; Sicily, 74, D-Day, 74
Aircraft industries
  ancillary firms, 146
  assessments of German production, WWII, 95
  British, 162
  British profits and losses, 4
  British wartime production, 2n, 15
  French, 162; Airbus Industries, 162
  electronics, 165, 166, 168
  machine-tool development, 41
  maintenance, 167
  post-WWII British, 143, 146
  post-WWII Japanese, 146
  post-WWII Soviet, 145
  problems after WWII, 128-129, 133, 143, 145-146
  Soviet, 162
  spares, 167
Airfields, WWII, 61
Airliners, 178
  inter-war, 41
  post-WWII, 140-143
Airlines, 162: the first, 40; expansion, 4, 40; inter-war, 40, 41; post-WWII, 132-133, 140; competition, 178; computers, 168
Airlines
  Aeroflot, 163
  British Caledonian, 166
  Continental, 163
  Frontier, 163, 166
  Mid Continent, Wichita, 170
  Northwest, 163
  O'Hare, Chicago, 170
  People Express, 166
Airmen:
  class supplying most, 3
  WWI, 4
  WWII, 61
  See also Pilots
Airships, 11
  inter-war, 41
  submarine-chasing, 22
  U.S. Navy Akron, 53, 55
Akagi, Japanese carrier, 118
Aleutians, 120
  Japanese attack, 117
Alksins, Gen., 53

Allenby, Gen., 20, 66
Allied Expeditionary Air Forces, WWII, 95
Altitude records, 42, 48
American Association for the Advancement of Science, 152
Anglo-American Guarantee Treaty, 29
Anti-aircraft defences,
  guns, 9
  in WWII, 63, 86
  in Vietnam, 9, 150
Antonov, Russian designer, 145
Antwerp, U-boats attacked by RNAS at, 22
Apollo moonshot, 183
Arab-Israeli War (1967), 135, 153-154
Argentina, aircraft industry, 146
Ark Royal, HMS, 104, 105, 107, 109
Army air arm, British, 31
Arnhem, airborne landing at, 73
Arnold, Lt. H.H., 2, 3, 72, 79
Asquith, H.H., 26
Atlantic/Mediterranean area, seaborne air power in WWII, 101-109
  British naval conservatism, 101-102
  naval defence against aircraft, 104
Atom bomb, 8
  discussion raised by, 128
  dropped on Japan, 128
Australia, Japanese attempts to isolate WWII, 116
aviation, general, 162

— B —

Balbo, Gen. Italo, 48
Ball, Albert, 17-18
Balloons, observation, 11
Béarn, French carrier, 102
Beatty, Adm. Sir David, 14
Beech, 168
Belgium, German *blitzkrieg* on, 68
Benghazi, 11
Bennett, D.C.T., 93
Berlin Airlift, 129, 147, 154
Biship, Billy, 14
Bismarck, chase and destruction of, 107-109
Blimps *see* Airships
Blitzkrieg, 6, 7, 63, 66, 124, 179: against Poland, 66-67; against Norway, 67-68; against Holland, Belgium, France, 68-70; in Balkans, 70; against Greece, 70; against Crete, 70-73; against Russia, 73-74, 179; faltering of German, 74; Japanese, 67, 111-112; Israeli (1967), 154; in USSR, 75
Blücher, 67
Boeing Air Transport stewardesses, vii
Boeing Commercial Airplane Co., 165
Boeing Corporation, 143
Boelcke, Oscar, 16-17
Boffins, 63, 99
Bombers, 13; first RNAS, 24; RAF inter-war, 37; RAF losses, WWII, 86; German lack of heavy, WWII, 91; US post-WWII strategic, 132; nuclear, 135
Bombing,
  atom bomb dropped on Japan, 128
  British inaccuracy, 93, 95
  counter productive, 8, 27
  effectiveness, on cities, 6
  Korean War, 148
  lessons learned from WWI, 27

of civilians, 24, 26, 37, 85
  strategic, WWI, 7, 24-27
  strategic air offensives, WWII, 91-95
  Vietnam War, 150, 152
Bombs,
  atomic, 89, 128
  buzz, 87
  early, 11-12
  for B-17, 87
  hydrogen, 128, 129
  incendiary, 8, 93
  WWII; 60, 93
Brabazon, Lord, 143
Britain: early balloon units, 9; early air force, 10; aircraft production in WWI, 15; Independent Bombing Force, WWI, 26; Air Mission trains Japanese, 30; inter-war rearmament, 41; night bombing of, 85, 91; air strategy problems in WWII, 92; Suez action and, 132, 154; rocket research, 135
Britain, Battle of, 7, 63, 79, 85, 98, 179
British Aerospace, 165
British European Airways, 140
British Overseas Airways Corporation, 140
Brooks Field, Texas, 23
Bulgaria, defeated in Macedonia, WWI, 21
Burma, WWII campaign in, 77-79
  lessons from, 179

— C —

Caminez, Harold, 31
Cape Matapan, battle of, 106, 109
Cape Spartivento, battle of, 107
Caporetto, battle of 19, 27, 33
Caproni, Count, 33, 163
Carriers, aircraft, 7, 179, 180
  actions in Pacific, WWII, 111-124
  as ferries, 105
  British losses, WWII, 103
  British shortage of (1939), 102
  European disinterest in, 101-102
  escort, 101, 103, 105, 120, 124
  merchant, 103
  prototype, 22
Cessna, 165, 168
Cessna, Clyde, 39
Chennault, Claire, 49, 53, 117
China, 48
  lessons from Japanese war in, 179
  post-WWII air force, 145, 147
  post-WWII nuclear bombs and missiles, 134
  post-WWII supply of Russian aircraft, 145
  war with Japan (1930's), 48-53
Chindit expeditions, WWII, 78-79
Chow, Gen., 117
Churchill, Winston, S., 21, 22, 24, 26, 70, 80, 85, 94, 99: sanctions bomber offensive, 92; his carrier tactics, 104-105
Clausewitz, Karl von, 5
Cold War, 128, 143, 146, 181
Command of the Air, Douhet's, 33
Convoying, 22
Coral Sea, battle of the, 117
Courageous, HMS, 105
Crete, 101, 106
  German airborne attack on, WWII, 70, 73
Cuban crisis (1962), 135
Cunningham, Adm., 106
Curzon, Lord, 26

— D —

D'Annunzio, Gabriel, 27
De Gaulle, Gen. Charles, 134
De Havilland Canada, 165
Derna, 11
De Seversky, Alexandre, 5, 19, 32
Dien Bien Phu, 149, 152
Doolittle, Gen., 116
Doolittle raid, on Japan, WWII, 116
Douglas Co., 30
Douglas, Donald, 30
Douhet, Gen. Giulio, 5, 24, 27, 29, 32, 33, 38, 177
Dowding, Air Marshal, 63, 80, 122
Dr. Strangelove, 129
Dresden, Allied destruction of, WWII, 95
Dunkerque, 105
Dunkirk, 69

— E —

Eagle, HMS, 105
Eaker, Gen. Ira, 73
Eben Emael, Germans capture Belgian fortress of, WWII, 68, 74
Egypt, 154
Eisenhower, Gen. Dwight D., 95, 149
El Alamein, battle of, 74
engines
    Dart, 164
    Fw-190, 183
    maintenance, 167
    Pratt & Whitney, 171
    Pratt & Whitney R 4360 Wasp Major, 129
    Pratt & Whitney SIC3-6 twin Wasp, 64
    Rolls-Royce Dart, 175
    Rolls-Royce RB-211, 129
    Rolls-Royce RB211-524 turbofan, 138
    unducted fan (UDF), 175
    Wasp radial, 64
    Wasp twin, 64
Enterprise, USS, 113, 117, 118, 119
Enterprise, USS, post-WWII replacement, 140
Essex, USS, 112, 120
Ethiopia, 48
    lessons from Italian invasion, 179

— F —

FAA regulations, 168, 170
Fairchild-Caminez engine, 31
Fairchild, Sherman, 31
Falklands/Maloinas War, 175
Fechet, Jaes E., 40
Fisher, Adm. Lord, 21
Fitch, Rear Adm. Aubrey, 117
Fleet Air Arm, 29, 30, 31, 102; poor design of aircraft for, 31, 102; actions against Italian navy, WWII, 104, 106, 107; carrier tactics, 104-105; actions in Norway campaign, 105; defence of Malta, 105; against French fleet, 105; Taranto action, 103, 105-106, 109; against *Bismarck*, 107-109; against *Scharnhorst* and *Gneisenau*, 109
Fletcher, Adm. Frank, 117, 119
Flight Safety International, 166
Flying, glamour of early, 1
Fokker, Anton, 15
Formidable, HMS, 106
Forrestal, USS, 140
Foulois, Benjamin D., 40

484th Bomber Group, 82
    aircraft, 83
    attack on Petfardo Oil Refinery, 84
France: early air force, 9; air losses in WWI, 13; strength of air force in WWI, 14, 19; aircraft production in WWI, 15; first bomber squadrons, 24; inter-war air force, 29; opposed to strategic bombing inter-war, 33, 38; rearmament inter-war, 41; air force in 1939, 62; Germans over-run, WWII, 69-70; single aircraft carrier (1939), 102; fate of French fleet, 105; retreat in Indo-China, post-WWII, 132; post-WWII *force de frappe*, 134; industry recreated, 164
Fries, Gen. Amos, 33
Fuller, Maj. Gen. J. F. C., 6, 124
Furious, HMS, 24, 105

— G —

G-suits, 130
Galland, Adolf, 94
Gallipoli, aircraft use in, WWI, 20
GAMA (General Aviation Manufacturers Assoc.), 165
Gavin, Gen. James M., 150
GCA (Ground Controlled Approaches), 165
Genda, Minom, 115
Germany: mistakes in Russian war, 7; counter productive attacks, 8; early air force, 9, 10; early balloon units, 9; strength of air force in WWI, 14, 19; aircraft production in WWI, 15; form *Jastas* in WWI, 17; naval air service in WWI, 6, 13, 24, 25-26; create secret air force inter-war, 29, 31; inter-war policies, 32-33; Condor Legion, 53, 54; air force in 1939, 62; *blitzkriegs*, 6, 7, 63-74; air defence in WWII, 85-88; attacks on shipping, 96
Gliders, 74
    Baka, 89
    Waco CG-4A, 77, 79
Glorious, HMS, 105
Gneisenau, WWII, 109
Goering, Hermann, 18, 30n, 32, 33, 53, 67
Graf Spee, 105
Graf Zeppelin, carrier, 102
Graf Zeppelin, airship, 41, 147
Greece, *blitzkrieg* by Germans in, WWII, 70, 101
Groves, P. R. C., 37, 177
Guadalcanal, 116, 119
Guernica, 53-59
Guns
    anti-aircraft, 11
    Lewis, on aeroplanes, 15
Guynemer, Captain, 21

— H —

Haig, Gen. Sir Douglas, 25, 26, 37
Halsey, Adm. W. F., 116, 119, 121, 122, 123, 124
Happe, Capt., 24
Harris, Air Chief Marshal Sir Arthur, 94, 96, 99
Heineman, Ed, 100
Helicopters
    carriers, 159, 160
    H-5, 124
    MA-25 Hormone, 159
    in Vietnam, 150-152
    post-WWII, 140, 149, 169
    Sikorsky HUS-1, 132

USN Sea King, 159
    Westland Wessex, 151
Henderson, Gen. Sir David, 26
Henry, Prince, of Prussia, 12
Hermes, HMS, 103, 115
Hindenburg, airship, 41
Hiryu, Japanese carrier, 118-119
Hitler, Adolf, 33, 66, 67, 69, 70, 79, 80, 85, 91, 94, 98, 99
HMS Bulwark, 151
HMS Eagle, 151
Hoeppner, Gen. Ernst von, 18, 28
Holland, German *blitzkrieg* on, 68
Home Defence Air Force, WWI, 2n, 181
Hood, HMS, 107
Hornet, USS, 117, 118, 119, 120
Hosho, Japanese carrier, 30
Hydrogen bomb, 128, 129
    deterrent concept, 129, 129n, 133

— I —

Illustrious, HMS, 105, 106
Ilyushin, Russian designer, 145
Immelmann, Max, 17
Imperial Airways, 40
Imphal, 78
Independence, USS, 120
India-Pakistan War (1965), 153
Indomitable, HMS, 106, 115
INS (Inertial-Navigation Systems), 166
Institute of Strategic Studies, 128
Intelligence, economic, in WWII, 61-62
International Air Transport Association, 178
Israel, 132, 156
    employs effective air power, 8, 153-154
Italy: early air force, 9, 11-12; war in Libya, 11-12; air actions in WWI, 19, 27; establishes Air Ministry, 29, 102; supports strategic bombing inter-war, 33; long-range flights inter-war, 48; Ethiopian campaign, 48; air force in 1939, 62; Allied air power in invasion of, 77; attacks on shipping, 96; lack of carriers, WWII, 102

— J —

Japan: mistakes in China war, 7; first carrier, 29; inter-war theories of air tactics, 30-31; air force in China war, 32, 49-53; inter-war production, 41; air force in 1939, 62, 67; *blitzkriegs* in WWII, 111-112; actions in Burma, 78-79; US air attacks on, 88-91, 95; airborne actions in Pacific, 108-124; naval planes and carriers, WWII, 112; impotence of submarines, 116; atom bomb on, 128; aircraft industry today, 146
Jellicoe, Adm. Sir John, 14, 22, 29, 114, 115
Jet engine, 128
Joffre, Gen., 37
Johnson, C.L. "Kelly", 37

— K —

Kabul, air evacuation of, 48
Kaga, Japanese carrier, 118
Kahn, Herman, 134
Khe San, Vietnam, 149, 150
Kingston-McCloughry, AVM E.J., 5
Kinkaid, Adm. Thomas, 122, 123
KLM, Dutch, 40
Königsberg, WWI, 20
Königsberg, WWII 105

Korean War, 2n, 128-133, 143, 145, 147, 154, 180, 181
Kurita, Adm., 122-124
Kursk, battle of, 76

— L —

La Stampa Sportiva, Turin, 11
Lanchester, F. W., 37, 177
Langley, USS, 30, 140
Lawrence, T. E., 20
Lee, Wing Cdr. Asher, 5
LeMay, Gen. Curtis E., 72, 91
Lend-Lease, 76
Lettow-Vorbeck, Gen. von, 20
Lexington, USS, 30, 113, 114, 116, 117
Leyte, 121
   US landings on, 122
Leyte Gulf, battle of, 122-124
Libyan War (1911-12), lessons learnt by Italians, 11-12
Liddell Hart, Capt. B.H. 5, 101, 124
Link, Ed, 60
Link trainer, 61, 181
Lloyd George, David, 26
Lockheed Corporation, 143, 146, 162
London, bombing of, 85, 91, 93
Lundendorff, Gen., 18
Lufthansa, 4
Luftwaffe, 41, 75, 91, 98, 179, 181: attacks Holland, 68; attacks France, 69; in Greece, 70-73; wasting effect of *blitzkrieg* on, 73; in Battle of Britain, 79-85; in air defence of Germany, 85-88

— M —

MacArthur, Gen. Douglas, 114, 116, 117, 120, 121, 123
McCain, VADM John S. 123, 124
McDonnell Douglas, 162, 165
Macedonian front, WWI, 21
MAGIC, 100
Mahan, Capt. Alfred Thayer, 6, 108
   on British sea power, 7
Malaya, in WWII, 115
Malta, 70, 97, 101
   air defence of, 88, 122
Markings, aircraft, 16
Martin Co., 8, 9, 10
Martin, Glenn L., 5
Maude, Gen., 20
Mers-el Kebir, 107
Messerschmitt, Willy, 100
Middle East, British success in WWII, 74
Midway, battle of, 31, 112, 114, 117, 118-119, 124
   Japanese losses, 119
Missiles,
   anti-ballistic, 124, 134-135
   ballistic, 4, 8, 134-135, 182
   Chinese, 134
   Exocet, 175
   Polaris, 134-135
   SAM, 154
   Skybolt, 135
   Thor, 135
Mitchell, Gen. William, 5, 19, 27, 28, 29, 30, 31, 33, 37, 40, 98, 177
   court-martialled, 33
Mitscher, Adm. M. A., 121-123

Moehne Dam, 81
Moffett, Rear Adm. William A., 29-30, 178
Montgomery, Gen. Sir Bernard, 74
Moskva, USSR navy, 140
Musashi, IJN, 123
Mussolini, Benito, 29, 33, 70

— N —

Nagumo, Adm., 113-116, 118-119
Napalm, 8
Narvik, 67
NATO, 168
Neosho, USN oiler, 117
New Jersey, USS, 150
Nimitz, Adm. Chester, 114, 116, 117, 118, 121, 123
Nomonhan War, 41
Norden bombsight, 94
Norway: German *blitzkrieg* on 67-68; campaign at sea, 105

— O —

Oil embargo (Arab), 166
Oldendorff, Adm., 122-123

— P —

Pacific theatre, seaborne air power in WWII, 109-124
   airstrips, 119
   loss of Allied ABDA fleet, 114-115
   US offensive from 1943, 120-124
   vastness of area, 109
Palestine campaign, Allenby's classic use of air power, WWI, 20
Pan American, 40
Parachutes, 10
Park, Air Vice Marshal Sir Keith, 85
Patrick, Gen. Mason, 40
Patterson, 3
Patton, Gen. George, 77
Pearl Harbor, 108, 112, 115, 116, 120, 121, 124
   Japanese attack, 113-118
Pepew, Dick, 31
Philippine Sea, battle of the 121-122
Phillips, Vice Adm. Sir Tom, 115, 124
Pilots, WWI,
   'aces,' 13n
   early training, 10
   fighter, 13-14
   losses among, 14, 27
Pola, 106
Poland: German *blitzkrieg* on, 66-67; air force, 66
Porte, S. C., 22
Pratt & Whitney, 64
Prince of Wales, HMS, 107, 115
Prinz Eugen, 107, 109
Propellers, 65
   Hamilton, 65
   24E60 Hydromatic, 65

— R —

R-101, 41
Radar, 8, 9, 60, 79, 103
   against U-boats, 97, 98
   at Pearl Harbor, 113
   British stations attacked, 80
   defences today, 150-152
   for naval aircraft, WWII, 103

German, 85
   in Middle East, WWII, 74
Rand Corporation, 128
Range records, inter-war, 48
Read's crew, 36
Record-breaking, inter-war, 42-48
Repulse, HMS, 115
Richmond, Adm. Sir Herbert, 101, 102
Richthofen, Baron Manfred von, 17, 18
   his Circus, 16, 18
Richthofen, Gen. von, 67, 69
Rickenbacker, Eddie, 3, 14
Rickover, VADM Hyman, 29, 33
Ridgway, Gen., 148
Robinson, Leefe, 18
Rockets, 8, 134-135
   Atlas, 134
   Blue Streak, 135
   for naval aircraft, 103-104
   V-2, 88, 134
Role of Pursuit Aviation, The, Chennault's, 53
Rolls-Royce, 146
Rommel, Gen. Erwin, 106
Roosevelt, Pres. Franklin, 53, 62, 121
Roskill, Capt. S.W. 101
Rotterdam, bombed by Luftwaffe, 68
Royal Air Force, 32, 37, 38, 102; losses in WWI, 13, 27; strength in WWI, 14, 19; in Palestine campaign, 20; formed, 26; inter-war cut back, 29; inter-war roles, 37, 48; belief in strategic bombing, 37; wins Schneider Trophy, 42; aircrew and training in WWII, 61; in 1939, 62; actions in France (1940), 69-70; defeated in Greece, 70; in Western Desert, 74, 77; in Battle of Britain, 79-85; night raids on Germany, 86; intruder operations, 88; bomber offensive on Germany, 92-95; Pathfinder force, 93-94; shipping attacked and defended, 96, 97; against U-boats, 97, 98; post-war V-bombers, 134
Royal Air Force College, Cranwell, 4, 38
Royal Aircraft Factory, 26
Royal Australian Air Force, 168
Royal Flying Corps, 13, 15, 17, 19, 31; strength in WWI, 14, 18; markings, 16
Royal Naval Air Service, 13, 15, 26, 31; flying boats, 16, 22; in WWI, 21-24; subordinate to RAF, 29
Rumania, occupied by Germans, WWII, 70
Russia: air force in WWI, 19; Soviet air force trained by Germans, 32; inter-war production, 41; air force in 1939, 62; failure of German *blitzkrieg* in, 73-74; revival of air force (1941-42), 77; post-war planes, 133; 'hot line,' 135; carrier development, post-war, 140
Russo-Japanese War, 7, 12

— S —

St Lo, USS, 124
Saipan, USS, 140
Santa Cruz Islands, battle of the, 120
Saratoga, USS, 30, 116, 120
Saxe, Marshal, 6
Scharnhorst, WWII, 109
Scheer, Adm., 14, 113
Schneider Trophy, 42
Sederström, Baron Carl, 51
Sheffield, HMS, 109
Shipping, harassment of, WWII, 96-97
Shoho, Japanese carrier, 117

Shokaku, Japanese carrier, 117
Sikorsky, Igor, 31, 32
Sims, Adm. William S., 30
Simulators, 166, 168
Singapore, 38, 122
    falls to Japanese, 115
Single-Side-Band radio, 165
Six, Robert F. 3
Slessor, Marshal of the RAF, Sir John, 5
Smith, C. R., 3
Smushkevich, Gen., 53
Smuts, FM Jan Christian, 26
SNECMA, 164
Society of British Aerospace Constructors, 146
Soryu, Japanese carrier, 118
South-East Asia Command, WWII, 78
Soviet Army Air Forces, 75
Spaatz, Gen. Carl, 75
Spanish Civil War, 32; Russian air force in 53;
    Luftwaffe in, 53-59; Italian air force in, 59;
    lessons from, 179
Speer, Albert, 95
Spruance, Adm. R. A., 119, 120, 121, 122
Sputnik I, 134
Stalin, Josef, 53
Stalingrad, 74, 78
Stempel, Major, 31
Stilwell, Gen. Joseph, 79
Strasbourg, 105
Student, Gen., 68, 73
Supply-dropping, 78
Survival in the Air Age, 133
Sykes, Sir Frederick, 37, 177

— T —

tactics, 160
Takagi, Adm., 117
Taranto, FAA night attack on, 103, 109
Tedder, Air Chief Marshal Sir Arthur, 74, 95,
    96
Tirpitz, 104
Tobruk, 11, 106
Torpedoes, 102, 104
Toyada, Adm. 122
Trenchard, Lord, 5, 13, 14, 27, 29, 30, 31, 37,
    38
Tripoli, 11, 12
Trippe, Juan, 3
Truk, 120, 121
Truman, Pres. Harry S., 133
Tunner, Gen. William, 147
Tupolev, Russian designer, 145
Turbo-props, 140-143
Turkey: war in Libya 1911 and, 11, 12; de-
    feated
    in Palestine, WWI, 20

— U —

U-boats: WWI, 21, 22; UC 36 sunk by flying
    boat, 22; WWII, 92, 96, 97; losses in WWII,
    98; destroyed by aircraft, 97, 98; U 29 sinks
    Courageous, 105; U 39 attacks *Ark Royal*, 105;
    U 30 attacked by *Ark Royal*, 105
Udet, Ernst, 30n, 99
ULTRA, 100
United Parcel Service (UPS), 170, 172
United States of America: early air force, 10,
    19; aircraft production in WWI, 15-16; La-
    fayette Escadrille, 19; naval air service, WWI,
    21; Nye Committee, 31; Chemical Warfare
    Service, 33; aircrew in WWII, 61; air training
    in WWII, 61; command and strategy in Pacific
    theatre, 114; 'hot line,' 135
United States Air Force, 183; peacetime prob-
    lems, 132, 133; post-WWII recommissioning,
    133; Strategic Air Command, 134; in Korean
    War, 147-149; in Vietnam War, 149-152
United States Air Force Academy, 4
United States Army Air Force, 32, 37, 181:
    supports strategic bombing inter-war, 33-37,
    38; obsolescent in 1939, 62; Ninth Air Force,
    77; daylight raids in Germany, 86; Eighth Air
    Force, 86, 94, 95; Twentieth Air Force, 91;
    bombing offensive on Germany, 94, 95; in
    Korea, 148; helicopters in Vietnam, 150-152
United States Marine Corps, 148
United States Navy: creation of carriers, 28-29,
    30; creates own air force, 29-30; wins Sch-
    neider Trophy, 42; world rank in 1939, 62;
    airborne actions in Pacific, 108-124; naval
    planes, WWII, 112; low loss of planes, 112;
    carriers in Pacific, 112; submarines in Pacific,
    116, 118, 122; Fifth Fleet, 120; Fast-carrier
    Task Force, 120; Third Fleet, 122, 123; post-
    WWII use of carriers, 132; post-WWII carriers,
    140
U.S. *Saratoga*, 55
USS *Forrestal*, 143
USS *Ranger*, 54
USS *Yorktown*, 54

— V —

V-1 flying bomb, 88
Vauban; Marshal, 111
Victorious, HMS, 107
Viet Cong, 152
Vietnam War, 132, 149-153, 180: failure of US
    air power in, 7-8; anti-aircraft defences, 9, 150;
    use of air power, 135, 149-152; herbicides used
    in, 152; S. Vietnamese AF, 152-153
Vietnamese, North, 6, 152
Vittorio Veneto, 106, 109
Vittorio Veneto, battle of, 19
Voss, Werner, 18

— W —

Wallis, Barnes, 100
War
    principles of, 5
    return to frontier protection (1960's), 129
    rise of guerrillas, 129-132
Warsaw, German attack on, WWII, 67
Warsaw Part, 168
Warspite HMS, 105
Washington Naval Conference, 30
Wasp, USS, 120
Wavell, FM Lord, 7
Wever, Gen. Walther, 33, 91
Wichita, Ks, 167, 170
Wilhelmshafen naval base, 24, 85
Window (foil), 86
Wind-tunnel, 135
World War, First, 7, 9; careers of airmen, 4;
    improvement in air power, 8, 14-15; flying
    training, 10-11; bombers, 13; fighters, 13-14;
    strength of air forces, 14, 19; command struc-
    ture of air forces, 14; aero engines, 15; aircraft
    production, 15-16; fighter operations, 16-20;
    Middle East actions, 20-21; air power at sea,
    21-24; strategic bombing, 24-27; War Product-
    ion Committee, 26; lessons from, 178-179
World War, Second, 4, 9; independent use of
    air power, 6; advances in technique, 7; im-
    provement in air power, 8, 60-61; flying train-
    ing, 10; early German successes, 63-74; turning
    point for Allies, 74; Normandy invasion,
    74-77; Soviet air revival, 77; Burma campaign,
    77-79; Battle of the Atlantic, 92, 93, 96, 97, 98;
    Casablanca Conference, 94, 120; Atlantic/
    Mediterranean area, 101-109; Pacific theatre,
    109-124; lessons from, 179-180
Wright Brothers, 9

— Y —

Yamamoto, Adm. Isoroko, 116, 117, 118, 119,
    120
Yorktown, USS, 116-119
Yugoslavia, German *blitzkrieg* on, 70

— Z —

Zeppelins, 9, 21
    L-22 and L-43 destroyed, 22
    L-50 and L-60 destroyed, 24
    L-59 in Africa, 20
    LZ-13, 25
    raids on London, WWI, 6, 13, 25
    sheds bombed in WWI, 22-24
    Z-IX destroyed, 24

Above: the author in training in Alberta, Canada, in early 1944, and, below, today.

Robin Higham was born in London and educated on both sides of the Atlantic. In 1943 he volunteered for the Royal Air Force and was sworn in in Canada, where he received his pilot's wings in 1944. He served thereafter in the United Kingdom, Belgium, and the Far East in Transport Command and as an airfield controller until demobilization in 1947, when he returned to the United States. He graduated *cum laude* from Harvard, took an M.A. at the Claremont Graduate School, then returned to Harvard to complete his Ph.D. in Oceanic History in 1957. His doctoral dissertation was published as *Britain's Imperial Air Routes, 1918-1939* and led to his being asked to do the as yet unpublished history of BOAC, 1939-1974. His next published work was *The British Rigid Airship, 1908-1931: a study in weapons policy* followed by *The Military Intellectuals in Britain, 1918-1940*. Intermingled with a series of bibliographical guides to British, U.S., and official, as well as various national military historical subjects, came the publication of *Air Power: a concise history* (a History Book Club selection), and with David H. Zook, Jr., *A Short History of Warfare*, with Jacob W. Kipp, *Soviet*

Aviation & Air Power, and with Abigail T. Siddall and Carol A. Williams, *Flying Combat Aircraft* (3 vols.). His latest book is a military, diplomatic, air study, *Diary of a Disaster: British Aid to Greece, 1940-1941*.

Since 1963 he has been on the faculty at Kansas State University, a full professor since 1966. From 1968 to 1988 he was Editor of *Military Affairs* (now emeritus) and from 1970 to 1988 of *Aerospace Historian*, as well as for many years President of the Consultative Committee on the *Revue International d'Histoire militaire*. Recently he became the first recipient of the American Military Institute's Samuel Eliot Morison Prize for distinguished service to the field of military history. Chosen Kansas State University's outstanding graduate faculty member for 1971, he teaches military, naval, and aviation history to students ranging from undergraduates to doctoral candidates.